music, and helped to launch a number of professional musical societies in the United States and abroad.

Two of Seeger's wives were gifted musicians: the violinist Constance Edson and the composer Ruth Crawford, the first American woman to receive a Guggenheim award for the study of music. Three of his children—Peter, Michael, and Peggy—have established international reputations in the field of folk music.

This first biography of Charles Seeger describes the boundless energy and creative undertakings of an astonishingly versatile figure. Drawing on Seeger's own writings as he explored his social and musical world, Ann Pescatello vividly portrays the experience of a pivotal figure in modern American culture. Musicologists, music educators, and all concerned with twentieth-century American life will be rewarded by this insightful study.

ANN PESCATELLO is Director of the national program, Scholars in the Schools, and Director of the Council on Intercultural and Comparative Studies and Senior Research Associate at the University of California, Berkeley.

Charles Seeger

Charles Seeger

A LIFE IN AMERICAN MUSIC

❧

Ann M. Pescatello

University of Pittsburgh Press
Pittsburgh and London

Published by the University of Pittsburgh Press, Pittsburgh, Pa., 15260

Copyright © 1992, University of Pittsburgh Press

Manufactured in the United States of America

Printed on acid-free paper

LIBRARY OF CONGRESS CATALOGING-IN PUBLICATION-DATA
Pescatello, Ann M.
  Charles Seeger: a life in American music / Ann M. Pescatello.
    p.   cm.
  Includes bibliographical references and index.
  ISBN 0-8229-3713-1
    1. Seeger, Charles, 1886–1979.   2. Musicians—United States—
  Biography.   I. Title.
  ML423.S498P5   1992
  780'.92—dc20
  [B]   92-4679
                                                              CIP
                                                              MN

A catalog record for this book is available from the British Library.
Eurospan, London

Contents

❧

Preface

❧

ON FEBRUARY 7, 1979, Charles Seeger died in his beloved
New England. He was a friend, a colleague; he was great
company, even though we bridged a generation gap of more
than half a century. Charles Seeger was an unusual man. Many people
attribute diet and exercise to their longevity and prescience. I attribute Charlie's to his mind, his constant concern with ideas, with
thought processes, always functioning with the highest potency —
sometimes twenty-four hours a day.

To know Charlie was a privilege. He was many things to many
people, some of whom he readily admitted could neither abide nor
understand him. Many, if not most, respected him. Some of us also
loved him. He could be cantankerous, insistent, maddeningly persistent, stubborn; he was more than occasionally curmudgeonly. He was
also kind, generous, willing, and able to share his ideas with all who
came along; thoughtful, a careful guardian of traditions but an
insistent explorer of new ideas and frontiers.

Relatively few people have the opportunity to survive into their tenth
decade, and still fewer to see that their activities and ideas have persistent and profound effects on those around them and those to come. The
history books have not yet — indeed, may never — record Charles Seeger
as a major figure of his time. But Charles Seeger was a major player, a
towering persona in some arenas, a preeminent figure not because he
was famous for any one thing, but for the collectivity of all his
contributions to the American music scene and to American society.

Charles Seeger was a participant-observer, a participant in and
observer of history. He had periods in which he was affected by history
in the making and latterly arrived at the fact that he should be
involved in the events of the time, as for example, his belated

awakening of social conscience—twice, first in his early professional years in California and later with the New York and Washington years. But he also was a mover and shaker, contributing in some small but important ways to the infrastructure of American history as it was being written, particularly after the 1930s.

Charlie was contradictory in nature and spirit, an aspect that perhaps made him empathetic with the dialectical approach. On the one hand he was a traditionalist and preserver of traditions, while on the other he was a creative genius and a champion of the new and untried. His approaches to music were both cognitive and affective; he wrote the densest essays on systems and ideas in music, while at the same time promoting lyrical tunes.

A most important way in which Charlie was contradictory was in his conflicting nineteenth- and twentieth-century views of women. On the one hand, he held prescribed notions against which he fought constantly about the proper role and place of women. On the other hand, almost all of his major contributions to the American scene were made in partnership with extremely strong and intelligent women whom he valued: both his first wife, Constance, and his second wife, Ruth; Margaret Valiant and Sidney Robertson of Resettlement Administration and WPA days; Vanett Lawlor of the Pan American years, are examples. And he was drawn to women with those qualities in his daily discourses on the matters of musical note.

Charlie and I met more than a quarter century ago when I was a graduate student in history at UCLA. We were brought together by our interest in Latin America and through mutual acquaintances in music. We became friends instantly and remained so until the end of his life. We enjoyed a warm, personal friendship and colleagueship. This book is one that Charlie and I planned to write together. It was to be a collaborative effort; it started that way and has since grown in perspective. Seeger had a sense of himself as being unique in American history but not ready to personally articulate that thought to the public, although he had sufficient ego to realize that it would make a great story. But, he did not wish his "story" to be rendered in the typical musicological mode. I am an historian not a musicologist, although I am a maker of music and a musically perceptive listener to music.

This was to be an historical-biographical study of the influence of the life and life work of Charles Seeger in the musical sphere in America. He was particularly intrigued by the implications of the thesis about the effect of the society on the creative individual and the effect of the creative individual on the society. How far behind or ahead of his society is the individual? How little or how much is one influenced by or does one influence the other? His vision of this book was that it be a historical record about a man whose life spanned revolutionary changes in American music, musical culture, and musical thought.

In a letter to me (May 18, 1976) Charlie suggested that the subject that would recommend itself would contain the words *music, society,* and *individual*—one who has seen the development of the twentieth century from before its beginning (he was fourteen at the turn of the century). He wrote,

[There is] a fairly strict theoretical parity between the singularity of the person, the singularity of the social cultural context of the particularities in which you have to talk to both. . . . I don't want to cramp your style or hold out for any false modesty in this situation. I gave a lecture at Harvard last week and in the course of the discussion, I had not the slightest hesitation to put myself in the position of creating a theory of my own for the socio-cultural historical development of musicology in the near future. I took the same stand of telling the world what was what, but at the same time welcomed discussion, especially of anybody who thought he had a better one. This is precisely what every composer and author of products in the compositional process of speech does if he is aiming to present the most comprehensive view of a case possible.

The book also is seen as a chapter in the social history of the United States for the span of nearly a century, of American life and music in which Seeger played such an important part. A theme is the historical case in which the society and the culture plays theoretically one half and the individual theoretically one half.

On January 6, 1976, Charlie wrote to me:

Make the central topic of the book the historical case in which the society and the culture plays a theoretical one half and the individual plays a theoretical one half. The crux of the matter being the interplay of the two, first the one then the other taking the lead and not forgetting the other individuals in the picture: [in the AMS] Kinkeldey, Cowell, Spivacke, Reese, Dickinson, Haydon, Strunck, Lang, C. S. Smith, the flock of Europeans that were stranded here by the beginning of World War II, Edward Dent, to name only the outstanding figures. The last two generations [of SEM] can be almost handled as a collective, but Merriam, McAllester, Rhodes, Kolinski, would have to be considered.

Other themes are part of this story, too; Seeger's constant concern about the hegemony of the Old World over the New, the dominance of high culture over folk culture, the missionary role of educators in "making America musical"; his role as a critic, a balancer between the dichotomies of the constraining conservative and pushing radical approaches; his idealism, always searching for an all-embracing unity, always seeking universes, embodying the old German concept, *Musikwissenschaft*, which encompassed all nonperforming, noncomposing investigative aspects of music; his encouragement of new ways of thinking about the perception and discussing of music.

He and I worked on this book together until he died. For some time thereafter, I did not return to the manuscript, thinking that I could no longer write the book. Time and perspective determined for me that the story of Charles Seeger as a figure integral to American society should be told. One of the aspects of this study was to analyze and to put into scholarly and cultural contexts the major tenets of Seeger's work: were they new, or just new to music, or were they new as a result of being honed in the American music context? Taken individually, each facet of his life has been important in American music: creator of a department of music; composer; writer; critic; inventor; musicologist concerned with the history and systems of music; ethnomusicologist; administrator of music programs for society; folklore exponent; founder of scholarly societies; educator; internationalist; teacher and husband to one of America's greatest composers—Ruth Crawford; father and appreciative audience of musically talented children—Peter, Michael, Peggy, Penny.

Taken as a whole, Seeger certainly made a contribution to American life. In fact, he was particularly concerned with how his life and ideas would be seen in the context of the society in which he lived.

Although he readily studied other societies, lived in and espoused the Latin American traditions, and apprenticed in Europe, Seeger was first and foremost a *norteamericano*—the quintessential American.

I see Charles Seeger as first and foremost a sage, a philosopher, about music and about the societies and cultures in which it abounds. In that regard, he is also an ethnomusicologist; although he might agree in terms of his understanding of what an ethnomusicologist should be—a scholar who must consider the context of the music integrally with the music itself, regardless of what music it is—he would, rather, say that this is what the term musicologist should mean, hence he is a musicologist.

Archie Green once told me that he thought that Seeger was a democratic humanist. I agree; I think he was that, as well; a thoughtful evolutionary, asserting the rights of all peoples and all musics. He was, from the beginning, and remained, always, a philosopher entranced by dualities. In a letter to Gilbert Chase (January 4, 1971) he commented that he had used the terms *raw* and *manipulated* adopted from Thomas Hart Benton in the late 1920s, and made first reference to them in his 1933 *Encyclopedia of Social Science* article, well in advance of Lévi-Strauss. Later, for example, he was intrigued with Wiley Hitchcock's distinction between *cultivated* versus *vernacular*, dealing with two sides to the problem of American music, the division occuring in the nineteenth century, with incorporation in the twentieth century of vernacular elements as a democratic social statement (See Achter). Similarly, he anticipated the anthropological-folkloric approaches as regards musics, and particularly folk music, of the structuralists—those who believe that folk music is contained in static reservoirs, formed before the advent of the mass media, with fragments left—and the functionalists—those who believe that folk music is a flowing stream, using whatever is available—an analysis nicely postulated by Kingman, and one that applies to other areas, as well.

I would like to acknowledge the help of several persons in putting this story together—Charlie, first and foremost. During his lifetime, I was able to study all his papers, professional and personal, discuss them with him, and sort through his correspondence, again discussing this with him. He made available to me all the family papers and histories that were in his possession or to which he had access, including many albums of family photographs. We reexamined his few remaining compositions, and talked endlessly about music and ideas. I made copious notes, eventually committing much to memory.

In addition to Charlie, several of his sons and daughters have been generous and enormously helpful with critiques of drafts of this book, with insights into personal contexts, and in offering whatever help they could to bring this work to fruition. Michael, particularly, and Peter have been good colleagues in this venture; Peggy, Penny, and Charles have contributed, also.

I want especially to thank Archie Green for his English scholar's critique of this book and his particular concern that this man of enormous activity not have his life framed in the passive tense. I also thank Trudi Olivetti who made available to me a large corpus of materials that she had been collecting and organizing for a study on Seeger that she did not complete. I also thank Bonnie C. Wade for her insights and editorial hand.

This was not an easy book to write. I lost my intended coauthor — who had promised to stay with it until he was at least ninety-six. Further, I wanted to find the right balance between the density of Charlie's ideas and writings, and the delightfulness of the person, interspersed with the triumphs and the trials of his personal and professional life. It was important to both of us that Seeger appeared as neither too much of a saint nor too much of a sinner.

To see the unfolding of Seeger's ideas as they complemented his work, I have followed a chronological structure. I found it impossible to go into enough detail on each possible theme or subject: there is simply too much to cover in a biography of such a many-sided genius. My hope — and I think his would be, too — is that this book will initiate more in-depth and definitive research into each facet of Seeger's work.

This one's for you, Charlie!

Charles Seeger

~

New England, New York, and Mexico, 1886–1908

⧢

CHARLES SEEGER, the quintessential nineteenth-century New England gentleman, was born in Mexico City on December 14, 1886. He spent some of his formative years in Mexico, in the shadow of a blatantly imperialistic North America with decided ideas about Latin America and any other civilization that sought to challenge its supremacy. Mexico and the relationship between North and South America remained a critical factor throughout Seeger's life, both culturally and intellectually. But this affinity was always carefully balanced by Anglo-Saxon traditions, for Seeger was a product of New England society, family structure, and values.

Boston, the home of many ancestors, was first a city of pilgrims and puritans, revolutionaries and proper citizens, bankers and ship merchants, and of education and culture. Since independence, Boston, like other northeastern cities, had benefited from immigration and industrialization. New England was booming and Boston Harbor, through which moved the ships of Seeger's great-grandfather, Thomas Simmons, was one of the most active on the eastern seaboard.

But in this era Boston was also becoming a city divided against itself. Before about the 1840s, most immigrants to Boston and the East were laborers from the British Isles, except for some like Karl Ludwig Seeger who came from Germany escaping from poverty, political persecution, or military conscription. After the 1840s, Boston attracted a more varied labor pool, needed to feed its numerous industrial and manufacturing concerns. The Irish led this new wave of migration, joined later by peoples from central, eastern, and southern Europe, and finally, after the 1890s, by Jews and Italians. Boston's population became increasingly heterogeneous and socially distanced from the aristocracy of the "brahmin" descendants of earlier immigrants.

Boston's working class and lower-income population dwelt in the inner city and in certain suburbs. People with money and "class" either lived in town on Beacon Hill or along the trolley lines stretching out to the suburbs, where remnants of that wealth may be seen today. Great-grandfather Thomas Simmons (1793–1866), owned a big home on a hilltop in Roxbury from which he could see his ships entering Boston Harbor. Neighboring towns and cities shared in this wealth, towns like Lancaster, New Hampshire—where some of Seeger's ancestors settled—and smaller Massachusetts cities, particularly Springfield, home of Seeger's parents. The enormous new labor supply and the abundance of old money, primarily merchant capital, gave New England prosperity and expansiveness that defined the world of Seeger's immediate ancestors.

The New England values of hard work, economy, and self-discipline were the philosophical underpinnings of merchant capitalism, the guiding values of Seeger's father. To succeed, to acquire property, to rise in rank and enhance one's middle-class standing were important to young Charles Seeger. So, too, was the Yankee-Protestant sociopolitical tradition. This tradition, as Hofstadter notes, "assumed and demanded the constant, disinterested activity of the citizen in public affairs, argued that political life ought to be run . . . in accordance with general principles and abstract laws apart from the superior to personal needs, and expressed a common feeling that government should be in good part an effort to moralize the lives of individuals while economic life should be intimately related to the stimulation and development of individual character."[1]

Seeger could chart the geneaology of his New England families for more than two centuries. His father was German on one side, and English on the other. The original Dr. Seeger, Karl Ludvig, from Wurtemberg in the Neckar River valley, traced his ancestry to a crusader, one Gebhardus de Seeg. As a student at the Karlschule in

Stuttgart, he had been a classmate of the poet Schiller. Karl Ludvig eventually settled in Northampton, Massachusetts. Charlie remembered singing German Christmas carols in the house on King Street in the company of many relatives, one of whom an aunt who was a very loyal descendant of old Karl Ludvig. As he related to his daughter Penny,

My great-grandfather Karl Ludwig Seeger came to this country in the late 1780s [1787]—this being as soon as he could possibly manage it after getting his degree as Doctor of Medicine in the famous Karlschule of the Duke of Wurtemburg. He came to Charleston, South Carolina, married, but his wife died and he moved to Holyoke, Massachusetts, and married for a second time Lucy [Sally] Parsons of Northampton. He had 14 children, but my children are the only Seegers in this line of the family. I know there are quite a number in the North Central states and there used to be a Judge Seeger in Newburgh, New York, but we never tried to trace any ancestry there. I give you below a couple of generations of ancestors of Dr. Karl Ludwig Seeger:

> Johann Friedrick Seeger 1720–1769 m. Charlotte Friederick
> Johann Seeger 1675–1747 m. Marie Margarete Dannenhauer?
> Johann Jakob Seeger no dates m. Euphroryne Schillin
> Johann Jacob Seeger 1588–1664 m. Katherina Steebin
> Georg Seeger no dates m. Juditha

The Austrian Heraldry Office, at the instigation of a friend of my father's, produced a coat of arms and a *Stammvater* sometime around the year 1067 —a typical fantasy of heraldry offices, skipping over 400 centuries of European turmoil with invasions of barbarian tribes. I don't put much stock in geneology myself, but I give this to you in case you happen to be interested.[2]

Henry Leland Clarke, a distant cousin, sent Charles a geneaological chart that demonstrated their relationship through the lineage of the Parson family of Sally, Dr. Karl Ludwig Seeger's second wife. These Parsons traced back to a Sarah Vore (d. 1676) who married Deacon Benjamin Parsons (d. 1689), whose brother, "Cornet" Joseph Parsons (d. 1683), married Mary Bliss, from whom descended Sally Parsons.[3]

Seeger's paternal grandfather, Dr. Edwin Seeger, was born in Northampton on May 10, 1811. He studied medicine at Jefferson Medical College in Philadelphia, graduated in 1832, and practiced medicine in Springfield and later in Northampton. In 1840 he married Harriet Foot, who bore him a daughter also named Harriet. When his wife died, Edwin married Elizabeth White in 1847. Dr. Edwin Seeger flourished financially and bought a large farm near Bridgewater, Connecticut, to which Seeger retired in 1971.

Seeger's paternal grandmother, Elizabeth White (1819–1905), traced her American roots to William White, who came to Massachusetts in 1630 and purchased land from the American Indians that later became the town of Haverhill. A descendant, Captain John White, defended that land in the wars between colonists and Native Americans. Yet another descendant, Major Moses White (1756–1833), was on General Putnam's staff in the revolutionary army. For his services, he received a grant of land in Lancaster, New Hampshire. Charlie frequently related a story that as the army marched through Philadelphia toward Yorktown, Moses White halted at a house where he asked a pretty girl to fetch him some water. When she complied, he told her that he would return one day and ask her to marry him. He did. She was an Attlee, whose father, Judge Attlee, apparently enjoyed some fame during the Revolution. Seeger's great-grandfather, John Hazen White (1792–1865), was probably their son.

Seeger's maternal ancestors included the Simmons, Adams, Pomeroy, Ashley, King, Robinson, Hamn, Twing, Simpson, Lincoln, Fosdick, Foster, and Brewster families. As Seeger told Penny, "Elder Brewster who was more or less the schoolmaster of the Pilgrims, was one of [Mother's] ancestors." Although he added that no ancestors arrived on the Mayflower, his mother, in a brief memoir, claimed direct descent from Mayflower passengers. Her family was long on New England tradition, ranging from seacaptains (whose cargoes Seeger suspected included slaves for the "triangle trade") to abolitionists.

In 1952, Seeger was asked to describe his family and religious background in a letter defending his son's application for conscientious objector status.

BACKGROUND. On my side, Michael comes of British stock, excepting only for a South German physician, Dr. Charles Louis Seeger, who settled in the United States in the 1780s. All the rest of the family who could be were in this country before 1700, one branch having come over in the Mayflower. Three men were officers in the Revolutionary army and another is said to have walked down Bunker Hill backwards "because he wouldn't turn his back on the red-coats." The family's traditions have been guided since 1800 by doctors and businessmen, all New Englanders, extremely independent and with strong puritanical leanings. Although many sons served in the wars as did my brother Alan, who wrote the well-known poem "I Have a Rendezvous with Death" and died in France as a soldier in the French Foreign Legion, others stayed at home. I myself, with these traditions well in mind, registered as a conscientious objector in World War I. . . .

RELIGION. My father and mother were Unitarians but not typical churchgoers, though they carefully sent me to a Unitarian boarding-school and always regarded themselves, and were regarded by others, as good Christian people.[4]

Seeger described his mother, Elsie Simmons Adams (born in 1861) in these words,

[She was] very pretty and as a young woman was as appropriately interested in young men as they were interested in her. She had a large number of beaux. She was almost disdainful of schooling, although she went to good schools. Her grandfather [the shipowner Thomas Simmons] brought her up—her mother died shortly after she was born and her father not long afterwards [five years later]. . . . The grandfather died and the money wandered off somewhere else. An uncle who had promised to leave her his fortune of $800,000 finally decided to leave it to an old seaman's home or something of that sort and my mother was left with nothing but a small competence, that her father had left her, netting her about $1,200 a year, which made her an heiress in those years. She was brought up in her late adolescence in [Miss Nourse's] fashionable school in Cincinnati where her aunt, who was her guardian, had taken her because her husband had moved there. Mother was brought up there with the well-to-do of Cincinnati: the Tafts, the Hollisters [one of whom was later a senator], and the Smiths, all multimillionaires.

Seeger's father, as Charlie noted in the same reminiscence, was

a brilliant student in high school and when he was sixteen a group of wealthy men in Springfield came to his mother who was by then a widow living on a small pension and offered to put my father through Harvard and the law school because he seemed to be a young man of great promise. His mother drew herself up in New England pride—she was a White, incidentally—and said "Seegers do not accept charity." So father went to work in a bank. The prospects of future life in a bank depended entirely upon the death of the president and the secretary and treasurer. He decided in his early twenties that he would have to leave banking and look for some more adventurous and promising occupation. By the time he was something like 25, he met my mother and became engaged to her. He had some letters to somebody in Mexico and that appealed to his sense of romance, so he left for Mexico to make his fortune. He worked on the *Mexican Financier,* the American newspaper of the American colony in Mexico City, became interested in working on the railroad which was being built, and presently branched out into an importing-exporting business with a friend named Guernsey. He went back to Springfield where my mother had been waiting for him and they were married in the Unitarian Church on State Street. . . . They took the ship back to Mexico, where I was duly born.

Mother's idea was that her husband would become a millionaire, that her daughter would marry a titled Englishman and her sons would all also become millionaires and would marry young women from the older Boston families. But their going to Mexico stopped all this romancing as far as practical life went, but not as far as reading Victorian novels, which kept on for the rest of my mother's life, not necessarily the best Victorian novels either. She used to read some of them over and over again [until] she practically knew them by heart and we all used to joke her about it.

My father was not by choice, I think, a merchandiser. He was a good amateur in music; played the organ and the piano in an amateurish way, composed some very pretty songs that I used to sing when I was 6 years old, dressed in a velvet suit, standing up by the piano when guests came. And he could draw very well. He had an instinctive "line" that you can recognize in any one of his thousand or more sketches of picturesque places in Mexico and later on in Europe and North Africa. He could write very well in English and later on could write a respectable sonnet; [he would] often write amusing poems for us children and eventually wrote and published a book of poetry, a book of verse called the *Ballad of Hatton Chattal*, and translated Iswolski's *Memoir*. . . . But his view of music, poetry, and drawing was definitely that of avocations. A respectable man went into business, earned enough money to keep his wife supplied with the necessary servants and convenient house [to] bring up his children, send them to good schools and to college afterwards, except the girls of course, who were slated to do something else until they got married. My father's activities in merchandising expanded from ordinary importing and exporting of things like coffee and other products of Latin America to the providing of sugar machinery and small railroads, etc. [Seeger's father also ran the first automobile bus line in Mexico City, in 1901, and was the first automobile importer in Mexico.] But he tended to trust people excessively and one time when he was in Mexico way off in the sticks trying to collect money due to him for a sugar mill his colleagues in New York precipitated a bankruptcy and he returned to have to appear in bankruptcy court. If he had been a regular merchant he would have simply said, "Well, I have no money; my creditors will simply just have to take the rap." But that was not my father's idea of doing things. He told the judge that he had arranged with his creditors to pay every cent back with interest and that they had complete confidence as letters he could show demonstrated. The judge dismissed the case with eulogies for an honest man. He eventually paid back every cent—the last debt to the Chicopee Bank in Springfield produced a letter of appreciation from the directors, that I still have.[5]

Seeger's family was a close, "traditional" one,[6] and his parents' New England values had lasting effects on Charlie's own world view. One was that love was important but religion was not. Seeger claimed to have been greatly influenced by his parents' Unitarianism—a strong sense of ethics and upstanding behavior. Also, in Seeger's tight-knit family, example was the main way of teaching; otherwise, one's principles had no foundation. Didacticism remained an ever present element in ways of acquiring knowledge in Seeger's youth and throughout his life.

Charles recognized a certain superiority in the Seeger view of the world. From the time of Dr. Karl, they all had firm ideas about how the world should run. Charles admitted to a mixture of family and Harvard snobbishness that surfaced sometimes in his own attitudes. According to his family, the world was composed of three classes of people: the Seegers, friends of the Seegers, and the rest of the world. A respect for hierarchy may also be observed in his life and work.

Seeger's mother shaped his sense of the place and value of women. He noted that, like most women of her day, his mother was "uneducated" in that she had little formal booklearning, but he was also aware of her intelligence and talent. This conflict between "education" and "intelligence" was bothersome to him, but still he grappled with the dichotomy of an educated father and an uneducated mother, about whom he commented:

She did, however, emulate my father who wrote a four-volume autobiography of his life up to 1930 or so, and her short skit is really good bedtime reading. She eventually learned to put capitals at the beginnings of sentences and to actually put in periods occasionally, although she was never known to use a comma or a semicolon as far as I can remember. Her spelling was so atrocious that in our earliest schoolroom days we remembered correcting her. So she got busy and learned to spell fairly well.[7]

Seeger also was initially influenced by the view of his parents, particularly his father, that the only real music was written music. When young Charlie expressed an interest in folk music, his father told him the only folk music in America was Negro spirituals. His father said that in his youth he danced to fiddle music sometimes, especially in cities like Springfield, but it was to "real" music, Strauss waltzes. Seeger's mother shared this prejudice. She was brought up on ballads sung by her nurses, and probably knew many of them, but when she became a debutante, she had to forgo ballads and sing the "usual" music.

Seeger was also deeply affected by his Latin American experience. His father's business ventures took the family back and forth between the Northeast sector of a United States vibrant with industrial and commercial activity and a Mexico flourishing in the wake of nineteenth-century romanticism. The effects of this bicultural environment remained with Seeger always.

The Mexico of Seeger's birth and part of his early years, and to which he returned annually as a teenager, was under the domination of Porfirio Díaz.[8] During the Porfirian Age (1876–1911) many of Mexico's chronic problems were in abeyance. Banditry, once endemic to Mexico, was brought under control by a national guard, the Rurales. Within a few years, Mexico had become a country of martial law, without courts but nonetheless safe. Once the threat of violence was quelled, foreign capital began to flow in. Trade, manufacturing, and agriculture flourished. Mining operations, mostly American, were revived and made profitable, with increasing quantities of gold, silver, copper, zinc, lead, and other important metals flowing north of the border to underwrite the United States' rapidly expanding industries and commercial ventures. Transportation, led by the railroads, developed, and foreign markets were expanded for Mexico's agricultural products. A final incentive to foreign investors and businessmen was Díaz's funding of Mexico's foreign debt at a reasonable interest rate and balancing the budget.

The centerpiece of the Pax Porfiriana was the capital. Mexico City was modernized, cleaned up, and electrified, despite a powerful gas monopoly. Streetcars were introduced. Elaborate mansions and public buildings were constructed. The creole class, those of Spanish heritage and citizenship or unmixed blood, once again enjoyed "the good life." Díaz also surrounded himself with a coterie of intelligent young lawyers and economists, followers of positivism and similar au courant doctrines. This oligarchy of *científicos* sponsored a revived cultural life, and the capital was home to artists, musicians, and men of letters. Material and cultural advancement was considerable.

The Díaz period provided an environment most hospitable for foreigners. Foreign money could buy anything, and the mines, plantations, and factories hummed, with any strife quickly and brutally suppressed by the Rurales. The clergy, most of them foreign, were again tolerated. There was great encouragment of European and North American influences and immigration, especially Yankee capital and managerial ingenuity. The families of foreign businessmen were isolated from the harsh realities of life for the average worker. Seeger's father was one of thousands enticed by the financial possibilities opened up by the Pax Porfiriana.

Seeger's father, now well-to-do, moved his family frequently between New York and Mexico. New York was the headquarters of his business enterprises, while Mexico was the source of the raw materials. In the later 1880s and early 1890s, the elder Seeger was an independent merchant in the sugar refining business. He moved his family back to New York City for the first time in June 1887. Charlie remembered his father's first New York office, on the Bowling Green by Battery Park, and the carriages and men with top hats who worked in the offices of lower Manhattan. Later, the elder Seeger was a vice-president of the American Rubber Company, which imported rubber from South America and then made imitations. Still later, after problems in the South American market made it difficult to do business there, his area became North Africa and Europe.

The Seegers purchased a home on Staten Island which Charlie remembered as in a gothic Swiss chalet style, with wooden walls nearly two inches thick and adorned with the heavy scrollwork that was popular in the 1870s and 1880s. He also recalled a living room below his parents' room, a nursery, and quarters for their four servants. Seeger remembered that when the house burned after having been empty for years, twenty new houses were built on the property. His recollections were vividly detailed:

The house was one of the old—no, I should say: The ridge above St. George (where the New York Ferry came in) had formerly been divided into sizeable suburban estates with substantial and commodious houses requiring a number of servants. Our house was not, I think, one of the older ones. These had a squat but monumental style, rather plain and dignified. Ours ran sharply up-and-down—steep gables and like a train of cars, stretching out behind. . . . There was a barn and we kept one or two horses and two cows, a chicken house and yard and a vegetable and fruit garden of more than half an acre, peach, pear and cherry trees. It was planted by someone who fancied exotic trees and shrubs. Oh, it was a lovely spot to grow up in. Nice lawns, two hay fields and lots of trees to climb. It was the after-school gathering place for the neighborhood. One of our teachers at the Staten Island Academy, wanting to show off before some visitors to her room, asked the class "And now, children, what place do you like best to be?" "Seeger's barn" was almost a shout.

[For the children] there was top-spinning in a cleared space on rainy days, [prisoners bars, colors, Indians, statues, on clear ones], coasting in winter and, off and on, cat hunts (a peculiarly savage institution that came to an abrupt end one day when we actually found we had killed a cat) and, I am sorry to say, occasional stone fights (with barrel tops for shields) with gangs of boys from the crowded slums down to the south of us. . . . From our hill-top, with all the comforts of those days, we looked down on Duck-Pond Hollow, a narrow, foul-smelling and looking place that ran from Tompkins-ville to New Brighton. Servants and service were cheap. Dennis Garvey, the

Charles, Elizabeth, and Alan, Staten Island, 1891

gardener and coachman, lived with quite a family in a converted barn that abutted on our garden. His wife took in washing. I remember once being sent to him with a message and for the first time entering the combined living, kitchen, laundry [sleeping and work] room. His children — whom I never saw otherwise — shrank from me into the shadow and his gaunt wife entered [from the steam of her tubs — for she took in washing to eke out Dennis' meagre pay]. . . . Yet we loved Dennis. Alan, especially, adored him and used to follow him around, asking questions and, I remember, often asking him to spell Constantinople. Bridget (alias Bibby), the nurse, ruled the nursery where we had supper (in winter before a glowing grate of coal) and later in company with my father's mother and my mother's aunt — two little old ladies, one an aristocrat, the other a plebeian, whom we used to tease delightedly by making our eggs taste like potatoes and our potatoes like eggs, the secret being dousing them with so much butter (we made our own, much of the time) that it was no wonder they resembled each other. Little Mary, the cook, and Nony, the waitress, were our devoted friends and allies and a genteel little old lady came in to sew endlessly. Apples, flour, and such were bought by the barrel. Store bread, pies or cake were unheard of.

The Lowe house was one of the more monumental, older mansions I mentioned above. It stood out on a meadow hillock behind our place and I never knew it except as deserted and gradually running down. There was another like it across Tompkins Avenue. It became a boarding house. I remember Janet Charlier lived there with her mother and father. She was one of Alan's "girls." On one St. Valentine's evening, I remember, he and I went out to deliver our paper-lace, anonymous valentines and after delivering mine we cautiously approached Janet's door—stalking like Indians so as not to be discovered until, with a wild whoop, we threw them in the door and raced off. This was after a period dominated by quite a bit of folklore. Boys were nicknamed by their "girls'" name and girls by their "boys'." I remember Alan made quite a point of being fickle. He had started out by adoring an older girl [Adeline Trask] two classes ahead of him. She was already pre-empted by a boy of her age-group who was, accordingly, called "Addie." Nothing daunted, Alan insisted upon his rights and became known as Little-Addie.

Alan was incredibly small for his age (I was too). We were wiry and agile. But while I kept out of serious fights by guile, fast action and tongue-lashing, Alan met everything head on. He was a terrific little scrapper. Nothing, he averred, could daunt him. One day, my sister and Alan found themselves in an argument who could ram their heads harder into a tree than the other. Sister started off and made a good but not too damaging exhibition. I remember Alan's drawing-off to get a good run a-butting his head into the big horse-chestnut so hard that it sent him sprawling. The trouble was, there was a four-inch nail—a spike—that we had driven into the tree to help us climb it. Fortunately, Alan just grazed it, getting a bad wound, but not killing himself. Once we were coasting down the well-iced hill toward St. George, Alan on his sled a little in front of me on mine—the old high sleds. Just as we came to a cross-street a horse and wagon came right into our path. I, of course, promptly fell off my sled but not Alan, who very neatly steered between the fore and hind legs of the horse and scooted on down to the bottom. It is a wonder he ever grew up, that boy.[9]

Charles also wrote a short remembrance entitled "Boyhood on Staten Island," an informative document about the social and cultural mores and conditions of the time.

Back in the 1890s, the ridge that marks the southern horizon of New York Harbor and stretches from New Brighton Staten Island on the east to Tompkinsville on the west was already occupied for the most part by dwellings on what have since been known as "city lots." The old estates of a dozen or more acres with pretentious houses that required sizable corps of servants had been broken into subdivisions and all but four of the old houses had disappeared. I remember the old Lowe mansion, empty and falling to pieces on a cow pasture out behind our house. There was another like it on the five or six acres to the west of us where a public school playing field now lies. It had been turned into a kind of superior boarding house. The only one still standing was lived in with its accustomed style by the Whitehouse family. Christine Whitehouse was in my class at school and the bosom friend of my flame Nina Perry. Portions of the original estate had given place to commodious, well-kept suburban cottages some of which were occupied by the familes of my school friends. Our house, the last of the four, with its steep gables and diamond-pane windows, was situated upon four acres on the crest of the ridge, on the corner of Tompkins (now St. Marks Place) and Hamilton Avenues [on a hill at the Southeast corner. The house stood on four acres, which ran through to the next street, along Tompkins]. Much of it, land had already been sold off. The old ferry slips were at the foot of Hamilton Avenue and my Father commuted to his office on Bowling Green each week day. The trip took about thirty minutes and the fare was five cents as, I believe, it still is. When there was any doubt about the time and the air, as it usually was in those days, fairly clear, a pair of binoculars focussed on the tower of the Produce Exchange, which cut the Manhattan sky-line, usually set us straight. At night, we could hear the bell-buoy on Robin's Reef and the whistles of the trains running along the Jersey shore through Communipaw towards Bayonne.

It was an idyllic spot for childhood. A fancier of exotic trees and shrubbery had landscaped it. There was a barn and we kept a cow and a horse—sometimes two of each—with the conventional hay loft, feed bin and tack room for the buggy, sleigh and surrey. A sizable chicken yard and a large vegetable garden together with a dozen or so fine fruit trees and considerable hay, made the household partly independent of much of the marketing that has to be done by suburbanites today. Supplies were bought in quantity and stored in the cold cellar: barrels of potatoes, apples, flour; tubs of butter were ordered from wholesalers, delivered by express and stored in the cold cellar. Sacks of coffee beans were imported direct from Mexico by my Father's importing-exporting company. The warm cellar housed the kitchen, laundry and the hot-air furnace. How well I remember waking up on stormy mornings with little piles of snow under the cracks in the windows, the contents of our china water pitchers on the "washstand" frozen solid because the north wind sweeping across the bay had blown into the "registers" and driven all the heat into the rear of the house! Still worse was the ice-cold tub awaiting each male member of the household. All gentlemen took cold baths every morning. The colder the better. That was all there was to it.

School was the Staten Island Academy that still stands on Richmond Terrace, though overshadowed now by modern office and apartment buildings that have made a borough center just above the present ferry landing. My first two grades, however, were in the old private house that was torn down, during my third year in school, to give place to the present building. Unlike the modern school, the academy offered only instruction. I haven't many memories of it; but our friends in it—my brother's, my sister's, and mine—circumscribed together with our parents, our universe. The gathering place for our friends was our barn and every afternoon the gang collected there. . . .

It was a homogeneous crowd of a dozen or two governed by an extraordinarily strict code of honor. It was that code, the folklore upon which it was based and in whose terms it was loosed or tightened, that gives the memory of those days the unique nostalgia that still haunts me. The cardinal principle was an exaggerated chivalry: never to refuse a dare, never to tattletale, always to give fair play and, for the boys, to maintain a storybook reverence and consideration for the girls. . . . [Here Seeger alludes to the practice of boys being called by their girl's names and vice versa.] My sister and I were the only ones to escape this, to us, somewhat unwelcome . . . private feeling. Her strategy was to pronounce herself so fickle that by the time anyone could label her she would have already changed the supposed object of her affections. I managed by refusing to divulge my six-year long loyalty to Nina, consequently becoming known as "Nobody," a title of which I was proud.

St. Valentine's Day was about the only time (outside of dancing school) where we were forced to select partners, so that it "didn't count" when positive declarations could be made. But anonymously. The procedure was exciting. After supper, one stalked the house of the favored one, dodging from bush to bush, Indian-fashion, finally creeping up to the porch and placing the valentine, with its paper lace protected in a strong envelope, under the door,

Elizabeth, Charles, and Alan, Staten Island, 1893

making a tremendous racket and dashing off to a preselected vantage point from which unseen, one hoped to see the girl pick up the envelope.

One day, the code of honor was broken. I don't remember how it came about, but during a recess at school some of the boys threw cockleburrs into the girls' hair, so that the next day many of them showed up shorn of their flowing tresses and with a couple of irate mothers to see that the teacher uncovered the culprit. Each girl was called upon to stand and name her assailant and our hearts sank as one after another of our cherished idols tattled. But when one of the Hasbrouk boys' girls tossed her head and said she wouldn't talk, such a cheer went up that all hope of disciplining us for the crime went by the board.

Rather early in these delectable days, we decided that there was not enough ice cream and cake circulating. So we organized a club whose only known purpose was to practically compel the parents of the members to give parties in turn. The stratagem succeeded amazingly until the mothers compared notes and decided that the thing had gone far enough. So, the club simply evaporated into thin air. But we were not to be easily discouraged. The next effort was a more restricted one—a secret society. We met in the basement of Nina's house and invented a ritual. The girls sat honorifically on barrels and boxes against the walls, a king or chairman was somehow installed, and the members called to order. The procedure was simple for a boy—to disobey, whereupon the offender was condemned to punishment, stoic reception of which earned admiring glances from the girls. But this, too, was ended by parental disapproval, partly, I seem to remember, because the refreshments demanded were a burden and partly, because things seemed to be getting a bit out of hand.

But aside from these conspiracies, the main occupations were group games, rather more healthy if sometimes a bit rough and, occasionally, cruel. They were mostly out-of-doors or, in bad weather, in our barn with the carriages pushed aside and the big doors thrown wide open. In winter, there were coasting and, occasionally, snowball fights—these latter, quite highly organized. There was hide-and-seek (with infinite variations), colors, prisoners' bars, statues (which could be quite rough) . . . cops and robbers, Indians, cat hunts, and top-spinning, including the curious trick of spinning a top with another (one especially contructed top with a long, sharp point, was occasionally used and not considered quite proper). Marbles never got a chance. It was discovered that we were "playing for keeps." And that was "gambling." The agates, bulls-eyes and micks were confiscated and that was the end of it. Indians, too, eventually ran up against parental disapproval. One day, Chief Russell Bell was captured, tied to a neighbor's clothes line and presently in the rush for supper, forgotten. Long after dark, his parents combed the neighborhood anxiously (this was before installation of telephones) until he was found shivering but mum, as a good Indian should be. Russell had perfected a sensational trick of falling flat, face downward, from a standing position. He would hide behind a fenced corner until a couple of girls were about to walk by, then collapse in front of them. They usually rewarded him with the expected screams and flight, while the rest of us watched from suitable cover.

Particularly savage was the cat hunt. We decided that there were too many of them around. So we concocted "poisons." A poison was made up of as many unpleasant and forbidden items as we could mix together in a sizable dish—cleaning fluids, ammonia, insecticides—I can still seem to catch a whiff of some of these terrible mixtures. No cat would come within miles of one. So, we went after them with stones, knives, spears, hatchets, bows and arrrows, and feet. This came to an abrupt end one day when we found we actually had wounded a little half-grown cat, that it was found dead the next day. We were overcome with remorse and could barely keep the tears back, but buried it with honor.

One could look back upon such days and sneer at the veneer of civilization and gentility that was continually being broken through by the tendency to a latent juvenile delinquency and then forced to cover up by exercise of authority from one source or another—usually the parents. Although we did not recognize it, our resentment was expressed in the classic pattern now very generally known. When, for example, electric lights were first put in our neighborhood streets, we considered it a point of honor to keep the bare little bulb on the pole behind our house broken because it kept the hens awake at night so that they wouldn't lay eggs. One mean compensatory activity was to hide high and quietly in the leafy tree over a sidewalk and drop ink on the passers by; another keeping the waters in a pond so peppered with stones from slingshots that a fisherman, annoyed to fury, would try to find us and give us the thrashing we deserved, but without success.

As I look back on it, there seems to have been a continual testing of the limits of our sheltered life. Our hilltop, I must admit, was an oasis. Shipping, manufacture, poverty, and near poverty surrounded it below. Jersey Street, running from Tompkinsville to New Brighton, ran through what we called "Duck Pond Hollow." . . . It was a grimy slum, on at least one of whose intersections there were four saloons with the traditional swinging half doors. . . . The boys and girls of our age living there went to the public or parochial school and rarely ascended the ridge. I never went down into the hollow without adult company. As we grew older, our gang would survey the southern prospect somewhat gingerly and one day a foreign gang walked through Hamilton Avenue by our house, observed attentively by ours, which had the advantage of high ground. The next time this happened, we were ready for them. Each of us had a sack of stones and a shield made out of barreltops. The first stone fight was never repeated. The intruding gang of larger boys surged toward the fence menacingly and we fled to the safety of the house. But the gang never appeared again.

Parents somehow put a stop to exploration of these limits. And we were . . . glad they did.

It was not what we would call, nowadays, a very democratic bringing up. My father was more of a Hamiltonian than a Jeffersonian. The household was run upon gentle but firm patriarchal lines. Servants, fresh off the boats from

Ireland, were almost a drug on the market. Ditch digging was only by hand and was paid a dollar a day. Our gardener, Dennis, who had a family of a wife and three or four small children, received a dollar and a half and worked from before daylight to as late at night as he was needed. The cook probably had the same wages, but little Nony the waitress began at fifty cents. Laundress and sewing woman came by the day. One dollar. The men of the family were supposed to ignore the fact that there was a kitchen. We boys were forbidden to enter it. Effeminizing influence. But patriarchy was a wonderful tradition. It allowed enormous leeway for the exercise of power and imagination—to the women in it, depending, of course, upon their ability to use it. My mother was an expert and ruled the establishment like a queen. We children were not slow in finding room for manoeuver and many were the days when the smell of fresh-baked bread signaled an invasion of the kitchen. (Father was "at the office.") Warm loaves . . . were hollowed out and filled with our own sweet butter, and the dough pressed into doughballs.

Inevitably, there were trials of strength between us and our mother. She usually won; but once she didn't. The case was that of the Parmalee boys. They were given to mildly profane language. One glorious afternoon, the Parmalees were told to get off the place and not come back. The gang took this personally and for several days foregathered at the Parmalees' house. This was too much for Mother. After a talk with Mr. Parmalee they were invited back provided they restrained their tongues; and I seem to have the impressions that they very sportingly did.

Somehow or other winked at by our father (though encouraged by our mother's example) companionship with the servants was almost continuous through the day. They were lovely people and we adored them—especially Dennis, with his store of Irish folklore, speech that sounded deliciously quaint to us and a sparkling sense of humour. All these relationships were, however, upon a strictly observed class basis. Although Dennis's family lived in the upper story of a large barn that abutted our garden, we were supposed not to know that he had a family. And to all intents and purposes, we didn't [after this episode]. Dennis's family's living situation was . . . like nothing I had ever seen or wanted to see again. Never afterward did I feel quite natural with Dennis, even when asking him the questions we dared not ask our parents or teachers or getting him to spell forbidden words.

Times away from this paradise were rare, principally because there were no better places to be. There were trips by horsecar, later by trolley, to South Beach for sea-bathing, to Silver Lake for skating, or to the Montgomery's on

The Seeger family, Staten Island, 1894

Todt Hill back on the Island where, one day, we were driven in a four-in-hand to one of the last fox hunts. There was much hanging around the railroad yard of the little belt line that ran to Tottenville on the southern tip of the Island the mere sound of whose engine whistle rang in our ears as mysteriously as once to the Celts the storms of the foggy Atlantic the siren call of the mythical island of Hy-brasil.

I rode my first bicycle when I was seven, meeting as bravely as I could the jeers of the younger generation who lived down below our hilltop. Golf was just beginning to be a fancy new game and I used to ride out with my father to the Fox Hill links to caddie for him Sunday mornings on the otherwise bare and useless land on which little holes had been dug and sticks put in them.

Keeping a catalogue of the ships in New York Harbor was a must for my brother and myself. To be entered, a ship had to be seen and classified. Old square-riggers, schooners up to five masts, barks, barkentines, sloops, yachts, warships, ocean liners, freighters, "tramps," excursion boats, tugs, and even barges were dated as seen. A hole in the fence of the local U.S. lighthouse tender base between St. George and New Brighton enabled us to slink into the secret domain unobserved and gain access to the piles underneath the docks, where, cautiously stepping from one horizontal to another we could traverse the whole works and examine many of the details of ship repair and maintenance.

It is sometimes hard to realize the great changes that took place under my own eyes, as it were, in the 1890s. My own experience involved the step from buggy and horsecar to trolley, culminating in a trip up Broadway in 1898 in a "Forecarriage" — a pair of wheels powered by a gasoline engine, behind which any rear part of a horse-drawn carriage could be attached at the horizontal juncture known as the "fifth wheel" of any vehicle. The telephone was a new gadget one knew existed, but there was none in the house. Kerosene lamps and candles alone illuminated the rooms of the house. Gas jets under ground-glass globes were used in the halls, bathrooms and kitchen. But meaning most to me, at the time, was escape from the Little Lord Fauntleroy ideals of my dear mother. Imagine, nowadays, a boy of four or five taking a Sunday walk with his parents, dressed in a long coat with white fur wristbands and collar, kid gloves, a cane, and a large round-brim felt hat crowned with a cascade of ostrich feathers in two colors and tied under his chin with a three-inch satin ribbon! There was long hair, in sausagelike curls down to the shoulders until my sixth birthday. In winter, underclothes were from wrist to ankle in heavy wool. Suits were of what is now overcoat-thick cloth. As we grew older, shirts were only white, with attachable collars and cuffs. Cloth hats or caps were worn at all times outdoors, except . . . in the hottest summer days.

This late-Victorian way of life was possible, of course, only by the existence of a social class structure fast approaching that of the contemporary European civilization; German education, French manners, English clothes and diction were the ideals. Superimposed upon the puritanical morality and professed egalitarianism of the still-colonial consciousness of the American people, these "foreign notions" were already baring the incompatibilities finally recognized in the Spanish-American War of 1898, Theodore Roosevelt's trust-busting, and rough, rich, out-of-doors men.

My father and the men whom he respected lived their lives trying to hold onto the kind of culture defined by John Pierpont Morgan as the way the life of culture could be lived only by people who left the kind of culture, people with two or more servants, protesting but having to endure the innovations that undermined the social conditions that made that culture possible. Life, as represented to us children by our parents, was a free enterprise, for those able and worthy, to compete in the open market. The known fly in the ointment was the fact that some men are able but not worthy, and some worthy but not able. It was also a fact that many of the former gravitated towards business and politics. And facts were facts. The well-brought-up, decent, honest man—that is, the gentleman—only went into business if he had to or because he inherited an obligation to; and, as a rule, he kept out of politics. The cards were, thus, not exactly stacked against him, but he had to work hard and take the slings and arrows of outrageous fortune without complaining. Our bringing up was, consequently, a disciplining in the use of . . . freedom. Education in schools merely gave one command of the techniques. These techniques were worthy of higher uses and necessary in the arts, sciences, and philosophy. Our testing of the limits of our freedom was accepted as natural, though disappointingly hard to explain when we went too far. And, when we did, the duty of the parents was to catch us up sharply, which they did.

Often as not, the ends to our excursions were brought about by our own volition. The discipline began to pay off before we were caught malingering. Sometimes, it was by considerations of prudence. We realized we had gone too far. Not seldom, one can see now in retrospect the emergence of the family discipline in our own moral, aesthetic, or even social decisions.

Although neither of our parents were churchgoers—they were married in a Unitarian church and professed that faith upon the required formal occasions—they were proud of their New England ancestry and of the family name. My father's belief was comparatively simple. Seventy percent of the human race was fit only to be governed; another twenty percent was intelligent enough to act under direction; the remaining ten percent was constituted by the competent who had the discipline, the sense of moral duty and physical ability to give that direction for keeping the remaining seventy from mere savagery and anarchy. It was taken for granted that we children inherited the qualifications and duties of membership in this ten percent. Sterling honesty, industry and self-sacrifice on the part of this segment of the population were what kept the human race on even keel. When his company failed, in 1900, my father scorned to take advantage of the bankruptcy laws and pledged himself to repay, with interest, every debt. He did. My mother attended an excellent "finishing school" for young ladies, whose textbooks seem to have been less read by her than Victorian novels. For her, this was a superb discipline and suited her abilities to a "T."[10]

When I was about seven, she decided that we should go to church and say prayers before we went to bed. I rather liked the simple little church back near Sailors' Snug Harbor. There was singing and a pretty little girl with long yellow hair sat in the pew just in front of ours. But the minister, hearing that Father was a good amateur musician, made the mistake of asking him to play the organ. And that was the end of the churchgoing. I have often had occasion to realize that we children received a more thoroughgoing religious bringing up than most of my churchgoing contemporaries in their churches. There was no specific religious instruction. But right conduct was clearly laid down, above all, by example, as well as by precept. As I look back upon it now, it was the example that counted. One could argue about the precepts, but one absorbed the examples. One could even consciously flout the precept while unconsciously actually living by the example. As the children grew, what had been a partnership of two time-lovers became a tight family community within which lives revolved. In the earliest days I remember, the climax of each glorious day was to run down the hill to the front gate to greet Father upon his return from the office. Then we would be taken off to the nursery for supper while Father and Mother were served in the dining room. As we went to sleep one could hear fragments of *Tristan* and the *Ring* in piano arrangements or graceful Mexican *danzas* floating up from the drawing room. When there were guests for dinner, we would slip out of bed and hang

Charles and Alan, Staten Island, 1894

over the banisters of the staircase in wonderment about what it could be that gave rise to . . . laughter.

As we grew older, we graduated one by one to dinner with the adults. Then began what became the most important tradition of the later lives of all three children—the evening after dinner with Father. Talk about business was taboo. Money or the cost of anything could not be mentioned at table or afterwards. Such things a mere unpleasant necessity, like "going to the bathroom," for the living of life, which was an entirely separate thing. There was reading, drawing and watercolor painting, [family game-playing—cards, lotto, dominoes], and later anagrams [which he credited with expanding his vocabulary], capping verse, and, for me, Haydyn and Mozart symphonies in piano four-hand arrangement [for duets with various family members, particularly his father]. The family evenings eventually turned into Sunday excursions, with sketching pads, and the founding of a family monthly magazine. Removal to New York City for two years and then to Mexico City did not hamper [our] development but expanded the range of experience and comprehension of the "great" world—the world outside of American provincialism. [11]

The Seegers lived in Manhattan at Park Avenue and Seventy-third Street for two years before their final Mexican sojourn, where the children were exposed to a much more cosmopolitan universe. Seeger believed that these years brought the family even closer, and he forever cherished an ideal of close-knit family life.

Except for those years in Manhattan, the Seeger children spent their formative years exclusively in Staten Island and Mexico City. In addition to Seeger's recollections of Staten Island, which ranged over the various periods when the family lived there, another fond memory was staging plays with his brother and sister. Below is an advertisement for one presented when Charlie was seven, during the family's second Mexican sojourn.

In The Teatra Casa Seeger, January 13, 1894 "for this night only, the following celebrated artists: Senor Don Louis Seeger, E. Adams, tenor, Monsieur Alan Seeger, the world renowned basso profundo, Mademoiselle Elsie, in their choicest selections." Decorator and general manager, E. A. Seeger. [12]

Charlie and his siblings had spent little time outside the family and immediate neighborhood before they went to school—a traumatic experience for Charlie. The prevailing family attitude was that "people came to the house to see the Seegers, but there was not much of the Seegers going out to see others." School was first the Staten Island Academy, a very good private school formed in the early 1890s. Although Seeger quickly adjusted to being "out in the world" in school, as can be seen in the above recollections of Staten Island, he also cherished the closeness of the immediate family in Mexico when almost all activities took place in the home, including private tutoring for the children.

Seeger made no recounting of his youth in Mexico similar to his Staten Island memoirs, but it is clear from fragments about those years that he was happy there. When he was nearly six, in 1892, the family returned from New York City to Mexico. They landed in Vera Cruz to learn that a typhus epidemic had broken out in Mexico City. Unable to reach the capital, they spent several months in Puebla, about 100 kilometers southeast, which Charlie always remembered with fondness. During this period, his father's Mexico City office occupied the first floor of the Seeger home, and the family lived on the second or upper floor, as was customary in Mexico.

The family's last Mexican sojourn began in the summer of 1900, and the Seeger children were again tutored at home. In these years Charlie expanded his range of interests. He started reading poetry and, being already practiced on the piano and violin, also studied guitar. In the process, he learned something about Mexican popular and folk songs.

In 1902 Charlie was sent back to the States for his final high school years to prepare him for Harvard. He was enrolled at Hackley, a recently opened Unitarian school in Tarrytown, New York. As he recalled:

Ostensibly my mother and father were Unitarians, but they never went to church and their religion was a very mild sort of thing as was also the Unitarianism of the school I went to. The various ministers who came to visit us, mostly very worried looking men, gave us lectures and that was about all. Oh, we did sing hymns which we took great pleasure in parodying when we could do so safely. [13]

Charlie spent every summer from 1902 through 1908, when he graduated from Harvard, in Mexico. His experience in Mexico had a

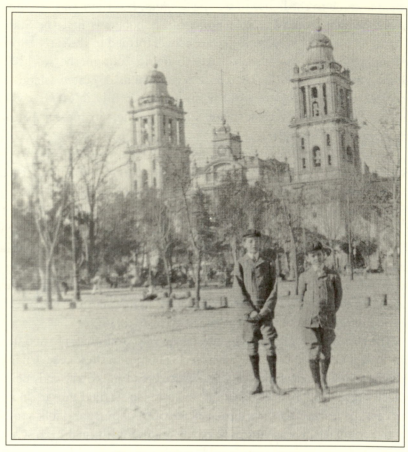

Charles and Alan, Mexico City, 1901

profound and lasting influence on him, and resonated in some of the important issues and activities of his later life. He always maintained an affinity for things Latin and retained vivid recollections of his youth there:

I never got to Acapulco although we started off hopefully from Iguala. (I was in my late teens and went with a businessman and his wife) and reached Chilpancingo, horses, guide, and two tents. We crossed a fairly broad stream, deep enough for us to have to take our feet off our stirrups, 75 times each way. No roads, of course. A few years later I started off with a college friend for Taxco from Cuernavaca, again, horse-back with an old bandit for a guide. First night was spent getting what sleep we could on the bare ground in a corn-husk shack on top of a high mountain beside the ruins of a pre-Columbian temple with the most gorgeous tropical storm reverberating all around us. The next night was in a small village in which we had heard there was an inn, but there wasn't. The only town official was the notary and he said we could take refuge (it was the rainy season) in his office, where there was a couch and a big flat-top desk. I gallantly gave the couch to my friend and I started in trying to sleep on the desk; but presently a camp-cot appeared and I got some sleep. Taxco was rarely visited in those days. It was quite a way from the railroad. No curio stores, restaurants, movie houses; just an almost perfect eighteenth century relic. The hotel was good and clean and for a bath, the *mozo* would bring a big round tin tub into which he put the charcoal stove to heat the water. This was the custom, even for middle class Mexico city-houses in those days. Man went through the streets, with tub and heater; and one could call him in for service. I don't remember his announcing his passage in song; but food of various kinds was vended with singing. Two melodies stick in my memory. One, I seem to remember was for tamales, the other for ducks, hanging alive by their feet over the vendors' shoulders. [14]

The Mexico of young Seeger's ideals, the Latin and Mediterranean ambiance, would have been an enviable experience for almost any well-to-do American family, able to have the best of everything, a contingent of servants, and a very patrician existence. As North Americans, they were privileged foreigners in the omnipotent shadow of the United States government.

It was not, however, ideal for most Mexicans. The bill for the Pax Porfiriana finally came due. Its cost had been great and its accomplishments, in some ways, artificial. The successes of Porfirian Mexico were largely a by-product of the United States' post–Civil War prosperity. The Mexican economy responded to U.S. booms and busts, a pattern that was clear by 1907. Haciendas reverted to feudal holdings. Rural people — Indians and laborers — were discouraged from moving to the cities. Mexico came under the twin tyrannies of an irresponsible native aristocracy and blatant foreign exploitation. In 1883–1894, Díaz's *caballada* (his derisive name for his lawmakers) passed laws opening up 134.5 million acres of the public domain (one-fifth of Mexico's land) to foreign speculators. Further, Díaz had been forced to throw open what remained of the Indian communities. When Indians such as the Maya and Yaqui objected, they were brutally suppressed and sold to slave gangs, primarily in the Yucatán, to cultivate henequen and tobacco. At the end of the Díaz period, fewer than 10 percent of the Indian communities had land. After 1911, Mexicans attempted to end this corruption by turmoil, uprisings, and finally revolution. These troubles eventually drove the Seegers—long after Charlie's graduation from Harvard—out of Latin America and to Europe. Bullets in the bathroom were the end of the family's twenty-five years in Mexico.

The Revolution of 1911 in Mexico put an end to a very prosperous business. My father had gone into the importation of expensive automobiles for wealthy Mexicans, for which he charged easily 100 percent profit, for everyone, so my brother and I went to Harvard with adequate funds to lead the life of young gentlemen. But the revolution put an end to this business and he started all over again keeping a store of goods supplied by the American Rubber Company in Havana. I don't think he actually sold behind the counter, rubber shoes and waterproof garments, but it was a pretty small business. But after a year or two the company transferred him to Europe as vice-president of the European branch of the United States Rubber Company, where everything went very well and he was able to live the life of a gentlemen that he'd always looked forward to. Until one day a brash young man came into the office and told him he was out; that the company was retiring him and that he was to return to America, which of course he had to do. He retired then to his place up at Patterson where he had bought the old Patterson homestead, Patterson, New York. [15]

Probably because the Seegers missed the bloody revolution that began in 1911, they harbored a romantic view of Mexico. The Mexico of young Don Carlos Seeger's childhood and adolescence was an idyllic, prosperous time for foreigners and privileged Mexicans alike. It was one in which the wealthy elite sent their children abroad, particularly to France, for education and the civilizing graces. This was the Mexico that entertained the European doctrines of positivism, a romantic era rich in letters and the arts. Seeger's memories of an isolated, comfortable existence of servants, serenades, and languid complacency left him with a love of Mediterranean civilizations. He frequently spoke of the influence of Latin culture on himself and his brother Alan. [16] Both identified with romantic poets; Mexico, along with the great learning of Europe, especially of southern Europe, Charles wrote, "laid hold of us and dominated our lives."

Seeger recollected his adolescent years in the following reminiscence:

Boarding school and college had left summers in which to resume the lifestyle of Staten Island, but [we] children entered a world totally at variance with the world in which their childhood had been lived. Within the decade 1900–1910, a centuries old way of life was shattered, first by the telephone and electrification, then the automobile. There was nothing left of Staten Island except the furniture and the tradition. The grandchildren have some of the former and, I hope, not too little of the latter. [17]

Elizabeth responded to her brother's letter with this comment:

I think that Father and Mother were perfect parents of small children; it was only when we became individuals that Mother failed and I don't believe that Father ever would have if we had not been separated by the (to me) fatal residence in Mexico. I think that Mother, too, would have been very different if she, (a) had not been ill because of Mexico and (b) had not been so isolated from all other families and social customs; it was a very sad ending to a potentially happy family life. Do you remember when we began spending our evenings together? I remember the time when we had supper in the nursery and maybe spent our evenings there, but I also remember going upstairs to bed and wondering, asking, in fact, what mysterious thing they did after we went? I think our evenings and the things we did with Father are among the best parts of our family life. To this day when I am staying with a family, it seems wrong to me when everyone drifts off to his or her room or job and I think they miss a lot. They both meant to and did to a great extent make a work of art out of their home, Mother primarily, but Father too, especially, in all he did with us. I can't see any account of [Staten Island] complete with that left out. Christmas! Do you remember marching in with Aunt Hattie leading us, singing Tannenbaum? And going to bed with the robins singing and the crickets and Father playing Wagner downstairs? By the way, Dennis's family must have come in for Christmas, because I remember that Mother always included the servants then; in New York I distinctly remember our current cook, whom we did not know well, bringing two or three children to our tree.[18]

While family life overall had been "idyllic" in Seeger's remembrance, he had suffered periods of distress, both physical and psychological. Through psychoanalysis and introspection he came to understand more about it. A physical handicap that began in his youth and worsened through life, was a hearing disability. As a boy, Seeger was plagued with increasingly painful earaches. His parents poured laudanum in his ears and applied hot water bags, and his father would try to lull him to sleep with piano music ranging from Wagner to Mexican *danzas*.

Yet Seeger also associated music with early stages of rebellion. As a boy he studied the piano, but rebelled against practicing. He also refused to read books and determined that from the second grade on he would be indifferent to school. This realization gave him another weapon: no one could force him to pay attention in class.

His analysis of this rebellious "anti-establishment" stance later led him to several conclusions about himself. He recognized that he had cultivated this posture from a very early age as a response to the birth of his sister in his fourth or fifth year, when she displaced him from his room next to his parents. Moreover, his brother Alan was frequently sick and garnered considerable family attention. As Charlie grew older, he began to see himself as relegated to a less influential role in his parents' world. At first he claimed not to have taken this out on his sister or brother, although he felt that he had given up many things because his sister was so small and his brother sickly much of the time. Seeger even attributed the inferiority complex which he believed he nurtured until his junior year in college to this resentment of his siblings. At that point, he reckoned, he had begun to accumulate enough independence, certainty, and rank among his colleagues to change his attitude about himself; indeed, he acquired a highly developed and honed superiority complex.

He vented his frustrations on his family by deciding very early that he was going to lead a different kind of life from what his parents expected.

He would not pursue business as a vocation. In analyzing his rebellion, Seeger frequently referred to a dichotomy in his personality. He saw it as allegiance to the structure and some of the ideals of the family but, at the same time, a resistance to doing what was expected.

In further introspection about childhood attitudes and traits, Seeger thought that a key aspect of his personality was forgiving and making allowances for other people's mistakes or misdeeds. Another strategem was to engage in a judicious fight and then to taunt his enemy from an advantageous cover or position. Forged to perfection as a child, he used this strategy all his life, intellectually. Seeger also suggested that his susceptibility to being beaten by bullies as a child contributed to his cultivation of nonviolence. This was supported by the ethics he learned from his Unitarian parents who supported the Christian ethos of love, kindness, and chivalry.

Seeger also inherited from his parents a respect for the "good life," being monied, and occupying a certain position in the world. When his father visited Europe on business in the early 1900s, according to Charles, he observed a class-divided society and decided at which social level he wanted to live; Charlie acquired this attitude, too. He and his siblings were indoctrinated in his father's conviction, noted earlier, that 70 percent of the people were born to be led, 10 percent true leaders, and that 20 percent would carry out their wishes in running the lives of the rest. Charlie also confessed, uneasily, to sharing some of his father's political ideas, though they conflicted with his more radical side. In Seeger's words, his father was the "snobbest of the snobs." A juxtaposition of philosophies was always there in Charlie's life. He was the classic nineteenth-century "liberal."

Seeger had a great respect for his father, whom he remembered as a handsome, distinguished man of integrity and strong character. He claimed that despite his father's conservatism he was very human, never stooping to extremes. He was intellectually and artistically alive; he wrote poetry and was an ardent sketcher with some talent, producing volumes of drawings of Mexico, Staten Island, France, England, Spain, Morocco, Italy, and other places. Some of these sketches Charlie kept in an old trunk in the Bridgewater house and, occasionally, proudly showed to guests. Eventually his father was able to live in Paris, which he had always wanted to do. There he enjoyed good friendships with several European artists, intellectuals, and political figures of import, among them Alexander Iswolsky, the former Russian minister of foreign affairs and ambassador to France, whose memoirs the elder Seeger translated and edited.

Seeger's development, then, was curiously divided between non-conformity and adherence to tradition. He fulfilled a long-desired family plan for college. In 1904, Seeger entered Harvard, where he acquired a coterie of close friends. One was a Reginald Sweet who, much to Charlie's delight, always went around in overalls. Another was George Foote, who became a banker. John Hall Wheelock became a poet of some note, and, as we shall see in the next chapter, Seeger set some of his poems to music. Edward Brewster (Ned) Sheldon, a future playwright, and Van Wyck Brooks, who became a noted essayist and critic, also were part of the coterie.[19]

At Harvard, Charlie and his friends all belonged to the Stylus club, which invited noted artistic personalities to the area. Charlie and his friends were able, for example, to work with the great Sarah Bernhardt on stage. In their senior year, Seeger and his friends were elected to the exclusive Signet Society.

About his later college days, Charlie wrote:

With my roommate, Dutro Plumb, I occupied the west front room on the second floor during my junior and senior years of happy memory. Kenneth Carpenter and Billy Kurtz lived in the front east room on the same floor. As you know, the house stood fairly free in the garden without being crowded in by the buildings of later construction. I had my Steinway grand piano in the corner of the room. There was a small bedroom just above the front door. My poor roommate, though he became a fanatical music-lover later in life, spent most of his time out of our room, for I was at the piano — or dashing between it and my desk — most of my waking hours. I regret having to tell you that I remember nothing more of the room or the house in those two years, 1906–08, but the music made in them.

Curiously enough, Mrs. John Tracy Edson, mother of my first wife, had purchased at a sale of the effects of the house, several fine pieces of furniture said to have been in it for generations. I remember one piece, especially. It was a mahogany sideboard of great simplicity, surely eighteenth-century,

Harvard Signet Society portrait, 1908; Charles is second from right, middle row

though whether of British or American make I never knew. It stood in my house in Berkeley, California when last I saw it, but was afterward burned in the great Berkeley fire that destroyed nearly a square mile of houses.[20]

While Seeger apparently enjoyed college, he and his friends had a poor opinion of their Harvard education. This is not surprising; Harvard had not yet attained a reputation as a major intellectual center; although it claimed famous men on the faculty and graduated others, it was chiefly known as a college for sons of the elite. Seeger worked with the famous literary scholar George Lyman Kittredge in his senior tutorial on Chaucer, in which he studied ballads. But he felt that music training at Harvard was very bad; students were frequently ahead of their teachers. Regularly assigned books and music scores had many uncut pages, indicating that students had never opened them and were not held accountable for the information they contained. All the while, Seeger continued to study the piano (but confessed to hating scales). As he noted to his daughter, "I didn't pay any attention to the other studies and in music I and my colleagues taught each other. By the sophomore year, we'd attained such a low opinion of our teachers that we didn't bother very much with the instruction except to pass the examinations."[21]

Even in Boston, where one could get the best musical training in the United States, one had to train oneself, Seeger observed. He spent considerable time at Boston Symphony Orchestra concerts. He would attend one day with musical scores of the works performed—scores obtained directly from Europe about which his professors had no knowledge—and the next day just to listen.

Seeger, like his friends, had very different opinions about music from the views of his professors. Perhaps they were simply ignorant of the works of Debussy and other modern composers, or perhaps they did not consider this music worth teaching. New works, particularly by Scriabin, Debussy, Mahler, Satie, and Strauss, were being introduced by Karl Muck and the Boston Symphony. Seeger's interest in these new styles and forms convinced him that upon graduation he should go to Europe. As he told Penny:

At that time, the latest composers which we were devoted to were Richard Strauss and Claude Debussy; . . . we did know Reger and Ravel and perhaps a few others of the lesser known. Schoenberg, Stravinsky, were unknown, unheard of. . . . Ruggles and Ives were not heard of. Webern, Berg, Bartok unheard of. In Europe they were just beginning to play some Schoenberg. I think I heard *Verklaerte Nacht* there—one of his earlier works and was not greatly impressed with it. Rimsky-Korsakov I heard with the Russian Imperial Ballet in the Paris Opera House, but there was not anything that presently became known after 1912–14 as "modern music." Wagner was supreme, with Strauss of course, and Debussy was beginning to be known. Although we were devoted to him, he was still a comparatively unknown person in America although *Pelleas and Melisande* was given at the Metropolitan in 1908.[22]

Just as the family expected Seeger to attend Harvard, they wanted him to become a businessman. However, the rebel in him prescribed a different course. Not only was he not interested in business, but

Seeger had sufficient interest and talent in music, particularly in composition, that he chose that area as the one on which he would concentrate, much to his father's great disappointment.

My youthful ambitions and ideals by the time I got to Harvard were to avoid going into business, even if to do so meant going to college which I was not interested in doing. But I found that I could study music in a music department at Harvard, so I said I would take every music course there and I suppose you can say that music became an ideal and being a composer — yes — becoming a composer became an ideal. . . .

I was slated to become a partner in my father's business in Mexico, and . . . hating business with a mortal hatred, I decided that almost anything would be better than going into business. Becoming a composer was a marvelous thing to do. But, when I told my father that I was going to be a composer, he was horrified. He said, "But gentlemen are not musicians. Come and work in my office for ten years and I can guarantee (alas, I might prophesy) that you will be able to put aside enough money so that you can retire for the rest of your life and then you can write all the music you want." That wasn't my idea; my idea was that I was going to be married as soon as possible, have a lot of children, and spend my life composing. He pointed out the impracticality of it and the argument closed.[23]

Seeger graduated from Harvard magna cum laude in music in 1908, and he and his friends scattered in different directions. Foote, Sweet, and Wheelock went immediately to Europe, while Brooks and Sheldon headed for New York. Seeger's decision to learn more about the new European music was complemented by his concern to enhance the environment for American music. "One did not pick up American music where American music was; you had to pick up American music where European music was," he mused. Seeger's father supported him during his European sojourn.

The word got back to Harvard that Mr. Seeger, who was just one of these cold businessmen, wouldn't support any of his boys beyond the time when we were twenty-one, or graduated from college. The daughter would be supported until she was married or if she didn't marry, for the rest of her life. The boys would have to go out and earn their living. So letters went back to my father saying that he was a very thoughtless parent to let this brilliant talent not go abroad and really seep up the knowledge that the great German

Graduation picture, Harvard University, 1908

and European—German musics—French and other musics didn't count in Harvard at that time—it had to be German music. So father relented and gave me enough money to go abroad and study music for a year. At the end of that year, the funds were going to stop so I managed to borrow some to keep me another year and then . . . another half year and my father was somewhat horrified, but I kept quiet.[24]

Seeger wrote in 1958,

In these last fifty years, I have lived successively three lives. At graduation, the world was most accurately described in terms of Shelley and Keats, and most deeply felt in the harmonies of Debussy and Strauss. It was a beautiful world, spoiled only by the meanness of some human beings who seemed to make it their special business to make as many people as possible as miserable as possible. They accomplished this mainly through the device of government. The result was what seemed to be an immutable socio-economic class system throughout the world, with the mean on top and the demeaned in a hierarchy burdgeoning down from their lieutenants to the lowest class of all, representing variously 70–90 percent of populations, of which it was most unpleasant to be a member. But the mean were not really on top. They only thought they were. The real top were those who made up the small minority that rejected the whole mess and floated free and untrammeled over it all, in communion with the realities of life—beauty, love and virtue. It was these alone who could see and feel things as they really were and not as the mean ones made them seem to be. The ethic and esthetic were simple: the attractive, lovely, beautiful and good were necessary and indispensable, the repellent, ugly, unbeautiful were unnecessary and, so, dispensable.[25]

The first two decades of his life had been molded by his familiarity with this hemisphere. Indeed, Seeger was a genuine American article. His creative life was a constant ebbing and flowing from North to South, and he remained preoccupied with the concept of verticality. In his early years it was with the immediacy of the border and the ease of movement between the northeastern United States and Mexico. Later it was with the pan-hemispheric links between the Americas. But his vision of South America was always that of a don, of the benevolent patron, a logical extension of the influence of his first twenty-one years.

If a vigorous, jingoistic United States, and a romantic, prerevolutionary Mexico were major contributors to shaping the ideas and attitudes of young Seeger, another formative influence would soon be at play—pre–World War I Europe.

2

Europe, Constance, and the University of California, 1908–1919

❧

SEEGER SPENT THE SUMMER after graduation with his family in Mexico, then left for Europe in the autumn of 1908. Seeger was ready to be impressed by Europe, influenced by what he had read and heard. Shortly after reaching Europe he decided that Europeans knew how to live and that Americans did not, especially in cities.

As a composer, Seeger preferred French compositional styles and techniques, but since conducting was his immediate goal, and because Germany was a center for conducting activity, he chose to go there, specifically to the opera in Cologne. His first stop was Munich, a bohemian city of painters, writers, and musicians, the artistic center of Germany at the time. Among German cities, it was most receptive to and displayed a French style, an *esprit frondeur*. It was avant garde. It was the home of Germany's best review, the *Simplizissimus,* an organ of irony, satire, and the impressionist artistic culture. The city attracted Thomas Mann and others, including spirited young Americans like Seeger. He stayed far longer than he had planned, six weeks and "a while." From Munich he traveled to Berlin, where he did not linger. Although it was a great intellectual center, to Seeger Berlin seemed too circumspect.

After arriving in Cologne on January 1, 1909, Seeger signed on as apprentice to Otto Lohse, conductor of the Cologne Municipal Opera. As he recalled,

Of my 2¹/₂ years in Europe, [one] was served as an assistant on the conducting staff at the Cologne Municipal Opera, so that I really knew the opera from the stage side out, attended rehearsals from nine o'clock in the morning to the end of performance at night, sometimes 11 or 11:30.[1]

Seeger liked Cologne, though he found it quiet; its streets were deserted by eight in the evening. The people were kind but distant. There he had his first love affair. He expressed his interpretations of his experience in terms of a relationship to things that he knew and things that he did not know. He lay awake at night, expressing in mental diagrams his feelings and his role in the relationship. Then, on the fourth day, he said, music began to flow. Those diagrams, he claimed, contributed to his later turn from composition to musicology; he could not separate talking about music from making music.

This love affair portended the complicated romantic relationships that Seeger seemed to cultivate throughout his life. He and his new love left for Paris, where he met his college mate Ned Sheldon, who invited them to dinner. There Seeger met the soprano Marie Doro, of Victor Herbert operetta fame, to whom he immediately took "quite a fancy." Despite the presence of Seeger's girlfriend, Seeger and Doro managed a few evenings of dinner and the theater together. Doro suggested that they should go off to Dresden to write an operetta which, she boasted, would be "better than Victor Herbert's." She would write the libretto and Seeger would compose the music. Enthralled by the idea, he agreed to meet her in Dresden after extricating himself from his "commitments." He did, but Marie Doro never kept their rendezvous.

Seeger returned to Cologne after lengthy stays in Paris and Dresden, but by the end of 1910 he realized that he would probably never have a career as a conductor. For one thing, he had neither perfect pitch, a disappointment to him, nor the ability to hear notes in the upper register. More important, however, his hearing was growing worse, and he often missed entrances in the music. He would never perform or conduct professionally.

Seeger returned to Berlin, which now had more appeal, with the intention of writing an opera. He spent several months on both music and libretto for a "choral opera with solo parts." He envisioned it as the "first American opera." Set in New York and Long Island, the work explored class differences and promoted a utopian vision of society. He described the project to his daughter:

My aim as a composer was to write the first American opera of any stature. I worked out a libretto on the basis of my friend John Hall Wheelock's *Poems of the City* in which the chorus was to be hidden to each side of the main scene on the stage as part of the proscenium. They were to sing through a netting which would conceal them and would keep up a continual comment on the action on the stage, more or less in the style of the Greek theater.

The plot was to begin with a tennis party down on Long Island and the first scene did get finished. I still have the score. It was very Straussian and perhaps impractical from that viewpoint because it needed a large orchestra. From there it made a journey up to the city where the hero was looking for his wife who was a poor girl (and he was a rich man) who had fled back to the city because she couldn't stand the frittering away of life in Southampton. He finds her and they go through a various number of experiences in the city and he finally decides to join her in the fight for unionization of the workers. Although I was not a Socialist at the time, it was all written more or less in the vein of Shelley and Keats and Byron—very romantic, and you can imagine the rest. I destroyed the libretto long ago, because it really was a bit mawkish.[2]

Once committed to composition, during the rest of his sojourn Seeger traveled frequently to France, especially to Paris, using Berlin as his base. German and French culture influenced his creative and intellectual growth and his developing social consciousness. He had known American jingoism, an Ivy League education, and Latin American life. Europe had been a missing piece of the puzzle. While he ceased to compose after 1919, Europe's impact on his musical ideas was profound; likewise, in Europe he first encountered the radical social and political ideas that remained with him all his life.

France was in the last years of *la belle epoque*, what Roger Shattuck has termed "the banquet years." Between the death of Victor Hugo in 1885 and World War I, the country was prosperous and Paris was the cultural capital of the world. In this time, audience and performer moved from the salon to the cafe.[3] The post-Wagnerian music world made a great impact on the impressionable young American musician, conductor, and composer drawn to French music. Although

Wagner's popularity was still growing in the early 1900s, eventually the impact of this "genius-artist of romanticism" declined. The new generation of French composers strongly influenced Seeger. While at Harvard, he had considered French music to be light years ahead of other contemporary work. Chabrier, Fauré, Debussy, Ravel, Scriabin, the expatriate Stravinsky, Satie—each in his own manner dominated the French music scene.

Because of the particular influence of Erik Satie on Seeger, his career requires a brief discussion here. As a composer, Satie went through two distinct periods, interrupted by a voluntary hiatus between 1898 and 1910. He had a major impact on modern music in both careers. Few composers, in Shattuck's words, "reveal more clearly than Satie the origins and early development of twentieth century music,"[4] an opinion Seeger shared. He was particularly drawn to Satie's musical intellect.

During Satie's first period, Chabrier and Fauré were the two most independent and original composers working in France,[5] and Seeger responded to their work partly through their impact on Satie. Chabrier influenced Satie, writes Shattuck, in his harmonic freedom and musical humor, while Fauré, although less influential, affected his pianistic style and techniques of melodic accompaniment. Satie himself said that Debussy was the greatest influence on his life and work. Debussy's *Pelleas et Melisande* launched a "new independence in French music" and moved French composition away from Wagnerism. In *Pelleas,* Debussy's great revision of vocal technique consisted in writing according to the emotional pressure of the words and in allowing a single pitch to carry a number of syllables without forming any melodic line. Such innovation excited Satie, who in his *Messe des pauvres* (1895) "carries verticality and unvarying dynamics to their extreme point. . . . Satie was approaching a style of disjunction, of separation rather than unity of parts." Two years later his work, *Pièces froides* for example, showed further experimentation and originality.

Between Satie's first and second careers, he spent some time at the Schola Cantorum, principally studying counterpoint with Albert Roussel and analysis and orchestration with Vincent d'Indy.[6] He and Debussy debated and experimented with harmonic "impressionism."

The idea of form for Debussy, Satie, and others was unlike that of the classical and romantic composers. Particularly for Satie, form was

a series of points which turn out to be one point. His music progresses by standing still. . . . Form ceases to be an ordering in time like ABA and reduces to a single brief image, an instantaneous whole both fixed and moving . . . extended only by reiteration or "endurance."

Ravel and Debussy experimented in different ways with the idea of readjustment of values.

French composers after 1883 adopted many of the ideas of the artistic school of impressionism, especially as exhibited in the paintings of Monet, Cézanne, and Toulouse-Lautrec. Later, by 1910, the musical world of France had found new allegiances to fauvism and cubism. Stravinsky's *Sacre du Printemps* illustrates the fauve rhythms at work, as do works by Debussy, Ravel, and Fauré.

Seeger's attraction to the French composers helped him in his own analysis of composition and musical experimentation. He thought American composers should be more experimental; America and most of Western Europe, he felt, were still enthralled by Germanic romantic modes, notably the work of Richard Wagner.

Seeger's attraction to the *new* has an explanation in what Roger Shattuck spoke of as a response to contemporary ideas, in art and philosophy alike, that were challenging traditional concepts of sensory perception. Instead of understanding phenomena in time and space as a "reasoned arrangement of events in a series," modern artists were experimenting with "a violent dislocation of them in order to test the possibility of a new coherence. . . . Just as a phenomenon in nature could no longer be understood as existing *there* in the simple location of classic physics, so a work of art . . . no longer had a simple *here and now*, but a very complex unity, a polytonal composition." This was not a search for the "self-forgetfulness" of romanticism but a new self-awareness on the part of the artist. Music in the period came to represent those "banquet years," writes Shattuck, in its effort "to be 'pure,' to be utterly self-reflexive."[7]

These dichotomies in the new styles of European music and art, and a growing affinity for dialectic, explain the appeal of avant-garde musical concepts for Seeger.[8] Juxtaposition was accompanied by simultanism, by which "the mutually conflicting elements of montage . . . converge in our minds as contemporaneous events." Simultanism, synchronicity (the coincidence of events in space and time as an interdependence of objective events among themselves), and superposition (imposing or enforcing juxtaposition of parts) were key elements. Simultanism is not simply a Hegelian resolution of opposites; it requires that we must accommodate "concurrently and without synthesis" two or more contradictory propositions—an intellectual challenge that found fruitful expression in the arts.

If France supplied an impetus for composition and musical concepts, European social thought, modified by the American context, changed Seeger's ideas on society. In the words of H. Stuart Hughes, "It was Germans and Austrians and French and Italians—rather than Englishmen or Americans or Russians—who in general provided the fund of ideas that has come to seem most characteristic of our own time."[9]

To a far greater extent than was the case on the European periphery, the countries of the Western and Central European continent shared institutions and an intellectual heritage—in philosophy, in law, and in the structure of higher education—that presented their leading social thinkers with a similar set of problems [and shared in] a wider experience of psychological *malaise*: the sense of impending doom, of old practices and institutions no longer conforming to social realities, which obsessed so many Continentals.[10]

The major figures of the period—like Freud, Croce, Pareto— ushered in an era of specialization in social theory, and an emphasis on discrete, finite problems. Yet they were philosophically adventurous and left behind more unproved hypotheses than answers. Their innovation was to erase the lines between science and the imagination. As Hughes observes, "Personally, they were humanists: they combined a philosophical with a scientific education, and they drew no clear line of demarcation between literature and social science."[11] Consciousness was a major concern in this body of thought.

The basic assumptions of Enlightenment and nineteenth-century social thought were being challenged, and novel ideas were emerging. The new social thought was at odds with a basic premise of the American republic—the ideal of rational beings freely choosing among properly weighed alternatives. European social thinkers who argued that human beings were in charge of their fate in strictly proscribed activities and for only brief periods—who argued, in other words, "the basic characteristic of human experience was the limited nature of its freedom"—expressed a concept that denied a fundamental tenet of American democracy.[12]

The early decades of the twentieth century saw a revolt against positivism. Key tenets of positivism—notably, a belief in progress, scientific rigor, objective investigation, realism, and a rejection of all metaphysical assumptions—first emerged in the eighteenth century as utilitarianism, but in the nineteenth century, with the advance of social Darwinism, a new recognition of the impact of heredity and environment on human development replaced a belief in the primacy of reason and logical choice. Along with these developments, perhaps paradoxically, these decades saw also the vigorous expansion of socialist thought.

The intellectual ferment of Austria, Germany, and France influenced Seeger both as a musician and a man of ideas. He became aware of new psychological concepts, such as levels of consciousness—the subconscious, the preconscious, the unconscious—and new concepts of time and duration in history, literature, and philosophy. These ideas had profound implications for a musician. In Hughes's words, philosophers and artists were seeking

to define the nature of subjective existence as opposed to the schematic order that the natural sciences had imposed on the external world . . . the task that Croce had set himself in trying to establish the qualitative and methodological differences between the realm of history and the realm of science. . . . It was the dilemma that obsessed the novelists of the first two decades of the new century—Alain-Fournier, Marcel Proust, Thomas Mann—of how to recapture the immmediacy of past experience in language that in ordinary usage could reproduce no more than the fragmentized reality of an existence that the logical memory had already stored away in neat compartments.[13]

Seeger's future colleagues on the Berkeley faculty—Teggart, Adams, Lewis, Loewenberg, and Pope—as well as visitors to Berkeley like Ralph Barton Perry, with whom Seeger would enjoy intellectual exchange, were affected by these European currents. It was Perry, influenced by Kant and by the theory of value posited by psychologists and economists in Austria, whose own theory of value would come to play such an important role in Seeger's thinking. Hegel and Kant both were idealists; indeed, Hegel's doctrine extended from the idealist's view that the ultimate reality of the universe lay in the idea rather than in the data of sense perception.

Kant became another intellectual force in Seeger's development. Kant's metaphysical and epistemological work reconciled the positivist and antipositivist. One of his convictions was that it was possible to transcend the symbolic world of science, to understand a phenomenon in terms of something else and to arrive at absolute knowledge — an idea Seeger would pursue in his work. Kant also tried to determine categories of thought and to distinguish between those used in cultural science and those used in natural science. Separating methods of study from the object or item studied was another strategem later employed by Seeger.

The neo-Kantians, in particular, argued that the cultural sciences tried to understand particular events, whereas natural science tried to formulate general laws. Men such as Heinrich Rickert of the school of southwest German philosophy and an influential figure in 1910–1911 Berlin, suggested that cultural scientists made choices. His theories promoted the avant-garde idea of the subjectivity of all knowledge. In Hughes's words,

In putting the whole emphasis on the notion of value, [Rickert] implied a radically subjective conception of historical knowledge. Value in the social and historical world could not be arrived at by any verifiable process: it could only be "intuited." Hence there was no guarantee of its validity. Ultimately the historian was reduced to an act of faith in his own values. . . . From this dilemma, the only escape-route was by way of metaphysics . . . as assertion of the absolute validity of the historian's value-system, [an implication] . . . that value had an independent and transcendental existence outside and above the consciousness of the individual historian.[14]

Wilhelm Dilthey also tried to solve this problem by undertaking a critique of historical reason, the problem of the scientific value of historical writing. For him, history was not fixed but changed with the time and culture of the historian; knowledge in cultural science was an internal, intuitive process gained through experience. These new ideas regarding the subjectivity of social science and history—blurring the lines between art and science—strongly affected the young musician as he absorbed the intellectual currents of prewar Europe.

The last decade of the nineteenth century and early decades of the twentieth were the crucible years of Seeger's intellectual development. He matured in the heady atmosphere of European thought at a time of Europe's political and cultural preeminence. Radical ideas about process, scientific method, criticism, aesthetics, and value changed Seeger's own thinking.

His original purpose, to become an avant-garde composer, was quieted by his increasing concern about being an American composer with an imported music tradition. This contradiction, perhaps first reflected in his attempt to write in Europe an opera of social message set in America, affected much of his later thinking and writing.

The spring of 1911 was a memorable one for all the Seegers. With the coming of the Revolution, his family had to flee Mexico. His mother and sister departed on the *Merida,* which sank en route to New York. They survived, but lost seven trunks filled with silver, silks, heirlooms, and other possessions. Seeger, himself, after two and a half years, returned to New York, having decided to pursue a career as musician and composer and to undertake a tour as an accompanist. As he told his daughter,

I came back to start in professional life in the distant colony of New York, which was then the only city that had an opera house and the only one that had a symphony orchestra except Boston. I think perhaps there may have been one being founded in Philadelphia, and shortly afterwards in Chicago. But there was only one decent quartet in the country and that was the Kneisel Quartet.[15]

His was a spartan existence in New York. Seeger lived in a little hall bedroom on Madison Avenue where he did much of his composing. Shortly after his return, Schirmer agreed to publish *Seven Songs for High*

Voice and Pianoforte, which included a setting for John Keats's "Asleep." Because Seeger composed in the contemporary French vein, his music was considered revolutionary in the United States. According to Seeger, Kurt Schindler, who judged the music for Schirmer, hailed him as the golden boy of his generation, THE future composer of America.

Nearly twenty-five, and proud of his incipient success, Seeger planned a life for himself that would lead to fame and fortune as a composer and musician. He did not envision making any permanent commitments, at least not for several years. That was not to be.

Six weeks after he landed in New York City, Seeger was invited to lunch with a teacher of violin at the Institute of Musical Art, Franz Kneisel. There he met one of Kneisel's principal students, a young violinist named Constance Edson. She was looking for an accompanist; Seeger got the job, and soon they were musical partners.

Constance came from a well-established New York family.[16] Her mother, a Charliere, was related to the Curtiss family of Philadelphia. Her grandfather was headmaster of the Charliere School on Fifty-ninth Street, which was attended by the sons of many well-to-do New Yorkers, among them the Damrosch boys.[17] An uncle, mayor of New York, presided over the opening of the Brooklyn Bridge. Constance's father, a physician and Annapolis graduate, fought at the battle of Santiago during the Spanish-American War, an experience from which he never fully recovered.

Dr. Edson became the company physician for the New York Life Insurance Company in Denver and came into a sizable inheritance. The family enjoyed a life of wealth and display during the 1890s, until the money was gone and they were saddled with debts. Bitter quarrels about Mrs. Edson's extravagance led to a separation and Dr. Edson's emotional breakdown. Dr. Edson later told Seeger that he could no longer endure his wife—a powerful, erratic, and difficult woman whom Charlie called a virago. Their conflicts over the children and property—she kept all the furnishings of the Denver home—occasionally came to near tragedy. Once a drunk Dr. Edson threatened his wife with his Smith and Wesson revolver; Constance prevented him.

Leaving her son Elie, age sixteen, in New York, Mrs. Edson sailed to Europe with eleven-year-old Constance. There they had an adventurous existence. For a time Mrs. Edson was the mistress of the governor-general of Tunisia, where she and Constance lived a life of luxury in a palace. When that relationship ended, they traveled to Paris where Constance contracted scarlet fever.

Their first night, Constance told Seeger, found them on the streets with no place to stay. A priest befriended them and let them sleep on the straw of his tiny room. Before long Mrs. Edson, obviously a survivor with a penchant for the good life, had settled herself in a well-connected coterie in Paris. Recognizing her daughter's unusual musical talent, Mrs. Edson arranged for violin lessons. In Charlie's words, Constance was "whipped" into being a violinist, although she had a true gift for the instrument.

Mrs. Edson returned to the United States, leaving Constance, now in her early teens, to continue her violin studies in Paris. She lived for a year with the Rices, a well-to-do American family living abroad. Mrs. Rice gave Constance much-needed moral and financial support during a difficult time. The Rices and Constance returned to New York together, but no one met Constance at the dock.

The Edsons and Charlieres had excellent connections in New York's music world, and Constance soon came under the watchful eye of the Damrosch family. She became like an adopted daughter, even calling Frank Damrosch "Uncle Frank." Constance's talent and persistence earned her a scholarship at New York's Institute of Musical Art, where she studied with Franz Kneisel (as noted above). She later studied at the New York Institute with Kaiser, another excellent teacher. In addition to the Damrosches, many of the wealthy people who supported the Institute—such as the Warburgs and the Loebs— opened their homes to her. Constance's music connections served Charlie well some years later when the couple returned from California to New York.

Having decided on marriage, Charles and Constance began a violin-piano concert tour of the Northeast, performing on Long Island and at Bar Harbor and Stockbridge, to earn money. They particularly liked the Berkshires, where Constance's family and friends summered. They accumulated enough to set up separate living quarters but not enough to marry. Constance, earning a better living than

Charlie, rented an apartment at 223 Lexington Avenue and Charlie a room around the corner. They were connected by a pulley clothesline that carried notes back and forth—Constance had a telephone, but Charlie did not. They continued to teach and give recitals, with some success.

On December 22, 1911, Charles and Constance were married in a simple ceremony in her brother Elie's apartment in the east eighties. Dr. and Mrs. Edson, Elie, Mr. and Mrs. Seeger, and Elizabeth were in attendance, and John Hall Wheelock was Seeger's best man. They had just enough money to pay for the announcements and the minister.

Seeger's plans, once so carefully laid out, had changed drastically. No longer could he do as he wished; accustomed to a comfortable life, he did not wish to live in penury with his bride, soon pregnant with their first child. A more substantial career was necessary, and the opportunity for that was soon to come.

In May 1912, Seeger was surprised to receive a call from Benjamin Ide Wheeler, president of the University of California, offering him a position, on the recommendation of a Harvard faculty member, as professor of music. He and Seeger met for lunch at the Waldorf-Astoria. Seeger accepted the position, which paid the "glorious" salary of $3,000 per year. That evening Wheeler invited Seeger and Constance to a dinner at the Plimpton's, of the Ginn book publishing company. At dinner, Seeger was introduced to Lady Murray, whose famous husband, Sir Gilbert, had been made a full professor at the age of twenty-seven. With satisfaction, Seeger later related that Plimpton was flabbergasted at the fact that Seeger was to be a full professor at twenty-six.

The young couple traveled west in the summer of 1912 to a completely new life. Charles and Constance quickly settled into Berkeley, an area of spacious farmland, eucalyptus groves, wildcats, wild dogs in the hills, and a gentle climate. It was a different ambiance, free of Yankee gentility, closer to the Pacific world and Latin America.

They moved into their first home, a rented house on La Loma, and prepared for the birth of the baby. Seeger had always had a curious fear that he would die before he had a child. He was released from that fear on September 16, 1912, when Charles III was born. With happy abandon Seeger walked the Berkeley hills, conquering another anxiety—a fear of woods and mountains.

On that same date, Alan sent a postcard from Paris. Having graduated from Harvard in 1910, Alan—already committed to poetry as a vocation—had left the States for Europe in the autumn of 1912. Alan's card said that he intended to winter in Paris and stay "for years and years, the best to explore the Old World."

When he arrived in Berkeley to begin work, Seeger found that there was no real music department; his position had been established by the state legislature as an appendage to the Department of Agriculture. Some classes met at the YMCA, while others were held in the foyer of the Hearst Mining Building. The first music building was what Seeger termed "an old, smelly house on Bancroft." Seeger's predecessor had been John Frederick Wolle, a quiet, unassuming man. When Wolle departed, all he left behind was twenty-five students and, in Seeger's view, no music curriculum.

The first year was an exploratory one for Seeger, learning what was being taught and what courses could be developed. He had been hired to teach theory, harmony, counterpoint, and music history. Because Seeger had a low opinion of what currently passed for music history, he set out to remedy the situation. The idea that music had evolved from primitive to folk to fine art, following the prevailing theory of the day, meant that early music, popular music, and folk music were given little attention. "Primitive" music materials were rare, so that genre was considered only perfunctorily. Folk music was given a few lectures as a remnant of a dying past, and popular music was not dealt with at all. Needless to say, Seeger vowed to make changes. Seeger's first year at Berkeley also provided a stimulus for his own further intellectual development. He realized that despite a Harvard degree, he was not well educated. With a new friend, Herbert E. Cory, he set out to educate himself in a number of new disciplines.

Moreover, he was coming in contact with fresh approaches to social issues and becoming aware of social problems he had never before encountered. Colleagues such as Alfred Kroeber, Robert Lowie, Richard Tolman, and many others, introduced him to ideas and concerns that differed radically from those he had known in the East. He acted on one of his newly developed opinions at a meeting of the Academic Senate, where Seeger seconded a motion by Alfred Kroeber that no student be awarded a bachelor's degree until he had supported himself with the labor of his own hands for one year. Such a suggestion would never have been made in the hallowed halls of the Ivy League.

The music professorship had been for one year, but the position was renewable. Liking California and concerned about his livelihood, Seeger asked President Wheeler in April 1913 about an extension of his appointment. The president assured him that there would be a second year, and many more, if Seeger were successful. Suddenly it was possible to undertake more ambitious long-range projects.

Seeger set about planning a summer session which, as in later years, was held in the old administration building auditorium. Although such programs were primarily training for public school teachers, Seeger considered this innovation the beginning of the "real work" of the department. In the 1913 summer session Seeger experimented with a new history of music course, which he offered to what was then considered to be a large class, 200–250 students.

Only a few American universities offered music history, and most followed a chronological structure, emphasizing dates and assuming an evolutionary development. Little attention was given to contemporary, living music; most courses stopped at about 1800. Dissatisfied, Seeger prepared a new course, although he did not deviate completely from the traditional approach. He found folk songs from around the world in numerous books and arranged to have them performed.

The custom in those days [was] that the great art of music—music that really was music, had as a forerunner, folk music and Greek music. So I gave a concert of folk music. It was in 17 different languages, one of them being English. Two of [the songs] were American—there was "The Hangman's Tree" and "Barbara Allen." Both with piano accompaniment just published by Schirmer, but it was taken for granted that these songs were just sung by some very old people and soon they would be out of existence. The singer learned how to pronounce the words by going around to the chairman of the departments of the different languages. There was one language that we couldn't get any advice about, and that was modern Greek. But the chairman of the department said, you know, there is a peanut vendor out on the corner of Bancroft and Telegraph and I sometimes hear him singing and whistling; perhaps he could help you. So we went around and he said well, what's the song? So we sang him the song. Oh, he said, I know that song and he gave us the pronunciation.[18]

Seeger also initiated and conducted a 120-voice chorus that sang music ranging from the ninth century to the present. He believed that this marked the first time in California that such "stuff," as he referred to it, was performed.

In his second academic year, the pace quickened. The young family moved to larger quarters, one block up on La Loma. Charles and Constance launched a series of chamber music recitals patterned after those given in Ivy League colleges, and Seeger began to formalize a department of music. In 1913, department personnel and teaching apparatus were moved to another location. Seeger initiated a full curriculum, a four-year course of study, although there was not yet a formal degree program. In a position paper called "Toward an Establishment of the Study of Musicology in America" (c. 1913), he outlined some of his basic approach.

The term "Musicology" comprises, in its widest sense, the whole linguistic treatment of music—the manual instruction, the historical study, the music-research of the psycho-physical laboratory, the piece of music criticism. But in the more restricted sense in which the term is properly used, it comprises only the small part of this work in which the higher standards of modern scientific and critical methods have been maintained.

In Europe, where Musicology is a well-established study, national and international societies, numerous periodicals and publications attest a vigorous growth. In America, practically nothing has been done, owing partly to a prejudice against the musicological point of view itself. For having been elaborated by the great continental Universities, the musical frontiersmen everywhere have felt that the linguistic bias of the academic mind has ever-born the musical element in the study and that the historical orientation, so long in fashion, has tended to a loss of balance whereby musical thought is led away from systematic work—that is, the study of the art of the present day. Consequently, contact between the living art and its study has been poor and the various branches of musical activity have pursued independent paths, without the co-ordination or strategy of a general staff.

When this sort of thing happens in any well-organized field, we know what the trouble is and how to go about correcting it. . . . Music is not founded upon language or upon language studies. But its conduct in our day depends customarily upon an extensive use of language. . . . The common attitude toward musicology may be seen, then, as a justifiable suspicion of its premises coupled with a wholly unjustifiable refusal to take the trouble to revise or rectify them—unjustifiable, because we not only make use of the results of European musicology but do a lot of more or less careless talking about music ourselves.

For obvious reasons, America fosters its own philosophy, its own science and its own criticism. It should also foster its own Musicology. There follows a brief outline of some of the work to be done either by an independent institute or by an adequately organized academic department. [19]

Seeger then proposed the components of a music department, which would become the basis of musicological study in America. It would require (1) research—scientific, critical, historical, and systematic—in musical theory and practice, history and comparative musicology, and an experimental laboratory; (2) conferences that would invite prominent musicologists for original work, consultation, and public lectures; (3) a library for books, manuscripts, and phonographic archives, including photocopying facilities; (4) publication of the complete works of important composers, unaltered texts of the best readings, important musicological works in foreign languages and in translation, a musicological yearbook that could eventually become a quarterly, and a music magazine; (5) a museum for instruments, music printing, trade, and industry; (6) education for students of all ages, from very small children to adults. Charles observed, "With musical education being rushed as it is today, the need is most urgent for a thorough investigation of the whole enterprise, to save endless mistakes by musicians who know nothing about teaching and by teachers who know nothing about music."

He also proposed some official or central encouragement of national and international musicological conferences and called for graduate programs in music: "Musicological work in Universities should be encouraged by the establishment of chairs and fellowships for graduate study here and abroad." And, he ended,

There can be no doubt that the field is a wide one. In view of the extraordinary development of music in America during the last two decades it is hard to believe that more of this basic work has not been done. . . . The structure appears, therefore, to one who sees it as a whole, still perilously lop-sided and lacking in some essential foundations. These will be cared for in time, but as time goes on the job will be increasingly difficult. [20]

As a key component of this curriculum, during the academic year 1913–1914 Seeger offered the first full course in musicology—history of music—in the United States. One of Seeger's students in this course was a student named Russick, later of MENC repute, and Glen Haydon, later a major figure in American musicology. Haydon recalled his enrollment in the first musicology course and its rarity among music programs in the United States, and remarked on its absence from the University of California curriculum after Seeger left. [21]

Regrettably, little remains of Seeger's plans for his courses and his work in establishing the Music Department. Almost all of Seeger's syllabi and records of the time were destroyed in the great fire of September 1923. But the University of California, Berkeley, Music Library contains Seeger's surviving syllabi and those he designed with E. G. Stricklen, another member of the music faculty—two works on composition: *Outline of a Course in Harmonic Structure and Musical Invention as Elementary Composition* (1913/16) and *Outline of a Course in Chromatic Harmony and Intermediate Types of Musical Invention* (1916).

Seeger greatly valued Stricklen, whom he brought to the Berkeley music faculty. He recalled their work together:

He was introduced to me by some local musician, I think his name was Weber, a piano teacher. I naturally needed someone to correct papers in my harmony course so I engaged Stricklen as what they call a "reader" and he turned out to be, in an emergency, a very good teacher, so as time went on, I turned over the harmony course to him and later an advanced harmony course to him, and he became a colleague. The books that we published were just handbooks—they were just syllabuses, they were not real books. My comment on the two books is they're very naive but they served the purpose and the one good thing about them—there were two good things about them. First, instead of teaching students to immediately harmonize melodies on basses in 4 parts, they harmonized them in 3 parts. Secondly, we started counterpoint along with harmony, where it belongs.[22]

In addition to his curricular activities, Seeger encouraged the main library at Berkeley to begin a music section. Until that time there had been no systematic development of a corpus of materials—books, scores, and other printed matter—necessary for regular study of music. By the time Seeger left Berkeley, the library contained an incipient music collection. Seeger was the first to recognize the importance of a first-rate library.[23]

At the end of his second year, things were going well. University recitals continued to be successful. Seeger had established a structure for the teaching of music, had instituted a four-year curriculum, had developed a real musicology course, had organized several performing groups and, to his special satisfaction, had initiated a music library. His relations with President Wheeler were good and working smoothly. He had money for books, instruments, and library materials.

Seeger was not contented with these accomplishments, however. He was also involved in myriad campus activities and intellectual enterprises. He decided to work with—almost in the sense of study with—Frederick Teggart in history and philosophy. From Teggart he imbibed the idea of process, and he began shaping his own theories of the history of music process.[24] In "The Circumstance or the Substance of History" (1910), Teggart discussed aspects of history, focusing on his own observations and also on those of Ranke (to put historical investigation on a sound basis we must put weight on the importance of fact in and of itself), the Hebraic theory of history (the record of God's dealings with man, that is, a teleological interpretation), and Teggart himself (history is the record of a sequence of changes and the desire is to arrive at an understanding of those transformations).

Also, from Teggart's *The Idea of Progress—A Collection of Readings Selected by Frederick J. Teggart* Seeger absorbed more completely than he had in Europe the ideas of Hegel ("History in general is the development of spirit in time, as nature is the development of the idea in space"), Comte ("the historical method verifies and applies in the largest way, that chief quality of sociological science, — its proceeding from the whole to the parts"), and Leibnitz ("the present is big with the future"). Seeger also found useful works by two other professors — H. M. Stephens and H. H. Bolton — who published *Prolegomena to History: The Relation of History to Literature, Philosophy, and Science* (1916–17), and *Processes of History* (1918).[25] He also worked with philosophers George P. Adams, Clarence I. Lewis, and an old Harvard classmate, Jacob Loewenberg, to hone more precise meanings for his words and to clarify *process* in the philosophical sense. Finally, Seeger expanded on his rudimentary knowledge of science, showing particular interest in scientific method and current scientific advances.

As a capstone to Seeger's continuing education, the visit of Harvard's Ralph Barton Perry to Berkeley, to lecture on the general theory of value, was of crucial importance. Perry affirmed his debt to Austrian psychology and economic theory and extolled Kant's critique of reason and his literary criticism. Seeger's concern with criticism and the history of criticism was newly stimulated by Perry and the theories he espoused. They led Seeger to his lifelong concern with aesthetic value and, most important for his future work, a keen interest in critics and criticism. He often attacked contemporary critics, whom he called "rascals distorting music," saying that they knew nothing about value and the history of criticism. To develop a history of criticism, he went to a colleague, Arthur U. Pope, an aesthetician, with whom he worked out an innovative grammar of criticism. Seeger used Pearson's *Grammar of Science* as a basis for discourse.

By the start of Seeger's third year, political clouds had gathered on the horizon. The Mexican Revolution was in full swing, and across the Atlantic Europeans squabbled among themselves, a distant threat to American security and complacency. Two letters from his brother Alan reminded Seeger of the precariousness of family and political life. In a letter of April 20, 1914, apropos of his own departure from the family world view, Alan expressed concern for the dependent and "poverty of existence" in which their sister lived with her parents. And, in a card of October 20, 1914, Alan spoke of the war in Europe and mentioned that he was in the second regiment of the French Foreign Legion.

A new world was dawning, and Seeger's social conscience was awakening, as was foreshadowed in his endorsement of manual labor as a requirement for graduation. At a faculty meeting, the economist Carlton Parker criticized Seeger and his friend, the young English professor Herbert Cory, as ivory tower idealists for championing the cause of migrant workers. In the spring of 1914, accepting Parker's challenge, Seeger accompanied him to the hopfields and fruit ranches of northern California where numbers of impoverished migrant workers were employed. Seeger was concerned by what he saw, especially the half-emaciated children. Some workers were of South Asian origin, called "Hindus" by ignorant Americans. The experience affected Seeger deeply; his observation of the migrants' deplorable working and living conditions, and what they revealed about California's entire social and economic system, were eye-openers.

California had long been a haven for migrants, both native and foreign. Beginning with the Gold Rush in 1848, California was host to constant and increasing migration. In 1850 the state had a population of 92,600, of whom some 70,000 were Americans.[26] By 1900, the population stood at 1.5 million, few of whom were native Californians, and it now ranked twenty-first among the forty-five states. After a large influx of midwesterners, by 1920 California had moved up to eighth place in population. The arrival of Latinos and Asians continued, although California's need for migrants was ironically countered by persistent attempts to exclude Chinese, Japanese, Mexicans, and South Asians.

They were all needed.[27] Not small family homesteads, but corporate farms have prevailed in California. The costs of irrigation—the great San Joaquin and Imperial valleys require abundant supplies of water—and the patterns of land tenure of the time of the major Anglo-European influx required large-scale farming, and intensive crop cultivation on corporate farms required enormous numbers of migratory laborers.

One crop after another—wheat, fruit, sugar beets, cotton—has been dominant in California. Wheat, the first major money crop, required only a few men to operate machinery, but drought and depression ended its reign in the 1890s. Wheat was supplanted by fruit, and later vegetables—crops that require many hands for picking, packing, and shipping. Although both were labor-intensive, the work was periodic in planting, harvesting, and thinning time. Thus evolved the type of labor structure upon which the state's agribusiness developed.

California's system of migratory agrarian workers also entailed some of the same problems of urban labor.[28] Intensive agriculture has a built-in flexible wage structure that allows workers to be squeezed to ensure the owner's profit. Low wages and labor surpluses were the rule, and the ethnic composition of the labor force encouraged exploitation.

There were two groups, the so-called tramps (or "bindle stiffs"), single white American laborers who, after 1906, swelled the ranks of the IWW (Industrial Workers of the World) and followed the crops by railroad, getting free rides by flashing their red cards. The other, by far the larger, group were foreigners who began to arrive after the 1870s. The Chinese came first, followed by the Japanese, with the rise of beet sugar (by 1909, numbering about 300,000), then by South Asians (Hindus and Sikhs from India, primarily) in the second decade of the century. In the 1920s, with the emergence of cotton as a major crop, Mexicans and Filipinos were dominant. Of this rich mosaic, it was mostly South Asians whom Seeger encountered in the fields.[29]

California was buffeted by the winds of radicalism in what Hofstadter calls the Populist-Progressive Age (1890–1917). Populism was "a kind of popular impulse that is endemic in American political culture . . . that expressed the discontents of a great many farmers and businessmen with the economic changes of the late nineteenth century." Progressivism was "the broader impulse toward criticism and change that was everywhere so conspicuous after 1900, when the already forceful stream of agrarian discontent was enlarged and redirected by the growing enthusiasm of middle-class people for social and economic reform."[30]

Influenced by these new political currents and inflamed by the workers' cause, Seeger and Cory read extensively and attended university seminars in anthropology, history, literature, and philosophy. They studied their American anthropologist colleagues Lowie and Kroeber, and read Freud, Kant, and finally Hegel. Outside the university, Seeger and Cory met and debated with anarchists, socialists, Wobblies, and "reformist agitators" such as Emma Goldman and Bertrand Russell, who became Seeger's "spiritual mentor."[31]

They became acquainted with Emil Kern, an old Kautskian socialist who lived with a pet cat in a corrugated shack in the Presidio area of San Francisco. Through Kern, the two began their involvement in the Radical Club, headquartered in an area called the Barbary Coast, a notorious red light district on the San Francisco waterfront. With Kern, they discussed the labor theory of value, began analyzing *Das Kapital*, and eventually read all of Marx and Kautsky. Seeger always claimed that Marx, and most Marxist writings, were beyond his comprehension, but he could understand Kautsky and particularly his conception of history, which he made required reading for his senior class. That Seeger regarded it so highly while calling it very conservative socialism was a clue to his own increasing radicalization.

By the end of the 1913–1914 academic year, Seeger felt that he had lost the "anti–lower class" attitude that he had imbibed from his father and from the rest of the Seeger clan. The experience in the hopfields and his new education had opened his eyes to the deep discrepancies between his life of relative comfort and the misery of migrants working not far from him. With the fervor of the convert, it also led him (perhaps rashly) to deliver his first lecture to the IWW club on what he had seen.

Seeger may have identified himself with the young Richard Wagner, for he spoke to the IWW on Wagner's role in the 1848 revolt in Germany. His talk prompted a retort by a George Bede, veteran of many IWW struggles, who said to Seeger, "You lily-livered bastard; sit down, you don't know anything about life." Obviously, Seeger was just discovering what many Wobblies already knew, and his lecture was received with some measure of derision at his naiveté.[32] Undaunted, Seeger and his friend Herbert Cory gave other lectures at the radical club and became quite friendly with several members. They participated in the development of the agricultural labor movement in

California by marching with the IWW through the San Joaquin and Sacramento valleys. However, as with other radical organizations, the cautious Seeger never formally joined the IWW.

In retrospect, Seeger considered his radicalization in the 1910s to be embryonic. He confessed that he did not read Hegel until 1914, but the culture in which Hegel had developed his ideas was one in which he too had been raised and had further imbibed in Europe. Thus he immediately felt attuned to Hegel, notably his notion of dichotomies, so that the concept of process quickly became basic to his thought. The Hegelian notion of dialectic as well as the Kantian notion of the transcendental dialectic from the *Critique of Reason* was to pervade Seeger's musical thinking later in life.

The political movements that were to draw his sympathy were also in their infancy, particularly the Russian Revolution. Seeger's political naiveté at this stage is reflected in a story recalled by his son Peter. One October evening, when Charlie read in the newspaper headlines of Lenin's followers storming the Winter Palace, he whooped with delight. "Of course Seeger whoops," said Robert Minor, a San Francisco socialist cartoonist. "He's an artist."

Seeger also became involved in the bitter debate about the war. Californians, as a whole, were not keen on U.S. involvement in World War I; in 1914, an estimated 80 percent of the population were opposed. In fact, Americans in general shared the idea that the Europeans were constantly squabbling among themselves and should be left to solve their own quarrels. For Seeger, the looming conflict was a toss-up between two undesirable powers: militaristic Germany and imperialistic Britain.

As the specter of war increasingly shrouded the campus, it was mirrored in internal academic problems. Seeger had developed differences with Professor William Armes Dalton of the English Department, a supporter of the British, about campus musical performances. When he arrived in 1912, Seeger recalled, the quality of campus musical shows, primarily the Sunday music programs in the Greek Theater, were "appalling." Under Seeger, the quality of both musical programs and performances at Berkeley improved greatly, and thousands now came to the afternoons of music at the Greek Theater and to the university recitals that he and Constance had initiated. Despite this success, and although he was now department head, Seeger was not named to the university's Committee on Music and Drama, probably because of his conflict with Dalton. He was, however, appointed to the Committee on Music Education, presaging his future work in this area. Seeger thought this a very stuffy committee, at war with the humanities, a problem he found elsewhere in the curriculum. But his committee service meant that he spent a few weeks each spring visiting public high schools in the California foothills. The urbanite took one step further into the countryside.

Seeger became more involved in activities in the greater Bay Area, developing what he termed his two San Francisco sides. On the one hand, he intensified his work with the socialist movement. On the other, he was equally comfortable at lunches, receptions, dinners, and other social events at the homes of the San Francisco elite, such as the Bournes and Kings. He was also concerned with the musical life of the Bay Area, which was growing, and the San Francisco Symphony, which was improving.

Aside from isolated campus political conflicts, Seeger's third year at Berkeley began auspiciously in the fall of 1914. His work continued to go well and his program solidified. Attendance in music courses increased, and he introduced new ones on voice culture that became a staple in the music curriculum. University recitals improved. And, to his delight, students advanced through his planned four-year curriculum in music for the B.A. degree. The library continued to grow, but it was hard to get music. There were few music publishing houses and a relatively limited distribution system in the United States. Most music was imported from Europe through a small import house in Los Angeles.

In the fall of 1914, sixteen-year-old Henry Cowell arrived at Berkeley to study music.[33] By the time he enrolled at Berkeley, the youthful Cowell had written more than a hundred piano composition. Through the auspices of Sam Seward and Jaime de Angulo, Cowell's father had brought Henry to meet Seeger the previous spring to seek his opinion of his son's musical talent. Seeger judged him brilliant and agreed to arrange a special status for the boy who, for lack of formal secondary preparation, could not be admitted as a regular student. Cowell recalled his meeting with Seeger:

I came away immensely invigorated by this first meeting with what I later came to recognize as one of the most acute musical intelligences that the United States has produced. For the first time here was somebody who didn't try to tell me that music couldn't possibly include the kinds of things I like to compose. I did a lot of writing the following summer, and when I had my first formal meeting with Seeger at the University in the fall of 1914, I remember so well his pleasure and excitement at discovering polytonality, dissonant harmony and counterpoint, and atonality, in the music I showed him. These were new terms to me, though such music was not. That first day Seeger showed me Schoenberg's Opus 11, with the tactful remark: "You might like to see how someone else has handled similar problems."[34]

Cowell became Seeger's composition student. There were no sound recordings in those days, only scores, so he developed a special course on dissonant counterpoint specifically for Cowell. He recalled, "I got Special Student standing for him at the University and Henry and I spent marvellous Thursday afternoons, not regular, quite sporadic, 1914–1917."[35] Seeger also arranged for Cowell to attend classes in theory under E. G. Stricklen and to receive lessons in counterpoint for two years from Wallace Sabin in San Francisco. In addition, Cowell met in a weekly seminar with Seeger, in a small group that included Glen Haydon, to discuss new ideas in music.

Cowell's work with Seeger from 1914 to 1916 revolved around Seeger's making his first tentative approaches toward a systematic use of dissonance.[36] Cowell himself had already used a type of chordal dissonant counterpoint in some of his compositions.

[He] had always been free of any preconceived notions about resolving dissonances. The suggestion of a theoretical "system" of dissonant counterpoint set him off into several notebooks of exercises, in the earliest of which he arrived at his "rules" by the literal opposite of those for sixteenth century counterpoint. Seeger gradually worked the study of dissonance into one of his theoretical courses, although the idea was so unheard-of that no course was so named in any of the University catalogs. Eventually Seeger wrote an outline, or syllabus, or manual, for use in this course—whether devoted wholly to dissonant counterpoint or including it along with other studies, nobody now seems to remember. It appeared sometime after 1918, when HC left the University.[37]

Seeger was particularly proud of his composition syllabus, for it was far in advance of its time. Although it was not called so then, Seeger was teaching what is now known as serialism. His own music, which he viewed as a creative expression of logical thought, included incipient tone clusters, unusual chord progressions, and other experimentation within a traditional context, leading some to compare his work with that of Charles Ives. The influence of Seeger's syllabus has been the source of considerable speculation, particularly as to its contribution to the musical development of several major twentieth-century composers.

Seeger was concerned that his syllabus would fall into the hands of those who might use it and even claim its ideas as their own. Henry Cowell, who championed Seeger's progressivism, agreed that Seeger was responsible for many theoretical and technical innovations for which he was not recognized.[38] Cowell admitted — indeed, swore — to Seeger some years later that he saw a copy of the syllabus on dissonant counterpoint on the desks of both Arnold Schoenberg and Paul Hindemith. Sometime during the early or mid-twenties, Cowell took a letter of introduction to Hindemith at the Hochschule für Musik in Berlin. Seeger's syllabus lay on the desk; Cowell had never before seen it. Hindemith showed it to Cowell, asking who Seeger was. Cowell never discovered how the outline came to be in Hindemith's possession — Seeger had not sent copies to either Hindemith or Schoenberg — but speculated that Hindemith's knowledge of the syllabus might have accounted for the change in his style after the 1921 Marienleben.

Despite his role as tutor, Seeger claimed that Cowell was an autodidact and that their relationship became more like one between colleagues. In Seeger's words:

Like all autodidacts (myself included), he swiped and made his own anything he wished. I made a point of telling him so and he knew perfectly well what I meant. . . . I fear that I am partly responsible for Henry's excesses in numerology. About when he came to me I had discovered the inferior resonance theories of van Oettingen, Rieman and Hauptmann and used it in my own theory, being something of a Pythagorean by nature. Henry, of course, applied them in a completely original way, paying no attention at all to mine. I was never able to impress upon him (indirectly, of course), the distinction between rhythm and metre.[39]

Cowell's widow does not quite agree, and has acknowledged Seeger's influence on Henry. She said that Seeger was Cowell's only real teacher of composition and that Cowell could state precisely what he had learned from Seeger.[40] Sidney Robertson Cowell reported that when he met Seeger her husband had been "immensely relieved to find a man who thought that music might reasonably include the things that he himself considered to be music against all contradiction, such as tone clusters and sounds from the piano strings." She also recalled her husband noting that Seeger had made two clear contributions to Henry's view of himself as a composer.

First of all . . . if you have new concepts for music, you have an obligation to create a full body of work with a systematic theoretical basis for each of them. Then, you yourself are responsible for disseminating your ideas. If people are to get used to them and come to accept them as natural, you are going to have to play the music yourself at first. And you must learn to play it well.[41]

Cowell himself also reflected on Seeger's influence on him not only as a young student but throughout his life. He considered the lessons he had learned and how Seeger had aided his development.

It was agreed that I should stop writing my own way for a year or so, but I soon found I could not do it, there was too much going on in my head. Seeger must have discovered at once that like most young composers I saw little connection between traditional musical techniques and the kind of thing I wanted to write. So he made two extraordinarily perceptive and practical suggestions: First, he pointed out that if I proposed to use new and unusual musical material I would have to work out a systematic technique for them so things would hang together. And, second, he told me that if my innovations were to establish themselves, I would have to build up a real repertoire embodying them, myself, letting them develop as I thought about them to make a sound world of their own. I have thought in these terms about my music ever since.

This is far from all that Charlie Seeger did for me: he found friends for me among musicians in New York and abroad, got me extricated from the U.S. Army when I got stuck there by mistake after World War I was over, and has been an unfailingly staunch and helpful friend ever since.

But it was the gift of a framework for my thinking as a composer, in terms I could accept, that was unique: no one else in America was able to think so freely about music at that time, and as for me — [it was] impossible to accept anything less. To be given a concept that would oblige me to establish relationships among my musical materials, without taking on the ideas of other people either for the relationships or the materials, was the greatest good fortune.[42]

Seeger returned this compliment in a warm assessment of Cowell, applicable not only to their university days together, but also their lifelong friendship. "My conservative friends have always wondered why I did not teach [Cowell] to be a respectable musician. My liberal friends have never given me credit for teaching him anything. He himself swiped many of his best (and some of his worst) 'ideas' from me, and occasionally [he] acknowledges it."[43]

Seeger continued to perform and compose, despite the burdens of administration, teaching, accompanying, and his other academic and social responsibilities. He and a student, Dorothy Pillsbury, designed a series of two-piano programs and the recitals continued.[44]

Seeger's experimental approach to composition was first publicly displayed at two performances of the Parthenia, outdoor masques presented by female students in the Faculty Glade each spring. *The Dream of Dedra* (1914) and *The Queen's Masque* (1915), both in collaboration with Ruth Esther Cornell (class of 1915), were written for sixty players, and entailed experimental rhythms, melodic structure, form, and orchestration. Some portions included a take-off of jazz and parodies of popular tunes, and Seeger arranged late sixteenth-century music for incidental accompaniment.[45]

The two masques were complementary, and Seeger's libretti illustrate what he referred to as his rebellion and naive social consciousness, not unlike his "first great American opera." The music and the lyrics were closely integrated, and each masque included a considerable narrative portion.

Both stories concerned a girl who was brought up in a fairytale type existence. Then, she goes into the real world and discovers that it is not what she thought it was. People tear her clothes from her, leaving her in tatters. As she stands forlorn, a huge haywagon comes in drawn by many of the poor people the girl had gone to help. The wagon has ten foot high wheels of poverty, ignorance, and sin. The crowd that had heckled the girl goes away. In the final scene, two children cling to the heroine who looks around, does not see anything left to do, and walks towards the audience, up the central aisle, and out. Some members of the cast threw a cloak over her as she departed.[46]

Since relatively few of Seeger's works survive, it is difficult to analyze him as a composer, particularly vis-à-vis his affinity to the new European (particularly French) music and his claim to the status of an innovator in twentieth-century music. His early compositions, especially the songs, were mixed in style and reflected the influence of the European and particularly French composers to which he had been so attracted, especially Satie, Debussy, Duparc, and Fauré. He was aware that few shared his appreciation of this influence, for in "On Style and Manner in Musical Composition" (1923) he sought to explain why the music of Debussy and others had not been well received. Other pieces, such as his early *The Lady of the South* (1908), anticipated Alban Berg's songs of 1915. Many of his compositions are "particularized by arpeggio figures, rich chordal texture, expressive tone painting [*The Pride of Youth*], clear reference to a model, or no keyboard at all."[47]

One of Seeger's more substantial works, his *Violin Sonata,* was completed for Constance. He had composed the first and third movements as a supplement to his honors application for graduation from Harvard in 1908. Seeger noted that it had "a lot of scales and chords in it which were the idolized devices of the music compositional process at that time." He wrote the second movement in 1912 and 1913, conceived as a dialogue between husband and wife, perhaps inspired by Strauss's *Symphonia domestica*, first performed in New York in 1904, but it was also musically akin to Messiaen's *Quatour* (1941).

Henry Cowell provides some insight into Seeger the composer:

As a composer Seeger has produced little, but all he has produced is of importance in the history of indigenous development in America. From the standpoint of precedent, one must concede to him the position of being the second in time to create works which are genuinely dissonant from beginning to end, and which in other respects are thoroughly experimental. The first is [Charles] Ives, who started quite independently on such explorations about 1897. I have no knowledge of anyone else before Seeger, who about 1912, broke away from the imitative style of his early songs and began a series of nervy experiments which resulted in his "Parthenia" music for two public productions at the Greek Theatre in Berkeley. A veritable wealth of examples of fantastic dissonances, curious rhythms, new melodic structure, and form, are to be found in these works, to say nothing of the orchestration! A germination bed for musical ideas. They are, however, not focused; they are scattered, and do not stand up as musical compositions. After their creation, Seeger became so self-critical that it was for many years virtually impossible for him to complete a work. He has discarded music which almost any composer in the world would have been proud of, because of some infinitesimal fault which no one but himself would have knowledge enough to mark. Thus the intellectualism which is one of his predominating features became so rigid as to quench the creative spark; that is, almost. Not quite.[48]

There is no question that as a composer Seeger seemed avant garde but he also desired balance. Perhaps the best summary available about the influence of Seeger as a composer and, more important, as a teacher or influencer of composers, is given by Cowell:

When the world thought Stravinsky and Schoenberg both insane, Seeger found them the most important new composers of their time. They were. He at that time, when the average musician could see no difference between the two, predicted that Stravinsky would become popular with the general concert public and that Schoenberg would be beloved by musical intellectuals. This has come to pass. Before Schoenberg eschewed thickness of sound and wrote the economically outlined "Pierrot Lunaire," Seeger worked for the downfall of over-voluptuousness and a return to thin lines of music. This at a time when, under the influence of Strauss, music was thought to be good inasmuch as it was full and thick, and to call music thin was to damn it utterly. Now the return to thin line has penetrated every circle of composers.

At a time when Debussian impressionism was the rage, Seeger advocated sharp definiteness of line. Now this definiteness is attempted by nearly everyone, and impressionism has all but disappeared. Before the idea of piling one chord on top of another as being the only line of musical development had lost its sway, Seeger suggested a return to counterpoint. The return has been made. Before Hindemith produced his works in dissonant counterpoint poured into a Bach mold, Seeger suggested this very idea, and created a system for such a counterpoint, worked out to the last detail of what the intervals should be and how they might move. Hindemith and Schoenberg both came out later with works embodying the principles of Seeger's suggestions. Long before Stravinsky supposedly led his group of followers into "neo-classicism," Seeger predicted the whole development of this return, or attempted return.

At a time when it was generally considered unaesthetic to use unresolved dissonances, Seeger predicted that in a very short time all possible dissonances would be freely used throughout all new music. They are. Away back, Seeger insisted on being enthusiastic about very ancient music; no one could see what possible musical value it had. Seeger also pointed out that it has similarity with modern music, in point of view; at that time no one could see the resemblances—people as a whole saw modernism as a "bunch of discords" only. Today, nearly all modernists have developed an interest in very old music, and the relationship between the very old and the very new is recognized.

Seeger pointed out the possibility of analyzing certain modern complexes as polychords, long before the word was generally known. He has often taken special interest in the works of certain composers who at the time were relatively unheard of, and insisted on his students studying them. A few years later, there has invariably been a wave of public interest in the direction of these composers. Monteverdi, Bruckner, and Stravinsky are examples.

One could go on indefinitely and not exhaust the number of subjects in which he has been a pioneer. Probably his most important standpoint, however, has been his open advocacy of the intellectual point of view in approaching music. This he started at a time when such a thing was utterly inconceivable—when it was considered that music had value only if it had nothing to do with the intellect, that the most damning thing that could be said against music was that it is intellectual, and that *thinking* about music not only has no value but destroys the musical impulse. Seeger almost proved this old-fashioned notion to be right by allowing over-intellectualism to stultify him. But he has brilliantly recovered, and has renewed activity in a great new outburst of fertility. And, as in the other cases, the public is gradually following him in this, his most important stand.[49]

The end of the 1914–1915 academic year tallied up more progress and more success for Seeger in his plan to build a comprehesive music program at Berkeley. And he was particularly pleased with the development of young Henry Cowell.

A second son, John, had been born (February 16, 1914) and the Seegers were able to secure a loan to build a house in the Berkeley Hills. Designed by John Galen Howard and Bernard Maybeck, placed in a lovely garden setting, it included a separate, round studio for Charles.

Autumn 1915 brought increasing agitation for entering the war. The students and younger faculty remained against U.S. intervention in another European dispute. Seeger's opposition to the war grew. He signed up as a conscientious objector and increased his involvement in the IWW and the Radical Club, actions that began to get him into trouble. Problems also arose because of his good relationship with President Wheeler, a Germanophile. He came into direct conflict with Dean Gayley, an Englishman, who became acting president when Wheeler was forced out.

Seeger began the 1915–1916 academic year with a bona fide Department of Music with an enrollment of several hundred students. Part of this success was undergirded by requirements: the music history course was required of juniors, and an introduction to musicology (historical musicology) for seniors was offered for the first time. In 1916, the Department of Music graduated its first class; Glen Haydon conducted the performance and Seeger hosted the party afterward.

In the summer of 1916 the family toured California for several weeks, visiting Yosemite and Indian reservations, traveling on dirt roads. As a result of that trip, Seeger became aware of approximately 1,200 wax cylinders of California Indian music available in the university's Anthroplogy Department. He was enthralled: these were the first field recordings he had ever heard. Seeger thought that the cylinders should not be used without some preservation, but he had no idea as to how to accomplish this. He was unaware that work on this process was already under way in Berlin. He told Penny,

So I started to listen to one. And I realized that wax was being peeled off the cylinder while I was listening, and I immediately stopped the machine and went to the curator and said, look, I'm ruining the record by playing this. Oh, he said, that's all right, everybody does it. And I said, you're a criminal, you ought to put these things under lock and key and not allow anybody to touch them, until you've made copies of them. I didn't know anything about copying at that time. Well, I don't know whether . . . I think he took my advice.[50]

Seeger's successful work over the next two years was enervating, however, and he began anticipating his sabbatical. The family planned to return to the East for the first time since 1912. Also, Seeger's increasing outspokenness about newly awakened social concerns and his conscientious objector stance on the war, which earned him some enmity among the Anglophiles on campus, likely contributed to his psychological distress.

The first open signs of incipient depression soon appeared. Seeger was invited to give several lectures at Harvard in December 1916. This invitation was partly intended as an opportunity to "look Seeger over," with the possibility of inviting him to come to Harvard. His first lecture focused exclusively on harmony, counterpoint, and basic musicianship. In the next lecture, he turned to "the individual."

Music is a somewhat abstract concept, a more universally empirical concept than that of the individual; so is society. The Individual has to be on that level of conceptualization. Then all three are equally perceptualized. A specific individual as an example of "the individual" can be handled in a more rational manner than historians usually do. How much of the individual is society and how much the individual varies it (intuitively). Society is the product of the ability to communicate.[51]

The meaning and relevance of his life as a professional musician whose work was meaningful to less than 5 percent of U.S. society, and the irrelevance of his work to changing the social conditions of the masses, had begun to plague Seeger. In one of the later Harvard talks, perhaps the key one, entitled "The Value of Music," Seeger's personal anguish came through. He digressed to discuss his generous salary ($5,000 a year) and his comfortable life in contrast to the penury and starvation suffered by so many Americans.

Perhaps because of the alarm aroused by the controversial nature of his talks, perhaps because his personal crisis had an effect on his behavior, Seeger's appearance at Harvard was not followed by an invitation to join the faculty. It is unclear what Seeger felt about this. Perhaps he wanted to return to Harvard, but felt out of tune with traditional Eastern conservatism and showed a bit too much of the Seeger disdain for what he did not approve of. That rejection came to gnaw at him in his final years at California and, combined with his unpopular position on the war, ultimately broke him. Possibly it became the culminating factor in the deep depression and breakdown he suffered at the decade's end.

A committed pacifist by 1917 — a conviction possibly cemented by his brother Alan's death on the battlefield — Seeger spoke out openly against the war on campus and to Bay Area radical and political groups.[52] Despite increasing pressure on the United States to enter the war and to recruit young Americans for the endeavor, Seeger remained a conscientious objector and refused to buy war bonds. By now, this stance had become unpopular throughout California. Once the United States entered the conflict, popular opinion swung almost 360 degrees away from pacifism and noninterventionist sentiment to extreme chauvinism. John Steinbeck's *East of Eden* provides a stunning look at this phenomenon.

Being antiwar in a country that had now been given over to a war economy and a war pyschology took a heavy toll. Some friends and colleagues now eschewed him. The distress of this loss of friends and colleagues was compounded by sheer fatigue. In the past six years, Seeger had built a department and taught fifteen to eighteen hours a week while continuing to compose. He had prepared half a dozen courses and had carried out endless other administrative duties. He was exhausted and ready to return east.

Such was the political, social, and intellectual matrix within which Seeger would weave his own schemes for music and society. The experiences of his first three decades undergirded the contradictions in his own personality and thought. As he reported to his Harvard classmates:

Europe, from 1908 to 1911 — in company with Foote, Sweet and Whee-lock — was something to remember, as was also the return to America full of the feeling that I was an American and that America was the place for me. Establishment as Professor of Music in the University of California came next, in 1912 — one of the strange things that professors of Philology do when they become Presidents of Universities and find themselves embarrassed by the need of filling a position in a subject that they know nothing about.

At Harvard, I had regarded the social life as mildly foolish and the life of learning as extremely so. Music and the experience of non-academic things seemed really worth while. So that in accepting the California position, the tongue was in the cheek and I gave myself over to one year of amusement, thinking I would not last much longer than that. Much to my surprise, I began to get a college education. The subjects in the catalogue, which had been mere names to me at Harvard, began to be seen as having connection with my main interest and it was not long before I started to study something for the first time in my life. In company with a colleague, Professor Herbert Cory, I took the subjects I should have taken at Harvard and bade fair to turn from a mere musician into a regular professor.

The industrial and migratory labor unrest of the pre-War period intervened, however, and led me eventually to make as much of a revaluation of my newly found academic interests as these had already [been] effected in my musical work.[53]

In his thirtieth anniversary report, he continued:

About the time I did my bit for the 25th anniversary volume, I had already brought to its final, complete organization an approach to musical composition which might have been labelled "technique for technique's sake." It will be recalled by those who have followed my musical and musicological activities that one of the chief reasons I gave up composition in 1915 was dissatisfaction with the "art for art's sake" approach which I had lived with up to that time — I could find justification neither for my nor for any other composer's work in the face of my growing realization of the social unrest and international war.[54]

And, as he wrote in his report on the fiftieth anniversary of his graduation from Harvard,

Two and a half years in Europe with Foote, Sweet and Wheelock profoundly modified this world outlook [he had earlier spoken of a hierarchy of the mean and the demeaned; see Chapter I]. It was to Jack [Wheelock] that I owed an awakening of a love of "sane and sensual humanity". The inevitable result was that loveliness and ugliness, attraction and repulsion, good and evil came to be viewed not as dispensable or indispensable but as merely existent. Neither term of any of these dichotomies was independent of the other. They were facts—things *given* to man whether he liked it or not. All that man could *give* was value—creation of beauty, love and virtue. Thus, ugliness as well as loveliness was equally a component of beauty, repulsion and attraction inscrutably and inextricably intertwined in love, good and evil equal participants in virtue.

Entry into academic life was accepted upon these terms and, so, as an almost Shelleyan flight into the empyrean—not from but into reality. In California, it was another poet, Herbert Cory, who initiated me into the world of scholarship; and an economist, Carleton Parker, who awakened a sleeping conscience. The earlier love of sane and sensual humanity turned out to have been objective, esthetic and without involvement of self. Though obviously shot through and through with inhumanity, no responsibility attached to it. There was no morality in it. . . . The value system could not cope with it. What I could do about it in music was problematic. Practically I could not maintain and theoretically I could not justify continued activity as a composer. In no uncertain sense this first life died of physical exhaustion and intellectual inanition.[55]

3

A Decade of Reckoning,

1918–1930

∽

I N OCTOBER 1918, Charles and Constance sublet their house and departed for the East with their two young sons. They stayed at Seeger's parents' antebellum estate, "Fairlee," in Patterson, New York, fifty miles north of the city. There they set about building a fourteen-foot automobile trailer—of Charlie's own design—in which they planned to live on their return trip to California the following year.

Charles was physically and emotionally spent. His opposition to the war and his increasing concern about the plight of the workers had brought him into conflict with society in general. A more personal afflication was an intensification of an intellectual conflict he had begun to feel between composing and academic life; he could not compose while teaching. He felt that he was infected by a "rigid intellectualism" and the "virus of musicology."[1] To his intense distress, he discovered that he could no longer compose, and he sank into depression. He told his daughter many years later:

I reached a point where I had found out so much about the composition of Schoenberg, Stravinsky, Scriabin, that—and Charles Ives and Ruggles—I realized I couldn't admire the music that moved me and I couldn't be moved by music I admired. It was a very serious situation and led me to two different styles of composition. One, in keeping with the movement which had been initiated in Europe, without my knowledge, before 1912, and the other by simply my own work in composition. I found that I was writing passages that were interesting but had no emotional—or, as I would say—no affective content to speak of, and then lapsing off into music that had an affective content but I couldn't feel were admirable.[2]

77

Henry Cowell had already noted the debilitating effects of the growing self-criticism that blocked Seeger's creativity. According to Cowell, Seeger discarded music that "almost any composer in the world would have been proud of because of some infinitesimal fault," including some pieces which were "short and all but perfection," such as *Solo for Clarinet*.[3]

Seeger's interest in musicology, initiated during his first year at Berkeley, had grown gradually. Not until he went east in 1918 and tried to put his ideas on paper did he realize the depth of that interest; he also realized that he could not yet effectively communicate those ideas. He continued his self-analysis:

At the same time, my musicology which I developed at the University of California . . . had also split. I found that I couldn't write, I could talk; but I couldn't write my musical thought although I could talk it, and the talking was not such that could be taken down at dictation; it was too costly in the first place—we didn't have tape recorders then and I found that even after I did dictate to a stenographer that it didn't make any sense. In other words, I couldn't make my writing about my musicological thought keep up with my musicological thought. So, in the period from 1919 to 1922, I was definitely posed on the horns of the dilemmas—couldn't compose, couldn't write my musicology. I did go ahead and do some composition. I revised my violin sonata and some of the songs that I'd written and I did get some of my musicology written down and it was published later in the *Musical Quarterly*, but I wasn't much satisfied with it. Meanwhile, I had become very much worried about another problem, that is, the living of these different kinds of lives— the life of the composer and the life of the musicologist, in contemporary America. I couldn't feel that either of them was of any value to the society that I found myself living in. The music that I liked to write, the music that I admired the writing of couldn't bring me an income, the musicology that I could think and the musicology that I could write couldn't bring me any living.[4]

Seeger reflected on the lectures he had delivered at Harvard in 1916, two of which he had framed without thinking much about the implications of the word *musicology*. In retrospect, as it was his wont to constantly change things, he planned to retitle them as one: "The Organization of Musical Knowledge: the Scientific Methodology and the Critical Methodology." His thesis was that only in the romantic era did composers write for themselves and not for what society wanted. In these lectures he anticipated his growing intellectual and social discontent, for had begun to believe that music *must have some relation to society*. And he was concerned with observing and determining the nature of *value* in connection with music. He was convinced that music should have value both to the composer and to society. Seeger attributed part of his growing resistance to composition to the development of his social conscience, which been been cultivated during his time at Berkeley and which forced him to question the validity of his position in society as a composer of "art" music. As he said of this period in his life and repeated often in later years,

I can compose music [and be paid a magnificent sum of] $5,000 a year. But . . . a very large percentage of people in this country are living on substandard wages. It bothers me to think that salary represents the difference between starvation and minimum living standards for people and a comfortable life for me.[5]

The pricking of his social consciousness and his quandary between "talking about music" and "writing or making music" and his attitude toward himself as a composer are suggested in Seeger's 1940 article on Henry Cowell:

A composer and his work are . . . integral elements in a world and in a total field of music. Can one remain entirely objective, scientific, logical about a complex of which one is oneself such an element? Are not the emotional and intellectual "fevers" inescapable correlates of the handling of this field in a reasonably complete manner? After all, is the known, in respect to which we may be objective, any weightier in the whole picture than the unknown, in respect to which another approach is necessary? Are the two so sharply separated from one another? Is it not, perhaps, one of the most important functions of the artist to explore both and to relate them, to convert them, as it were, in unknowable as well as knowable ways? Do we not by adopting either a purely objective or subjective attitude, merely avoid not only half our difficulties but half our opportunities? I believe this to be a fact. Dat ol' debbil, subjectivity, gets us even when we flee him.[6]

Shortly after his return to the East, Seeger suffered an emotional breakdown, which was confirmed by a physician and the Life Extension Institute. He spent most of his sabbatical year in Patterson recovering. Constance loyally supported him through the crisis, but the strains of managing work and two small boys—and a third child was on the way—were beginning to tell on both of them. They worked out an arrangement whereby they would share the housework and care for the children on a fifty-fifty basis. And they reduced their performing, together and separately, because neither had the energy nor the time.

As the sabbatical year neared an end in the spring of 1919, Seeger decided he needed more time. He was concerned that he would not be welcome at the university because of his unpopular pacifist views and involvement with "revolutionaries," and would be unable to resume the increasingly demanding job of department chairman. Eventually, he realized that he would not return at all. As he wrote many years later,

I jolly well was fired by the Acting President of UC, Gayley, a dear fellow, but a properly chauvinistic Britisher. I had been quite frank in saying that I was philosophically in agreement with Bertrand Russell. I was a pacifist. And I supported my stand with asking how anyone could fight for Czarist Russia, and claiming that it was high time that the British Empire were taken apart. I had lived $2^1/2$ years in Germany and loathed Prussianism, but could not see it was or could be as bad as the [British Empire]. I felt that the Committee on Musical Instruction was favorably inclined to me and had stood by me as long as I was in Berkeley and might, if I should return and try to fight it out. But California, four to one against the war in 1914 was 40 to one chauvinist by 1919. I hadn't the heart, the funds or the desire to go back. I simply was not the proper university professor I have now come to be—or nearly, for I don't wear a tie, I sit on the desk when I lecture (but not if there is a platform, though I have sat on the edge of the platform crosslegged).[7]

Not until the 1930s did Seeger renew his association with radical ideas and organizations.

They welcomed a third son, Peter, on May 3, 1919. Charles and Constance wanted him to be born in a big city hospital. As Charlie recalled:

We were living in the big family house in Patterson, a four-hour drive at that time to New York City, so I took Constance down to New York City to stay with our good friend, Agnes Holden, wife of an architect, while I went back up to Patterson to take care of Charles and John because I didn't feel that I could entrust the boys to the care of the two servants my parents then had. Peter was born in the city and when he was two weeks old, I returned to collect him and Constance.[8]

Charles and Constance planned to return to California, where they still owned a house, after touring the South and Southwest in their caravan. To raise money, they would give violin-piano recitals and small concerts at the homes of well-to-do families—friends gave them letters of introduction—and small organizations. They would also give less formal concerts, as they had done before their marriage. In this manner they hoped to earn enough to support themselves, as well as to offer free performances in schools, churches, meetings—indeed, for anyone willing to listen. Americans did not hear enough "good" music, they believed; they would bring "good" music to the people.

We looked down on popular music—folk music didn't exist, or except in the minds of a few very old people, who would die shortly and then there wouldn't be any. And this new thing that was coming, called jazz, was simply filthy—it was of the gutter and the brothel and wasn't fit to pay any attention to.[9]

In November 1920, sporting a beard (he had stopped shaving after his first trip through California in 1916), Seeger, Constance, and the three boys started out in a Model T Ford and the caravan that had taken a year and a half to complete. In the trailer they had a portable pump organ, a big iron pot for laundry, and hand-lettered signs announcing the musical events they planned to sponsor. However, their plans had not accounted for the difficulties of travel in the hinterland. Except for main highways, most roads were in deplorable condition, Seeger recalled, and virtually impassable in bad weather. Deciding to go no further, they wintered at MacKenzie's Mill, outside Pinehurst, North Carolina, in a two-room log cabin on land owned by a family named MacDonald.

We found a place where they would allow us to park off in the pine woods away from the highroad where nobody would bother us. And there was a pile of old metal near by and we didn't pay much attention to it; it was just junk, and the people were friendly. They tested us out by coming around half past five in the morning and knocking on the door of the trailer and asking if I would take them over to a neighboring town because their truck had broken down and they needed to get a new tire. Course I got out of bed, got dressed, invited them in—couldn't invite them in because there was no room to invite them in to—but I gave them coffee in the little porch outside. Then another time we were tried out—oh yes, we were taken around and shown the place where we might park and we chose just the wrong place that we might park for the winter, next to what they knew was their still. I just thought it was a pile of junk—they thought we might be revenue agents, you see, and when we paid no attention to that pile of junk, and it was hauled away before the next morning, we were accepted by that group, but not until the patriarch of the family came around. A little old man, about 5 feet, 2 inches, with a great white handlebar moustache, old man MacDonald, very handsome, a real aristocrat, came around in an old wagon drawn by a single mule and after performing the courtesies, he departed and evidently gave out the word that we could be trusted. [10]

Through a letter of introduction to the Hall family in Pinehurst, Charles and Constance were able to arrange a violin-piano concert at a local country club, which had a grand piano. The success of this event convinced them to stay for the winter, but their income was uncertain and they had to take odd jobs to make ends meet. On one occasion Charles was offered a temporary job loading roof tiles from a freight car onto a truck, for which he earned three dollars. There was some irony in this event: the tiles were for the new garage being built for the Halls, with whom the Seegers were going to dine that very evening. As Charlie remembered: "I changed from work clothes to my black tie and boiled shirt, and Constance was in her Parisian dress."

The winter in Pinehurst took some of the romance out of the prospect of a nomadic life of music making while living in a trailer with three small children. Abandoning their western objective, Constance and Charles decided to return to New York. Their ambitious scheme had failed, but they had learned much from the experience. For the MacKenzies and MacDonalds in North Carolina they played classical works, while their new friends reciprocated with banjos and fiddles. The "good" music—Bach, Mozart, and Beet-

*Charles, John, Constance, Charles, and Peter, Rock Creek Park,
Washington, D.C., 1921*

hoven—that they had set out to bring to the people did not impress
their audiences, for they had their own music that they valued.

They left North Carolina in April, giving concerts along the way. A
major stop was Washington, D.C., where Seeger had a very good
friend, President Harding's Secretary of Commerce Miller, an economist who had been a colleague at the University of California.
Possibly through Miller's influence, the family was able to camp in
Rock Creek Park where he and Constance performed every afternoon.
A story in the *Washington Sunday* rotogravure section featured photographs of the trailer, the big cast-iron pot, and other belongings.

Through Miller's auspices, they booked the National Theater on
Lafayette Square, opposite the White House, for a family concert in
May 1921. Constance's brother Elie Edson, a publicist, was their

Charles, Constance, Peter, and Charles, Rock Creek Park,
Washington, D.C., 1921

advance agent. They sold very few tickets, but the house was full—
the boxes occupied by diplomats, cabinet officers, and Mrs. Coolidge,
the vice-president's wife. Mrs. Coolidge had met the young musicians
through the Millers and had taken them under her wing. She saw to it
that the house was full.

The first half of the program was classical—Beethoven, Bach,
Mozart, and Brahms. After intermission, the curtain rose to reveal the
Seegers' trailer, with the cast-iron pot over a make-believe fire and a
rural backdrop. Seeger spoke of what they had been trying to
accomplish—to support free concerts for the people by entertaining
others who could pay for tickets—confessing that they had run into
difficulties. They were not skilled at arranging performances and had
not managed to make enough money to make the venture worthwhile.
He then showed them the kind of program they gave, using a portable
organ rather than a grand piano. Charlie and Constance performed

Constance, Peter, Charles, John, and Charles, Washington, D.C., 1921

while the boys watched from the wings. Then baby Peter ran onto the stage—a touch inspired by Constance's brother, a shrewd press agent with a sense for the pulse of an audience. Peter told me, "[Elie] put me down and aimed me," and he ran toward his father. Charlie played the portable organ with Peter on his lap. The occasion made headlines in the Washington papers.

The Seegers arrived in New York in June 1921 and set up the trailer on the grounds of a beautiful home on Peconic Bay, Long Island. They remained there for most of the summer, Charles commuting to the city for miscellaneous work. He and Constance performed in various places in New York and New England, but eventually admitted that their grand scheme to bring "good" music to the people of America had failed. With a growing family, they needed more security. "We had given in to comfort," Seeger later acknowledged ruefully, "we were not cut out for the rough and tumble life." Seeger again turned to professional "art" music, at the time displaying little evidence that he had been affected by political or social concerns arising from either his California or Carolina experiences.

In August 1921, Frank Damrosch, a family friend and Constance's adoptive "uncle," invited the Seegers to teach at the Institute of Musical Arts, later to be called the Juilliard School of Music. Constance would teach violin and Seeger would develop a new curriculum. Their salaries would enable them to live comfortably in New York, so they accepted, sold their Berkeley house, and stored their California possessions there in a friend's home. [11] Constance and Charles, with Charles, age nine, John, age seven, and Peter, just over two, moved into a "very nice" apartment on Madison Avenue at Sixty-eighth Street.

Seeger's new career began well. His colleagues at the Institute were exceptional: Percy Goetschus taught harmony; Franz Kneisel, his wife's former teacher, was still the leader of the string quartet; and the concertmaster and other members of the New York Philharmonic were on the faculty. Seeger, considered by his colleagues to be an excellent teacher, taught a series of required courses on musicology and on myths and epics, which he thought important for understanding Wagner and other composers. As a result of his course on myths, he began a serious study of anthropology, fulfilling a desire harbored since his earlier association with Kroeber and Lowie at Berkeley. In 1922–1923, Seeger asserted, he and Henry Cowell gave the first course on general musicianship ever offered in the United States; indeed, Seeger claimed to have invented the word *musicianship*.

But the Seegers' family existence had begun to deteriorate. Throughout the 1920s, their personal life was marked by a series of separations and reconciliations. This pattern was reflected in the solutions they attempted: sending the boys to boarding school; taking turns caring for the children (once sending young John to France to be with his grandparents; experimenting with various living arrangements over the next several years—including renting adjacent apartments in the city and taking meals together—living in Patterson with Seeger's parents, Seeger commuting from Nyack, N.Y., keeping a pied-à-terre in Greenwich Village, and spending summers in Patterson. But the marriage continued to disintegrate. Seeger became sarcastic, Constance hysterical. Touched by agoraphobia, she feared going out into the streets and also suffered from vertigo. Seeger speculated that an unstable childhood and family life contributed to her emotional problems.

At various times Constance gave up teaching (probably at Charles's insistence) to devote more time to the children; at other times she and Charles arranged to have classes on different days so that they could alternate caring for the household.

A crisis arose in 1927 when Constance announced that she had begun to put her earnings in a separate bank account and that she could no longer care for the children—upon which Seeger walked out, taking the boys with him. In the autumn of 1927 they vowed to give the marriage another try. Sending the boys (now fifteen, thirteen, and eight) again to boarding school, they moved into a "railroad" apartment near One hundred twenty-fifth Street. Charlie and the boys summered in Patterson in 1928, and in the fall of that year, Constance, Charles, and young Charles made their last move as a family to yet another apartment, on One hundred twenty-third Street near Claremont Avenue. The reconciliation failed, and in 1929 Seeger moved into the Harvard Club, his perennial retreat during the 1920s.

To be sure, if Constance was unstable, Seeger was often a very difficult and demanding person himself, with his own frustrations and disappointments. While he was always attracted to intelligent and creative women, and though he respected Constance's ability and tried to understand her desire for a career, Seeger held the standard ideas of his generation about the position and responsibilities of wives and mothers. At the same time, Constance was a sensitive, gifted woman who chafed at the limitations of the traditional female role. Moreover, Seeger had begun to spend more and more time away from home, enjoying the stimulating company of a new circle of musical colleagues—following fresh intellectual interests, as he had done in California. Meanwhile, Constance did not grow with him intellectually, according to Seeger, and disliked many of his friends intensely. "She was a violinist, never more than that; [she] tried to tie me down too much."

At various times Charles tried to analyze the failure of his first marriage. In later years he mused about his family's New England tradition that perhaps had led him to have such exalted expectations of matrimony: "It is a highly romantic tradition dating from 1620," he said, that in marriage one can "find heaven in that place." However, "in New England, from the Puritans to the present, the level of God went down, down, down." By Seeger's time, "the level of God was a marriage of the love of man for woman and vice versa, and that's how I had been brought up." By the early twentieth century, he theorized, the Puritan concern with the otherworld had been exchanged for a focus on the successful union of husband and wife. His marriage had failed to live up to this lofty standard; it "began to taper off after nine or ten years and finally ended one life," he concluded. Constance refused to grant him a divorce for several more years. Their marriage was finally dissolved in October 1932.

Seeger began to extend his social network, meeting new and stimulating people on the New York cultural scene. At the home of Blanche Walton, a well-to-do music patron, he met young composers and rising young musical stars. Among the group were his former student and friend Henry Cowell; the pianists Richard Buhlig and Carlos Salzedo; a musician friend of Cowell's and of Ruth Crawford's (Seeger's second wife), Dane Rudhyar (born Daniel Chennevière, he had taken a Hindu name); Edgard Varèse, the expatriate Frenchman who was to be one of the founders of the International Composers Guild; Edmond de Coppets, founder of the Flonzaley Quartet; and the composer Carl (Charles) Ruggles, whom Seeger had met earlier. Seeger told his daughter Penny,

Henry Cowell, who had been drafted in the army for three years, had been transferred to Governor's Island where he was playing in a band. This continued for some time after peace was declared and I remember having to undertake strenuous efforts to get them to release Cowell—they had no business to keep a draft soldier going beyond the time of his usefulness. And he shortly became acquainted with Ruggles and introduced me to him. Ruggles was then living in Leonia, New Jersey, across the Hudson River from 125th Street.[12]

Cowell, commenting on the group of radical musicians gathered around him in the mid-1920s, said that Seeger, as teacher and colleague, "influenced just about every composer around" with his systematic viewpoint and his view of music in a conceptual sense. However, according to Cowell, many composers who used Seeger's ideas were not completely aware of their source. This was due to "timing," the people to whom he presented his ideas, or to the perverse manner in which Seeger presented them.[13] In Cowell's words,

[Seeger] has a new idea—he imparts the idea to a few important acquaintances, usually in such a way as to cause instant repulsion on their part and to irritate them greatly; but Seeger does not mind irritating: he knows that if he irritates his subject enough, the idea will be remembered, and passed on. And this is what actually happens.[14]

In tandem with his busy musical and social life, Seeger began a new romantic relationship. At Blanche Walton's he met a fascinating young Englishwoman named Mona, to whom he agreed through a friend to give piano lessons. Soon he realized that he was in love. It was a psychological liberation for him, and a revelation: he had not realized that one could fall in love more than once—perhaps because of the expections with which he was raised, to which he alluded in his comments about New England matrimonial traditions. The romance lasted several months, and the couple discussed matrimony. But Constance's refusal to grant Seeger a divorce was perhaps fortunate in this instance; he came to realize that Mona, with her difficult upbringing, domineering mother, weak father, and her ambitions for Charles to "be somebody," was another Constance. The relationship ended painfully.

The upheavals in Seeger's life coincided with the onset of the Great Depression, which was paradoxically another liberating experience for him. He felt that the old establishment was being destroyed and that a new social era was beginning. At forty-three, he was ready for a new life. In his words,

It took an abortive effort to carry the three B's [Bach, Beethoven, and Brahms] to the backwoods, the better part of the twenties and a lot of physical rehabilitation work to set things to rights. When the decks were clear, a second marriage and the Great Depression combined in the conception of the second life. Nothing remained of the first but restored health, three fine sons, a sound musicianship and a theory of supremacy of value over fact. But finally, at almost fifty years of age, I had to admit that I could not make the theory work in twentieth-century America. The world of scholarship, toward which I had long been groping, had long before made the Copernican twist from the value-primacy of the Middle Ages to the fact-primacy of the present day. Not yielding an inch with respect to their theoretical parity, I nevertheless had to concede their practical precedence of the latter. Since then, my musicological work has progressed, though slowly. [15]

In professional terms, the twenties were years of great musical activity for Seeger. He later confessed that earlier in the decade he had attributed too much of his loneliness to personal problems when, in fact, they had been compounded by his professional dilemma. He had decided to give up composition, yet he was unable to resolve his problems with musicology. For Seeger, it was the resumption of the conflict between speech about music and music-speech.

Three articles, all written between 1918 and 1920 and published during this period, reveal his concerns at the time. In "Music in the American University" (1923), [16] he noted that music as a serious mode of study was still an outcast in many U.S. universities. There must be some university "grading system" for it. He believed that the United States needed more music literacy and that the study of musicology belonged in the university and should be on a par with language.

In "On Style and Manner in Modern Composition" (1923), [17] one of his earliest efforts at musicological analysis, his key purpose is clarification:

As a fundamental definition in any sound critique of music, . . . *style* is to be recognized upon the basis of the balanced articulation of all the essential resources of technique, in contrast with *manner*, which is to be recognized upon the basis of the special cultivation of a few of the resources and the comparative neglect of others. [18]

In the article Seeger discussed articulation of resources, by which he meant the "physical materials of the art (tonal and rhythmic) in the three main branches of composition (melody, harmony and form) or, in other words, the manipulation of the former by the latter." [19] He suggested that *style* defined close-knit or organic composition, while *manner* referred to loose or diffuse composition; the distinction between the terms had to do with the extent of the development of the strict implications of a musical subject, examples of which were Bach fugues and Beethoven symphonies. Style and manner should be understood within two contexts: the situation of musical art at any given time, and the character of the composer.

Seeger posited that music is created in three phases: *prevision* or the acquisition of the idiom; *vision* or inspiration; and *revision*. The first and third periods are cool, deliberate, and experimental, the second heated and hasty. Seeger's aim in this essay was to outline a set of preparatory disciplines by which one could produce qualifiable work, balancing discipline with talent, tradition with innovation. He addressed himself primarily to composers, but subjected the composing process to an analysis more characteristic of a social scientist or historian.

"On the Principles of Musicology" (1924)[20] dealt with the central problem that emerged in a number of his writings: the relationship between music and language, or the musical and the nonmusical points of view. Arguing that the assumptions governing talking or writing about music needed revision, he presented axioms and criteria that became the foundation for his later ideas on music and language. Judgment has to do with nonmusical views, writing and talking *about* music. On the other hand, music is an art; it resembles certain classes of language usage that can be classified as art in the same way that music as a whole is so classified; music has a "mysterious quality that allows it to place upon it a value for which we cannot logically account." Put differently, there is an art of music and there is an art of language; they may enter into a relation with one another; and they are technically in some respect homologous. To this postulate of facts should be added a postulate set on value, Seeger wrote:

(1) The art of language and the art of music are technically peers both in and out of relations entered into between them (i.e., they are equally directly used by us; function with equal degrees of autonomy) and are equally important or valuable; (2) the lack of balance introduced into musicology by the choice of instrument (language) may be compensated for by the

predominance of a musical point of view; (3) both on the whole and in whatever particular respect homology is hypothesized it must be equi-valued in respect to the two terms (i.e., music is as different from language as it is like it and until the contrary is proven each resemblance found must be considered as offset by a proportionate difference in the same respect.[21]

How does one talk logically about music? Seeger asked. Because of language, discussions of music have acquired definitions like those used in other fields such as physics and physiology to describe observed phenomena. In yielding to philosophers exclusive control over the grounds, data, and methods of talking about music, musicians have lost control of the situation. Therefore music becomes something else — sense data, sound waves, and the like. The musical view, wrote Seeger, is that to the musician, music is music, not something else. Thus, we are faced with two tasks: organizing musical knowledge and effecting a revision of music in terms of musical technique.

Musicology demands equal skill in language and music; to be logically sound and musically acceptable one must break down the splendid isolation of music and deny the claim of language that it can legislate for everything. Methods for studying music include both the historic approach — subject to inequality and myopia — and the sys-tematic, in which one approaches music as the artist or craftsman does: working in it to see how it has come to be as it is. A key point for Seeger was that modern musicology had reinstated a vast amount of the music of former times without keeping track of improvements in the methods for studying them or of present-day works with which musicology is out of touch. That is, it has tended to judge the history of music in terms that belong to the history of musicology — in terms of *former* systems.

In discussing *fact* and *value*, Seeger asked, what are the answers to the struggle between these antipodes? First, he suggested establish-ing a study of music so as to provide a give-and-take between fact and value — that is, a legitimate purpose. Then language should be held in check, and music should be allowed autonomy. The facts are that there is an art of music and an art of language, they may enter into relations with one another, and in some respects are homologous. As for value, language and music are peers, as much alike as they are different.

While Seeger had generated these theories in the years between Berkeley and the Institute of Musical Arts, he had also begun postulating others which he elaborated upon in the 1920s. He published several articles that reflected his two prime interests during this time: composition and musicology. "Reviewing a Review,"[22] a companion piece to "Carl Ruggles and the Future of Dissonant Counterpoint" by Dane Rudhyar, reflected Seeger's involvement in Blanche Walton's music circle. Shortly thereafter came "Prolegomena to Musicology: The Problem of the Musical Point of View and the Bias of Linguistic Presentation,"[23] continuing his preoccupation with the linguocentric predicament. The pendulum swung back again to a musicological problem in "A Fragment of Greek Music,"[24] followed by "Dissonance and the Devil: An Interesting Passage in a Bach Cantata."[25] Then "On Dissonant Counterpoint,"[26] and "Lines on the Grace Note."[27]

"On Dissonant Counterpoint" is of historical interest; in this essay Seeger dates the use of the term *dissonant counterpoint* to describe a particular technical procedure to about 1913, although he acknowledges the use of tonal dissonance by both Scriabin and Schoenberg before that time. It also analyzes the difference between consonance and dissonance in composition. Seeger argues that the effect of the use of dissonance has been to purify composition. He suggests that it had moved from being a "mere adjunct of the craft into an integral unit in the technic of the art," a procedure that involves the use of several new principles.[28] These are: the recognition of rhythmic harmony as a category on a par with tonal harmony; forecasting of the possibility of separate "harmonies" of dynamics, tone-quality, accent; the recognition and cultivation of an art of dissonant melody; the percentile ratio of consonant and dissonant tonal and rhythmic materials; and the fact that from the point of view of form, music had declined over the preceding fifty years.[29] Seeger concluded that for the first time in many centuries, Western composers were unfettered by the conventional European vocal range in the choice of intervals larger than the octave and that in rhythm and form there was a wider range of materials from which to choose.[30]

These were his last writings in the early compositional mode and other protomusicological issues. Seeger became increasingly interested in musicology as he grappled more successfully with its issues. He had determined historic musicology to be a study of music or a way of looking at music in general space and time. He had determined systematic musicology to be a study of music or a way of looking at music in its *own* space and time. Seeger presented this viewpoint and dual analysis to John Erskine, then a literary light in New York and head of the new Juilliard School of Music.[31] Erskine liked Seeger's idea very much, but did not think there was a place for it in the Juilliard curriculum.

Seeger's publications from this period indicate a new attention to musicological ideas and to social activism in music. In writing about composers, he is less interested in their compositional processes than in their character and opinions: he writes paeans to figures such as Ruggles, Ives, Crawford, Cowell, and others. Seeger frequently referred to his work written during 1918–1930, most specifically between 1923 and 1930, as "juvenile," under the influence of European traditional historical musicology, specifically that of Guido Adler. Adler's then path-breaking distinction between systematic and historic musicology affected Seeger before he was to be influenced by Ferdinand de Saussure's terms, *synchronic* and *diachronic*, as conceived in the linguistic structuralism of the time.

Seeger's teaching load at the Institute of Musical Arts was reduced by two-thirds because of Damrosch's displeasure at the breakup of his marriage to Constance. To compensate for this reduction in income, Seeger began teaching at the New School for Social Research, a radical institution for its time, both politically and pedagogically, and a far cry from the traditional, academic, highly prestigious music institute patronized by old and wealthy New York families. Teaching at two such different schools presented a philosophical dilemma. Seeger was less formal than other institute teachers, but he made a point of never having contact with students outside of class. Yet those with political black marks against their names came to him for help. They wanted a place to meet and to organize to advance various radical causes. Seeger agreed to find a meeting place for them at the New School.

The New School and its curricula presaged the changes then occurring in American society and in Seeger's own sociopolitical views. An innovative part of the curriculum being tested there was non-Western music. In 1929, with Seeger's encouragement, Henry Cowell, one of the first professors at the New School, had toured the Soviet Union and brought back recordings of Asiatic music, which he introduced to his classes.

Seeger now also began to show a penchant for forming and joining societies. He became involved with the International Music Society, forerunner of the Union Musicologique, now defunct. At the same time, Seeger was attempting to establish a musicology society because he felt the need for musicological contacts. He made inquiries and found that those currently prominent in music — Sonneck, Lewis, and Pratt — were not immediately interested. The most helpful person was Otto Kinkeldy, a German-trained German-American historian, who was then chief of the music section of the New York Public Library. Seeger and Kinkeldy began discussions on the idea of starting an American "musicology" society.

American society during these twelve years had changed dramatically. The United States had been involved in a European War, one in which Seeger had lost his brother Alan, a rising and respected poet, followed by a decade of boomtown mentality, of well-being, of that proverbial "chicken in every pot, car in every garage" goal to which the Republicans seemed to be directing the country. America had moved inexorably from a land of the frontiers and rural life to a cosmopolitan, urban, modernist society. The bourgeois mentality had taken hold, and Americans had begun to believe in the good life of consumer hedonism made possible by industrial capitalism. But eventually the nation's financial and political leaders acquired enough power to speculate disastrously with that security, and eventually it all came crashing down.

Seeger's life up to the 1930s had been one of upper middle-class gentility, of old-boy ties and connections in high places, of membership in the privileged elite, the establishment. It was as if there was a hiatus in Seeger's own thinking during these dozen years from his flight from California to his reincarnation in a new scholarly life in 1930. The angst he suffered because of a sense of failure — professionally and personally — overshadowed the immediate impact of historical events, political radicalism, and new cultural influences. But the Depression would change Seeger's life forever.

Western classical music, tuxedos, fine art, the best places—the life of the privileged elite was regarded as the "best" in American life and what should be achieved by the rest of the population. Seeger had been caught up in it. The 1920s, though the decade began with a caravan tour that ended because the Seegers could not make a go of roughing it, pointed toward a new direction. The changes in American society were accompanied by a broadening social awareness that was more and more brought home to Seeger. His awareness of social inequities had already been precipitated by his work in California and his glimpse of the laborers in the hopfields, the IWW, and the socialist activism of the wartime era—all came to play against the more intellectual and elitist traditions in which he had been raised and which characterized the twenties.

His publications of the time indicate little of what Seeger thought about the rural conditions he witnessed on trips with his family and the activities of populists and progressivists at work in America. The man who at Berkeley was so wrapped up in the plight of the migrant workers seems almost to have filed away in some corner of his mind the increasing abjectness of the rural American. He seemed as yet unable to cope with what he had seen in the early 1920s and was caught up in a very different ambiance for the rest of the decade. Little of the socialist ferment of the decade seemed to interest him, and even more, he was removed from the activities and ideas of Europe, the far more dramatic intellectual and social turmoil there.

As Seeger recalled this period of his life,

I spent my sabbatical year's leave in "the East" (1918–1919). The War had given me, as it gave to so many people, an opportunity to realize and express points of view with a clarity not ordinarily evoked under the conventional considerations of living up to that time. My opposition to the international war lost me many friends: my partisanship in, indeed even my recognition of, the class war alienated others.

Meanwhile, in 1915, after the performance of my most ambitious work, the "Queen's Masque" in Berkeley, I had decided to give up musical composition. Three reasons for this stood out beyond others. In the first place, it could not afford me a living and support for my growing family; second, I could not reconcile the "ideals" that had dominated my composition up to that time with the growing consciousness of the nature of geographical and social struggles of large masses of people; and thirdly, my musical education had been so bad that a complete revision was necessary before any more composition could be done. The strain of the conflicts involved in these considerations led me to take three years off and finally to decide to abandon all artistic, intellectual and social life of all kinds I had hitherto known, in favor of a back-to-the-soil and tramping kind of life.

After building a handsome automobile trailer and trying to gypsy it about the country for a year, I at least recovered a good deal of my natural health. An invitation to teach at the Institute of Musical Art came in 1921 and put an end to that adventure. Since that time I have earned a meagre living by teaching a few hours a week, enjoying the leisure that most men only promise themselves after sixty. By the help of a good friend I learned a little about keeping physically in good shape and the musicological life has gone well.[32]

Drastic change would come in the 1930s, with the Depression, with the attempts to reorder his life, with the new directions for music, for society, and for Seeger. There were many new fronts on which he could work and there were many new areas that needed attention. The next quarter century would provide a series of different platforms, new avenues, and varied activities in which Seeger would test out and expand the dichotomies in his life: woman's career versus home life; music versus speech; the life of privilege versus the world of work. Once more, history, society, politics, ideas would come to the fore with Seeger.

In sum, during the 1920s, Seeger's whole being and musical life was torn by his attitude that he could not approve what he liked and he could not like what he approved, an example of which was that he loved pre-1900 music and admired post-1900 music. The same dichotomy applied in his concern for society and his concern for self. He had to find a way to put into equal balance the resolution of head and heart, the intellectual and the emotional. The 1920s, then, clearly were a dividing point and gestation period for Seeger and, through that decade, the ideas that had taken root in California began to develop and, in particular, the Hegelian ideas surrounding life, society, and work.

4

Ruth and the New York Scene,

1930–1935

❧

S EEGER'S INTERESTS were shifting from writing and publishing his ideas on composition—many of which appear in the unpublished treatise sometimes called "Tradition and Experiment"—to teaching composition. One of his most brilliant students was Ruth Crawford, who in 1932 became Seeger's second wife.[1]

Ruth Porter Crawford, born on July 3, 1901, in East Liverpool, Ohio, was the daughter of Clara Alletta Graves, a teacher, and Clark Crawford, a Methodist minister. As a minister's daughter, Ruth moved frequently with her family, living in Akron, St. Louis, Muncie and Bluffton, Indiana, and Jacksonville, Florida, where her father died when she was thirteen. Her widowed mother supported herself, Ruth, and Carl, Ruth's older brother, by managing a rooming house.

Ruth Crawford was serious and introspective, with a strong social consciousness and an interest in poetry and music. She took her first piano lesson at age six, continuing her studies despite the family's many removals. In high school Ruth played the piano with a group of amateur musicians. She also wrote for the school paper, was class historian, and directed the senior class play.

Ruth's interest in music intensified in her teens, and she became an accomplished pianist. She studied at Jacksonville's School of Musical Art with Bertha Foster, its owner, and briefly with Beryl Rubenstein, and then gave piano lessons herself in the summer before her senior year. Foster offered her a teaching position effective after Ruth's graduation. Ruth continued her piano studies with Madame Valborg-Collett, another faculty member, who encouraged her to undertake more professional study. Collett was a taskmaster with whom Ruth felt uncomfortable, yet from her the young musician acquired the determination to study piano seriously and a fascination for things foreign.

Ruth remained at the School of Musical Art for three years (1918–1921). She attracted more students and began to gain a reputation as a pianist; now she could support her mother. In addition to giving lessons, Ruth continued to study piano and began to compose music.

Looking beyond her limited horizons, Ruth began to dream of studying in a larger musical center such as New York or Chicago. Through the school-sponsored concert series, she heard well-known performers and met correspondents for the Chicago-based music magazine, the *Musical Leader*. Mrs. Edward MacDowell, widow of the American composer and associated with the celebrated MacDowell Colony, presented a lecture-recital in the series.

Although encouraged to study in New York with Godowsky or Harold Bauer, Ruth decided on Chicago. Chicago was a major musical center in the 1920s, both in performance and music education. Great artists visited Chicago to perform in concerts, operas, recitals, and other musical events. The city's rich musical life was to be a major stimulus to Ruth Crawford's development as a composer.

Supported by a mysterious grant of money, Ruth enrolled at Chicago's American Conservatory in the fall of 1921.[2] There she studied with renowned artists such as the Polish pianist and composer Heniot Lévy (once a student of Max Bruch) and violinist and conductor Adolf Weidig, a student of Hugo Riemann (in theory), himself highly regarded as a teacher of theory and composition. Ruth also worked with pianist Louise Robyn and studied theory and composition with John Palmer.

Ruth's piano teacher, Heniot Lévy, was so impressed with her talent that he suggested that she complete two years of required harmony training in one. Her teachers of harmony, Weidig and Palmer, were similarly impressed with Ruth's originality, especially with her harmony assignments, several of which expanded upon early pieces she had composed in Jacksonville.

Having intended to stay in Chicago only a year, Ruth remained until 1929. She at first rented a room at the YWCA. To earn a little extra money, she ushered at concerts, recitals, and other events in downtown theaters. When she took a position teaching piano in South Chicago, six pupils supplemented her usher's income. The talented young musician was encouraged to continue at the conservatory for another year, then a third. In 1923, having received her certificate, she brought her mother to live with her. They shared an apartment until Clara's death in 1928. Ruth earned a bachelor's degree in 1924, at which time she performed her *Kaleidoscopic Changes on an Original Theme, Ending with a Fugue*, at Kimball Hall. In 1925 she enrolled as a graduate student at the American Conservatory and received her master's degree, summa cum laude, in 1927. In addition to teaching at the conservatory, Ruth also taught piano at Elmhurst College of Music, in the Chicago suburbs, while studying with Djane Lavoie Herz, former student of Arthur Schnabel and Alexander Scriabin, and wife of the impresario Siegfried Herz.

Ruth's ambition to become a professional pianist was blocked by a painful muscular condition in her arms. These pains had long troubled her, and she had followed osteopathic and electric treatments to no avail. Exacerbated by long hours of practicing, the condition forced her to discontinue her studies with Lévy for a time. In November 1922, Ruth changed teachers; Louise Robyn seemed more sympathetic to Ruth's muscular condition. Unable to play as she had before, Ruth's interest shifted to music theory, and she began to produce very fine counterpoint and harmonic exercises. While Adolf Weidig insisted on the traditional study of harmony, he also encouraged students to demonstrate their originality in composition.

Ruth began to envision another source of income in addition to teaching: writing songs and educational pieces for children. She also wanted to learn to write chamber music, but realized that she was not skilled enough yet. With Robyn's and Weidig's encouragement, Ruth moved into a different music sphere.

Through the Herzes, Ruth met an entirely new circle of music cognoscenti and intellectuals, some of whom later became celebrated musicians. In the late 1920s, Ruth was part of the Nietzsche group, which included the Herzes as well as University of Chicago professors and other prominent figures such as Clarence Darrow, Max Otto, and Ben Hecht. It was also in the Herz circle that Ruth first met Henry

Ruth Seeger, about 1931

Cowell, Dane Rudhyar, Edgar Varèse, Adolph Weiss, and other musical innovators who were to be important to her when she moved to New York. It was through Madame Herz as well as the French-born Rudhyar that Ruth came to be so influenced by Scriabin.

Ruth's attraction to Scriabin was as much philosophical as aesthetic, particularly during the 1924–1929 period: her *Piano Preludes* (1924–1928) reflect Scriabin's influence. Ruth's growing fascination with Scriabinesque technique—panchromaticism, serial procedures, use of the tritone and contrapuntal techniques, dissonance—grew as the influence of her teacher Aldolf Weidig declined. From Rudhyar she learned much about chording and rhythmic experimentation, and non-Western music; through Weidig and the work of Schoenberg, atonality; however, she was never merely an imitator. Others' ideas informed her work, but her compositions were her own.

Ruth became good friends with Henry Cowell, who was intensely involved with the encouragement and promotion of new music. In 1925 he had founded the New Music Society in California for the presentation of ultramodern works by unknown composers, and in 1928 organized the Pan American Association of Composers. In his journal, *New Music* (founded in 1927) Cowell published compositions that were by-passed by the music publishing establishment.

Cowell's compositional techniques did not greatly interest Ruth, but he encouraged her to experiment with new forms. Further, he arranged for the performance and publication of some of her pieces, and Ruth in turn joined several groups organized by Cowell in his campaign to promote unknown new composers.

The music critic Alfred J. Frankenstein, a neighbor and amateur clarinetist, also became a lifelong friend. The two occasionally attended musical soirees together, and Ruth would accompany him on the piano. Through Frankenstein, Ruth met the poet and folk singer Carl Sandburg, who lived not far from Elmhurst College. Frankenstein was currently working with Sandburg on *The American Songbag*, a book of folk songs published in 1927 and invited Ruth to contribute several piano accompaniments for the book. Ruth set to music *Those Gambler's Blues, Lonesome Road, There Was an Old Soldier,* and *Ten Thousand Miles Away from Home.*

Working with Sandburg opened up a new world to Ruth, who had had little awareness of folk music before this time. Nor had she ever encountered anyone like him, not only an internationally renowned poet, but also a good amateur musician who traveled the country lecturing, giving poetry readings, and singing folk songs. Ruth was soon included in musical evenings of folk singing at the Sandburg home — infectious informal performances led primarily by Sandburg himself.

This was the beginning of a lifelong friendship; Ruth became almost part of the family. When the Sandburgs needed a piano teacher for their two children, Frankenstein recommended Ruth. This was also a catalyst for an interest in folk music that developed over the next decade. Not only Sandburg's style but also his subject matter attracted Ruth, and she began to include his poems in some of her own vocal compositions.

In Chicago Ruth not only met many of the composers and major musical ideas that were to dominate twentieth-century American music, but also she herself was beginning to be known as a composer. Her works received praise and were widely performed in the Chicago area. She began to win competitions. In December 1925, Ruth's first three piano preludes were performed at a League of Composers concert in New York's Town Hall, with Gitta Gradova the pianist. She won a Julliard scholarship for 1927–1929. Her *Preludes* 6-9 (1927–1928) were performed by Richard Buhlig at a Copland-Sessions concert in New York in May 1928. Ruth was exhibiting much more maturity in her compositions, as is evident in the powerful *Two Ricercari* (1928) and, later, in *Three Songs* (1930–1932), with lyrics by Carl Sandburg, for voice, oboe, percussion, and piano with orchestral ostinato.[3]

After her mother's death in 1928, Ruth began to look seriously toward New York. No doubt her decision to go east was influenced by Henry Cowell, as well as Dane Rudhyar and other friends, who were now living in that city. She was awarded a scholarship to spend the summer of 1929 at the MacDowell Colony in Peterborough, New Hampshire.

Ruth's summer at the MacDowell Colony provided a necessary transition from a Chicago that had become a beloved home to a more intense professional life in New York. At the colony Ruth worked on setting more of Sandburg's poems to music and completed the collection known as *Five Songs*. There she met a lifelong friend— Marion Bauer, the New York correspondent for Chicago's *Musical Leader*.

Ruth quickly adjusted to New York. She knew a number of composers and musicians, and some of her work had already been performed in the city. Blanche Walton's New York apartment was what the Herzes' home in Chicago had been—a center for the presentation of "new music" and a gathering place for critics, art lovers, and performers.

Henry Cowell prevailed upon Blanche Walton to house Ruth and persuaded Seeger to teach her. Despite Cowell's championship of Ruth's remarkable talent, Seeger at first "turned up his nose" at the idea of working with a woman composer, because of a deep-rooted skepticism about the ability of any woman to compose music. He was unimpressed by samples of her work, which he criticized as excessively influenced by Scriabin. But Cowell was adamant. Moreover, Seeger needed the money, for the Depression was beginning to make itself felt and he was losing students.

After a week's trial, they agreed that Seeger would give six lessons of one to two hours' duration each week for a year. After that time, if both parties wished, the agreement would be renewed. Blanche Walton would pay for the lessons and would take Ruth into her home on Sixty-eighth Street, where teacher and student would enjoy the use of Walton's new Steinway grand piano. Lessons would begin at five in the afternoon, after which Ruth, Charles, and Blanche would dine together.

The first lesson was a portent of things to come. Seeger recalled that he began with a critique of early contemporary European and American composition, with Scriabin the culprit, using the overreliance on harmony he saw demonstrated in Ruth's work as a prime example of what he disliked. Because Seeger's approach to composition was conceptually linked to dissonant counterpoint and rhythm, he instructed Ruth to begin with dissonant melodic lines. When a servant knocked to signal that dinner was served, they ignored the knock — they were too wrapped up in heated discussion about compositional principles.

Ruth worked like a demon for thirty weeks, determined to prove herself not only as a composer but as a woman composer. Seeger later praised her as the best student he ever had.

Unlike Adolf Weidig, Ruth's teacher in Chicago, Seeger stressed musical form, and his assignments entailed a disciplined approach to composition, complete with rules. He insisted that each assignment was to be not merely an exercise but a composition. Most were eventually published.

Charles was the right teacher for Ruth at this time. She possessed enormous raw talent, but he helped to refine the mature composer. Seeger's disciplined approach to composition helped Ruth to organize her musical material, both in melody and rhythm. Soon this discipline and new compositional techniques of dissonant counterpoint, dissonant rhythm, and single melodic line were integral to her work. As she wrote to her friend Alice in January 1930, "Busy on counterpoint. Very much thrilled with it, for it is dissonant counterpoint, and breathtaking. As full of discipline as the old, and plus that, imagination. Charles Seeger has evolved this, and it is with him I am having the luck of working."[4]

Ruth also encountered the more radical music ideas of the time. Hitherto she had paid little attention to twelve-tone works, although she had found Schoenberg's ideas interesting when they were introduced to her by Weidig. When Seeger required Ruth to study Schoenberg's twelve-tone compositions, she was intellectually drawn to them. Through Henry Cowell she had become exposed to the new European vocal experiments and the use of vocables (meaningless syllables), with which she began to experiment in her own compositions. Although she wrote little choral music, her experimentation with vocable phonemes is displayed in such pieces as *To an Unkind God*; *Chant, 1930*, and a third untitled piece. Before 1930, relatively few serious composers (Darius Milhaud and Ralph Vaughn Williams are exceptions) used the musical and textual techniques that have since become commonplace. As she began writing new compositions and revising earlier ones, Ruth drew on the highly organized principles of twelve-tone music combined with redefined dissonance to produce new works of heightened maturity, ones that reflected her receptivity to Seeger's views on modern music.

Seeger later analyzed Ruth's compositional style before 1930 as basically homophonic, somewhat traditional. He saw great intellect in her compositions, particularly a strict logic in structure, and applauded their unpretentiousness. He predicted that her music "could very well find a permanent place in a small repertoire of an intellectual sort for a particular group of people who were interested in that sort of thing." Yet, he felt, she might have a profound influence on modern music.[5] In 1933, believing he was being complimentary, Seeger said of Ruth's work, "One can find only a few men among American composers who are as uncompromisingly and successfully radical."[6]

They became good friends. This was a year in which both came increasingly to rely on each other's friendship, working through old romances and, unexpectedly, laying the groundwork for their own. Ruth noted about him in February 1930,

Blanche calls Charlie a tragic figure. She tells me sadly that she has come to believe him to be the most utterly hopelessly selfish man she has ever met. . . . Charlie is so immersed in selfishness, that he is not conscious of it. To cover his extreme self-consciousness as a boy, his hyper-sensitiveness, his intense emotional nature, he built a wall of ice, of stone, to save himself. He was once so self-conscious that entering into a streetcar was agony. There I can sympathize with him. I have been there too. Charlie deliberately killed in himself the milk of human kindness, according to Blanche, to save himself from suffering.

There are intense beauties in Charlie. There are exquisite finenesses of feeling. . . . Anyone who can be as excited as Charlie was last week over — a counterpoint lesson. Anyone who can be so emotionally upset that he can't eat and his hands are trembling and his whole evening is a flare of sparks — all because of a so-called abstract thing as a bit of new music . . . they call him cold?[7]

Although he was no longer composing, Seeger continued to work on his treatise on composition that had its origins in his work at California.[8] Based on his old dissonant counterpoint studies, it began as a resumé of lessons he had developed over the years. But, as he instructed the extremely talented Ruth, he refined his lessons and examples and polished their presentation. Their partnership gave him a strong impetus to complete the manuscript, and he asked Ruth to help him with the project. Ruth's lessons could also continue. They agreed to work together at Seeger's parents' home, where he planned to spend the summer with his sons, as he had done since his separation from Constance. Ruth first found lodging at a nearby farmer's house, every morning walking to Charlie's. In August they changed venues, she living at Blanche Walton's summer cottage, he and the boys at a friend's cottage. They worked daily on the project, Ruth taking dictation and typing a new draft. By summer's end, she had completed a typewritten draft of the two volumes. Ruth got along well with the boys and drove up to Connecticut with Charlie to take them back to school.

Ruth was awarded a Guggenheim scholarship to live and travel in Europe, the first woman composer to win this honor. They agreed that she would not study with anyone else; she was twenty-nine, a mature musician, and it was time to show her work to the world. In the fall of 1930 Seeger drove with her to Canada in Blanche Walton's "flimsy Model A," spending the night en route with the Ruggles. It was during this stay in Vermont that they realized they were in love. When they reached the dock in Quebec, Seeger was momentarily tempted to board the ship with her, but he reflected that it was important for her to go alone.

The 1930–1931 year abroad was a rich experience for an aspiring composer. The International Composers' Guild was in full flower, and Ruth spent part of the year meeting many prominent European composers and music publishers, and attending concerts, festivals, and conferences in Berlin, Vienna, Budapest, and Munich. In Berlin and Hamburg she heard performances of her own *Diaphonic Suite no. 3*, one of four suites for bassoon and cello that she had written in New York in 1930. Ruth found Berlin, a showcase for contemporary music and new ideas not yet received in America, most stimulating. Soon after her arrival, at the International Festival of Contemporary Music at Liège, Ruth encountered alien compositional currents with which she had little empathy, but which widened her knowledge of the musical avant garde. She met Bartók, Honegger, Ravel, and Alban Berg, whose music she held in the greatest regard, and had a brief and unsatisfactory meeting with Hindemith. To her disappointment, she was unsuccessful in obtaining an appointment with Schoenberg. Among other discoveries, she was somewhat disillusioned by the politics and "business" aspects of music promotion in Europe, especially in the great capitals of Paris and Berlin.

In Europe Ruth was determined to put into practice the techniques she had learned with Seeger, free of his constant supervision. She completed several pieces for small groups, some of which she had brought with her in draft form. She planned to undertake a major symphonic work and a choral piece commissioned by the Women's University Glee Club of New York.[9] She was also eager to continue her study of orchestration and composition. After spending several months in Berlin, she moved to Paris in June 1931, hoping that her Guggenheim would be renewed. Charlie planned to join her there, after which "they would see what would happen."

In Ruth's absence, Seeger left Constance for good, living first at the Harvard Club and then in Blanche Walton's apartment. He and Ruth exchanged frequent letters, planning a fruitful holiday together. Ruth would get well into her orchestral piece, and he would complete his treatise on composition. But they did neither that summer. When Ruth received word that her Guggenheim would not be renewed, she was devastated, concerned about what would happen to her next, whereupon—as Seeger recalled—he simply put his arm around her and said that they were going to get married, have some lovely children, and that was that.

Ruth remained several more months in Europe, finishing some of her work and cementing contacts. When she returned to New York in November 1931, she moved into Seeger's small apartment on Thirteenth Street in Greenwich Village. Seeger began introducing her as his wife for appearances' sake; however, they did not marry for another year. On October 2, 1932, Seeger's divorce became final, and he and Ruth were married.[10]

While Ruth was away, Seeger returned to the variety of interests and relationships that had characterized his Berkeley period: scholarly societies, composer groups, music criticism, new political ideologies, and persons involved in the new social movements.

Seeger was encountering difficulties in his professional life. Walter Damrosch still disapproved of his breakup with Constance and looked askance both at Seeger's renewed radical sympathies and taste for avant-garde music. He did not want Seeger teaching or lecturing on any twentieth-century composer and reprimanded him whenever he did. During 1930–1931 Seeger's work load there was reduced. At the Institute he was put in charge of preparatory centers, small children's classes, conducting classes, and assigned to other noncontroversial activities. The Institute was experiencing economic difficulties and soon thereafter taken over by the Juilliard School of Music. Eventually, Seeger lost his job, partly due to budget cuts, his loss of favor with Damrosch, but primarily, Charlie claimed, because of his association with dissident students.

Although not out of favor at the IMA, Seeger's work at the New School for Social Research increased. Designed to develop and implement innovative educational programs, the school was a hotbed of new political ideas, which flourished as the Depression worsened. Henry Cowell had been giving lectures there on various music cultures based on what he had learned in Berlin and notably through Erich von Hornbostel, the celebrated comparative musicologist. In January 1931, Seeger and Cowell together offered the school's first course on music cultures of the world, which combined lectures with performances given by members of various non-European groups.

Another stimulus to Seeger's changing musical interests and developing social conscience was the Composers' Collective of New York. This was a coterie of professional musicians seeking to forge a relationship between music, society, politics, and the economy. Like Cowell and others, Seeger was concerned about the deepening economic depression and the plight of working people, among whom he now counted himself. One night in the winter of 1931–1932 Cowell visited Charlie and Ruth, and they discussed their feelings of guilt at being unable to connect their music with the present social catastrophe. One way to make a social contribution, he and Cowell agreed, could be the Collective. Yet while Seeger was becoming disenchanted with "art" music, he was as yet unimpressed by folk and popular music.

A radical group with informal ties to the Communist party, the Collective was at first a special section of the Pierre Degeyter Club, named for the French composer who wrote the workers' anthem, *L'Internationale* (1871). Made up of professional musicians, the Degeyter Club had its own orchestra and chorus, and organized study courses, lectures, and concerts. The Degeyter Club, in turn, was a wing of the Workers' Music League, founded in 1931 as the U.S. section of the International Music Bureau. The League had approximately twenty branches in Boston, Chicago, Philadelphia, and New York. The New York City federation boasted between eighteen and twenty workers' organizations—choruses, bands, orchestras—all representing various nationalities. Their slogan was "Music for the Masses."[11]

The composers drawn to the Collective, like many other artists and intellectuals of the period, sought solutions to the political and economic problems growing throughout the world. They attempted to link their interests with those of the unemployed, trade unionists, and other left-leaning artists and writers.[12] The Collective was to develop guidelines for a new workers' music—songs for the masses. Art was to be a weapon in the class struggle; the music to be composed was to be revolutionary in content and form, aimed toward redirecting and refining the workers' musical tastes.[13]

The loosely organized group met weekly in dusty, often unheated lofts in various sections of lower Manhattan, usually in the late afternoon. Members paid twenty-five cents a meeting; that paid the rent for a while and bought songbooks. Seeger used his earnings as the writer for the *Daily Worker* (discussed below) to pay for his activities in the Collective, considering his wages from the newspaper to be a reimbursement for what the Communist party had done for the group.[14]

Seeger remembered that they sat in rickety chairs arranged around an old upright piano, presumably rented by the Communist party, and played their compositions for each other. Each work was criticized on two counts: its suitability for the masses and overall musical technique (they were concerned as much to raise musical taste as to generate political consciousness). Seeger later thought that guitars, banjos, or ukeleles would have been more appropriate accompanying instruments than a piano.

The Collective was a small, genial group—at first only Seeger, Ruth, Henry Cowell, Earl Robinson, Norman Cazden, Marc Blitzstein, Elie Siegmeister, Wallingford Riegger, Herbert Haufrecht, Henry Leland Clarke, Jacob Schaefer, Robert Gross, Alex North, and intermittently Hanns Eisler, George Antheil, and Aaron Copland.[15] At its height in 1933–1935, the Collective embraced twenty-four composers, men and women who ranged from conservative to radical in their musical opinions.

Seeger viewed his role in the Collective as providing a stabilizing influence, since—in his later forties—he was older than the rest; most members were in their twenties and thirties. Seeger led Collective activities for about three years, while Ruth was relatively little involved and attended meetings only occasionally. The birth of Michael (August 16, 1933) and Peggy (June 17, 1935) brought new responsibilities for Ruth.

Most of the composers in the Collective had been trained at Ivy League schools or at Eastman and Juilliard, and they shared common views. One was an initial disdain for folk music. They were, after all, "professional," "classical" musicians, as interested in bringing "good music" to the public as Seeger had been earlier. And good music was European art music. They were less interested in writing music for ordinary people to perform than works for people to hear, even though they had established workers' choruses. While several became celebrated composers who later used folk motifs in their works, they never completely shed their prejudice against grass-roots America nor professed an abiding interest in folk music; Seeger himself did little with folk music until 1935.

These attitudes were perhaps understandable. Like H. L. Mencken, Sinclair Lewis, Sherwood Anderson, and many others, postwar intellectuals condemned the "booboisie" and the philistinism and provincialism of rural and small-town America. Many fled to Europe, like Seeger's brother Alan who had found a haven in Paris. In this they differed from their European counterparts, many of whom were famous composers sympathetic to the folklore and folksong of their countries and who used the folk idiom in their music.

The links between the Collective and the Communist party varied. Some members belonged to the party, but most, including Seeger, never formally joined. However, they shared the larger vision of the party in searching for solutions to the disastrous economic conditions brought on by the Depression. The early Communist movement had paid little attention to the role of art as an instrument of social change. However, by the late twenties the party began to explore the relevance of the arts for the working classes, a phase that resulted in "politicizing artistic expression and removing bourgeois influences from the cultural media of the working class."[16] This did not necessarily mean a new emphasis on folk music, which according to official ideology, tended to be "defeatist and melancholy," exhibiting "morbidity, hysteria, and triviality," and did not characterize proletarian music.

The Collective attempted to work within the Communist tradition of worker songs, but, as Seeger noted, that tradition—most notably, that of the German workers—had been able to accomplish what the U.S. workers' song tradition had not. Collective composers tried to employ "ordinary fragments of technique in an unusual way because [they] thought *that* was revolutionary and therefore suitable for the workers to use."[17] An example that Seeger offered of his own "misguided" efforts in this regard was *Lenin, Who's That Guy?*, which uses irregularly recurring sequences of four chords.

Hanns Eisler (1898–1962), a leading leftist composer and part of the German Workers' Music Movement, visited New York in 1934 and actively participated in Collective discussions. His talk, "The Crisis in Music," delivered at New York's Town Hall, was a major influence in the movement.[18] A celebrated pupil of Schoenberg, Eisler had written the music to Bertholt Brecht's *Massnahme* (*The Precaution*), a highly political work. The play involved a collaboration of workers' choruses and orchestras, agit-prop troupes, and revolutionary texts, all of which transformed the production into a political meeting. Songs of struggle, both unison and polyphonic, choral recitations, and ballads acquired great political significance, and

Massnahme endured for quite a while as a focal point of proletarian cultural discussion.

Eisler's works, especially his choral and marching songs composed between 1926 and 1933, were widely published and sung throughout the world. Ironically, he held a low opinion of folk art, although he used folk songs unconsciously as the basis for his compositions, which used techniques similar to those found in European workers' songs. Members of the Collective thought that Eisler's approach would work for American workers' songs, too.

As a Marxist, Eisler sought to combat the influence of capitalist entertainment music and create new forms and practices that would both satisfy aesthetic needs and educate the proletariat. He believed that a cultural organization out of touch with political realities becomes bourgeois; that a workers' chorus must teach a song of struggle at each performance; that classical, particularly a capella, music was useful for teaching polyphonic singing; that the conductor must educate the worker-singers into being functionaries; that revolutionary songs must express political utility; and that worker-singers should learn revolutionary songs of other countries to encourage revolutionary fraternization. [19]

Eisler's choral works were novel "in that they clarified the contradiction between revolutionary statement and the concert form, by the radicalization of their political and musical content—without destroying the concert form. Extremely difficult to sing because of their modern structure, they demanded the highest measure of discipline and painstaking rehearsal."[20]

Increasing contact with New York's ethnic communities, which had active workers' choruses, changed the Collective's direction. One Collective member was Jacob Schaefer, choral director of the Yiddish-language Freiheit Gezang Farein, which sang and played folk songs as well as classical works in a Workers' [Women's] Mandolin Orchestra. Schaefer also conducted the Workers' Symphony Orchestra. Although various ethnic groups performed in their native languages, making communication difficult, Collective members gradually came to appreciate the contributions of folk song as a vehicle for communication among workers and other social groups.

The Collective's compositions were played at concerts held by the International Composers' Guild and the League of Composers in the 1930s. The Olympiad Concert was entirely devoted to Collective compositions, one of which was a vocal work. Ruth wrote only two pieces for the movement: *Sacco, Vanzetti* and *Chinaman, Laundryman*, both sophisticated musically and carrying a strong message of social justice.[21] She also wrote several rounds, often collaborating with Charlie, that were included in the 1933 Workers' Music Olympiad concert.

Despite its good intentions, the Collective never succeeded in developing a viable proletarian music. Its work had limited appeal. While the lot of the workers was difficult, America had its own home-grown populism and progressivism in which workers could gain a platform. A more important reason was that these composers were classically trained and their music—often complex, dissonant, and difficult to perform—had limited appeal to the average worker. Seeger cited as a prime example the winner of the Collective's 1934 May Day competition, Aaron Copland's setting of Alfred Hayes's *Into the Streets May First*. Seeger thought Copland's song the best musically, but doubted the feasibility of using a piano on workers' marches.

Moreover, Collective composers were too intellectual, too unrealistic; they wrote music more to be heard than played, perceiving their audience to be passive rather than active comrades in making music. Seeger believed that the composer who met the group's goals most successfully was Marc Blitzstein, but even his musical, *The Cradle Will Rock*, appealed to a rather narrow audience.

By the mid-1930s, Seeger "had less and less to do with the compositional end of things." He ceased to try to make music in the written tradition for those who created and performed in an oral tradition. Three people were influential in bringing him to this realization: the legendary Aunt Molly Jackson, of Harlan County (Kentucky) fame, who set union lyrics to traditional ballads and performed them in New York in 1931 as part of her fundraising tour for striking coal miners; his friend Thomas Hart Benton, a New School colleague with whom he played and sang folk songs; and George Pullen Jackson, a Vanderbilt professor who had recently published an important work on nineteenth-century religious folk music in the South.

By 1935, Collective composers had begun to reassess their works in light of their own American folk music traditions; while hitherto whenever they used folk materials they had borrowed from the German or Russian tradition, now they realized that the native idiom would make their music more accessible to the public. Two books of American folk music came to the Collective's attention: Carl Sandburg's *American Songbag* (1927), which had become popular in the early 1930s, and George Pullen Jackson's *White Spirituals in the Southern Uplands* (1933), a pioneering study of shape-note singing. The short-lived Composers' Collective even published its own song collections, published through the Workers' Music League (sometimes referred to as *Workers' Songbooks I* and *II*): *The Red Song Book*,[22] which included fourteen songs (only three based on American folk and popular songs), and *The New Workers' Song Book* (1934),[23] compiled by Seeger and Lan Adomian, which offered twenty-two songs, modeled on Eisler's work, designed for trained choruses.

In 1935 the Collective issued a third volume, *Songs of the People*,[24] nearly half of which were folk or worker songs set to American folk or popular tunes. By this time it was more fashionable for U.S. composers to use American folk motifs, as in Aaron Copland's *Appalachian Spring*.

Also by 1935, many Collective members, including Seeger, had begun to question the group's political and musical assumptions and to doubt whether they would ever achieve their goal of meshing music with social concern. Further, government agents were watching the Collective and, as Seeger recalled, he began to worry about the personal consequences of his membership in it.

Though Seeger ceased to participate in the Collective by fall 1935, his association with it had rekindled the radical feelings he had nurtured at Berkeley. He had welcomed the Russian Revolution in 1917 and had thought at the time that, despite its limitations, Communism represented the only viable alternative to laissez-faire capitalism. Seeger said that the Collective shared the idealism of early Bolshevism, which stressed experimentation in all the arts. He described his political attitudes of this time:

There is no reason why you should not take me to task for some of the outrageous things I said and did during the early thirties. I was in an overwrought state of mind as any sensitive person must have been at the goings on during the Depression. And remember: I had been something of a Roy Harris myself not so long before that time. Perhaps not so much of an opportunist. And certainly not a careerist. Both music-technically and socially conscious, I was way out.

The Carl Sands activity and the musicological professional activity had nothing to do with each other. I was as strictly partisan in the former as I could be and as strictly scholarly as I could be in the latter. . . .

The lecture on the "Dictatorship of the Linguistic" was never written out. The *Music Vanguard* paper comes near to it. The lecture was a polemic. Marx influenced me greatly, but I never could take some aspects of it. As to the double life, I had always been conscious of that from early childhood on. When I ran into Freud, I was delighted to find that I was not the only person in the world that knew it. . . . I was not "made" to insert the paragraph I spoke of at the end of the *M{usic} V{anguard}* paper, but I "learned" to do so. In all my relations with politicos of whatever shade of nefariousness, I never admitted to being "made" to do anything. And I must admit: it was very rarely attempted. If the Democratic party had set up a Composers' Collective for active use of music in fighting the Depression I would have joined it just as wholeheartedly — as I did, when I was seeing the failure of the actual one I had worked so hard for in switching over with just as much enthusiasm to the Resettlement Administration, for this was down to earth, practical and all economically and politically as the C[ommunist] P[arty] never was or has been in [the] USA.

Jacob Schaefer was a "friend" but not a member of the Collective, as was Copland, Cowell and several others. The Collective was a bunch of crazy idealists. Schaefer was not of that kind.

No, I am not a Wobbly. I was nearer the Lunarcharsky kind of Communist in those days and in the later days of the Collective. It took me fifteen years to discover the nature of Stalin. You *must* realize: I have *always* gone my own way. If anybody or group run along beside me, I give them loyalty in proportion to whatever of my goal they share with me. When it comes to government, I have never departed from the conviction formed in my school days: government is at once a desired good and an unavoidable evil; individuality is to be valued above collectivity, but owes its very being to collectivity.[25]

Henry Leland Clarke, himself a Collective member, provides the following retrospective assessment of the Collective:

The Composers' Collective of 1935 was a rare institution. It was a club. It was a camerata. It was a Society for the Propagation of Good News. Rarely have creative artists worked for a common cause with sufficient dedication to make them WANT criticism from each other. Without the Composers' Collective there would have been no *Abe Lincoln Song* by Earl Robinson, and without his *Lincoln Song* there would have been no *Lincoln Portrait* by Aaron Copland. Without the Composers' Collective there would have been no *Cradle Will Rock* by Marc Blitstein, and without his *Cradle Will Rock* there would have been no *West Side Story* by Leonard Bernstein.

The Collective was all set up and busily working on its second *Workers' Song Book* when Hanns Eisler arrived to give it his encouragement. Among the reasons why Bertholt Brecht turned from Kurt Weill to Hanns Eisler as the man to set his words to music are these: Weill wanted his music to be immortal; Eisler wanted his to be instructive. Weill was a Walt Whitman; Eisler was a Tom Paine. The one proclaimed liberty; the other, fraternity, this is, not the individual, but the collective.

Eisler was a great teacher. He insisted on métier, craftsmanship. . . . He never deviated from common sense. When one of the collective pounced on his peers for composing too much like Schumann, Eisler said, "But the point is, is it good Schumann?" Eisler had some special words for Earl Robinson on the subject of simplicity. Earl has to be simple; won't be complex. . . . But Eisler pointed out that simplicity is not enough. Even an ordinary pop song to be successful has to have some special twist or trick. This is why Earl Robinson's *Joe Hill* has reached tens of thousands of people all over the globe. It is that extra repeat of the last line at the end going up to the high octave.

There were reasons why my own *United Front Song* was chosen to be the first song in the *Workers' Song Book No. 2*, which we were then preparing. It was not because I was a bright boy. There is no doubt that Aaron Copland was a bright boy, too. But his *Into the Streets May First* never got anywhere. The chief reason is that my song went through the entire *collective process*. First, it was the only one of mine to be accepted at all; some had been rejected with near derision. Second, it summed up the one thing we all really agreed upon, the danger of fascism. . . . The one thing we were all absolutely correct about was that the fascists were threatening the world with a second world war. Third, my text was edited (some would say censored) by V. J. Jerome, the Yale man then recognized by the left as the arbiter of all things esthetic and ideological. By altering a single sound in my verse he redirected the entire thrust of message from a Platonic meditation to a call for action. I had written: ·

> Fascists want our blood and sweat —
> That's what they will never get.
> Once we KNOW we are one,
> They must go — their day is done.

The revised third line reads, "Once we SHOW we are one." As a matter of fact, any creative artist anywhere is always censored — often more drastically than he realizes. I was fortunate in having so constructive a critic. And finally, I had a constructive critic for my music as well: Hanns Eisler. By altering a note or two in my left hand, he effectively added an augmentation of the main motive to the bass line.

Twenty years later I had the privilege of belonging to another words-and-music collective, the Hymnbook Commission that put together *Hymns for the Celebration of Life*. The same collective process had the same beneficial results. But it was not quite the same. The Composers' Collective of 1935 was on fire with something both urgent and inspiring. Recalling it brings to mind the lines,

> Bliss was it in that dawn to be alive,
> But to be young was very heaven. [26]

Although Seeger cultivated the worker ideology, he never truly relinquished his membership in the establishment. He claimed always to have been interested in the bourgeois-proletarian opposition, but pitied those who made an ideology out of it. Similarly, he sought to balance feeling and thought; because he was interested in the emotional side of himself at the time, he could "put up with" the intellectual. Seeger learned from the Collective the crucial difference between writing music that people would sing on specified occasions, and watching trained musicians try to do it. They were "trained out of doing things that way." Yet he had believed that developing a proletarian music was the responsibility of the disciplined composer; the proletariat lacked the musical technique to complement its revolutionary ideas.

Seeger's article, "On Proletarian Music" (1934)[27] sought to explain to the "establishment" the goals and activities of the Composers'

Collective and to rationalize the contradictions entailed in using bourgeois "art" music for proletarian ends. A revolution cannot be forced; the Collective's music should be *of* the proletariat, not *for* the proletariat. He defined three historical phases, proposing that music *for* the proletariat dominated a first period of music history. During the present, second, period, the proletariat was becoming critical of what music it takes from the bourgeoisie; the people understood clearly the music they heard and made themselves. He suggested that proletarian music was on the rise, while bourgeois music was on the decline. Finally, there would be a third stage, music *of* the proletariat, and the critical criteria would be reversed — "Content first, technic second." Seeger concluded, "Art, then, is always and inevitably a social function. It has social significance. It is a social force. It is propaganda: explicit, positive; implied, negative. . . . The better the art, the better propaganda it makes." Composers had three paths from which to choose: "fascism, which means positive propaganda for the older order; isolation, which means negative propaganda for it; and proletarianism, which means propaganda for the new order," for which, of course, there would be an audience not of hundreds, but of millions.

Continuing to pursue scholarly and intellectual issues, Seeger wrote many articles for *Modern Music*, the principal "serious music" journal, and became intensely involved in scholarly music organizations.

Just before joining the Collective, Seeger and Cowell had sought to create a forum for musicological scholarship. This included reestablishing earlier contacts with Europeans and European emigrés. While at the New School, Cowell had traveled to Europe, where (at Seeger's urging) he stayed with Erich von Hornbostel in Berlin in 1930–1931. There Cowell encountered not only the Berlin Phonogramm-Archiv and a small group of comparative musicologists, but also learned that before World War I there had been an American Section of the Societé Internationale de Musique. Efforts to reorganize it had been unsuccessful, despite the exhortations of W. S. Pratt, a leading American music figure. O. G. Sonneck also had attempted to revive the Section and had corresponded with Carl Engel toward that end, but Sonneck's death had halted the revival. Now, Seeger took up the project.

In 1929 Seeger had stepped up his acquaintance with Otto Kinkeldey, who had once been a member. They were joined by Joseph Yasser, a Russian emigré who in 1932 was to publish *A Theory of Evolving Tonality*,[28] a work Seeger thought remarkable; by Joseph Schillinger, another Russian emigré involved in Bolshevik music and in writing a novel theory of using algebraic formulas in composition;[29] and by Henry Cowell. In January 1930, the five met and laid the foundation for a permanent organization; the first meeting would be held in February at Blanche Walton's apartment. At first females were excluded, although two women were interested in joining: May DeForest, a musician, and Ruth. Women were later permitted to attend meetings, however.

In 1931–1932, the constitution and by-laws of the New York Musicological Society were drawn up. The society would continue to work with the Russian Group of Musicologists of New York City and with the American Library of Musicology, whose purpose was to publish classic musicological works with original texts and English translations side by side, and a series of original American works.

This was an important new enterprise. Musicology was still an incipient discipline; "Any serious discussion about music was carried on only in newspapers," Seeger noted. Most U.S. music professors were older men, comfortable in university sinecures, who were not interested in a scholarly society. The great influx of German-trained music scholars that would stimulate scholarship had not yet begun. Nonetheless, the New York five started organization with a great sense of urgency for, as Charlie believed, remarkable things were happening in music for which there were no scholarly spokespersons.

Because Seeger and his colleagues were greatly interested in the ideas of Guido Adler, an important aim of the fledgling society was to promote Adler's systematic approach to musicology. The rule of the meetings was that everyone present *must* comment on a presented paper, whether they knew anything about the subject or not. They devised once- or twice-yearly round robins and themes that led to occasional marathon discussions (similar to the later ubiquitous Main Seminar at UCLA's Institute of Ethnomusicology); one on the correlation of color and tone had contributions from artists, composers, acousticians, and the like. Seeger estimated that they met about thirty-five times and published three bulletins, which he edited. None of the papers presented between 1930 and 1935 was historical — most musicology then was systematic musicology — and almost all were delivered by members. In Seeger's words,

Henry [Cowell] . . . was one of the founders. You should have heard the first meeting: Kinkeldey reading a report of a piece of Japanese polyphony played by two shakuhachis. Obviously, Henry knew more about it (some of the rest of us did too). But the most amusing was K. reading a paper on a Javanese equal-tempered pentatonic scale. He had had a very nice little set of bronze slabs made at the Cornell Physics Department. Henry made mince-meat of it, for he had studied under v. Hornbostel and had played in a gamelan led by a Javanese musician in Berlin and knew that there was no such thing as an equal-tempered pentatonic scale in Java.[30]

Seeger, and later Harold Spivacke, usually chaired meetings. They began to think of expanding the society into a national organization. Although Spivacke found considerable interest in New York, he reported that the group could not expand unless Charles Seeger (who must have ruffled a few feathers) agreed to step down from the leadership. On June 3, 1934, George Dickinson, Carl Engel, Gustave Reese, Helen Roberts, Joseph Schillinger, Charles Seeger, Harold Spivacke, Oliver Strunk, and Joseph Yasser (although a member, Otto Kinkeldey was absent) — gathered in Blanche Walton's apartment at 25 Washington Square North and formed the American Musicological Association. (English-oriented scholars objected to the term *musicology*; they preferred *musical research*.)

Charles hoped that the organization would unite the historical study of elite European music and the systematic study of all world music — the latter then known as *comparative musicology* but is now known as *ethnomusicology*. In September 1934, the name was changed to the American Musicological Society, and the first official meeting was held in Philadelphia later in the year.[31]

The society's Greater New York chapter was formed on January 15, 1935, the first of several regional branches. Most of the leadership for the new national group was drawn from the New York Musicological Society. New names were added, so that the first AMS membership roster read: Jean Beck, Archibald T. Davison, George Dickerson, Carl Engel, Otto Kinkeldy, Paul Henry Lang, Gustave Reese, Helen (Heffron) Roberts, Joseph Schillinger, Charles Seeger, Carlton Sprague Smith, Harold Spivacke, Oliver Strunk, and Joseph Yasser.

Seeger had recognized the need for a publications arm for the organization. In 1932 Blanche Walton had given $2,000 for a first volume to be published by the above-mentioned American Library of Musicology. As president and editor of the enterprise, Seeger intended to publish only works on cross-cultural theory and non-European music, because there was already so much in print about Western classical music. Yasser's *A Theory of Evolving Tonality* was first published, followed by Helen Roberts's study of the music of southern California Indians. Schillinger's mathematical theory of the arts was also scheduled, as was Schillinger's and Yasser's *Medieval Quartal Harmony*, but funding was cut off after the first two volumes and in 1936 the American Library of Musicology folded. Seeger reflected many years later:

I can't help wishing the American Library of Musicology were resuscitable. It had an auspicious beginning—Yasser's *Theory of Evolving Tonality* (still quoted) and Helen Robert's *Form in Primitive Music* [a study of songs of the Luiseno, Gabrieleno, and Catalineo Indians of southern California]. . . . Norton carried its commercial distribution. It folded up just 40 years ago.[32]

Seeger had envisioned the American Library of Musicology as providing the scholarly materials and notated music for performance of world cultures' musics, for these publications as well as his organizational activities were closely tied to his teaching at the New School. From 1931 to 1935 Seeger annually taught a course in music cultures of the world. Following a practice developed in California, he required that live performances accompany every lecture in his "music cultures of the world" courses at the New School.

Seeger also used various other scholarly organizations to promote music study and to cultivate a broader forum for new musical ideas. Under the aegis of the New York Musicological Society, Seeger had been in contact with several German scholars who were contemplating emigration from their homeland because of the deteriorating political situation there. At his suggestion, the comparative musicologist Erich M. von Hornbostel, who had fled at a moment's notice from Germany in the summer of 1933, was offered a professorship in the University in Exile at the New School. Upon von Hornbostel's arrival, he, Seeger, and Cowell designed the first seminar in world music cultures at the New School. The first session used the old Edison cylinder phonograph; while in Germany, Cowell had bought two sets of the *Demonstration Sammlung* of the University of Berlin Phonogram-Archiv of 120 cylinders each; one set was for the New School and one was for himself.[33]

In 1933, Seeger, Helen Roberts, and George Herzog (the latter two with the Institute of Human Relations at Yale) founded the American Society for Comparative Musicology (1933–1936), initially called the Society for Research in non-European Musics.[34] It had an erratic existence. Its primary aim was to give financial support to an organization formed in Berlin in 1930, the Gesellschaft für Erforschung der Musik des Orients of von Hornbostel, and their journal, *Zeitschrift*, the only publication on non-European musics in the world. Only two volumes of the journal had been published when von Hornbostel, Sachs, and Lachmann fled the country. Wolf was forced to resign, and this left Seeger with reponsibility for the organization.[35]

Undaunted, with von Hornbostel Seeger drew up a proposal to found an Institute of Comparative Musicology in New York to which emigré scholars and others could be attracted. Likely patrons for such an idea would be the Warburgs, but since they were Constance's friends, Seeger was reluctant to approach them. By a fortunate chance, von Hornbostel was a cousin of the Warburgs, who had wanted to buy the Berlin archives, including the Phonogram Archives that von Hornbostel had headed; he and Seeger designed a project to retrieve the Berlin archives and set up the planned institute in New York. It would be supported by Warburg money and headed by von Hornbostel, but he died before the plan could be carried out.

In addition to promoting scholarly organizations, Seeger also developed other interests in the thirties. One major intellectual focus was the problem of criticism and value, which had become increasingly important to him. He felt that for years he had been living in two different philosophical and ideological worlds—one disdainful of the other. Related to his interest in criticism and value was a concern for the difficulties encountered by avant-garde musical groups and, in particular, the hostility of music critics toward modern classical music. The Metropolitan Opera, for example, refused to perform new music. Seeger was amazed by this neglect, for he saw much interest in contemporary music, as well as classical music in general. This, he concluded, was largely the result of sound recordings; their enormous growth in sales, particularly recordings of symphonic and operatic music, which flooded the market, indicated a growing public fascination with classical genres. Opera houses, symphony orchestras, and string quartets had begun to bloom throughout the nation. Stravinsky was becoming famous, while Schoenberg, Debussy, Dvorák, Ravel, and others were gaining new audiences.

In 1934 and 1935 Seeger surreptitiously undertook the role of music critic for the *Daily Worker*, an activity that drew together several prongs of his professional interest. He was aware that his involvement with the Communist newspaper was a dangerous venture, and since he was achieving success at the New School and prominence in the New York Musicological Society, he did not want to jeopardize these gains. Therefore, Seeger assumed the name "Carl Sands" because, as he confessed, he could sign his contributions "C.S." "Secrecy was not mentioned, however," he bemusedly recalled, revealing how he learned that his identity as music critic for the newspaper had become known. In 1934 he met a man at a meeting of the Professional Workers' Union who expressed an interest in *Daily Worker* articles written by a man named Carl Sands, which he had heard was Seeger's pseudonym.

Seeger as "Carl Sands" and Elie Siegmeister as "L. E. Swift" supplied the Collective's major ideological statements published in the *Daily Worker* between January 1934 and November 1935. The *What's On in Music* column covere a variety of current cultural events. Seeger discussed issues such as Leopold Stowkowski's battles with the trustees of the Philadelphia Orchestra. Another column focused on

Shostakovich, for whom Seeger had great respect. He also wrote about the Pierre Degeyter Club in Philadelphia and reviewed the activities of the New York Composers' Collective.

In his articles, Seeger analyzed the nation's values and was concerned with its uncritical and lowbrow musical tastes. He still considered art music as "good" and folk music as "lowbrow," not yet recognizing the cultural wealth inherent in the music of the people. Only later did he come to respect its vitality: "People make the music they want to make and if they are prevented from doing so, they will still try to make their own music, against all odds."

Seeger tackled the question of "revolutionary" music, and debated the relative importance of music and language for promoting ideology and social change. Later he changed his view: "There is no such thing as revolutionary music; . . . music does not recognize the dichotomy between revolutionary and nonrevolutionary." Further, he did not believe that folk music could be revolutionary; for him, it was simply the music of another class; the question of revolution was unimportant.

Finally, Seeger challenged the New York music critics, specifically their views on modern music. He considered Alban Berg's *Wozzeck* one of the great operas of the generation and the innovative Berg a great composer. He also wrote on Shostakovich's *Lady Macbeth* which, he believed, also moved in the new vein. He commented that the scene in which the hero commits a murder to a Viennese waltz had a terrific emotional effect and was a brilliant departure from the tradition of Wagner and Strauss.

Seeger's writings for the *Daily Worker* were uneven, sometimes the work of a professional scholar, sometimes the writing of a hack Marxist propagandist, in accord with a theme of Communist thought of the time that music should be nationalist (American) in form, but revolutionary (working-class) in content. Always aware of dualities, juxtaposing scholarly reasoning with the emotional appeal of the propagandist, he assumed the latter role because of his belief in socialism; a socialist organization of society would assure all workers, including musicians, a better life. Any conflict between that idea and music theory could be reconciled.

During this busy period, Seeger contributed two articles—one on Ruggles and one on Ruth Crawford—for Henry Cowell's *American Composers on American Music: A Symposium* (1933). This provided a forum for certain ideas he had been formulating about American classical music and the place of composers in the United States. In the article on Ruggles, for example, he strongly endorsed American music, suggesting that the nation should support its composers to enable them to compose music that reflected the American context and developed native ideas. Otherwise they would be nothing more than a pale reflection of European styles and concepts.

At the request of Alvin Johnson, he contributed two articles on music (with the help of Helen Roberts and Henry Cowell) for the *Encyclopedia of the Social Sciences*.[36] In "Music and Musicology" he was able to refine long held ideas—"old saws," he called them—about music and language, criticism, and the social function of music. He lamented that by eschewing the sciences musicology had grown "backward looking," and had "produced a wide gap between musicology and music." Criticism, he said, should address both the intrinsic value of music and its value to society. Music is an element in building society: "Music is a phenomenon of prolonged social growth—a culture. It is not only a product of a culture but one of the means by which the culture has come to be what it is and continues."

The lengthier "Occidental Music" outlined ideas that Seeger would return to again and again. After a brief historical summary, he turned to the twentieth century, when "for the first time music has become a mass commodity." He noted the implications of the control of music by educational, manufacturing, and distributional institutions, and discussed the changing social status of musicians, noting the relationship of social versus technical control of music vis-à-vis the place of musicians in society. He ended by describing the gradual professionalization of music and musicians, and seeing the education of amateurs as of crucial importance. A modicum of musical literacy should be expected of all U.S. high school graduates, he asserted.

In "Preface to All Linguistic Treatment of Music,"[37] Seeger elaborated on the relationship between music and language. As he began, "Music exists, with us, in a frame of language. . . . Language, on the other hand, is the 'universal' art in terms of whose technique the organization and the management of our individual and social life are cast. . . . Thus, as in our social system at large music performs a function far inferior in scope and power to that of language, so, even in the performance of this inferior function, it is viewed as incapable of action without the aid of language." He argued that language and music both communicate a content but that the particular nature and extent of the relationship between language and music have been ignored.

Seeger suggested that in the interest of music, language, and social organization, six questions should be asked: Does the state of affairs in our culture exist in others? Has this state of affairs always existed in our culture? Are there elements that suggest its continuation or modification? What expectations would we have from a comparative study of the techniques of language and music? Is it desirable for social organization that one art be so much more extensively cultivated and relied upon than the other? And, finally, is it possible that in the future we might see a gradual increase in the development of music as a social function, even to where it might find a balance with language? He suggested that most people find it difficult to place the two arts on a single plane but that "we must insist upon the acceptance and definition, inherent in the above questions, that music and language are both arts." And, he noted, "There is no evidence, biological, sociological, or other, that leads to the conclusion that one art is necessarily more suitable than another to the needs of social organization by man."

Seeger answered three of his six questions. First, he observed that the state of affairs he outlined "does obtain in all large ("advanced") cultures of the world, though possibly not everywhere in so extreme a form." However, it seemed that in "small, tribal, 'backward' or 'primitive' cultures, so much variety existed that the domination of language might not be so severe as in our own. But this must be seen in the context that "the development of arts such as language and music comes to be regarded as a 'progressive' step from a lower to a higher stage of social organization."

He provided an "evolutionary" scheme for explanation of this as a phase of the struggle for material existence which is, in turn, a condition of succeeding phases of that struggle. He concluded here,

With the rise of classes and the consequent differentiation of relationship between the individual and the group as a whole, comes a separation of the arts and the economic, political and social functions with which they were formerly integrated. Music and language emerge as separate arts. Their use as idioms by people in general become separated from their employment as media for set constructions by a few increasingly more highly trained specialists. At the same time, comes an ever increasing reliance upon language, especially by ruling classes, and a decreasing reliance upon music in the struggle for or maintenance of power.

In the second deliberation, Seeger suggested that in Western history "the relations between music and language began long before the time covered by our present technique of study." He chronicled Western civilization from the earliest music survivals—to the "earliest dependable references to language and to music . . . by 1000 to 500 B.C. [However, at that time] the two arts of language and music were differentiated, but were still viewed as two branches of one and the same artistic process, in India, China and Greece." Continuing through time, Seeger noted that "of the music of the non-ruling classes before the last century or so we have little or no knowledge" but that the music we know about was made by a small group of professional musicians and was the property of the dominant classes for which it was made. Overall, though, language "served in the same way as a 'fine art,' but kept its social function."

Finally, Seeger examined the conflicts that existed and new ones spawned in the process of classes fighting for supremacy. Seeger cautioned, "The professionalized art is . . . not a product of the ruling class whose property it becomes. It reflects and is used to perpetuate the peculiar relationships upon which the dominance of the class depends, but its actual producers are drawn from the ruled classes." He reflected on Western society from the period of the French Revolution, the English parliamentary reforms, and the Industrial Revolution and noted that "the strength of professionalized art is found in the works of exceptional mastery that were possible only under the conditions of extreme specialization." In his opinion, the "lowest level" of musical culture may have been reached around 1900.

Bourgeois professional musicians were increasingly losing contact with the class they were supposed to serve and had not found other, more satisfactory, connections. The class restrictions of bourgeois art kept them walled off from the masses. The vast majority of populations were drifting farther and farther from vital musical experience of any kind.

Soon thereafter occurred the technological innovations that revolutionized language art and music art.

Seeger then observed, "Once language abdicates the position of being supreme arbiter of all things, music will have a chance again, suggesting further an uptrend, first and foremost, through increasing musical activity by the masses for their own ends; second, through the linguistic study of music — musicology — which must be made to bend its efforts to the freeing, rather than the further imprisonment, of music by language."

Seeger concluded this essay by noting that in a subsequent issue he would deal with the last three questions, beginning with a brief comparison of the techniques of language and music. He never did, but in later decades tackled all of the issues in subsequent articles on language and music.

By the mid-1930s, many strands of Seeger's life and career were fading in importance, while new avenues of professional and personal endeavor lay ahead. Seeger enjoyed newfound professional directions compatibly allied with personal happiness in his marriage to Ruth. Looking back on this period in his life, he wrote:

The three reasons for having given up composition in 1915 now do not exist any longer, together with another reason not mentioned here. It has been a slow process, undistinguished by academic honors or external evidence whatever, for the simple reason that American universities do not yet recognize musicology as a respectable subject. In a lecture at Harvard in 1916 I set 1941 as the date at which a general academic acceptance of musicology could be expected. I see now, in 1933, no reason to alter that estimate. My book "Principia Musicologica" has already waited seventeen years of its twenty. I have, however, become more active during the last three years and all of the fundamental problems are settled, time only being needed for undisturbed work of revision and final retouching.

I was one of the founders of the New York Musicological Society, of the American Library of Musicology (of which I am editor) and of the American

Society for Comparative Musicology. Besides my work at the Juilliard School of Music, I have lectured for the last three years at the New School for Social Research upon Music and Musicology. [38]

Five years later, he wrote:

From 1915 to 1933, therefore, I occupied myself with a drastic revision of the whole technical and stylistic discipline of Occidental music. The result was embodied in a text-book [unpublished] "Tradition and Experiment in Musical Composition." By 1933 it was apparent to all but the most isolated observers that the conflict within the vanguard of twentieth-century music between the traditionalists ("neoclassicists") and the experimentalists ("dissonant writers") had been practically settled in favor of the former. As one of the diehards of the defeated faction, I was especially anxious to bring the work out quickly, if only to mark a grave. The depth of the Depression, however, with its even more intense social unrest and the threat of even greater war, again led me to a revision of my orientation. Whereas in 1915 it had centered around the futility of one ivory tower, aestheticism, the focal point in 1933 was the futility of another, the studio where one tried to lift oneself by the bootstraps of technique. Instead, however, of leaving me without an answer, as 1915 had done, 1933 provided the answer I have never been able to formulate for myself, for the times thundered a veritable cultural ultimatum that few could fail to hear. "Culture first, form afterwards." I devoted myself, therefore, to two years of intensive work in composition and music criticism along these lines. The controversy upon which I had spent so many years appeared in what I still believe is the true light, as a phase of the superstructure of musical development—certainly not the essential stuff of it. Most valuable was the association, first with a group of younger men in the Composers' Collective of New York City, of which I was one of the founders, and later with Hanns Eisler. During this time I was able to learn something more of the non-European musics. . . . Another brave attempt was a journal of music criticism, *Music Vanguard* which lasted but two issues. . . . funds made available by the ASCM [American Society for Comparative Musicology] and the ALM [American Library of Musicology] and other sources promise to put the study of world music back upon an international footing. 1935 found me, along with many other musicians, scoffing at the efforts of the New Deal to cope with the Depression. Believing that a rational social order would have to come as much from below-up as from above-down, and believing myself more adapted to the methods of the former than those of the latter, I had been active in the organization of workers' musical organizations, not only in New York, but throughout the United States. So, when an invitation to head the music unit of the Special Skills Division of the Resettlement Administration came late in 1935, I undertook the job with enthusiasm, since the field offered an unparalleled opportunity to demonstrate the superiority of the group-guidance technique over the conventional imposition of a program from above-down.[39]

Charles and Ruth, living in Greenwich Village, were not only active professionally and socially, but also busy raising their family. Despite the Depression, they earned a steady income from Ruth's piano pupils and Charles's teaching at the New School, odd jobs, and consulting, although it was an increasingly precarious economic existence.

Ruth put aside serious compositional work, and did not resume writing original music for another twenty years. Why she abandoned her own career as a composer may seem difficult to comprehend. Unquestionably avant-garde, her strong and original compositions used the most advanced compositional techniques, such as serialism, tone clusters, *Sprechstimme*, metric independence of parts, and spatial separation of performing groups. Yet perhaps her decision to devote herself to family and her husband's undertakings is not so hard to understand, given the times and her personal situation. She had two babies who demanded attention, and she needed to teach to contribute to the household income. Very likely she had little support from her busy husband for following an independent career; Seeger believed that it was appropriate for Ruth to be at home with the children and to use her talents profitably.

As the Depression deepened, unemployment spread, and more and more businesses failed, people lost their homes, their savings, and their faith in the system. The alarming economic collapse and attendant social upheaval had spurred artists and intellectuals to seek new solutions to the crisis, such as Charles's work with the Composers' Collective and his contributions to the Communist *Daily Worker*.

The administration of Franklin Delano Roosevelt, inaugurated in 1932, just as the nation seemed to hit bottom, slowly led the way to economic recovery through the New Deal. By the mid-1930s, the spirits of working America were reviving, along with a fresh interest in rural and working-class culture. As one manifestation of this new trend, the federal government sponsored various projects that directed the attention of professionals to the rich store of U.S. folk art and music. This effort was in many ways parallel to the Comintern's concern with the lives and cultures of the people and attempts to cultivate a popular front coalition. The popular front was more than a political tactic; it was "a kind of culture" with application in almost any intellectual area.[40] Thus it was possible for U.S. communists and militants to drop their confrontational and proselytizing stances and to join in the government's New Deal programs—a natural identification for Americans, centered on their folklore.

Until the mid-1930s, Seeger had resisted the popular movement. True, he had witnessed the exploitation of migrant workers in California in the early 1920s and had become aware of levels of society that had been largely invisible to him during his youth, but this did not lead at once to an acknowledgment of the vitality of U.S. folk art. He continued to see folk arts as dying—or at least "simply not suitable to an American revolutionary movement." Part of this attitude was encouraged by his feeling, noted before, that much folk music communicated a "downtrodden," melancholy, resigned attitude, songs to "keep the slaves happy," as it were. It was as if he had bought the Comintern's ideology as expressed in its third phase when it had supported the Collective. In a *Daily Worker* article, "A Program for Proletarian Composers," Seeger voiced his concern that folk tunes might sound musically pretty but were "not the stuff for a militant proletariat to feed upon."[41] Ultimately, Seeger dropped some, modified other radical views, and opted for "the ideology of reform,"[42] because he saw that the Collective was failing. He began to look again at folk art with new respect. People made the music they wanted to make, he observed, the music they themselves valued. This realization contributed significantly to his reevaluation of American music and his exploration of the social significance of the folk arts—folk music in particular.

Ruth had already been introduced to U.S. folk songs by the Sandburg family and had transcribed for piano several tunes for

Sandburg's *American Songbag* (1927). Now she, too, began to experiment with American folk music. Both she and Charlie were astounded that they, as American musicians and composers, had known so little about the rich folk song traditions of the United States, such as those noted in George Pullen Jackson's *White Spirituals in the Southern Uplands*. Ruth eventually transcribed some six thousand recordings in the Library of Congress Archives, edited collections, wrote song accompaniments, and published her own songbooks for children. As a teacher, she developed methods for using folk songs.

Seeger's latent interest in folk music was awakened in the winter of 1929–1930 when, at one of Thomas Hart Benton's weekly gatherings, he heard the painter Bernard Steffan play *Pretty Girl Milking Her Cow* and was startled by the song's beauty. "Modal!" he exclaimed, "And a plagal tune, besides!"[43] Benton, who made a specialty of rural and folk motifs in his paintings, joined his students in a string band that regularly performed Ozark folk music in Greenwich Village. Through Benton Seeger heard recordings of performers such as Dock Boggs, the Appalachian banjoist and balladeer, and other commercial folk recording artists. Seeger played "folk" guitar with Benton's "hillbilly" band at the dedication of Benton's *America Today* murals at the New School in January 1931. The program included many of the artist's favorites such as *Cindy*, *Ida Red*, and *My Horses Ain't Hungry*—all new to Seeger.[44]

He told his daughter Penny of his earliest acquaintance with folk music and his performance at the New School with Benton:

I'd been playing some Mexican folk-popular songs [at Berkeley] that my father heard, and I realized that I'd been challenged once on the ship going to Europe [after graduation from Harvard] by saying that folk song is not music; that's just the beginning of music. The people don't know how to sing, but they do the best they can, and its rather elementary. Any good composer can write a folk song. Well, this was in the smoking room of the ship and there was an old man who said, Go ahead, you're going to be a composer, you're a musician? Write me a folk song. Okay, simplest thing. So I pulled out my little notebook that I always carried and I pulled out my pencil and went off to one side and presently came back with a fine folk song. And he said, well, that's damn good. . . . And I said, of course it's good. Want any more? Well, that's enough.

Well, it was about this time, or some later, about in the thirties, that I happened to run across that book. And there was a notation. And it was one of the best known of the English versions of *Barbara Allen*. Not American, English. It's not known in America, except in schoolbooks. But copy it out of English books. . . . Very much a composed tune, I think. I wouldn't say, I wouldn't swear — it's some folk singer who's pretty darned near a composer might have done it, but it sounds to be transposed by some English composer. It had been sunk in my unconscious [it was one of the tunes performed in his first history of music course at Berkeley] and it came off. Well, that accounts for a good deal of that folk music business that we went into, but I discovered that I had a friend named Tom Benton who had a good collection of hillbilly records and he was shocked that I didn't know anything about them. And when he wanted to dedicate his room with paintings at the New School with some of his own harmonica playing and his students' guitar and banjo playing, all they could play was what was on some of these old hillbilly records. *Cindy* and *Ida Red* and *Red River Valley* and things like that, and he said, You know, I can't make the bunch — we just can't get together — you're a musician — you think you could make them jell? Did you ever play the guitar? I said, yes, when I was a boy [in Mexico]. Well, come around, I'll give you a guitar. See if you can't pull us together. Well, it was no trouble. I pulled them together all right and we got a program of about twenty minutes together and we sat in the middle of the little room at the New School and we started playing. And the well-to-do people who were giving money to the then almost impoverished New School, just in its new building and almost no money to live on, flocked into the room. In time we were so crowded we could hardly finger our instruments. We came to the end of our twenty minutes, and stopped and the crowd shouts of More! More! and we just had to play that whole program over and over again, to the plaudits of the group, and I hope they came forth with the money; at least the school kept going.

Well, that was one thing; then were was a nice old gentleman who wrote a book called *White Spirituals in the Southern Uplands* — George Pullen Jackson — and I discovered that sometimes a hundred or more American families would gather on the greens of county courthouses and for two days would sing out of a hymnbook, written in queer-shaped notes. And here was I, an American musicologist, and had never heard of it. And they'd sometimes sing for two days, and sometimes they'd be conducted by children and then everybody would cry.

Well, I realized that something was wrong. And then it happened that old John Lomax wrote a book called *American Ballads and Folk Songs* and submitted it to Macmillan for publication and Macmillan got Henry Cowell and me around to advise them whether they should publish it or not. Well, we'd taken one look at it and although the music notations were simply god-awful, the stuff put together with the music and the words were absolutely marvelous, and both Henry and I thought it was first-rate for publication. . . .

Well, these various things came together and on top of it I was trying to write music for protest marches and union gatherings. An old woman named Aunt Mollie Jackson had come to one of the meetings of the Composers' Collective, and I learned her songs and discovered that they were folk songs simply dolled up, with new words and perhaps a few touches of her own, and that the people could sing their songs and they couldn't sing our songs. So I went up to her and I said, Mollie, you're on the right track and we're on the wrong track and I gave up the Collective. We were all on the wrong track — it was professionals trying to write music for the people and not in the people's idiom. Well, those four things all came together with [the] invitation to go to Washington.[45]

Slowly, Seeger expanded his scholarly interests by including folk songs and discussion of its social value in his academic repertoire. He never became a proselytizer, but worked to win the acceptance of academic and social audiences for folk music through his writings. He was instrumental in legitimizing the folk repertoire in scholarly circles and in time gained an international reputation for his work, adding immeasurably to music scholarship. His growing awareness of folk and American music would be the focus of his work for almost two decades in Washington.

The New Deal and Music,

1935–1941

ᴄᴡ

I N NOVEMBER 1935, Charles Seeger's career took a dramatic turn
when he accepted an appointment in the newly created federal
Resettlement Administration (RA). In the spring of that year,
President Roosevelt had appointed Rexford Tugwell, a Columbia
economics professor, to head a federal program to combat rural
poverty and especially to address the problems of displaced farmers.
Seeger was recommended for a role in the RA by the painter Charles
Pollock (Jackson Pollock's brother), a student of Thomas Hart Benton,
who recognized in Seeger a sympathy with the RA's progressive ideas.

The New Deal had established myriad agencies to revitalize the
nation's battered economy. A large program of direct relief for farmers
was enacted in 1933 through the Federal Emergency Relief Act
(FERA), directed by Harry Hopkins. Section 208 of the National
Industrial Recovery Act was earmarked to develop rural-industrial
communities that combined small-scale farming with factory enterprises—a type of workfare as opposed to welfare—and also to design
programs for planned land use.

This Subsistence Homestead Division, under Interior Secretary
Harold Ickes, encountered legal and operational problems almost
from the start. Because agencies bogged down in bureaucratic tangles
were unable to deal effectively with emergency problems, Roosevelt
transferred various agencies to the Resettlement Administration.[1] He
also directed that other Interior Department programs, such as
FERA, its component projects, and units from other agencies, be
placed under the RA. The RA thus became the emergency organization designed to relieve the poverty of rural and urban groups that

either had not been reached by other federal agencies or lacked adequate political representation.

The Resettlement Administration was born of grandiose, idealistic hopes, but it faced overwhelming odds. FDR had to cope with a legacy of depression that went back much farther than the stock market crash of 1929—the most recent in a series of economic downturns over the previous half century. By 1929, the U.S. economy was already in a state of decay, especially in agriculture; rural poverty was a chronic problem, the legacy of bad farming methods and cycles of drought. Massive areas of arable land were eroded, land under cultivation was declining in nutrient value, prices were depressed, and many farm workers lived at the lowest possible subsistence level as tenants, sharecroppers, itinerant laborers, or harvest tramps.

The Resettlement Administration's broad objectives were: (1) to establish an effective land-use program; (2) to resettle destitute low-income families from rural and urban areas and to construct model communities in suburban areas; (3) to offer rural rehabilitation loans and grants to help small farmers purchase land; (4) to move rural populations to new farms and communities.

Director Rexford Tugwell was an idealist who, like many intellectuals of the time, shared a vision of a new United States, one of more social and economic equality than had previously characterized individualist, capitalist America. His long-range plan was to encourage new cultural attitudes and patterns based on collective interests. He intended that these newly mixed communities of displaced small farmers, agricultural laborers, and industrial workers, would develop a strong community spirit.

Of course, this utopian plan was impossible to implement, and tensions developed immediately in the model communities. The "collective," "cooperative," "organic" conception of the new homesteads smacked of a new social ideology that was repugnant to many people. Moreover, to throw together people of such diverse backgrounds, with little time to adjust and to appreciate their common interests, was an invitation to failure. Most settlements were, Seeger later noted, "a disparate bunch of families gotten together on good land, shown how to buy good seed, how to fertilize, how to plant, how to harvest, and how to sell cooperatively and meanwhile fight, sometimes disastrously, with their religious beliefs."[2] In search of ways to smooth over the difficulties, community directors requested programs in the arts as a means of alleviating tensions and fostering common goals. "There were painters [among them Ben Shahn and Charles Pollock], a drama man, a weaver, a textile expert, furniture designers and a complete wood-working shop, a sculptress, etc.,"[3] Seeger remembered. To develop and implement the musical component of such programs was to be Seeger's job.

The appointment came at a fortuitous time. The Depression finally had taken its toll on the Seegers' income, and Ruth and Charles, now with two small children, had been living on the edge. In addition to steady employment, Washington offered new intellectual possibilities and the chance to act on growing political beliefs. So in November 1935, Charles, Ruth, with young Michael and Peggy, and a friend, Margaret Valiant, packed the Chevrolet and drove to Washington. As Seeger remembered:

A telephone call came in asking me if I would be interested in a position in the Resettlement Administration, putting thirty-three musicians in 300 Resettlement communities within six months. Well, I could have laughed at the idea of such an impossible thing, but the salary was adequate, so I went down and was approved for the job, and one night we drove down and I began work in [the Special Skills Division of] the Resettlement Administration.[4]

Charles and Ruth bought a house in Silver Spring, Maryland, where they settled down in a modicum of comfort. Seeger's move from the heady radicalism of New York to the more sober environment of New Deal Washington reflected changes in himself. He had already become disenchanted with the Composers' Collective. In Washington, he found himself caught up "by deep conflict between radicals and liberals, between activists and academicians,"[5] just as New Deal reformers were caught between doctrinaire radicals and campus conservatives. But, needing the money and ever the pragmatist, Seeger made a practical decision to adjust his ideology to suit the climate. As cited above, when asked years later about his political allegiances, he said, "I have *always* gone my own way. If anybody or group run along beside me, I give them loyalty in proportion to whatever of my goal they share with me. . . . When it comes to government . . . government is at once a desired good and an unavoidable evil."[6]

The Special Skills office was set up on Connecticut Avenue, near the Mayflower Hotel. A primary responsibility was to employ artists, designers, and technicians to assist other agency divisions and to help homesteaders to develop practical skills and to express themselves through music, drama, graphic art, and handicrafts such as woodworking, weaving, and landscaping.[7] The music program was intended to encourage social integration, to act as a corrective to the disruptions suffered by people uprooted from their homes and thrown together in new communities by using familiar music idioms, particularly folk song.

As technical adviser in the Special Skills Division, Seeger set out to make sense of the music program. His organizational talents, as well as his readiness to commit ideas to paper, were immediately called into action. He approached the project with several strategies in mind, using techniques he had learned from the Composers' Collective. His long-range goal was to place 300 trained musicians in thirty-three resettlement communities throughout the United States. (Only a fraction of this total was ever realized.) Each community was to be made up of one to three hundred families, most originally from cities.

Although the music program was short on ideology and certainly was less partisan than the Collective and the Workers' Music League, such a program for promoting the arts was exceedingly radical for its time. Seeger established program guidelines in 1936 and issued an instructional manual, "General Considerations for Music Directors in Leading Community Programs."[8] The division's music workers were directed to survey what human and material resources they had to work with, to try to gain acceptance by community members, and to encourage music that the people liked, not what the RA workers liked.

Seeger first placed ten musicians in ten communities. As professionally trained artists, they still favored classical music. It took some time before they, like Seeger, understood the musical culture of the people whom they were assigned to serve. Seeger explained:

They were to go into the Resettlement Camps as somebody from Washington; they couldn't help that . . . they couldn't help it being known that they were musicians. "But for God's sake," I said, "there let it stop." From there on, you're a human being . . . The first thing for you to do is to find out what music the people can make. Then put that to the uses for which you're sent to the community—to make the people in that community get along.[9]

By the spring of 1936, Seeger was beginning to develop rural music programs and to organize music festivals that included folk music—but not popular music. Dance bands were supported in various places, however.

Resettlement Administration music workers were also to teach music in the schools, but Seeger did not want to distribute songbooks. Rather than teaching songs they themselves favored and looking down on the music of the local culture, RA workers were to encourage the singing and playing of songs the children already knew and loved. This practice sometimes ran counter to community attitudes; some parents opposed the singing of certain songs with lyrics they considered risqué.

Seeger also wanted to gather community songs and to retrieve nearly forgotten old songs and ballads from old-timers. Important sources of traditional music were the churches. However, this posed a potential problem for a government-sponsored program. Seeger thought it permissible for workers to help in religious services as long as they did not become embroiled in local antagonisms or sectarian disputes. To avoid conflict, in communities where there were several churches RA workers were directed go to all of them; otherwise, they might not gain the cooperation of a particular target group.

Workers were also to seek other ways of introducing music into the communities. Seeger's friend and favorite field worker, Margaret Valiant, was particularly adept at involving people in music making. Valiant had phenomenal success in the Florida community to which she was assigned.

To preserve a community's traditional music, one of Seeger's first acts as technical skills adviser had been to obtain a Presto sound recorder (it made channels in aluminum discs) for his workers to use in collecting folk songs. Sometimes he went into the field himself, but usually he sent others. A young woman named Sidney Robertson, who later married Henry Cowell, was a favorite with Seeger. Robertson made 150 recordings, of which Seeger thought the best to be the entire repertoire of Mrs. Emma Dusenberry, an elderly blind woman in Arkansas. Many of her 120 songs were old English ballads; others were passed down from her husband, who had sung a Great Lakes repertoire of songs and ballads. [10] Seeger's approach, according to Robertson, was at the time unheard of among most ethnologists:

"Record EVERYthing!" he said as emphatically as he could. "Don't select, don't omit, don't concentrate on any single style. We know so little! Record *everything*!" What he was trying to do was to innoculate me against contagion from the local collectors I was to meet, for each of them as a matter of course picked and chose items for his collection according to some personal standard of authenticity, or taste, or esthetic quality, or topical interest. Charlie knew it was important to disabuse me of any notion I might have that any particular part of the tradition was more important than any other. Nothing should be omitted!

And except for the fact that no three lives would suffice to get all this done, he was perfectly right. [11]

Seeger reached several important conclusions as a result of the RA music program, which had enlarged upon his recent experience with the Composers' Collective and five years of study and experimentation. He believed that the arts could enter the lives of the common people through both education and recreation. The idea of *participating* in music, as contrasted to passively listening to it, was gaining ground; one need not attend a performance merely to hear a *performer*, but to enjoy the music itself. To advance music as a vehicle for improving the quality of one's life, Seeger decided, one had to look beyond "art" music and work with the music people valued. Therefore, this music had to be collected, analyzed, and disseminated among the very people who had once created and preserved it.

Further, Seeger realized that any government activity in the arts was a propaganda effort; if one brought "a singing teacher or a record player to a Cumberland Plateau homestead or to a San Joaquin Valley migrant labor camp . . . [that was] more than an act of entertainment; it was also an act of political commitment."[12] This was a popular view in the Resettlement Administration. Director Dornbush wrote: "The music and dramatic activities of the [Technical Services] Division are not engaged in as ends in themselves, but rather as means by which larger social aims may be readily achieved."[13]

Seeger had long believed in the social function of music; he was convinced that music must serve the people. He did not want his workers to enter the communities with "hifaluting" attitudes, as he clearly stated in his advice to the workers:

The main question . . . should not be "is it good music?" but "what is the music good for?" And if it bids fair to weld the community into more resourceful and democratic action for a better life . . . , then it must be conceded to be "good for" that. The chances that it will be found good in technical and stylistic terms will probably be more than fair.[14]

His valued assistant, Margaret Valiant, commented on Seeger's ideas and goals:

What he had in mind I don't think was written out precisely, but it was basically to restore a sense of confidence in the people at the time who were very frightened by changes that they did not anticipate . . . and his idea, and I surely joined in with it, was to restore a sense of confidence in the old pioneer spirit of exploring and learning, and then sharing what we had learned and explored.[15]

One of Seeger's best workers was Herbert Haufrecht, a friend from the Composers' Collective whom he had brought to Washington. Haufrecht was a socialist and Communist party member in 1936, so he concentrated on collecting workers' songs in the southeastern United States. Rather than using the Presto recording device, Haufrecht captured union songs and other songs of social and political protest by notation.[16]

Although not all of Seeger's appointees succeeded—indeed, he considered most to be poor at their jobs—he was extremely fortunate with Robertson, Haufrecht, and especially Margaret Valiant, a conservatory-trained musician. Ruth had met her on the ship when she returned from Europe in 1931; like Ruth, Valiant had been studying abroad, particularly opera. The two women became the best of friends and, with Charlie, shared in many New York activities, including gatherings at the Bentons' home.

Perhaps one reason Valiant succeeded in her Resettlement Administration work in the South was that she was born in Mississippi. Moreover, she implicitly understood Seeger's aims. More than being an educated and sensitive musician, Margaret Valiant possessed other useful skills. She worked well with children; she knew how to appeal to each community and combined music making with other events. Sensitive to the situation of women in particular, she once organized a fashion show at which local women could display their craft skills as well as their voices. (She had formerly been a New York clothes designer for such fashion houses as Bergdorf-Goodman.) In addition, Valiant was able to convince her cadres to raise money by presenting music programs in unusual settings. In one instance, she encouraged the women to play along with the local hillbilly band, after which all performed during the intermission at a local prize fight. Seeger described Valiant's interpersonal skills:

She was singing all the children's songs with them and learning from them; . . . then she could get them to sing some songs of that same type that they didn't know.

Well, the next thing she noticed was that the women were dressed in old hand-me-down clothes they didn't know how to alter, or in flour and feed sacks. . . . [so she] put on a fashion show for the women. And each woman would model her own creation, aided by Miss Valiant who was a good seamstress and made her own clothes, [along] with their favorite song. If they couldn't sing their favorite song [she] would sing it, with the old cracked piano in the schoolroom.

Then the local hillbilly band . . . came around . . . and after the pleasantries were over [she] says, Oh, I see you brought your instruments with you. Will you play me something? . . . They played customarily for money in honky-tonks in the hot joints between Jacksonville and Tallahassee. So presently they got their instruments out and they tuned up and they looked at her and said what shall we sing? So she gives them . . . the title of something she's darned sure they know. Oh, they can play that and she praises them, of course . . . and . . . she gives them another. . . . So she got them going now. When finally they stopped and said, Well, what next? Then, she chooses something that perhaps they don't know. How many times she had to wait I don't know or whether she hit it right off. So she reaches over and takes the guitar and sings it very prettily. Well, it's made, she's one of the bunch. Now that's the hot bunch as far as the community goes.

And then the next thing that happened was that the baseball committee wants to play the local baseball team from the neighboring county, or . . . town. Well, they don't have any uniforms. So, they think up a prize fight and charge a small admission. They don't have much in the way of prize fighters, so their intermissions have got to be long and they've got to fill them in and, of course, the hillbilly band could do it.

So, the management of the baseball team comes around to see Miss Valiant; . . . they don't go to the hillbilly band, they go to Miss Valiant, she was so much identified with them. Oh, the arrangements are all fixed all set to go. But just before they pack up to go, she said, Gentlemen, there's just one thing we haven't settled and that's the divvy at the gate. Oh, divvy at the gate, we can't divide the gate, we need every cent for the uniforms. No divvy at the gate, no music. So, she gets a substantial part of the gate for music and the children in the schools. . . . And the prize fight comes off, and the music functions. [17]

Seeger also encouraged field workers to perform in theatrical productions. Again, he recounted the success of Margaret Valiant in overcoming community opposition and mounting stage performances on a shoestring.

The main job that [Valiant is] sent down there to do is to get as many of the people as possible, including the babies, onto a stage where they will all act together in some kind of a music show. Where they will sing what songs they can sing and where she'll help fill in the gaps and have the hillbilly band help out, too. But there's one obstacle. There's a very bigoted religious sect that can put a stop to it.

Well, the outcome of the long story is she first telegraphs me for transcripts for plays of a certain kind and the answer was to follow instructions — no play was being sent — make the scipt out of the life of the people. She goes to the wife of the leader of the most belligerent sect—no music in that sect at all—not even singing. And that woman does the hairdos for the women of the town for an egg or a cup of flour or something, and she gets this woman to do her hair. And she said she'd never lived through such an experience and she hoped she never would again, but for the sake of the program she would. And she talked to the woman and the woman says no, Miss Valiant, we can stop that in its tracks before you get started. My husband will simply stop it. And we're powerful enough to do it. Oh, but says Miss Valiant, listen to my idea, this is something different. No, she says, the theater is the instrument of the devil.

But Miss Valiant plugs ahead and finally describes her own script which is the life story of these people. She's looked them up, discovered where they came from, why they moved to the city, got on relief, how they're suffering there in the city because the relief isn't sufficient, and so forth. . . . Oh, she says, this isn't theater. This is life—I think my husband would approve. So there was a meeting that evening with the husband who was one of those grim southern religious leaders with a mouth just tight closed. No, no music, nothing. But after she reads the story with the help of the wife, he said, OK, you're right, that's life. And he takes the leading part, and his wife takes the women's leading part.

Well, the thing was put on and it was a whale of a success. They hear about it in Washington—it has to be repeated several times and Mrs. Roosevelt and others go down to hear it, simply showing that's the way that music can help.[18]

Valiant kept a diary, later published as *Journal of a Field Representative*,[19] about her experiences at Cherry Lake Farms near Madison, Florida. In the foreword, Seeger outlined the principles by which he organized the Special Skills Division music program—principles that reflect his larger conception of the function of music in American society:

1. Music, like any art, is not an end in itself, but is a means for achieving larger social and economic ends;

2. To make music is the essential thing—listening is only accessory;

3. Music as a group activity is vastly more important than music as an individual accomplishment;

4. Every person is inherently musical, and music can be associated with any human activity;

5. The nation's musical culture is to be evaluated as to the extent of the participation of the whole population, rather than the virtuosity of a fraction of it;

6. The basis for musical culture is the vernacular of the broad mass of the people — its traditional, often called *folk*, idiom; popular music, such as jazz, and professional, high art music are elaborate superstructures built upon the common base;

7. There is no ground for quarreling between various idioms and styles, provided a proper relationship between them is maintained — jazz need not be scorned, nor professional art music artifically stimulated, nor folk music stamped out or sentimentalized;

8. The point of departure for any worker new to a community should be the tastes and capacities of the group; and activities introduced should be directed toward developing local leadership rather than encouraging dependence on outside help;

9. The main question is not be whether music is good, but what music is good for; and if it can help people become more independent, capable, and democratic, it must be approved;

10. Workers should combine music making with whatever other activities and arts that help to make music serve a well-rounded function in the community.[20]

As program director, Seeger edged closer to an understanding of the function and value of different kinds of music. He modified his own musical values and recognized the music values of the people whom he was trying to reach. As he noted in a letter to the Special Skills Division chief, Adrian Dornbush,

I want it put on record that better men must be put in [the homesteads] if any approximation of our program is to be carried out in music. Where we are to find them, I cannot say. Perhaps we will have to train them. Unquestionably, however, the items are: first personality. Secondly, musical ability. For me to have to make this concession is a contradiction of a lifetime of holding the opposite. But in RA communities there is no escape from it.[21]

Sidney Robertson Cowell commented about Seeger's pathbreaking work in recording and according new respect to native folk musical culture:

A number of people in various parts of the United States had of course been collecting folk music long before Seeger came on the scene. But with only two or three exceptions these were people whose orientation was literary, not musical at all; and the direction of their efforts was strictly centripetal. Seeger was the first American of standing among the best-trained musicians to interest himself in American musical traditions, so his interest gave folk music a position it had not had earlier in this country. Moreover, his experimental quality of mind, applied to traditional music, gave rise to a dozen or more suggestions as to what might be done with the music hitherto unwritten in the United States.

Seeger involved young composers in the problem and he stirred up all sorts of other people with ideas for the uses to which archives might be put. Few people had thought beyond the collection of the material, in those days. Seeger said "What for?" to all of us, a very unsettling idea to a lot of people. This question, along with Seeger's famous ability to spur people to action, set all sorts of people off, in all sorts of directions, to provide whatever answers they could. This I think is what brought about the great change in attitude toward folk music in the United States, beginning in the mid-1930s.[22]

There was no question, for Robertson, that Seeger "led the first effective attack on the barriers that separated sophisticated musicians from the music of the American oral tradition."[23] His keenness for sound recordings and his respect for their historical value and cultural context is underscored by Sidney Robertson Cowell:[24]

Once in Washington someone phoned our desk to say that two Negro members of the Tenant Farmers' Union were in town from Arkansas, one of whom had composed some songs we should be interested in. These men had been brought to Washington for a congressional hearing, had given their testimony and had about two hours before their train left for home. I asked to have them meet me at the distant warehouse where the equipment was, left a note for Charlie to say where I was going, and I dashed off. One of the men proved to be a young, vigorous peronality who had indeed composed songs that were magnificent and musical protests. His companion, an elderly minister with a shawl over his head, sat by while we got one fine song after another onto aluminum.

Less than fifteen minutes of their precious time remained, with several great songs still unrecorded, when Charlie caught up with us. Perhaps because he was aware that I had paid much more attention to the singer than to his quiet companion, Charlie took over firmly and squandered (from my point of view!) our last few minutes in a courteous scientific explanation of the principles of sound recording, addressed to the gentle older man. This senior guest was far from able to follow him, but could, and I'm sure he did, as Charlie intended, appreciate the courteous implication that he would understand the technical description of what we had been doing.[25]

Seeger documented everything thoroughly. Accompanying the recordings deposited in the Library of Congress is a set of song sheets for use in the RA music program.[26] This additional documentation had its origin in the first month of Seeger's stint. He returned from a reconnaisance trip to Westmoreland County, Pennsylvania, homesteads and wrote a long report to Dornbush[27] suggesting that the Special Skills Division provide a songbook for the adult chorus; since none of sufficient quality existed, they should either develop one or provide supplementary materials to existing songbooks.

Dornbush approved and supervised production, and by March 1936 a new songbook was under way. Charles Pollock designed the dummy and Seeger got estimates of costs, selected the songs, transcribed about sixty of them, and experimented with samples of seven. First printed were: *The Farmer Comes to Town, Cooperation Is Our Aim, Young Man Who Wouldn't Hoe Corn, We Ain't Down Yet, Down in the Valley, The Dodger, The Buffalo Skinner, Wayfaring Stranger*, and *Bethlehem*. Each song sheet was in effect a music pamphlet, complete with fine drawings. Charles Pollock designed the covers; some were pen-and-ink sketches, others lithographs from grease crayon drawings. Seeger was particularly pleased that the drawings reflected American rural life and tastes.[28]

A tenth song sheet — *Sweet Betsy from Pike* — was prepared but never printed because of a lack of funds; others, such as *Cindy, Solidarity*, and *Phoebe* (*Old Grumbler*) which had been in preparation, never were completed. In Seeger's words:

The *Wayfaring Stranger* got its start from the [song] sheet I put out. A field worker of mine, a descendant of Wade Hampton, was specifically charged with collecting industrial folksongs and sent this text in. I showed it to Alan Lomax and he taught it to Burl Ives. Hampton also collected a ballad on the shooting of . . . a union organizer — in Rockwood, Tennessee, written by his daughter to the tune of *April Girl*. Sidney Robertson [Cowell] made the Dusenberry collection from which we drew the *Candidate's a Dodger*. The notations on the sheets are mine, the lettering, Pollock's. Ray, the drama man, and I made a comic strip on cooperatives and planned a tremendous movie, *John Henry*, in the frame of the diary of an old codge named [N. C.] Carpenter who went down to the store to get a bag of flour and came back with it—after twenty years. . . . John Henry was Leadbelly.[29]

Sidney Robertson Cowell commented on the quality and multi-faceted character of Seeger's work and attention to detail:

Once I had to draw up technical specifications for upright pianos (dimensions of every constituent part, kinds of alloys permissible for strings and pegs, allowable moisture content, wood, etc.). And Charlie held up my report for days because he thought it would be nice to add some pages on the history of keyboard instruments, and he could not make up his mind at which date to begin. When I mentioned that it was possible that the people who wanted specifications might not be interested in going back quite so far, he replied loftily: "That's just the trouble with those people—no historical sense!"[30]

Seeger's placement of no more than a dozen workers into the resettlement communities, considerably less than his mandated goal, mirrored the shortcomings of the RA. Although the Resettlement Administration had set up communities on good land, with technical aid and cooperation, they met with minimal success. Ultimately, disappointing results caused a fight between the Resettlement Administration and the Department of Agriculture over control of the land.

The RA program had been politically controversial from the start. Tugwell, who had become the target for all those dissatisfied with Roosevelt's "socialist" policies, resigned in December 1936 and was succeeded by Will Alexander, the son of an Ozark farmer. Alexander, with a divinity degree from Vanderbilt, was a liberal who had been involved in some of the earliest interracial activities in Atlanta, but somehow lacked Tugwell's clout or ability to defend the Resettlement Administration; thus, with Tugwell's departure, major support for the Special Skills program was removed.

At the end of 1936, Roosevelt transferred the RA to the Department of Agriculture; Congress, under severe pressure, voted to continue the RA for 1937, but by spring and summer the Special Skills Division's scope had been reduced. In September, following passage of the Bankhead-Jones Farm Tenant Act, it became the Farm Security Administration. Dornbush was transferred to the new entity, while Seeger floated through various agencies until settling into the Federal Music Project of the Works Progress Administration.

The brief life of the Resettlement Administration was yet another symptom of the political battles waged over the New Deal. Seeger concluded that the RA succumbed because the idea upon which it was founded had lost legitimacy among the Washington establishment. Local politicians began to attack the system as communism, and real estate agents collaborated in the effort to discredit it. They killed Eleanor Roosevelt's pet project in Arthurdale, West Virginia, because they wanted the federally appropriated land. After most of the people had been driven away, real estate interests resold the houses and subdivided the property. State and regional directors could have controlled things, but did not. And the homestead residents themselves had grown discontented.

Seeger had had a very difficult time finding people to send into the field. The entire program was premature, he decided, although it might have succeeded at some later time; in the midst of the Depression, people were still more interested in survival than in idealistic notions about engineering new communities and fostering utopian enterprises through the arts.

Further, faith in the government's power to foster beneficial social change had begun to decline, and disenchantment permeated the federal administrative hierarchy, from Tugwell down to functionaries. Although Tugwell had the solid backing of Eleanor Roosevelt, there were not enough other powerful people in Washington who cared to support him. Administrators who developed the schemes, including Tugwell himself, rarely understood the people whom they had placed in the homesteads, and even community residents were skeptical about the plan's objectives. Seeger concluded, years later:

[Resettlement Administration planners] didn't know the country well enough. They were politically naive, they were culturally naive, and they didn't realize that to build these resettlement communities, they'd have to build them up in terms not only of the techniques of learning and engineering, but in terms of the folklore of the rural people and the folklore of the political parties that governed upwards from town to township to county to state to region to government. They were utterly naive there; they learned their lesson in the process by being turned out of business.[31]

Seeger and his workers faced manifold problems in their campaign to retain and promote old musical traditions among the rural population. One barrier was an unresponsive bureaucracy. When he sought help from the head of the Agricultural Extension Bureau in his attempt to encourage "farm people to make music of the farm people" rather than merely listening to records or the radio, the official said, regretfully, that Seeger's notions were not feasible: the bureaucracy was too unwieldy.

Seeger, you're new in Washington. Secretaries come and go, but the Agriculture Department goes on as it always has. I sit in this office and I make recommendations. They go to each one of the twelve regional directors. Each regional director sends it to each state director under him. Each state director sends it to each county director under him, and the county director, if the memo gets to him, looks at it and throws it in the ashcan. The four million men singers and women singers and the 4-H clubs, they all do what they want.[32]

Finally, Seeger concluded that the only way one could accomplish anything was by operating outside the rules, which he "tried to do as often as possible."[33]

The communities were accepted as a desperate stopgap to stave off social chaos; but once things started to improve, many were concerned that such activities might develop into socialism. Because of reactionary fears, one federal agency after another was closed, or their functions scattered among other units, thus weakening their effectiveness. For example, the Federal Art Project was placed in the National Gallery, while the Photography and the Farm Security Administrations were housed in other units.

The Works Progress Administration was another response created by the New Deal to alleviate the effects of massive unemployment.[34]

Its Federal Music Project, first suggested in 1933, was created in July 1935 as a relief project, not a model for government aid to the arts. Because WPA arts projects were little involved with politics, the WPA escaped controversy, with less criticism from Congress or public accusations of communist influence than other entities received. Under the direction of Nikolai Sokoloff, the FMP was initially charged with maintaining the highest professional standards for musical performance by employing music teachers, singers, and instrumentalists, and serving the public by disseminating the knowledge and appreciation of music across the nation. This was integral to the social service ideals of the Roosevelt administration.

To meet these goals, the Federal Music Project offered free, inexpensive concerts, provided music lessons for poor adults, music appreciation for children, and training programs for music teachers, including techniques for group instruction. These activities stimulated amateur participation in music making and raised public standards for the professional performance of music. Musicians were placed, through audition, in new orchestras formed in cities that had never had them; some survived to become permanent organizations. The FMP also supported bands, vocal and instrumental ensembles, theater groups, black music groups, dance and opera troupes, and sponsored radio broadcasts. Summer performances in the parks became widespread, and arrangements were made to use high school auditoriums for concerts given by traveling musical groups. In addition to composers, teachers, and performers, the agency employed copyists and librarians who prepared and catalogued scores, compiled indexes, bibliographies, and other materials that were stored in libraries throughout the United States. One objective was to create a permanent corpus of unpublished orchestral works by American composers.

The FMP also promoted other important developments. One was the Composers' Forum-Laboratory, first established in New York in 1935 and then in other cities, which encouraged new musical creativity by sponsoring performances of the works of American composers.[35] These concerts not only provided a public hearing for new works and a forum for discussion, but also attempted to define American music itself.

Although the FMP did not commission works directly, project officials selected what was to be performed in laboratory concerts. Composers themselves rehearsed the musicians, conducted the orchestra, and otherwise oversaw the performance so that their pieces were presented as closely to the composer's intention as possible. Afterward, the audience was invited to discuss each work and other works in the artists' repertoire, with the dialogue frequently focusing on what made the music characteristically American.

The Seegers themselves benefited from the Federal Music Project's opportunities for new composers. Charles's *John Hardy* and the *Scena for Middleman, Farmer, Consumer* were performed in Washington, and his *Three Songs* were given a first performance on November 17, 1937, to celebrate the seventy-fifth anniversary of the Department of Agriculture, all under FMP auspices. The next year, on April 6, 1938, Ruth's compositions made up the first half of a concert given by the Composers' Forum Laboratory in New York (the second half devoted to Hanns Eisler). Among the works performed was her *String Quartet*. Afterward, Ruth discussed her music and her future plans for composition, revealing a developing appreciation of American music and folk idioms.

Federal Project No. 1 (or Federal Number One, as it was generally called) was innovative in several ways. For the first time in U.S. history, federal money was used to support cultural undertakings. It was also the first time the federal government assumed responsibility for improving the quality of American cultural life and fostering the creative and productive use of leisure time. Also, the project was vastly egalitarian; again for the first time, the U.S. government officially espoused the idea that the arts were for all people, of all ages, social classes, and geographical locations.

There were a number of unanswered questions, however. What kind of culture was being transmitted, preserved, and valued? Was it highbrow, lowbrow? Should the federal government support one or the other, or both? Whose definition of artistic quality applied? Indeed, whose conception of the *quality of American life* would be used?[36] What should be the role of fine arts in American life?

There were of course contradictions in encouraging the growth of the arts in the United States and calling for a national music that was both indigenous and of high artistic merit. The question of what criteria would dominate reactivated the old controversy concerning Old World influences in American culture, recalling a frequently heard injunction—dating from Emerson's time—for American intellectuals and artists to free themselves from Europe. Some chafed at the idea of a cultured Old World tradition imposing external standards of training, performance, and composition. Since even into the 1930s, musicians preferred to study in Europe—Germany, if possible—and to perform abroad before returning to the United States, the American musical elite was dedicated to foreign standards and lauded European artists and conductors. Opposing this was a spontaneous, organic, and highly popular musical life, thus exposing a polarization of art and popular music in American culture.

By creating the Recreation and Education divisions of the Federal Music Project, the Works Project Administration tried to resolve the dilemma by identifying two areas in which the arts would enter the life of the common people, and by emphasizing projects that included all genres except for "art" music. The role of the participant in art, as contrasted to the role of the performer, was gaining in importance. This meant a sponsorship of music education. The FMP's emphasis on teaching led to a promotion of music programs in public schools. The WPA began to develop rural music programs in 1936; however, the programs consisted still of "art" music, although theoretically they were intended to cultivate indigenous forms of expression.

In November 1937, Seeger was named deputy director of the Federal Music Project, a post he held until 1941. Seeger's responsibility was to develop folk music and recreational activities to promote it. He outlined his goals and published guidelines on how they should be accomplished in a pamphlet, *Music as Recreation*, that revealed a balance of Seeger the pragmatist and Seeger the bureaucrat.[37] His conclusion was that the aim of recreation is to meet the real need that exists to have everyone singing or playing an instrument, or both.

Much of the project's fieldwork was—inevitably—carried out in the South and Appalachian mountain areas, where rural poverty was widespread and yet where a rich, vital folk tradition of the British Isles survived. To extend the project into other areas, in June 1938 Sokoloff called for more emphasis on folk music, for example, where there had been little such activity. Seeger was happy to oblige. Until that time, interest in folk music had tended to follow composers' uses of it. Spanish-American folk songs were collected in New Mexico by the state university's Hispanic Studies Department. In California, a WPA technician trained in medieval materials notated liturgical chants of the California missions for performance by modern choral groups.[38] Other projects were undertaken in Mississippi, South Carolina, and Kentucky (ballads), Oklahoma (American Indian songs), Louisiana (Creole and Acadian songs), and the Northeast.

During his tenure at the WPA, Seeger made valuable contributions to the new study of American folklore and music. He added to the discs already deposited in the Library of Congress, the fruit of his work with the Resettlement Administration, his collections from the WPA, bringing to approximately 1,000 the number of recordings he placed in the Library of Congress's Archive of American Folk Song during 1935–1941. Another major achievement was Seeger's three-volume *Check-List of Recorded Music in the English Language in the Archive of American Folksong.*[39] Collected, compiled, and sometimes grudgingly assembled by WPA field workers, it has long been highly regarded by folklorists.

In December 1938, a Joint Committee on Folk Arts was established to coordinate the ongoing activities of the FMP in folk music, with folklorist Ben Botkin (of the FWP) as chairman and Seeger the vice-chairman. This was conceived as the "folk" complement to the WPA Music Project, the Historical Records Survey, and the WPA Theatre Project, which was to produce Marc Blitzstein's *The Cradle Will Rock.* Botkin and Seeger developed a plan for a folk arts collective and an expedition to gather folk materials. Seeger was designated the troubleshooter of this joint committee.

Seeger was also a traveling representative and consultant on another project to establish federal music centers in a number of rural areas. He would cover the same territory he had been responsible for as deputy director of the FMP, a vast area stretching from New York to Florida and extending west to New Orleans, Texas, and Arkansas. He traveled to the field as often as possible and also continued his Resettlement Administration pattern of sending field workers to collect folk arts materials.

Seeger had become convinced that many genres of American music were worthwhile and should be promoted more vigorously. As deputy director of the Federal Music Project, he believed it his responsibility to emphasize a variety of musical genres and to interest key government personnel to support them. He pursued this idea in one of his several meetings with Eleanor Roosevelt. The first lady asked Seeger to draw up a program of American folk music to be played at a concert for the visiting king and queen of England; the concert would serve as a forum in which to promote American music.

Seeger wanted to enlist the educational establishment in promoting American music, so a major activity of the Federal Music Project was teaching. He wrote a collection of memoranda on music education and addressed various educational organizations on the subject. In 1939, speaking to teachers of the Florida Music Project in Jacksonville, he lamented the slow progress made in advancing the musical arts relative to other arts sponsored by federal programs:[40]

The really great problem of the Project is to catch up with the other Arts Projects. Why is the Music Project behind the others? Because we have made no permanent or evident accomplishment. Once a big concert is over, what have we to show? The Art Project has pictures, the Writers' Project has books and articles, state guides, etc.; the Theater Project presents American Plays that have been published (many of them). These plays have runs if they are worthy. When the Art Project was inaugurated, the question was "What to paint?" Shall we copy the old masters, paint madonnas, Dutch windmills? The answer was "No—paint America." One is immediately struck by the freshness of the work we view in a Federal Art Exhibition. It IS America—it makes one see things in America that one had not noticed before.

In the Writers Project the people write about America. One reads things about America one did not know. The Federal Theater Project produces American plays, by American actors. These three projects have put their work in appreciable form because they have produced America, because they are interpreting America to Americans, not imposing old and foreign forms upon America. Writing and painting and the theater will be different from now evermore because of the WPA.

This is sadly untrue of the Federal Music Project. Any one of the activities of the latter could be taken over by any organization and carried on, so that in a few months, the Federal Music Project would be forgotten. We have not registered as the other Arts Projects. We have made the contribution but we have not made it show. What then should be done? We have up to now been merely recreative not creative. Why not interpret the musical America? This problem faces instructors in public school music also. The music for public schools and bands is written by academic gentlemen who imitate Europeans.

There are many truly American folk songs. American music education is based on the classics and on the folk songs of European nations. There are of course, mountain ballads, Stephen Foster songs, which are not truly folk songs although they are labelled that. They are the "popular" songs of Foster's day. Ives, Ruggles and Gilbert founded a school of American music, but their work cannot be performed before American audiences, to Americans. It must be done for Europeans to be appreciated. The rank and file of American musicians can carry on this school but they are still in love with European musical standards, still ignorant of America's possibilities.

In every ethnic group the music has begun to figure in the great history of music when it began to present its own country in music. This is true of Great Britain, Germany, the Netherlands, France, Italy, Finland, Norway, Spain, and all countries. Each rose to its height musically because of its national group significance. America is the first great nation in which an attempt has been made to found a music NOT on a national racial basis. When the founders of this country came here they brought with them the finite and folk arts of the old countries. Only the folk arts lived. Of these music was the best preserved, and flourished best. Music from the British Isles took the firmest hold. Only 75 percent of our people are of that origin, and the folk songs of the British Isles are traditional. An oral tradition, however. The oral tradition is usually supposed to be dead. On the contrary, America has one of the most vigorous collections of folk music of the day, including old English ballads, early American ballads, singing games, square dance music, etc.

Europeans come over here and discover our own folk music. We now have a large collection of folk song records in Washington, amounting to some 150,000 recordings. America has folk music that is more alive than any other country with the exception of Spain, Hungary, and Russia. Only

2 percent of the American people are interested in opera, etc. America has simply quietly resisted it. Why not do as every European nation has done? Why not get down and really study American music?

Europeans say America has made the greatest contribution to music that has been made in 20 years and Europe has been trying, very badly, to imitate it. Jazz is penetrating far farther than Beethoven ever went, because it is expressing not just individual thoughts of composers, but expressing the heart of a great people. The Negro, especially around New Orleans, has given a distinct character to American folk music. So we have three sources of folk music, the British Isles, colonial America, and Negro music.

American music, deserted by professional musicians has made music from its own soil and from the common people, from whom we have the old folk songs, the Negro songs, the hillbilly songs, and the cowboy songs. Composers, critics, historians, in fact all but teachers, have come to recognize American music. European music is killed in Europe by Fascist domination. Only in Russia is music still free. The real folk music is now centered in Russia and America.

Seeger realized by 1939 that the Federal Music Project was in trouble. He had expected to have more responsiblity for administering it, but by the time he joined the agency Sokoloff was firmly in control and the project was nearly past its heyday. Almost immediately after it was established, the FMP began to experience funding cuts, as did other federal agencies. Monies were reduced in 1937 and again in 1938. In September 1939, the FMP was renamed the WPA Music Program and transferred to state control—which meant that the states were required to contribute 25 percent of its funding. Congress officially discontinued the Federal Music Project in 1940.

In Seeger's estimation, his work with the WPA music project lacked the joy, camaraderie, and imagination he found in the Resettlement Administration. Much of his work for the WPA, particularly in the Recreation and Education section, was deskbound, although he occasionally undertook field trips to oversee projects and workers. He was often carrying out orders, not formulating policy. Whereas Seeger had the support of Director Dornbush in the Resettlement Administration, his efforts to promote traditional and folk music encountered Sokoloff's resistance, even though Seeger had been hired specifically for that purpose. Further, most of Seeger's staff, many of them unemployed musicians, usually knew little and cared less about collecting and preserving rural music. Most preferred European classical music, reflecting Sokoloff's preferences and training, while the Resettlement Administration had been able to promote public school and rural music programs in addition to an art music agenda.

In evaluating his government work between 1935 and 1941, Seeger summarized his achievements, his failures, and how he had approached his task. He always tried, he said, to live on the technical level—to do the job demanded of him, not promote ideological causes. In this regard, he considered his Resettlement Administration work successful, while the Works Project Administration's Federal Music Project—poorly organized to begin with—never reached the level of the RA's Special Skills Division. Another problem was that the WPA represented more special interest groups that had to be monitored with a watchful eye. And the WPA's work in many communities was hampered by bigots, particularly those representing religious groups; he believed that their opposition and intransigence had retarded the recovery of many areas of the nation from the Depression. But like Eleanor Roosevelt and Rexford Tugwell, Seeger continued to believe in the role of the arts in fostering social harmony—an idea he had cherished ever since his days with the Composers' Collective.

Seeger noted that these government-sponsored projects seemed to accelerate changes in social roles. For example, in Louisiana and elsewhere, women were in charge of the arts projects and most of them employed other women, or (in Seeger's words) "some subservient men."

The cultural impact of these programs was unmistakable. The American theater never returned to what it had been before the Federal Theater Project came into being; "The slate was wiped clean of all the old ideas. A whole new view of theater, which was actually au courant with European thought at the time, entered the American scene." The theater project tried some of the daring approaches of the experimental theater in London and on the Continent, but just as they were being tried successfully in the United States, the Federal Theater Project was shut down.

The years in Washington under Roosevelt, particularly the early years, were a period of splendid innovation, despite a mixed record of success. It is easy to understand Seeger's sympathy with Roosevelt's vision and ideas. FDR was, after all, of the same social class, a patrician, Harvard-educated, with a liberal bent, an establishment figure who swam against the tide with new and innovative ideas. FDR collected bright people from all over the country for his New Deal programs.

Tugwell was another good example of the kind of leader Seeger admired. He was a very impressive person "who had many stodgy assistants" through whom Seeger frequently had to "ram his ideas." Some of Tugwell's best ideas also were stymied by that bureaucracy. Yet there was a prevailing attitude in Roosevelt's Washington that everyone had some worth. The goals of educating everyone, making certain that all citizens had something to eat, clothes to wear, and a decent standard of living should be the ideals of any society. In particular, now people could buy from some other source than the company store. Farmers were able to plant with the aid of books published by the Department of Agriculture "instead of just planting. It was like an evangelical event."

For the first time, Seeger had been given oversight of workers in a government bureaucracy and responsibility for how they functioned. Everything "had to be kept at a low profile, the musicians in a community had to keep a low profile." He, too, cultivated modesty and begged everyone in the Special Skills division to avoid publicity, but instead to "spread around good ideas, good deeds, and those sorts of things. Work from below, work from within, bore from within, that was the only way to survive." Seeger attributed his success both to the agency's organizational structure and to his own procedures, honed during the years of the Composers' Collective. "It was just good common sense."

When the invitation to Washington came suddenly in November 1935, just as he was leaving the Composers' Collective, Seeger had a program all ready for the Resettlement Administration. He knew what he should do: "to work in the vernacular that was in the heads of the people," not what he could superimpose on the people, but what they already had. "The vernacular was to be folk, popular, mixed; whatever the people wanted."

Although the Federal Music Project died, Seeger did not stay idle. While he waited for another appointment to be approved, and since he remained on the federal payroll, he was kept busy with several government music projects. Seeger worked temporarily with the National Resources Board where, among other tasks, he completed a bibliography of WPA publications. Another responsibility was overseeing the editing of the above-mentioned Archive of American Folk Songs List. And he was commissioned to undertake another project. General Spatz of the Air Corps, a guitar player and singer, called for a compilation of army songs. So, with the help of Helen Bush, a Library of Congress cataloguer, Seeger edited the *Army Song Book*, which had a print run of five million copies. He included some eight or nine folk songs in the book.

The family grew by another daughter, Barbara Mona, born May 4, 1937. Peter lived with the family from time to time, often spending summer vacations from college until he lost his Harvard scholarship in 1938. In keeping with the family's growing enthusiasm for folk music, Peter played banjo and sang, to the delight of Mike and Peggy. Ruth contributed financially to the household by working with Charlie on various enterprises. She made transcriptions and arranged archival materials for various folk music projects for him for both the Resettlement Administration and Federal Music Project, as well as for Library of Congress activities. At Charlie's request she became a serious student of and researcher in native folk idioms, primarily as his assistant.

A natural offshoot of Seeger's work was a new interest in folklore and folk art. The family attended folk festivals, although they were somewhat rare in the thirties: there was a national festival, one in Asheville, N.C., and "a couple of fiddler conventions. White Top . . . was nothing like it is now," according to Michael Seeger.[41] The *Three Songs* Seeger prepared for the seventy-fifth anniversary of the Department of Agriculture in 1937 were something of a lark, but also symbolized a meshing of Seeger's lifelong love of composing and his recent foray into a folk idiom.

Seeger's interest in folklore was stimulated by his friendship with John Lomax, author of *Cowboy Songs* (1910) and *American Songs and Ballads* (1941). Lomax held a dollar-a-year post as honorary curator at the Library of Congress's Archive of American Folk Song, where Seeger spent much time reading. When Lomax asked Charles to make transcriptions for his book, *Our Singing Country*, Charles was too busy, but recommended Ruth, who "did a beautiful job." Both she and Charlie began to share Lomax's "evangelical" enthusiasm for collecting folk songs.[42]

Seeger considered himself a "johnny-come-lately" to folklore. Now, in addition to his appreciation of Lomax and Sandburg, and admiration of Cecil Sharp's folksong collections, Seeger was also impressed by the studies of folk music made by several early twentieth-century German and Scandinavian musicologists. To get some idea of the history of folklore, Seeger also read the work of the eighteenth-century Bishop Percy, and of Scott, Burns, and Herder.

Seeger learned from other leading folklorists, as well. During the 1930s he became close to Ben Botkin, Herbert Halpert, and others. He also joined the Folklore Society, although he was skeptical of the academic approach to folklore found in U.S. universities—a study of "archaic survivals in the form of mostly library sources." He was also doubtful about the federal agencies that attempted to study and preserve folklore, even though he had worked for them; they were attempting to homogenize the American people—to reconcile city and country, urban and rural life. He came to understand that "people, regardless of what stratum of society, have a desire to make music in the tradition of that stratum. And the music from other strata that some people might listen to, they might not want to make."

Continuing his scholarly writing, Seeger published various articles promulgating his idea of folk music as a "musical vernacular," promoting American classical music, and exploring the connections between American composers of "classical" music and "the life about us."

In "Music in America,"[43] Seeger set forth an important new direction for the discussion of music in the United States. Claiming that the American music tradition could be divided into three areas: academic, folk, and popular, he observed an individualistic, sophisticated, and learned national energy that flowed into popular and academic music, different from the common spirit and shared experience that flowed into folk music, and a complementarity between visible cultural diversity and constant integrative drive.

Seeger began by comparing the United States with China, India, and the USSR in having the "four largest, most active and most diversified musics in the world today. It differs from them [however], first, in that its indigenous primitive music . . . is still undigested by the dominant culture; second, in that the traditions of this culture were more lately imported and have been thrown into contact with each other for a shorter time; and third, in the rapidity with which its musical diversity is being integrated in one recognizable whole." His thesis, that both the wide diversity and rapid integration are desirable factors in American music, is the now vivid argument in American society of assimilation versus pluralism. Diversity did not become a respectable idea until the civil rights movement demanded it be.

Of the three American musical traditions, folk music was the possession of the greatest number of Americans, their musical vernacular, Seeger said. He pointed out that folk musics in America derive from almost the entire world and that unlike popular or academic musics thrived in the harsh new conditions of America. In contrast to folk music, the traditions of academic music are the possession of a small class of highly trained professional specialists. "The very essence of academic art is to be found in the fact that it can be made only by the professional" whose traditions are "predominantly of German extraction . . . with strong infusions of . . . Italian opera . . . and French salon music." Popular music in America, as elsewhere in the world, is not so easily distinguishable. "By its very nature, popular music is more unstable, volatile, more markedly hybridised an art. . . . It is partly an oral, partly a written tradition, the former seeming to be the case when the art is closer to the folk, the latter, when it verges upon the academic."

Then, popular music was possessed by a population smaller than that of folk music and larger than that of academic music (this is no longer the case). He thought it significant that American music made its first success in the popular music tradition, a triumph of the assimilation policy.

Concluding by noting the countervailing influences that each of the music traditions applied to each other, he predicted a musical coming of age in America:

What we may confidently expect will come out of all this is, on the one hand, a stabilizing of the too hectic change in the styles of urban music and, on the other hand, a socializing of the over-individualized forms of rural music. Unquestionably, the musical soul of America is in its folk music, not in its academic music; and only in its popular music to the extent popular music has borrowed, stolen and manhandled folk music materials. On the other hand, the gestures, the nervous energy, the characteristic flair of America— industrialized, sophisticated, learned America—is in its academic and popular, not in its folk music. It is quite as necessary to have both! But they should not fight with each other; for there is every reason to believe each has something the other needs for its well-being and for the well-being of the country. Great musics in the past have been formed out of just such interplay of diversity and integration as can be seen now in American music. There is some reason to believe it is happening again.

In "Grass Roots"[44] Seeger lamented that American composers were too modern or too uninterested to explore our own rich artistic heritage. He thought that in 1925 or 1926 "the jazz boys had hit upon something the academic or fine-art composer had missed." The success of jazz was "due not alone to its technical innovations but . . . to its basic root in an art totally unknown, or unrecognized, by the bulk of American professional musicians . . . the folk music of America. . . . Our hymns and spirituals have parallel fourths, fifths and octaves, ballads without expression and accompaniment, instrumental music that defies 'laws' of harmony." It was shameful that it had taken Americans—himself included—until the 1930s to discover America's rich musical traditions.

Pointing to the 12,000 records in the Archive of American Folk Song and the composers' resistance to their use, he suggested several remedies. "The first thing, it seems to me, is for the professional composer to make up his mind that his place in world music will depend upon finding his place in American music and in American life." His second suggestion was that composers should discover America, get away from the urban areas and into the countryside. "The third step in the making of an American composer must be the digestion of this experience. . . . So there we are. Plainly, if we are to compose for more than an infinitesimal fraction of the American people, we must write in an idiom not too remote from the one most of them already possess—their own musical vernacular." Noting that music is the most highly developed of our native arts—except for speech—and that it is a dynamic folk art, he concluded, "But our culture has definitely graduated beyond the colonial phase. The people as a whole know it. Professional musicians seem to be among the last to admit it. Is it not time for a change?"

This theme continued.[45] In "The Importance to Cultural Understanding of Folk and Popular Music," Seeger reiterated his strong view of folk song as the backbone of the American music heritage and as an untapped source for American composers. He pointed out that folk and popular music is the musical communication most common among men and that when the history of music in America is presented, it would show that the main concern had been with folk and popular music. His key point was that if we wished to have music serve the ends implicit in the Inter-American Music Conference (discussed below), we should put our major emphasis on folk and popular musics, with art and primitive musics playing, respectively, "dominant and recessive minority roles."

He presented his argument by applying the general theory of acculturation to the particular field of music in the new world. He noted that the music-acculturation processess operating in the New World from the first conquests to the present must exhibit a fundamentally identical pattern, although their elaboration in various regions could be quite diverse—a Redfieldian "big culture, little culture" idea. He presumed that a full array of musics were present in the beginning of culture contact and that, through a multitude of factors, some musics came to be prefered over others. The first casualty was fine art music but, in the twentieth century, with the advent of technology, the colonies looked back to Europe and its fine art music became "the envy of the pseudo-nobility of wealth and power in the new world countries rapidly emerging from the colonial phase." This "contra-acculturative" process had met with varying reactions in diverse regions of the United States.

He suggested that the existing music-cultural situation and the point of departure for programs proposed by concerned agencies would entail three degrees of interest: acceptance, interest, and participation. In the case of the Inter-American Conference, the group could pursue two likely avenues: either contributing its idea of the "right" kind of music, or serving as a planning board using rational principles and scientific methods. He hoped for the latter, putting themselves above the battle, using anthropological techniques to be objective. They should do several things: first: to start work immediately on the serious study of music in the new world, its history, resources, needs, and potential for development, through surveys, depositories, and indices. Second, collect new data and develop maps of musical stocks. Third, encourage the development of such studies by providing the means for scholars and students to travel, to exchange ideas, to use auxiliary fields such as folklore and archaeology. Such a comprehesive program could result in benefits to international relations through music. Efforts resulting from the conference must be viewed as acculturative or contra-acculturative, according to the form those efforts took.

In a still-standard essay in folk music scholarship,[46] Seeger based his analysis on George Pullen Jackson's studies on the relationship between the melodies of shape-note hymns and the tunes of American secular music. Jackson had not really considered that living musical traditions existed beyond his range of knowledge. Seeger pointed out the vigorous, disciplined beauty that appeared in the shape-note hymns, composed in the backwoods. He carried Jackson's work further by tackling the musical paradox between the homophonic style and the contrapuntal functions of the hymns, analyzing them as derivative of both oral and written traditions.

Seeger intensified his preoccupation with Americana and folk music through the 1940s, not only from an intellectual concern that American scholars recognize their own worth, but by his socially impelled idea on the value of music and, in this case, the value of American music.

At the American Historical Association meeting in 1939, Seeger gave a paper in which he delineated some cultural approaches to history, and argued for the legitimization of folk sources as keys to understanding a culture.[47] Seeger began by noting that the term "folk music" is used to designate three or four socially and historically determined music idioms found in most cultures, but contended that it was impractical to discuss the external relations of one of these types of idioms without looking at the inner mechanisms and the points at which they intersect. He proposed some hypothetical values to historical study from inquiry into folk music and began by asking: "Why has the study of music-culture relationships been neglected?" and "How shall we go about remedying the situation in which we are at present?" He first blamed the general historian but conceded that he cannot be responsible for techniques in every area under his purview, concluding, "The general historian would seem to have done as much as, if not more than, has the musicologist to effect a *rapprochement* of musical and cultural studies." He answered the second question by stating, "It would seem that alignment of the fields of music and culture must be approached from both sides. Gain will be measured, I would say, as much in terms of what the social historian can see in a music-continuum . . . as in terms of what the musicologist can see in social history."

The musicologist and historian had approaches in common. Since the advent of technological improvements, sound recordings, and video materials, unwritten and nonverbal sources could now comprise a rich, hitherto untapped source of data for both musicologists and historians, who so greatly relied on written sources. Seeger proposed, "In place of the single concern with inner, technical operations of music, viz.: the presentation in language of an account (1) of the nature of music-technical processes, (2) of the relation between the universe of music and the universe of discourse, and (3) of the function of the total field of music in the total field of culture."

He then focused on the hypothetical values of folk music as a source of social history. The first is the universality of the folk idiom—the musical vernacular of the "common man." The second, the anonymity of folk idiom, makes it possible to feel "that one is dealing directly with a socially molded thing, with a deep-set cultural function expressing not so much the varieties of individual experience as the norms of social experience." Other hypothetical values include the fact that forms of folk idioms do not show rapidly changing fashions, therefore express the more enduring characteristics of a culture; that use of an oral tradition allows the content of folk idiom to come directly to us without intervention of the written word; that as a means of cultural expression and communication, the folk idiom is more familiar to the average student of history than is fine art music; that it is similar to other materials used by social historians; that emphasis on folk idiom will tend to break down barriers set up by the theory of the "otherworldliness" of music; and that the non–fine art idioms "constitute the field into which the normal expansion of both comparative and historico-musicology seems likely to take place." Seeger further suggested that folk music offers a quantitative criterion to the study of history; that the anonymity of the folk idiom allows for expression of norms of social experience; that since it is an *oral* tradition, its content comes without the intervention of a social censor; and that as a means of cultural expression and communication, it is more familiar to readers.

Particularly because of new technological advances, folk materials was an area in which historians, anthropologists, musicologists and others could easily converge. The problem was that history used one art form—language—while music used another, and studies using language tended to exclude music as "unmethodical thought." He concluded, "In our exploration of folk music as a source of social history . . . we should not look for any such fantastic result as ability to express in language the content of music" and wished that musicologists would provide as receptive a forum for discussing such innovative approaches as had historians.

Continuing for another audience his role as educator,[48] in "Music and Culture" Seeger focused on the function of music in the theory of culture as a whole. It required scientific method, but to Seeger music thinking was overwhelmingly critical with a qualitative view of art owing little reference to our culture. Noting that the critical standards accepted by professional music circles have little validity outside of it, that we do not know nor speak the same musical tongue, Seeger said that we need to know the quantitative and qualitative distinctions among music's idiomatic variations: "(a) fine art music which has a tradition and written sources, and is urban; (b) folk music, which has tradition and oral sources, and is rural; (c) hybrid popular art idioms, which are partly written and partly oral; [and] (d) fringe idioms: jazz (popular and fine arts) fine orchestrated and blues (folk and popular)." Each idiom has its own language, fact, and value to be learned.

He noted problems; one was between making music in a traditional idiom and people listening who do not possess the idiom; as example, listening implies being active culturally as well as musically. Another was that excessive diversity was beyond the capacity of integration. He thought the two ways to control music-culture relationships were through competition and cooperation. Finally, he cautioned against the fallacy of regarding music as a "universal language."

Despite new activities and expanded professional horizons, Seeger continued and enlarged upon his previous musicological interests. He served as vice-president of the AMS from 1935 to 1937 and as president of the American Society for Comparative Musicology from 1935 to 1938. In 1939, he presented a paper at the American Musicological Society meeting that demonstrated his attraction, and that of other U.S. music scholars, to the widely accepted methodological work of Guido Adler.[49] Since the 1880s, Adler had dominated music scholarship (with a few powerful adherents even today). In the 1920s and 1930s Seeger, Sachs, Strunk, Welch, and others began to question some of the strict Adlerian methodology. Seeger suggested discarding Adler's two separate branches of music study and designating musicology as one study in which two *orientations* are possible: *systematic* and *historical*. In *history*, one uncovers the processes of events, "how things came to be as they were"; in *system*, its material is a process, therefore connected with other complexes of points and processes, "How things are and are coming to be what they will be." The essay is a forerunner of many such attempts, an early display of his complicated theoretical writings, and evidence of his propensity to invent new terminology when he felt that the old terms would not do.

In another publication from this period, Seeger decided to "throw down the gauntlet" to musicologists.[50] Noting that both government and music are functions of a culture, he suggested six steps toward an applied musicology:

(a) analysis and description of the field of music in a culture;
(b) estimation of trends;
(c) prediction — the need for improved statistical apparatus and controlled experiments;
(d) development of a critical method and a value theory for musicology;
(e) definition of objectives;
(f) checking the critical dicta versus the scientific data.

This shifts emphasis from the logic of structures to the dialectic of functions, from objectivity to subjectivity. To Seeger, the prime concern for an applied musicology must be to integrate music knowledge and music practice, and to achieve this government facilitates the development as a cultural function and regulates it.

About his career in government service to this point in time, Seeger noted:

I undertook the job with enthusiasm, since the field offered an unparalleled opportunity to demonstrate the superiority of the group-guidance technique over the conventional imposition of a program from above-down. The history of this unique and practically unpublicized experiment with the arts in government will be written in due time. For the present, let me say only that I feel certain at last that I have, as a result of these two years' experience, come to grips with the musical reality of our American culture. What any ordinary textbook should have taught me in school, what twenty years of teaching in universities and conservatories had steadfastly to blind itself to, what seems so unthinkable in the concert hall or the studio, I have now, after thirty years of professional life, seen clearly. . . . The development of programs along these lines, national in scope and involving the cooperation of many agencies and individuals is now my chief work.

He wrote his parents in 1939:

[I am in] continual touch with people from all over the country. Phonograph recordings of unusual and interesting music come in from many states. Projects of merit involving long-term, large-scale planning are continually

Charles Seeger, Sr., and Elsie Seeger, Patterson, N.Y., 1940

under discussion and promotion. Altogether it is a very exciting life. The
feeling that perhaps one's efforts do a little something to counteract the
oncoming of fascist developments is no little part of the satisfaction. And
many fine and able colleagues is another.

I work most closely with a group interested in the study of American
culture. We are discovering so many things we did not know about America,
its people and its customs, that one almost feels as if one were watching a
drama unfolding where one had thought there was nothing but a burlesque
show. Seeing, for the first time, America through American, instead of
European eyes, is perhaps a better way of putting it. And many of the traits
that I most abhored—the jerry-built houses, the very efficient factories, the
main street and the bungalow street, take on, sub specie American culture,
new interest and often beauty. . . . I always felt the best and most productive time of life would begin in the fifties. I suppose everyone has a different
feeling about it. But for me it is working out that way.[51]

In 1939, the winds of war were blowing more fiercely. Already
under way in Europe, the Second World War would bring to the
United States many European musicians and musicologists who were
to make a strong impact, for although they established musicology
firmly in America, they also brought a particularly scholarly bias that
still pervades the study of Western music in the United States. Seeger
would become intimately involved with the results of this artistic
migration.

6

The Pan American Years,

1941–1953

∾

SEEGER'S "Pan American" years were a period of great achievement and activity. Seeger deepened his involvement in music education—a lifelong concern—and in international organizations. Cultural relations linking Western Hemisphere nations increased after 1939, because communications between the United States and Europe were greatly reduced. Instead, there developed a lively exchange of students, professors, artists, composers, printed music, discs, and radio broadcasts among the twenty-one American republics.

To organize hemispheric communications more formally, in 1939 the U.S. State Department, through its Division of Cultural Relations, set up conferences on inter-American relations in four areas: philosophy and letters, education, fine arts, and music.[1] The objectives were greater cultural cooperation and a better understanding of Latin American countries.

Seeger, as a member of the organizing committee for music, gave an address to the music conference entitled "On the Importance of Folk and Popular Music to Inter-Cultural Understanding."[2] The conference devoted to music heralded the musical activities of the Pan American Union (PAU), which Seeger was shortly asked to lead. In February 1941 he was appointed director of the PAU's Inter-American Music Center and chief of the Music and Visual Arts Division, with an impressive annual salary of $4,600. Seeger was pleased with his new colleagues; he had great admiration for Leo Rowe, director-general of the Pan American Union, as well as for Assistant Director William Manger and Harold Spivacke of the Library of Congress.

Seeger's job entailed enlisting the aid of national organizations and governments to promote the interchange of music and musical activities between the Americas. It included the exchange of leading musicians and musicologists, publication and performance of musical works, building up a library of printed music and sound recordings, sponsoring publications, and ultimately establishing an Inter-American Music Council (IAMC) that might serve as a model for a world federation.

Seeger summarized his responsibilities:

My duties at the Pan American Union were first and foremost to persuade Latin American ruling classes, which meant government officials and wives of government officials and wives of ambassadors, etc. that the United States was not a nation of mere money-grubbers, jazz addicts, and—what's the other, I think it was alcoholics or something. The object of this was to keep German airplanes off of Colombian airfields so they wouldn't bomb the Panama Canal. That was the first job. In the broader sense it was to help make the Good Neighbor policy of Franklin Roosevelt a reality.[3]

In an early statement of his prime objectives for the next dozen years, Seeger declared that his ambition was not merely to promote cultural dialogue but in so doing to change music education in the United States and in the Americas.[4]

Our lives and our living of them are conditioned by many things— geography, climate, economic, social and political history. I sometimes wonder, however, whether any of these affect our life and our living of it more concretely than does the art of speech. It is in terms of speech that most of us—even musicians—distinguish and study the art of music and organize music activities. . . . [Because so] much of the time we spend at conventions and conferences is spent tightening up and extending our musical organization by means of speech . . . an occasional review of our manner of talking about music would be a good thing. This would seem to be especially desirable when we come to such a subject as that of "Inter-American Relations in the Field of Music." . . . Most of us are at home in the field of national organization. Music in the field of international organization is a brand new departure. There are vast stores of data, but no tested or even tried techniques for handling them as functional entities— that is, as factors in going concerns. Scholars have written . . . on "primitive" music, on folk music, on the fine or high art musics of the world, and . . . popular music. But of the relationship among these, of their functions in the social orders they are found in, of their significance to us, and, least of all, of the problems of their social organization, comparative musicology tells us nothing.

Seeger suggested that with the increased organization of music we might be able to determine whether any kind of music can penetrate the considerable barriers of language and culture. Further, by examining our own culture prior to our involvement in international activities we could clarify both the international picture and our own.

Once again, continuing his preoccupation with the hegemony of the Old World over the New, Seeger cited the danger to Americans of depending so much on European musical precepts. He saw this in terms of the conflict between exoticism and (American) nativism, between old authoritarian educational methods and more modern democratic teaching techniques. The Americas should work together to assure that music is a major factor in cultural cooperation.

Seeger's plans for the Pan American Union's music division built upon the issues raised in "Inter-American Relations." He first set out to forge an alliance with a large, effective organization through which he could argue for inclusion of folk music and Latin American music in the curricula of U.S. public schools.

The Music Educators' National Conference (MENC), a well-established organization of public school music supervisors, had several advantages to commend it: an efficient central office, a forward-looking leadership, and a well-published, widely circulated magazine. The MENC's associate director, Vanett Lawlor, agreed to participate in Seeger's inter-American project in November 1941, and accepted a half-time position with the PAU, effective February 1942. Vanett Lawlor was indispensable to the success that Seeger enjoyed in his music activities with the Pan American Union.[5] As in many of his successful projects, he was aided by the intense involvement of a competent woman whom he respected, such as Blanche Walton, Margaret Valiant, Sidney Robertson, and of course Constance and Ruth. Seeger also hired Spanish-speaking Gustavo Duran, and Luis Heitor Correa de Azevedo, a professor at the Rio de Janeiro Music Conservatory, who knew Portuguese.

The PAU music division's first project, designed by Lawlor, was to publish the music of Latin American composers. Seeger set up a committee of musicians that included Henry Cowell and Pedro San Quan, a Cuban, to collect as much Latin American music as they could find. On the advice of qualified music educators, the committee considered all available Latin American music and selected for publication over two hundred "good" works that could be sung and performed in the U.S. public schools. Cowell was responsible for selling the compositions to major music editors and textbook publishers. Music publishers such as Schirmer and Presser were interested in these massive textbook projects because with the profits from the schoolbooks, said Seeger, "they could afford to lose money on what were called 'prestige' compositions, among them my own songs."

Also, at Seeger's direction, Cowell drew up a uniform contract for Latin American composers that would give them maximum, equal benefits.[6] In Seeger's words,

The first thing I had my eye on was the contract with the Latin American composers. Up to that time, the contracts were drawn up by the American publishers, very much to the benefit of the American publishers. One of the most prolific American publishers, I needn't mention his name, was a very clever man who would go to the bar where the Mexican popular composers used to meet, treat the crowd to drinks, get the composers sufficiently inebriated and then say, "You know, I like your work, I think it's pretty good. I'll give you fifty dollars for anything you write. Well, naturally one of the most prolific sent him, I think, eventually something like 150 songs.

This one man—I think his sister and I think his brother and aunts may have written some of them, but he put his name to them—well, I went to this gentleman and said, "Look, there's a man named Ponce down in Mexico who has written a song named *Estrellita*. It has been copyrighted in the United States by eleven of you publishers and Ponce has never received one single cent. It had been pirated. It's made thousands of dollars for you people. I don't think this ought to keep up and you're too rich a man to sit by and let it keep up." He said, "Well, what's your proposal, Mr. Seeger?" I said, "You draw up a contract with the Latin American composers just as you would draw up with American composers. You submit specimens of the two to the Latin American composers, show them that you're reformed now, just as [the] Good Neighbor policy has reformed you." Well, he fell in with it; he was a good sport. And as I was going out the door, I said, "Mr. So-and-So, you know that the songs of such and such a man—he was the man, I think, who bought 150, you haven't published all those songs." "Oh," he said, "by no means, not more than three or four of them." "You haven't lost on that, have you?" "Oh, Mr. Seeger, I'm a businessman."

All of those 200 compositions that were selected for publication were signed for with contracts where there was somebody to sign a contract with. They were printed and they were sold and the things were played all over the United States. Well, the word got around through Latin America that the old pirates up there in the north had reformed.[7]

To obtain Latin American support, Seeger's next project was to send North American composers and other musicians to tour Latin America. Three groups—who had previously toured under the auspices of Nelson Rockefeller, from whom he had good cooperation—all met with "phenomenal success"; they were the Yale Glee Club, a dance group, and a chamber wind ensemble. These groups were successful because they spent their budget judiciously and brought not only goodwill but also good equipment, some of which they left in the countries they visited. They also ingratiated themselves with the Latin American ruling class, a crucial ingredient for future Pan American success. As Seeger recalled,

The Yale Glee Club, boys in tail coats, white ties, [sang] Palestrina, and Bach, and Brahms. It knocked the ears off the Latin Americans. They had no such choral organization. They'd never heard better singing, even in Europe. But, they said, these boys are all the sons of wealthy Americans. We must have funny ideas of North Americans who are nothing but dirty money grubbers, who adhere to nothing but jazz, or as a man who came in to my office, one time early in the forties and sat down at the table and said, about this nice place you have, Mr. Seeger, but in the United States, don't you have any composers? And I said, what do you mean by composers? Oh, he said, composers, I mean composers of symphonies and quartets. Fortunately, I had some published music at hand. I don't think he believed me. . . . He thought we had nothing but jazz and popular Broadway things. So, this basic policy of simply making friends among the Latin Americans was the same sort of thing I had at [the] Resettlement [Administration].[8]

The next goal was to reach both urban and rural populations in the Americas, first in the United States. To awaken them to music of other countries, Seeger's group devised a program for fall 1942 for the MENC outlining the scheme. Although public school music educators were hostile to musicology, Seeger thought that the best way to highlight Latin American music was through comparative musicology. The next approach would focus on folk music and they would publish folk music, in English, in music textbooks. They attempted to enlist the services of younger U.S. composers, like Aaron Copland, Virgil Thomson, Henry Cowell, Roy Harris, and others, in public school music programs.

To target popular audiences in Latin America, Vanett Lawlor traveled throughout the region to establish exchanges between musical organizations and other agencies. Fortunately, many Latin American directors of music education were also leading composers who were grateful for the PAU's new contract guidelines, so they were pleased to cooperate with Lawlor. To encourage solidarity and cooperation among Pan American nations, projects were inaugurated such as having Chilean songs performed in Mexico, for example, or Guatemalan songs in Uruguay. Seeger judged that perhaps these cooperative schemes succeeded because so many Latin American countries had shared a common colonial experience.

The PAU initiated many other music projects, including a program that fostered an exchange of music field workers between North and South America, but Seeger always kept a guarded eye on what he termed the "polyphonic" development of the work of the Pan American Union. Too many projects, though worthwhile in themselves, were unconnected to the others. Seeger worked toward designing projects that would complement each other and produce concrete results such as founding permanent organizations, programs, and publications.[9]

One such effort sent Lawlor on an official visit to Chile for six months, which resulted in the Inter-American Institute for Music Education, headquartered in Chile. Another project, initiated almost at the beginning of Seeger's tenure, was the publication of a series of brochures about Latin American music. These included general works such as *Music in Latin America*[10] and works on individual countries such as Argentina and Brazil.[11]

Seeger also commissioned bibliographies of Latin American reference materials available in English.[12] He also began the systematic release of music scores and sound recordings available in the United States, a fine example of which was produced by Gustavo Duran.[13] This activity complemented another of Seeger's prime goals: to build a music library at the Pan American Union. Components of that library would include a section for scores and parts of the works of contemporary composers in the Americas and an archive to house a major collection of recorded music and lore of the Americas. In 1950, Seeger began the *Boletín de música y artes visuales* which in September 1957 was divided between the *Boletín interamericano de música* and the *Inter-American Music Bulletin*, which survived until 1973. Also in 1950 Seeger generated a series of radio programs to air popular Latin American music in the United States.

During 1943–1950, Seeger had served as music editor for the *Handbook of Latin American Studies*, the principal reference work in the field. Each of his annual essays contained an assessment of Latin American music research and listed current music periodicals. Familiar themes were the wealth of Latin American publications available despite the war in Europe; the value of bibliographic coverage of Latin American folk and popular music in addition to art music; and continued efforts to enforce copyright laws to protect Latin American composers. The last was particularly vital to Seeger, especially regarding performance fees for both Latin American and U.S. composers.[14]

In retrospect, Seeger was proud of his accomplishments at the Pan American Union. He was pleased with the PAU's capable secretary-general, Alberto Llerga Camargo, a liberal Colombian, and he was fortunate in working with a larger budget than he had ever been given charge of during his adminstrative career. The PAU library collections of books, music, and phonograph records had grown considerably under his leadership. The newly established Inter-American Music Council had spawned the Inter-American Institute for Musicological Research, headquartered at Tulane University and directed by Gilbert Chase, and then the Inter-American Institute for Ethnomusicology. These institutes and a Latin American Music Education Council sponsored conferences attended by musicians and musicologists from throughout the Americas.

A frustrating feature of Seeger's work was the pervasiveness of politics not only within the PAU, but also in the international councils and societies with which he was increasingly entangled. Particularly troublesome were United Nations operations—specifically UNESCO (the United Nations Education, Social, and Cultural Organization), founded in 1945 and associated with the United Nations in 1946. Of course, Seeger was himself a very political animal and had helped these international associations come of age, often for his own political reasons.

Because of Seeger's involvement in other international organizations, his influence in Pan American affairs began to suffer owing to political realignments over which he had no control. At the Ninth Conference of American States in Bogotá, Colombia, in April 1948, the Pan American Union became the secretariat of the Organization of American States (OAS), a regional unit within the United Nations. As Seeger saw it, the OAS bureaucracy began at once to insidiously usurp control of the PAU.

Seeger had sensed the changes at a joint UNESCO-PAU committee meeting. When UNESCO officials suggested that the PAU's Inter-American Music Council, which he directed, was unnecessary, "the Pan American Union people said nothing"; when Seeger himself was silent, the IAMC was terminated. A proposal to eliminate the International Music Council did not pass; it was retained, within UNESCO, with Luis Heitor Correa de Azevedo as its head. Eventually Seeger decided that his usefulness to the Pan American Union was over. He felt straitjacketed by the system and foresaw the defeat of his ideas, proposals, and projects.

Despite his concerns about the changes that threatened the OAS, Seeger managed a successful organization until his retirement in 1953. He had been given sufficient money to hire Latin American consultants and to bring to Washington Latin American specialists—such as the Chilean Otto Lange and Guillermo Espinosa, a Colombian—to replace several key people. First to leave was Vanett Lawlor, who returned to full-time duty with the MENC. Then Correa de Azevedo left to head the IMC, and Gustavo Duran went to work for the United Nations.

With the birth of the United Nations and its agencies, Seeger's dream of forming an international music federation to embrace myriad regional councils had become a possibility. He had advanced the idea of an overarching international music organization when the Pan American Union was first established, suggesting that once an inter-American music council was created, European, African, and Asian music councils could follow—as components of what could eventually become a federated world music council. Seeger saw such a world council as a logical parallel to other global institutes and commissions such as the International Theatre Institute, the International Commission on Folk Arts and Folklore, the International Federation of Library Associations, and the International Commission on Museums.

But UNESCO soon announced a music program that Seeger considered to be as impractical as it was inadequate; further, it was certain to be dominated by Europeans. To counter European influence over American programs, to find a firm place for music in UN organizations, and to promote his own federation idea, Seeger presented a proposal to the second UNESCO conference, held in Mexico City in 1947. (For political reasons, Professor Helen White of the U.S. delegation presented his plan.) It asked the director-general "to make preliminary enquiries for the establishment of an International Music Institute and prepare proposals for furthering such a project for submission to the Third Session of the Conference in 1948." However, upon the direction of UNESCO's Secretary-General Julian Huxley, and against the judgment of PAU representatives, only propositions relative to particular musics were to be presented to the Mexico City meeting. Foreseeing his proposal's defeat, Seeger requested another member of the U.S. delegation to present a brief resolution directing the secretary-general to enquire into the feasibility of setting up an international music *council*, rather than *institute*. This was done, the Huxley-directed propositions were overwhelmingly defeated, and Seeger's resolution enthusiastically adopted.

Three PAU Music Division staff members went to Paris to implement elements of the proposal to establish the International Music Council (IMC). The project needed approval from twelve committees;

with each review it was revised, and each time it asked for less money. By the time it was finally approved, it received an appropriation of only $2,500. As the "father of the International Music Council," Seeger was on the organizing committee, and a year later he traveled to Paris as a member of the prepatory commission to finalize its formation. The plan was confirmed in 1949.

To promote the cause, Seeger prepared a paper on the music aspects of UNESCO.[15] Seeger commented on the inspiration promised by a union of intellectual rationale and political common sense and discussed the practical difficulties of making the union work, the notions that "peace can be taken by storm, the spreading of too little over too much and the pressure of special interests." These were largely political difficulties, but there were technical ones, as well. A lag had developed between the enormous degree of modern intellectual progress and that of political thinking and action; intellectuals were naive in minimizing this lag, which endangered the organization's health. Seeger noted the difficulty of uniting so many different genres—the arts, theater, dance, folklore, cinema, letters, museums, libraries, etcetera—under the rubric of "cultural" organization.

UNESCO had distributed music activities among six different sections. *Music* fell into the section of arts and letters, budgeted under cultural interchange, while *musicology* fit into the philosophy and humanities section, and *music education* under arts and letters in cooperation with education ($8,750 had already been budgeted for music education). *Music library work* was divided between the library section and arts and letters.[16] Several dozen related projects were classed under *mass communications*, and, more particularly, under the *library* section, where at least fifteen projects were under way. The picture Seeger painted in the 1948 report was one of an intergovernment agency, UNESCO, dealing only with governments and other international organizations, "surrounded by a planetary family of autonomous specialized organizations with which it can deal, but which are controlled and directed by private initiative." Although UNESCO was sufficiently funded, Seeger had two words of caution: when working through government, patience, ingenuity, and watchfulness were important. He listed thirteen steps the United States seemed to be taking to ensure concrete results. Second, although the fields covered by UNESCO were hopes for peace, they were also essentials for war, so UNESCO should first show how education, science, the arts, and humanities could be used specifically for peace and against war, then how to be used specifically in their own right.

As one of its activities, the IMC helped to form an International Association of Music Libraries (IAML). This was in keeping with Seeger's practice of starting a library in tandem with each music agency. As before, he played a familiar behind-the-scenes role, nominating the IAML's first president. The still successful IAML has sponsored some major projects; for example, it continued the Robert Eitner bibliographies of musical sources. It also publishes its own journal, although Seeger thought that it quickly came under the influence of the "great composers" syndrome and should emphasize other musics, such as those of Asia. For many years, though, he remained interested in IAML and considered that it had produced excellent work.

Seeger soon regretted the International Music Council, however. Because UNESCO was primarily based in Paris, European hegemony was inevitable. Seeger would have preferred locating the International Music Council somewhere in the Americas. He disdainfully noted later that when it was founded documents had already been drawn up "in the European fashion of a bureau of control not disturbed by voting," and that the founding committee of the IMC was presented with a constitution already written. "So the International Music Council got started and it got off on the wrong foot . . . and it's been on the wrong foot ever since."[17] Although his resolution had passed at the 1947 meeting, Seeger never was able to have his ideas fully developed in UNESCO as he had envisioned them because director Julian Huxley and his cohorts had a different perception of international music organizations. Also, Seeger observed that UNESCO music personnel were far more interested in promoting European music rather than a wider variety of types of world musics.

There were some positive results. Four major organizations emerged from UNESCO activities: the IMS (International Musicological Society); IFMC (International Folk Music Council, now known as the

ICTM, the International Council on Traditional Music, with a wider range of musics under its consideration); the Jeunesse Musicale; and the IMC (International Music Council). Seeger was active in all and traveled to their international meetings between 1949 and 1952, getting to know the European leaders well, all of whom had, in his estimation, a "true European style of benevolent dictatorship." He came away with a low opinion of both the British and the French and suggested that the organization had been "English disk-jockeyed" ever since the Huxley years at UNESCO.

Seeger's frustration at the European hegemony over international music organizations reached its apogee at the 1952 meeting of the International Music Council, at which he was "like a bull in a china shop," objecting to everything. It seemed to Seeger that his pet project, the IMC, had become increasingly an organization sponsoring sessions such as "We know who great composers are," and "similar useless topics." Seeger wanted them to concentrate on people, not professionals, and especially not on the elite. Worst of all was that as a result of the European and, especially, French influence in and domination of UNESCO, the growing Latin American–United States unity disintegrated.

In 1953, Seeger again stated his goals for a system of international music education.[18] Seeger identified many problems posed by a proposed conference on music in general education. Why limit the conference to music educators alone; why not include the whole problem of musical education? Which viewpoint should predominate, that of the professional musician or the professional educator? Music education has three principal aims: education of the professional musician; education of the scholar-musicologist; and education of the layman and his children. Because, until recent times the professional taught the professional and the layman the layman, each group inherited, carried, and transmitted a different music tradition than the other. Their separation as social classes maintained the separate traditions in comparative purity, but changes in civilizations and technological advances has thrown this out of balance, enlarging the distribution of some traditions and narrowing that of others. This coincided with the skills that the diverse groups had, those of the cities, with popular and fine art traditions dependent on the written traditions, while those in the rural areas, the great majority, depended on the older tradition, the oral tradition. By the mid-nineteenth century, the professional musicians decided to teach "the hordes of children that were coming into state supported schools how to appreciate and read written music." This was a disaster, he protested.

For unless the teacher is competent as a musician, the professional musician will judge, quite rightly, that the work is worse than none. And unless the musician is competent as a teacher, the educator, equally rightly, will make the same judgment. The effort to build a musically literate public in the image of the professional musician has, furthermore, been resisted successfully by generations of children—particularly boys. . . . The cake has lovely frosting, but is hollow inside. For music is mainly in the making of it—not in the listening to someone else making it.

The implications are that small segments of the population will continue serious study of the fine art and popular traditions and an increasing minority will mix the traditions, but the great mass of people will continue to be taught by persons like themselves. A new type of lay teacher must be evolved "one who can utilize some of the professional techniques but who will steadfastly resist the effort (that has failed so disastrously) to cast the layman and his children into the mould of the utterly incompetent professional." He continued,

It is here that the scholar, that shadowy and almost unrecognized figure, who has remained in the background of the controversy, must be called from his preoccupation with history to study oral tradition, discover how it works and how it may be adjusted to written tradition and to the new conditions under which both flourish today. With his mediation, too, it may be possible to answer our second question: Which should predominate—the viewpoint of the professional musician or that of the professional educator?

The musician, says Seeger, sees man as serving art, while the educator sees that art must serve man. "Any sane policy must allow leeway for both."

At the IMC conference in 1953, on Music in General Education, Seeger proposed yet another organization, which became the International Society for Music Education (ISME).[19] Seeger praised the teaching of music as a profession requiring special abilities and training and lauded the music teacher. However, throughout the world, in the first half of the twentieth century, they had moved relatively little toward a common goal: "that every child shall have a chance to develop to the utmost the music traditions of his culture and that when he grows up he will continue to do so." People could not rest on the idea that a good teacher never lacks pupils, and that, as a direct result of technological innovations, we have mass communications and with it universal elementary and secondary education. Technological innovations did not supplant the old teacher-student relationship, but rather extended and modified it, as well as music and the teaching of it. Thus educators needed to become informed about mass communications.

Seeger suggested that these developments are controlled first by government and private companies, or "policy groups," then technicians, or "technical groups," and finally consumers. Policy groups have effectively assured unanimity of agreement among its members, and technical groups—musicians and teachers—have carried out the detail of policy group directives. All such entities have molded music traditions through time and place. "During the nineteenth century, the external control of policy groups and the internal control of technical groups began to turn toward the masses of the populations with a view to increasing the consumption of products of the fine and popular arts." Seeger asserted that by 1900 professional musicians had nearly complete control of fine art, businessmen and semiprofessionals popular art. This "accentuated the corruption and near abandonment of folk music in all industrialized countries" and contributed to the loss of control of the professional musician and music teacher over the fine art tradition. To compensate, professional musicians and music teachers entered government, business, and other institutions or agencies; specialized more or broadened their fields through interdisciplinary activity; and simultaneously reacted to the era of mass communications by developing professional organizations. Music is undertaken for two main ends: "interest or protection," which inevitably brings a third end: "planned, concerted action to build, promote, and . . . assure administrative and public approval and support of a programme of work under virtual control of the organization," with the MENC as a conspicuous example. The result is that teachers, not the government, control the materials, methods, personnel training, and instruction in music.

Seeger noted that the IMC statutes provided for the establishment of an international institute for music education and an international journal of music education. Seeger proposed three standing committees—for music in general education, for education of the professional musician, and for education of the scholar or musicologist. "[This] union of the three main categories of music education is purposeful, and those of us who framed the document believe, conforms best to reality and is in the best interest of all." He stated the reasons and lauded the faith in the oneness of humanity that produced UNESCO, and in the oneness of music that produced the IMC.

The International Society for Music Education worked up a constitution—under Seeger's direction—which became a model for international organizations: delegates would represent not only countries but also all branches of music. Seeger was scheduled to present the constitution at its first meeting in Liège, Belgium, but, as he noted in a letter,

I was so deeply involved with the founding of the International Music Council and the International Society for Music Education, of both of which I was "the father," that I stayed on [at the OAS] unpleasant as it was. Then, the same year that Ruth died, 1953, the State Department refused me a passport, although I was supposed to present its [ISME] constitution, which I had drafted, to the official organization of ISME. I had two years to go before retirement but promptly resigned.

(These events are discussed in more detail in chapter 7.)

Seeger's involvement first in national, then hemispheric, and finally international music activities was complemented by his activity with the American Musicological Society (AMS), which had been quiet during the war and which he now served as president (1945–1946). With a small membership, a ruling committee of three—Seeger, Glen Haydon, and George Sherman Dickinson—mapped changes and a new constitution and nominated Dickinson to be the next president to carry out these changes. They established regulations for membership: a written application and the signatures of two AMS members in good standing. The purpose was to prevent dilettantes from joining the society, although he, Kinkeldy, and others, opposed classifying the membership by class. Its 1946 meeting, during the last year of his presidency of the AMS, "was stormy." Two controversial issues were the new constitution, which "raised some hackles" and, despite considerable opposition within the membership, a fully planned project for a journal which was to be launched in the second year of Dickinson's presidency (1948).

The postwar explosion in music education and the sudden upsurge in AMS membership, due to the growing number of European musicians who had sought refuge in the United States, made the AMS more cosmopolitan and international. But musicology in America was forever changed by the enormous influx of European-trained scholars. Again, Seeger felt a prevailing bias in favor of European art music over all other kinds and himself soon out of sync with the AMS. In 1952 he failed to persuade the International Musicological Society at its annual meeting in Utrecht to include a society for comparative musicology (or ethnomusicology) within its ranks. Seeger sought to reconcile his belief in the viability of scholarly study of musics of the world and the promotion of an American approach to the scholarly study of music — that is, to study music in context as well as for itself. It was some years before the Society for Ethnomusicology was formed, but the need for a branch organization that served interests outside the mainstream had began to gain credence.

Seeger continued to be an indefatigable contributor to the work of professional music organizations. In addition to his other associations, he had served on the Commission on Musicology of the American Council of Learned Societies (ACLS) since 1942 (and as its chair 1950–1952), in which capacity he encouraged the development of a total view of music in the United States and comprehensive program of U.S. music education — from grade school through university. He planned a conference for the commission to address sixteen facets of American musical life.[20]

In fact, he had anticipated this twenty years earlier.[21] He said then that it is easier to say what music is *not* than what it is. Musicology is the methodical treatment of music by language, but the method of criticism in that treatment was still lacking. Seeger noted two types of literary criticism: *impressionistic*, nonmusical, and *scientific*. In musical science, there are music technique requirements, which include a basic plan to fit music of any time and place, a standard of measurement, and a clear definition of domains of musical and nonmusical considerations. The problems are that musical processes are regarded as fixed, rather than continually changing, standards. In music-physical characteristics, there are six variables: pitch, loudness, and timbre; tempo, accent, and proportion. Noting harmonic or chord, dissonance/consonance in Western achievement, he suggested that music is a phenomenon of prolonged social growth—a culture, not only a product of a culture but one of the means by which culture comes to be what it is.

Increasingly displaying his primary love of scholarship and the philosophical analysis of music, Seeger used the American Musicological Society meetings as a forum for his ideas, both practical and theoretical. His thinking on the arts and international organizations gained a hearing at the fourteenth annual AMS gathering, and he persisted in his work on musicological matters with a paper read at the sixteenth meeting in 1950.[22]

In "Systematic Musicology," Seeger called attention to his earlier work on the complementarity and interdependence of historical and systematic orientations in musicology: while the two orientations "cannot in fact be totally joined, neither can they for long be held entirely separate." Seeger again juxtaposed the problem of the art of speech with the art of music, noting that many disciplines, musicology in particular, use the power of the art of speech but suffer the limitations of the semantics of the art of speech. Historical musicology was the history of systems; systematic musicology, the system of history. Although students of musicology lean toward one or the other, a balance should be made between the two. He favored a systematic methodology, but was interested in exploring historical and comparative approaches to music study. He broached the idea of a cumulative approach to the field of musicology, and even began promulgating a universal one. Seeger was coming to believe that music, any music, should be treated as "dynamic wholes."[23]

Seeger used "Systematic Musicology" to advance a proposal and several propositions he thought valid for Western fine art music, as it was then known. This essay introduced *general spacetime* and *musical timespace*, as a key to distinguishing between historical and systematic approaches. According to Seeger, the distinction between historical and systematic orientations in musicology was best made on the basis of two separate but related concepts of spacetime, general and musical. The historical or diachronic approach saw music as occurring in time and space—that is, general spacetime—while the systematic or synchronic approach saw music (music as time itself and space itself) as occurring within a smaller time and space, or music space-time—tempo, duration, phrases, regularly recurring beats, and such.

After discussing the concepts involved in this proposition, Seeger posed a second proposition: "Elaboration of a concept of music spacetime rests upon its distinction from a concept of general spacetime," which he reviewed under seven headings: occurrence, provenience, identity, continuity, control, measurability, and variability:

(a) *occurrence:* general spacetime is universal; Music spacetime occurs within it;

(b) *provenience:* general spacetime is a given; Music space time is man-made;

(c) *identity:* general spacetime is unique; music spacetime is multiplex;

(d) *continuity:* general spacetime is uniform and endless and beginning-less; music spacetime varies infinitely;

(e) *control:* general spacetime is outside our control; music spacetime is within it;

(f) *measurability:* general spacetime is measurable by norms of the art of speech but is not itself constituted by any known norms of its own; music spacetime is measurable as a phenomenon in general spacetime by the same speech norms, and is constituted by norms of the art of music known by carriers of the music tradition or traditions in which any structure is cast;

(g) *variability:* general spacetime has invariables; music spacetime has variables.

He concluded that the relationship among the three spacetimes—a fixed one, general, and a variable one, music, both reported in a second variable, speech—required no further elaboration.

Seeger's third proposition was that the "concept of the music event [occurred] in both general and music spacetimes. In the former, the music event may be regarded as a phenomenon: in the latter, let us say tentatively, as a "normenon." An example was the *Eroica*: each performance of it is a separate event in general spacetime, but in music spacetime all performances have been of one event.

The organization of an apparatus to deal with the problem of a universally valid foundation for the study of music rested primarily with systematic musicology, elaborated in a table, entitled "Conspectus of the Organization of Musicological Study upon a Basis of the Systematic Orientation." The task would rely on two equally important criteria—the musical, or intrinsic, and the nonmusical or extramusical, or extrinsic viewpoints—on both systematic and historical orientations, and on both scientific and critical methods, all of which are presented in the table. The table outlines eight possible operations, each using one term of each of the three types of time dichotomies of criteria noted above. The order of the operations provides an organization of musicological work in which the core is the systematic study of a particular tradition, or traditions, of which the student is a carrier or has sufficient knowledge and around which additional layers of comprehension can be wrapped, including those offered by historical study. Seeger concluded that the entire apparatus could not be carried out by any one person and that each person needed to carve out a section, according to interest or competence, upon which to work. He then reminded his audience that the music event is not to be confused with the verbal report of it. "The task is to find a terminology and a method of handling it most suitable to the particular idiom under investigation." The successful completion of the project would provide a base for comparative musicology and thus "a world view of music envisaged."

In another paper presented at an international congress in 1952,[24] he focused on an idea that served as a major building block for his later works: by the particular musical tradition which the student carries, she or he sees music in terms of that personal tradition as well as the tradition of the music—a type of musicological juncture. Seeger needed to recharge his intellectual batteries with such thinking and writing as a counterbalance to his exhausting administrative duties and his focus on more practical topics such as education, American studies, and his involvement with UNESCO and other international organizations.[25]

"Wartime and Peacetime Programs in Music Education"[26] follows the pattern of his almost missionary effort to advance the dual causes of American music and the role of U.S. music education. While lauding the conference in progress, he identified an area upon which "a recapitulation or even some further discussion may be profitable—the relation between the programs of war emergency and of peaceful development—between what we HOPE is the short-term and what we KNOW is the long-term program of music education in the United States," and urged that the panel discussion center around the interrelationship of wartime and peacetime programs.

Noting that war and music are both normal functions of culture, he warned that "until the culture of which it is a part is destroyed, music development proceeds in war as in peace and in the times of mixed war and peace, sometimes more intense, sometimes more relaxed, though it is difficult to say why this difference takes place." He chided the AMS for canceling its 1942 meeting and abandoning any study of the relationship between war and music. The current conference, however, had accepted the challenge and put itself and its resources on a war footing; praising this decision, he asked if all realized that there should be a logical continuity of having music as "good for something" follow its logical conclusion from "good in itself." "After a century of music as a 'good in itself,' we swung into a program of music as 'good for something.' After a century of music as the "art of peace" and "universal harmony," we are pressing it as a weapon in war—and at that not only as a defensive weapon for the home front but as an offensive one in the armed services!" This was not a break in the program of U.S. music education but rather a logical continuity. Although the United States was ill-prepared for war, it was well prepared in music education, having at the ready thousands of trained musicians for the armed forces and the home front; after such an astonishingly successful "lead-in," it was faced with the "follow-through."

Seeger enumerated several strong points in music education: a steadily improving teacher-education program; a sizable group of music educators in the field; an incredible number of performing units; a broadening base of operation; increased integration with other subjects; good working relations with various government and nongovernment agencies, and favorable public relations. Weak points were lack of development of creative techniques in schools; an underused oral tradition; lack of contact with contemporary fine art composers and, consequently, failure to use music as a vehicle of living thought, feeling, or other mode of expression from one person or group to the other; and improving but still poor public relations with some so-called prestige fields. But wartime developments in music education, such as the program "American Unity through Music," have made some strides. "Far from hamstringing our music education program, it would appear the war emergency has been the occasion for a tremendous spurt of growth," of improvement, tuning us into twentieth-century realism instead of nineteenth-century romanticism.

The MENC journal was a major vehicle for Seeger's ideas on education.[27] In "Music Education and Musicology," Seeger wrote, it seemed obvious that of all fields of U.S. musical activity, music education and musicology should be most closely coordinated. "Both are concerned with musical knowledge. Both are concerned with the handing on of this knowledge. For the most part [both educators and musicologists] are practical musicians. And . . . in a broad sense of the term, teachers." Why have they "flourished side by side with so little recognized connection and with so much antipathy between their respective personnel?" First, music educators are concerned chiefly with the knowledge *of* music gained with direct experience of the art, while musicologists take knowledge of music for granted and are chiefly concerned with knowledge *about* it. Second, music educators are concerned with the established domain of musical knowledge and its cultivation in schools and teacher-training centers, while musicologist are concerned with the general extension of musical knowledge and its sytematization as a whole. Third, music educators are interested mainly in the progress in musical knowledge and ability of their pupils, while musicologists are interested mainly in their own progress and musical knowledge and ability. Fourth, American music educators have been very *local* in their viewpoint, concerned with the "here and now" of their place, while musicologists have been very Europe-minded and centered in the past. Both groups are broadening their space and time visions and values.[28]

Despite constraints on convention travel, there was a roundtable discussion held in New York, attended by G. S. Dickinson, George Herzog, Curt Sachs, and Hans David of the AMS and Lilla Belle Pitts, Vanett Lawlor, John C. Kendel, Alfred Spouse, Glenn Gildersleeve, Louis Wersen, Peter Wilhousky, and Jacob Evanson of the MENC. Sachs summarized the results of the meeting in the published account.[29]

In other articles Seeger honed his wide range of interests and spectrum of ideas, as well as his goal to publicize folk, American, and Latin American music, and music in schools.[30] These writings all reflected Seeger's views that the Old World had hegemony over the New, that "high" culture held sway over folk culture, and the role that education must play in "making America musical." He lamented that most U.S. citizens remained musically illiterate, thus forming a loose "folk society," absorbing and creating vernacular music, its folksong revivals comprised of survival/revival/arrival elements—of which survival was prime. Folksong was persistent and should be understood in terms of colonization, industrialization, and urbanization. In "Folk Music in the Schools of a Highly Industrialized Society,"[31] he suggested that folklorists should be in charge of *survival*—that is, preserving traditional songs—and educators in charge of *revival*, and he proposed that the point of beginning of the revival is where the *child* is.

He heralded his entry into yet another intellectual sanctum with a "sociological" paper[32] and once again became a founding member of a new society: the American Studies Association. Concerned that U.S. scholars always put themselves in an inferior position vis-à-vis European scholars, he was determined to show that U.S. thinking was not stymied by tradition. Seeger carefully noted that by referring to "American" music or studies, he was not equating them exclusively with folk traditions. Indeed, American folk music was only one element of American music; he was specifying all American cultural idioms.

Early in his tenure at the Pan American Union, Seeger had published several articles on American music. He campaigned for the development of both European art music and local and regional music-cultural movements throughout the Americas, stressing a "oneness" in the hemisphere.[33] Earlier he had made several points about American music.[34] One lament was that conflicts developed between "folk" and "elite" musics, pitting oral traditions against written ones and the resultant disparities of music taste and usage between city and country. Although he posited that the one essential basis of music education in a country is the folk music of that country, he stressed American unity through music. He lauded the movement toward knowing and accepting itself and its music which seemed to him to be underway in the United States, following the path of the Latin American countries. The program, "American Songs for American Children," was "the most momentous single step to be taken" toward the time when the United States *will be at home with its own music.* "This step is the adherence of the music educators of the United States to the principle that one essential basis of music education in a country is the folk music of that country; . . . it gives substance to our effort to make music serve in the larger picture of hemisphere relations. And this is perhaps the most practical path toward the eventual setting up of a world community of musics." Seeger set conditions for using folk music as a basic component of music education.

Music education [should be seen] as an integral part of American music as a whole—as possibly the most effective agency we have for the integration of American music within itself and within the culture of which it is a part. . . . The term "American music" (that is to say, United-States-of-American music) may be used in two senses: first, as designating the music and music activity actually existing in the United States; second, as referring to the part of this music that expresses or characterizes the American people as distinguished from other peoples.

Children needed to experience "all" musics of America, in American terms as American products. Four elements that aided the development of music in the New World were: the native American; European; African; and those Americans of wealth and professional music students who went to Europe during the nineteenth century "and acquired, with the psychology of the colonist returning to the mother country, a musical attitude and taste of distinct and peculiar character." It was in terms of this fourth element that music education had grown, and although some progress was being made to consider all of the world's and varieties of American music in the music education sphere, more must be done. "[If the integration of] our national culture is our most important present task, we shall have every stimulus to deepen musical knowledge and broaden musical taste, but also the satisfaction of knowing that music education is already in a clear position of leadership in the national music picture."

Seeger demonstrated an abiding concern for government and art networks, a concern he did not share exclusively with the music educators, bringing his ideas directly to the musicologists.[35] He observed that conceiving of the arts as useful in the development of political relations among nations had been one impetus behind the creation of the PAU and UNESCO. He opened with the idea of viewing political relations among nations as a given, with the usefulness of the arts to be considered in that context. He discussed the problem primarily in terms of "politics in art," and a fourfold continuum by which this problem would be viewed: political relations among the arts and within each; political relations among culture communities; political relations among social strata; and political relations among governments and within intergovernment organizations. The prime example of political relations among the arts was, to Seeger, the rise of language over all the other arts. The prime example of political relations involving the arts in the domain of culture was "mostly of the catastrophic kind—the flood of East Mediterranean art into Western and Northern Europe, of Chinese art into Japan, and of European and African traditions into the Americas—all accompanied by economic and military movements of one kind or another." The outstanding example of political relations partly causing and partly resulting from the social stratification of mankind has been the development of "various classes of art tradition: primitive

art, fine or professional art, folk art, and popular or commercial art."
Finally, he saw the government and intergovernment continuum as
superstructure.

Seeger provided several anecdotes on the use of music in government activities, commenting, "Experience has shown again and again
that the political frame in which the arts are used is of paramount
importance in the effect obtained. Thus, 'poor' art in a politically
'good' frame yields better political results than 'good' art in a
politically 'poor' frame," adding that 'good' art in a politically 'good'
frame was best. The general dilemma of art programs in the foreign
relations of all national governments is that "to gain best reception
they must appear to be objective, but to have continued financial
support they must be propaganda."

Intergovernment or the development of international agencies
were, Seeger observed, in an embryonic stage. Some binational
exchanges, such as between Germany and France, had been carried on
for thousands of years, yet their conflicts increased in bitterness and
frequency. Making a case for international cooperation, he recognized
that the arts provide fodder for both competition and cooperation. In
cultural and social confrontation and reconciliation, the arts function
fairly independently of each other and are themselves causes of and
vehicles for conflict and rapprochement. He urged artists, scholars,
and amateurs to help governments realize that the arts can be used to
provoke war or promote peace. Much depended on how they are used,
yet to a certain extent they cannot be controlled. Intergovernment or
international programs then existed at the pleasure of national
governments, but he hoped that in the future the roles would be
reversed: "It seems there will be much more use of art both by national
and by international government before there is less. . . . Long after
these agencies have ceased to exist, the arts may be expected to
continue to flourish, and, indeed, rise to greater heights of accomplishment than any we, in these primitive days, have known."

In another "sociological" challenge, Seeger took on another pillar of
establishment power in "Musicology and the Music Industry."[36] He
confirmed that musicologists agree on the nature of intrinsic music
value—that is, in terms of itself—but that it had not been system-

atized. He thought that musicology has practically nothing to say on extrinsic musical value; it is in the hands of the U.S. music industry, which is little concerned with knowledge *of* or *about* music in the past; it is absorbed with the present and future.

Seeger continued to proselytize on behalf of folk music and oral lore.[37] In "Professionalism and Amateurism in the Study of Folk Music," Seeger supported the view that there is room for both in the study of folk music, but in the future professionalism should outweigh amateurism. An aspect of personality could change any of the norms [discussed] as regards folk music. Concerned with the linguocentric predicament, he believed that one should know one's "own" music and spoke of the importance of integration, interaction, acculturation, and the need for music in schools and music in organizations.

In "Oral Tradition in Music" he noted that orality, a concept of basic importance in the study of folk speech, has served folk music well. However, while it was a useful device for potentially tying the fields of folk and fine arts together, such a union might fail for several reasons. One was the lack of use or acceptance of "oral tradition" in musicology. Indeed, the "increasing dominance of instrumental music in the Western world since 1600 has pushed consciousness of *oral* processes into the background and placed main emphasis upon *aural* processes." Further, the term is used loosely to mean accumulation, transmission, and the means by which both are employed. Finally, he suggested that the popularity of European fine art music, and its concomitant near universal adoption of the theory of unilinear evolution from primitive, to folk and popular, to fine art, has taken root.

Thus there were two major difficulties in the more widespread use and acceptance of "oral tradition" for the fine arts. One is the ambiguity in the word "oral"; the other is the lack of attention to the basic conditions and process or dynamics of music tradition in general. "Oral tradition is only one of many kinds of tradition." Seeger accepted the notion of *tradition*, the handing on of acquired characteristics, as a basic distinction between man and other animals. He provided a scheme for using the term, beginning with *music tradition* as a function of culture, a dynamic conception. In the sense of *accumulation* of material products such as repertoire, this is structural in character. In the sense of *process*, there is a combination of various oral and written modes. And, in terms of the *technical* it is students of the field who are the controllers, with two types of tradition of control: intrinsic, operating within the music activity, and extrinsic, operating from outside the music activity.[38]

In using the term "oral tradition" to integrate folk music with the general study of music, the crux of the problem arises when one encounters the written tradition. For Seeger the key was that "a very vigorous oral tradition in speech can flourish among people who are literate in speech. . . . But without a very vigorous *oral tradition of writing*, neither speech nor music writing can be learned." For Seeger, a unitary music idiom was being forged by a resurgence in orally learned singing and playing, not only in folk song revival movements but also in blues and rock.

Seeger concluded that it would be wise to confine the use of the term *oral tradition* to "bona fide word of mouth (*os, oris*), substituting for it, as the main technical process of folk music, the less picturesque but more accurate "unwritten tradition." He referred to the occidental (international) technique of music notation—"probably the most accurate and most widely used throughout the world"—as a development of the fine art of European music. . . . *Ur-texte* have become defined by their composers, during the last century, with increasing precision."[39] Seeger saw this system as a control system, par excellence, and noted that "the gap between the highly individualized identity of the product of fine art and the highly generalized identity of the product of folk art must not be underestimated" and that their treatment demands two different techniques. To use a control product of the fine art tradition to notate a product of the folk art tradition produces a reproduction that is a secondary rather than a primary datum.[40]

Finally, on the usefulness of a revised concept of oral tradition in correcting unilinear theories of the evolution of music, Seeger stated, "There can be no folk music in the proper sense of the word until there had been for sometime a fine art of which it can be *in part* a dying survival," but this was an observation he was willing to make solely for the occidental family of music tradition.

Seeger furthered his reputation in things American by continuing to press for research and fieldwork that would result in a comprehensive American music tradition. In addition to his articles, he published penetrating, substantive book and record reviews. His first, important for several reasons, initiated the practice of including record reviews in the *Journal of American Folklore*.[41] Here Seeger elaborated on folk music study sources, the often pioneering role of business in field recordings, and the emergence of serious standards in evaluating recorded data.

Framed by his idea of acculturation, his review emphasized the commercial setting in which oral and written traditions converged. He posited that both the oral and written traditions of America had two mainstreams to which the larger folk and some fine art traditions owed allegiance: the African and the European, primarily British. Indeed, Seeger pointed out the increasing importance of African elements in American hybrid musics long before it was common to do so. His purpose was to provide a guide by which record purchasers could make judgments on recorded performance. Listeners could categorize any kind of performance by understanding style and having some knowledge of a performer's background. Seeger concluded that the acculturative process — of which this was a part and in the context of which the evaluative process could occur — was unending and that, at least, folksong records could be further distinguished by poles of "what has been" (that is, *Mountain Frolic*) and "what is coming to be" (*Deep Sea Chanteys*).

Broadening his parameters, Seeger wrote on the direct attribution by society to the process of the transformation of music.[42] Tracing American music through various European influences and elaborating the idiosyncrasies that emerged in American musics, particularly those of the United States and Brazil, during the eighteenth and nineteenth centuries, he also dealt with the problem of collectivity versus singularity. Seeger pinned his analyses on method and process. He wanted to develop a method or approach to the study of Latin American music that would encompass acculturation of all native musical traditions with the tradition of European art music, and to learn the process by which transplanted European musical traditions established their domination over native Amerindian and imported African traditions in the Americas.

Acculturation was a key concept for Seeger; he framed it with his own emendations that reflected a deep concern for the social context as well as cultural traditions and became a fruitful definition to be used by ethnomusicologists.[43]

In another article on acculturation written expressly for teachers, "Music and Musicology in the New World 1946," Seeger mapped out a possible methodology for studying the movement of musical ideas.[44] He suggested seven criteria:

(1) the traditions—music culturally evolved ranges of forms and contents inherited, practiced, modified, and propagated, as, for instance, the Amerindian, the European, and the African, acculturation among them and the products that embody them—all inherited from cultures antedating the dominant Euro-American;

(2) the idioms—variations in type of usage of traditions upon different cultural levels or to serve different social functions, as, for instance, survivals of the primitive or tribal art derived from Amerindian and African sources, and the folk art and popular art derived from Europe, the hybrids among these and the products that embody them;

(3) the methods of transmission—oral, written, and mixed oral and written, and education both formal and informal;

(4) the quantitative distribution among the population of the traditions and the idioms;

(5) the qualitative factors employed in evaluation of traditions and idioms, particular products of these, and their distribution, by area, social stratum, and so forth, with reference to style and manner;

(6) the development of services to the traditions and idioms, as, for instance, through publication, library, implementation (including radio, film, photograph, etc.), management, property rights, organization of special fields, and so on;

(7) the integration of the traditions and idioms in the culture, as, for instance, their relative autonomy and dependency, and their control from within and without.

Seeger's emphasis on the need for research and field work in U.S. music, combined with his lifelong love for Latin America, resulted in a comprehensive undertaking on the cultural, historical, and social components of music in the Americas. He wrote numerous papers, some brief, some substantive, on the development of music in the Western Hemisphere. He reflected on the West European origins of much American music and the transition of this to an American corpus with individual, sui generis, music characteristics. Seeger saw the tremendous influence of North American music in South America and vice versa, as a result of Pan American Union activity.

The 1941–1953 period was, then, an important one professionally for Seeger, for international connections, for the various politico-educational movements, and for his writing on a variety of subjects. In personal terms it was also quite satisfying, despite the lengthening shadows cast over him and his family by the red scare of the McCarthy era.

During their busy life in Washington, Ruth kept a household, served as hostess, and was her husband's partner in countless professional endeavors. In addition, she wrote song accompaniments, published her own songbook, taught folk songs to children and developed teaching methods in her work at a number of schools. She transcribed and arranged thousands of recordings of folk music from field recordings for the American Folk Song Archive in the Library of Congress. She wrote and edited many articles and books, primarily on folk music, all of which sold well and brought good royalties.[45]

Key to Ruth's success was that not only was the material well chosen and substantive, but the presentation of the material was scholarly, rare for the genre. Each book contained valuable information. For example, the introduction to *American Folk Songs for Children*, which had its genesis in her contact with the Sandburg family, discusses the songs' musical, social, and education contexts, how the works were gathered, and the traditions associated with each song. It also includes suggestions for authentic performance. Further, Ruth grappled with the problem of how to most accurately transfer sounds to print. She experimented with many devices from her compositional techniques, seeking to combine authenticity with practicality.

In addition to her songbooks, Ruth also transcribed and edited other highly successful works.[46] Other folksong projects to which she contributed were those of John and Alan Lomax, father and son, with whom she worked on transcription, authenticity, authoritativeness, and practicality to produce *Our Singing Country* (1941),[47] a beautiful synthesis of the scholarly and the practical. Each transcription was authoritative in providing context, concept, and authenticity of performance, yet each song could be sung with ease. As Ruth wrote in the preface, she wanted to include "as many characteristics of singing-style as is possible, yet to keep most of the notation simple enough to be sight-read by the average amateur."

She also made the transcriptions for George Korson's *Coal Dust on the Fiddle* (1943) and his *Anthology of Pennsylvania Folklore* (1948–49) and was the music consultant for Ben Botkin's *Treasury of Western Folklore* (1951). Ruth's transcriptions for Botkin's book, her last to be published during her lifetime, show the elegance and substance of her work.

Ruth and Charles together served several publishing houses as consultants on American folk music for children. They also supplied musical arrangements for the Lomaxes' collection of 111 best-loved American Ballads, *Folksong: USA* (1948). The foreword to this volume enunciated their basic principles of transcription and arrangement of folk songs. They distinguished between arrangements and accompaniments, unaccompanied and accompanied singing, the use of various instruments and styles of performance. They noted the problems in using the same tune for all text verses, of "irregular" rhythms and nontempered pitches, and stressed the need for harmonic simplicity and cautious use of phrasing, tempo, and dynamics.[48]

Ruth planned the programs and chose the music for a series of State Department broadcasts entitled "Music in American Life," maintained a heavy teaching schedule at two schools, and gave private music lessons from eight in the morning to six in the evening on Saturdays.

With all of this professional activity plus the care of a large house — after the arrival of Penny in 1943, the family moved to a comfortable old house in Chevy Chase in 1944 — frequent company, and many professional commitments, Ruth had little opportunity to return to the composing career. Her intense involvement in folk music activities was not only economically rewarding but also meaningful to them both. Charles and Ruth were attracted to exploring the socioeconomic contexts of folk music and in analyzing its relationship

Michael, Penny, Charles, and Ruth; Barbara and Peggy in foreground

to art music. Ruth did not abandon her earlier modes of composition; she was engrossed in other activities. Even one of the few pieces from this period that employed a more traditional style—a work entitled *Rissolty Rissolty*—was based on folk tunes. Written for chamber orchestra, it was commissioned by CBS radio in 1941 for its "School of the Air" program. Ruth's son Michael commented on her career: "Any creative person, I think, makes these choices between family and their work. Ruth did, as well. And I know that she felt a good deal of conflict in her choices."[49]

During the last five years of her life, Ruth began to return to composing. As she noted in a letter to Edgard Varèse,

I am still not sure whether the road I have been following the last dozen years is a main road or a detour. I have begun to feel, the past year or two, that it is the latter—a detour, but a very important one to me. . . . Until a year or so ago I had felt so at home among this (to me) newfound music that I thought maybe this was what I wanted most. I listened to nothing else, and felt somewhat like a ghost when my compositions were spoken of.

Whether I ever unfold the wings and make a start toward the stratosphere again, and how much of the dust of the road will still cling to me, is an interesting question, at least to me. If I do, I will probably pull up the road with me.[50]

Indeed, it is as if that prolonged yet useful detour for Ruth had finally begun to come to an end. In 1952, writing to a Mr. Ussachevsky, Ruth seemed to reassert her own individuality by noting that she was now going to be known as Ruth Crawford-Seeger.[51] Her intense intellectuality and creativity began to be refocused on her original love—art music composition. She claimed that the many years of work with folk music materials provided a gestation period for thinking about the relations between folk music and art music and for analyzing compositional ideas and techniques in a new light. Yet, her composing in these last five years, and particularly her last piece, the *Suite for Wind Quintet*, written in 1952, shows none of this later folk influence; instead, it recalls her style of the early 1930s.[52]

The exhausting pace of life for the Seegers was immensely fulfilling.[53] As Charles wrote in 1953:

Apparently, one of the things I find most difficult to do—or, more precisely, things I am inclined most to postpone doing—is to give an account of myself and what I have been and am doing. Not that I dislike the task. To the contrary. But it takes a lot of time and one has a tendency to purl along like a summer brook that has nothing else to do. So after doing my biennial stint for "Who's Who in America" and the usual things of that sort, and the quinquennial report of the class of 1908 of Harvard, I rest on my laurels and put requests in that interesting drawer of my desk: to be answered sometime. Not long ago what still remained in such a drawer was thrown away. It had a wedding invitation for some place in India in 1927.

Having retired last February [1953] from the Pan American Union . . . I supposed that by getting off of as many committees and boards as I could I would have time to have a paragraph reach you for the March number of the Hackley Alumni Bulletin. I have never been busier than in the last three months and should not be taking time for this leisurely letter except that I have worked down far enough in the pile to reach yours of February 16th.

I live here in Chevy Chase, Maryland, just over the District of Columbia line in a comfortable old house on a wide tree-shaded street with my wife and four of my seven children, ages 9–19. For the past fifteen years, my interests have been channeled into (a) production of my musicological papers and (b) activity in music organization, especially international. At present, I am setting about making three thin little volumes out of the papers, which need revision (of course) and additions to make rounded wholes of the separate collections.

Embellishing on this, he wrote in his forty-fifth anniversary report to his Harvard class:[54]

My seven children and six grandchildren are all doing well. My wife's books are increasingly successful. My own work takes two directions: one, the drawing together in more definitive form of scattered papers read over several decades; two, the participation in projects of world organization of music interests, activity, and work. . . . These projects of international cooperation are closely backed by a number of United States national organizations in which I have served in varying capacities.

Michael, writing of his father and mother (whom he called "Dio"), spoke of "the pleasure of Charlie and Dio's relationship for both of them and how important it was for both Charlie and Dio to be able to talk of all these issues. They had a very close and physically warm as well as intellectually warm relationship."[55] Little did the Seegers dream that this idyllic existence would so soon and so suddenly end. In the late spring of 1953 Ruth began to be noticeably unwell, and by midsummer she was diagnosed with cancer which, though operable, was considerably advanced. Although their love affair never ended until the day he died, the happy and full life of the Seegers came to a close with the death of Charlie's beloved Ruth November 18, 1953, thus marking a volatile and accomplishing period, professionally, and the happiest time of his life, personally.

7

California Dreaming,

1953–1970

∽

S EEGER'S DEPARTURE from his position at the OAS in 1953, at
the age of sixty-six, did not mean a withdrawal from active life.
More than a quarter century of accomplishment lay ahead for this
polymath; in his later years Seeger refined and produced some of his
most seminal work. Concentrating his creative energies on ethnomusicology, in the last decades of his life Seeger revitalized his name and
stature in the field of academic music, not only by work in this newer
field but also in other areas of music scholarship and technology.

Washington and the nation had been living in the shadow of the
cold war since the end of World War II. While son Peter, now a
successful folk musician and performer, had fallen victim to innuen-
does and accusations,[1] Charles — mindful of his own political involvement during the thirties — was loath to protest the increasing assaults
on civil rights and political freedom.

Seeger felt constrained by his professional responsibilies to remain
quiet. He had been serving in sensitive government positions and also
was keenly aware of his duty vis-à-vis his international musical
affiliations. And he was older and more pragmatic than he had been in
the 1930s: he had a family to support and thus made a conscious
decision not to be an outspoken activist against the repressive spectres
of the times: the House Un-American Activities Committee and the
chief vigilante, Senator Joseph McCarthy. But, with the hysteria
reaching its apex and the stepped-up onslaught on Peter — along with
rest of his well-known singing group, the Weavers, Peter had been
blacklisted — the ominous shadow of the red scare fell over the family.
Seeger feared that the net would soon descend upon him.

As a result of this ugly political atmosphere, as well as his increasing disenchantment with the growing bureaucratization of the international music organizations with which he was involved (see chapter 6), Seeger decided to retire two years earlier than he had planned. He recently had had run-ins with various government agencies and was anxious to avoid trouble and jeopardizing Ruth's very good income.[2] The Pan American Union/Organization of American States, his primary forum, was a sensitive organization, involved as it was with hemispheric politics; Seeger thought that by announcing that "Dr." Seeger was retiring, he might avoid further government harassment.

However, the nation's reactionary political environment encouraged attacks on agency officials such as Seeger, active or retired, and ultimately he became a target. The pretext for the FBI's investigation was that, as a vigorous opponent of the United States' entry into the war during World War I, Seeger had been a conscientious objector and had refused to buy war bonds. But in reality the FBI used those long-ago events as an excuse to interrogate Seeger about his more recent membership in international organizations and alleged connections between that involvement to his decades-earlier activities with the Composers' Collective of New York.[3]

The culmination of the persecution process can be seen in the chronicle of his passport. As a Pan American Union official and one of the founders of the International Music Council, Seeger had possessed a diplomatic passport since 1949, which accorded him the privilege of not having to pass through customs as well as numerous other benefits. In 1951 his passport was renewed, but only as an ordinary passport; then, in 1952, he received only a limited passport. Finally, in 1953 he was refused one entirely, even though he remained a UNESCO representative—one of only three personal or non–government affiliated members—and the recognized founder of UNESCO's infant music group, the IMS, and was scheduled to travel to Belgium to present its constitution.

Only in the last years of Seeger's life was he able to analyze the emotionally intertwined professional and personal tragedies of this crucial, painful period in his life. Not only was his patriotism assaulted; he also bore the burden of Ruth's rapid deterioration and death only three months after the fatal diagnosis. Seeger's response to official harassment revealed a combination of guilt, defiance, and a desire to cover up the past. For many years Seeger seldom spoke of the events of those weeks and months; when he did, it was clear that he was never certain that he had performed properly in the FBI investigation. He had admitted to involvement in the Composers' Collective but, since he had never held membership in the Communist party, he could not admit to having been a Communist. He somehow distanced himself even from his son Peter's affirmed Communist party membership and Stalinist views, and perhaps always felt somewhat guilty for his stance.

Ruth's death in November 1953 left Charles with increased family burdens. Three daughters were still in school: Peggy was at Radcliffe, Barbara was in high school, and Penny was in the sixth grade. In 1954, six months after Ruth's death, Seeger sold the Chevy Chase home and moved with Barbara and Penny to Boston, to be near Peggy.

Feeling that his daughters were still "all too young [for him] to handle," he began to feel a pressure to marry again. At first Seeger was optimistic about reestablishing his acquaintance with an "old girlfriend" who had once been his "valentine." He should have married her in 1911, he said, instead of Constance. Margaret Adams Taylor, a financially secure widow and mother of five children, was now living in Santa Barbara, California. Seeger hoped that by remarrying he would provide his youngest children with security in a new home. Margaret's large family also pleased him: in his enthusiasm he claimed always to have wanted a dozen children—and now with her five and his seven, his wish had come true. They were married in March 1955 and went to live in Margaret's house in Montecito, near Santa Barbara, that summer.

Of this transitory time he noted in his fiftieth anniversary report to the Harvard class of 1908:

Why it took me so long to make the change [regarding musicological work] is more than I can say. Suffice here to report an immersion in the day-to-day struggle of national and, finally, international conflicts. First, in the

Penny, Peggy, Margaret (Seeger's third wife), and Barbara;
Peter and Charles standing

suffocating misery of the depression era in New York City. Second, through government appointments (shades of 1908—a bureaucrat!), it was the same thing in the remote countryside, and then in the cities of the Southeast. Third, by appointment to the Pan American Union, an intergovernmental agency, the same upon a hemisphere scale, but this time with the aid of many national professional organizations, under guidance of the incomparable Vanett Lawler. Finally, after the end of the war, came activity upon a world basis in connection with UNESCO, the International Music Council and various international professional organizations, of some of which I was one of the founders.

Suddenly—not gradually, as had the first—this second life came to an end. Death of the beloved Ruth within three months of diagnosis of unsuspected cancer, my retirement from the Union, from public life in general, and removal from Washington followed in quick succession. Again, in contrast to the end of the first life, the rich and varied life that Ruth and I had built together, the host of friends and professional connections we had made throughout the world and, above all, our brood of four young children, constituted not only a basis for a third life but a moral obligation to lead it.

Then say, O Erato, or maybe Euterpe, Melpomene or even Clio, how shall I sing this third life beginning at the age of threescore and ten? How sing of Margaret, my Valentine of 1900 whom I had seen only once since (in 1911, when I should have married her, instead of 1955, when I did)? I had always wanted twelve children. Now, her five and my seven, all living and doing well, make up the dozen. . . . Jack, if he would cheer up a bit, could make a poem out of it. Alas, I cannot. Suffice to say, that translated to heaven—I mean California—for a second time, if the best is yet to come, I'm ready for it.[4]

Happiness did not endure long; by the end of 1960, the marriage was finished. Seeger commented, "It was nice while it lasted," although later he wrote to his stepson Rufus, "I am trying to . . . forget the whole miserable business."

Back in California, Seeger became acquainted with new developments in music, particularly on the West Coast. Margaret's house had a wonderful study,[5] and it was there that Seeger began seriously to tinker with the melograph, which was to become an important tool at UCLA's Institute of Ethnomusicology.

Seeger had become increasingly interested in the visual graphing of sounds and in his new leisure time began to read widely on this subject, with special interest in the application of technology to the task. One early idea he had was to put electrodes on people while they were making music and listening to music "to find out whether people who hear music hear what music the music maker is making." He had earlier toyed with the idea of an automatic transcription tool in "An Instantaneous Music Notator,"[6] which advanced the idea that a machine could create a graph based on sound frequencies provided by an oscilloscope; the recording device would have separate curves for amplitude and frequency.

Because of his increasing interest in non-notated musics, which form the bulk of repertoires studied by ethnomusicologists, Seeger sought to devise a new transcription tool.[7] In collaboration with his oldest son, Charles, an astronomer at Cornell, Seeger developed an instrument that would allow for the objective transcription and analysis of music. Seeger's invention was based on an idea that technicians had been working on for years. Early in the century, in Russia, Eugenia Eduardovna and others had attempted to capture sounds by ear from recordings by using hand graph notation. In the 1920s, U.S. experiments in "phonophotography" had created hand graphs made by the mathematical reduction of sound wave photographs.[8] And in the early 1950s, a Norwegian researcher named Gurvin had used an oscillogram made by electronic-mechanical reduction and photographed on film,[9] while Alan and Barbara Merriam had devised an oscillogram by electronic-mechanical reduction written directly on paper.[10]

In 1956, Seeger ordered built for him the first electronic music writer in the United States, employing a type of notation useful for both notated and non-notated musics. The melograph, as it came to be known, was designed to meet three basic problems encountered by ethnomusicologists when transcribing from live performances or sound recordings. One was the subjectivity of the transcriber and of each transcriber's perceptions of the same body of music. Another was that conventional notation was not designed for musics of oral traditions. Third, conventional notation could not translate, except in gross terms, the subtleties, qualities, and styles of a given body of sound.

Three models of the Seeger melograph were developed over a fifteen-year period. At first the Bell Laboratories expressed interest in the project, but when support was not forthcoming, Seeger financed model A himself.[11] Soon he and Mantle Hood began to plan for model B. Seeger was interested in using the machine in a broad way.[12] Referring to the earlier "Instantaneous Music Notator"—his attempts to graph instantaneously a single melodic line, its mathematical interpretation, and handwritten graph, so as to permit ready correlation with the auditory sense without using costly and time-consuming photographic apparatus, film development, and printmaking—he commented on what progress had occurred and on work under way in Norway, Switzerland, Belgium, and Italy.

He also presented information on the apparatus, input, response (within which he discussed instantaneity, range, ambit, chart, and accuracy), operation (including information and legibility), and material considerations for producing the melograph. Seeger included nearly two dozen photos of notations made on the machine to demonstrate progress on its development. He observed:

We are working our way, for the first time in history, toward a bona fide universal technique of music-sound-writing. All that is now necessary, besides perfection of the equipment, is to standardize: (1) width of chart; (2) square co-ordinates; (3) two pitch norms (A = 440 and the octave); (4) one time norm (the second, with decimal divisions).

For Indonesian, Indian, and other musics, certain additional items might be investigated. "Graphs on charts of musics other than one's own could be "translated" by reading through a properly calibrated transparent mask laid upon them." And, for Seeger, this was clear:

Our conventional notation will not serve—and we should no longer pretend it can serve—the need of a universal music sound-writing. To no one would I recommend abandonment of traditional techniques of writing music for the novel and still undeveloped graph. For the present, I would urge the two to be used side by side.

In 1958, Hood convinced UCLA to provide $2,500 to construct model B of the melograph. The improved model included filters enabling it to transcribe the singing voice. Soon Hood and Seeger were planning a more advanced model. As Seeger reported:

The Institute of Ethnomusicology has finally been set up here at UCLA and I have a position for research in it that will keep me here a good part of each year. The first task is development of the Model C of my electronic-mechanical melody-grapher, nicknamed the "melograph." First comes the engineering design, for which we have funds; next, the procurement of something like $50,000 to manufacture it; third, development of techniques and procedure of its use. Meanwhile, Models A and B give us occupation in a limited way. [13]

In 1968 the Institute of Ethnomusicology finally received the melograph at a cost of more than $85,000. Model C gave musicologists a universal means of writing single melodic lines and under certain conditions more than one line. While this universal music writing does not do away with specialized writings that are traditional in many musics, it delivers a scientific display of physical fact rather than a normative symbolic representation of the pitch, loudness, speed, relative duration, and tonal density (tone quality) of the phonology of the single line. A model D, which will display also the rhythmic density (if possible), has long been in the planning stage. The device also provides a visible speech that can be read by persons who know the language in which it is spoken or recorded.

The sophisticated model C possesses an electronic sound analyzer that uses computer logic circuitry to produce a photographic record of amplitude, pitch, and spectrum. It offers an amplitude range of forty decibels, a pitch range of seven octaves, a spectral range of 15,000 Herz, and can reproduce thirty minutes of music at a time. The melograph's frequency has a top discrimination of about 1/14 tones and can reproduce rhythm and tempo to show changes with a 1/1,000 margin of error. It also displays accurate fluctuations of the basic pulse represented by notational symbols such as meter and bass.

Seeger assessed the development of the melograph:

There are—or, rather, there have been made—three models. The first, Model A, I had made at my own expense of ordinary components available in 1956 in any radio supply house. It cost me $1000. I gave it to Wesleyan on condition that they would pay for its renovation, which I think they did. I would not recommend having a duplicate made. You would have to buy a sharp filter that would cost three or four hundred dollars more. It is at best a primitive device though it can make a first-rate pitch-time graph of materials that it "likes" or, separately, a loudness graph. The graphs made of the Irish song in IFMC IX were made by it.

Model B was a more sophisticated device and was purchased by UCLA for $2,500. It makes the pitch and loudness graphs simultaneously. I used graphs by it in my MQ [*Musical Quarterly*] paper on "Prescriptive and Descriptive Music Writing" and in the *Selected Reports* of this Institute for the graph of Molly Jackson's "Barbara Allen." This type of device has also been made in Israel, Sweden, and Czechoslovakia. But dated 1962, I would not recommend its duplication. I have directed enquirers about it to Sweden and Israel, where offers to "custom make" copies of their models have been made. I think Indiana bought one from Sweden. The prices run around $4,000–5,000.

I enclose description of our Model C. Designed six years ago, but with refinements added during its five years of building, it is already far below what could be designed today. It does do remarkable things, though. For example, a student here who is working with muezzin singing can read the Arabic words even though he may not have seen or heard them before. . . . It is an enormous thing; big as the console of a five-manual church organ. It could be rebuilt now in one-third the size. It cost us $85,000 but could probably be redesigned and compacted for the one-third size for much less. The manufacturers of all three of our devices is: Research Manufacturing Corporation of San Diego.

As I look at the matter, we want such a device, if it is to be a scientific, precision instrument, to show six factors as the musician knows them: pitch, loudness and density of sound (timbre) and speed, relative proportions of long and short, attack and release, plus rhythmic density. Our Model C does remarkably for the first five. I am working on a project for a Model D that will give also the rhythmic density—number and nature of rhythmic events. . . . One of the most important things you can do with a properly designed one is to hitch it into a computer. Our Model C has five outlets that can be hitched up. But we cannot use them because we lack the little "black box" that must serve as intermediary. It costs $15,000 and we haven't been able to find it. We are told that the larger computers could probably do a better job with visual display than our tricky camera. [14]

Model C has had widespread, successful use and has spawned similar machines used throughout the world. It was experimented with at the UCLA Department of Music and changed somewhat by Professor Nazir Jairazbhoy. After leaving UCLA, Mantle Hood also improved upon it at the University of Maryland. Despite the revolution in the electronic processing of music, the melograph that Seeger developed, and the model C, with which his reputation has stood, was and remains a useful device for study and transcription of non-Western music. It is particularly valuable for recording vocal music because it can display the tone quality of sound as well as provide information on vocal pitch, loudness, vibrato, and ornaments. [15]

Seeger worked on the solutions for years. In the process, he developed ideas that distinguised two types of music notation which he came to call prescriptive and descriptive.[16] In "Prescriptive and Descriptive Music Writing," he refers to the simplest kind of music—unaccompanied melody—and ways to notate it. He describes three hazards inherent in practices of writing music:

The first lies in an assumption that the full auditory parameters of music can be represented by a partial visual parameter, that is, by one with only two dimensions, a flat surface. The second lies in ignoring the historical lag of music writing behind speech writing, and the consequent traditional interposition of the art of speech in the matching of auditory and visual signals in music writing. The third lies in our failure to distinguish between prescriptive and descriptive uses of music writing—between a blueprint of how a specific piece of music shall be made to sound and a report of how a specific performance of any music actually did sound.

He then delineated the differences between prescriptive and descriptive notation. Prescriptive notation, which is subjective, aimed at and reflected in performance, is the type most prevalent in music. Its success or failure hinges on the performer's perception and ability to fulfill the composer's intention through his notation, which is seen to be a variety of mnemonic devices. Descriptive notation is objective; Seeger developed it as a form of graph notation, the use of which could complement prescriptive notation; the machine for producing graph notation was the melograph.

As Seeger observed, part of the problem of notation as it related to folk music was that its tools were developed along with the repertoire of the Western art tradition. The notation system is mixed symbolic (linear) writing in which the symbolic element is the most highly organized and dominates. This type of musical notation is almost entirely prescriptive, emphasizing pitch and meter; when we apply it to music of other cultures, we pick out structures familiar to us in the notation of Western art music and ignore all other music qualities for which we have no symbols. To devise a notation that would consider factors of style and the relation of music to culture, to include function as well as structure, Seeger applied the techniques of the automatic graph which produces a visible notation of any desired aspect of the music. This he called *cantometrics*, methods that provide a means to a descriptive music writing that can be recorded and read with maximum objectivity.

Mantle Hood was Seeger's colleague, champion, and friend for many years. Originally interested in composition, Hood had become intrigued by other musical systems. After studying in Holland with Jaap Kunst, he went to Indonesia, the colonial laboratory for Dutch Studies. After returning to the United States, Hood had begun a fledgling program in ethnomusicology at UCLA in 1954, which combined teaching with performance of Japanese, Persian, Indian, Balinese, Greek, African, and other musics. In 1961 Hood established the Institute of Ethnomusicology at UCLA.

One of Hood's first actions was to have Seeger appointed to a research position at the institute, a position he held until 1971. In Hood's words:

It must have been one of the most remarkable appointments in the history of the University of California, because Charles was in his mid-seventies, by University standards a really difficult age to justify in appointment. He was with the Institute for almost eleven years; and, I learned as he approached his eightieth birthday, the position had to be defended each year before the Board of Regents by the Chancellor.

His invitation to join the Institute was on terms worthy of the man. No duties were required, no responsibilities, no classes or seminars, no publications demanded. He was free to spend his time any way he desired. We hoped he would elect to spend some of it with students; and he did, most freely.[17]

Seeger's new attention to academic music involved him once again in professional organizations. Just as he had been a founder of the American Musicological Society decades before, in his latter years he was again an originator, on the ground floor of the Society for Ethnomusicology (SEM), founded in 1956.

As a pioneer in researching, cataloging, and bringing scholarly attention to folk and American musics, Seeger had long campaigned for the recognition of comparative musicology as a significant academic field. By the late 1940s and into the 1950s, interest in world musics grew and others joined the crusade. (Indeed, in 1954 Seeger urged that the Macmillan encyclopedia of music should include comprehensive coverage of all musics. He declined Oliver Strunk's invitation to be on the steering committee to resuscitate the project, but suggested that Mantle Hood, the rising ethnomusicological scholar at UCLA, should head the AMS committee to oversee the enterprise.)

At the 1952 American Anthropological Association meeting, Willard Rhodes, David McAllester, and Alan Merriam discussed forming an organization to deal with the new interest in musics of the world. Charles Seeger was added to the group because of his organizing genius and international connections. Seeger was not enthusiastic about the implication that the new field was somehow separate from musicology. As he said, "Musicology is the proper name for the study of the music of the world . . . everything in the world. . . . Ethnomusicology is no name for a separate discipline of the study of music."[18]

In the spring of 1953, a slightly larger group began to communicate by mail on the "ways and means whereby the members of our field of study could be brought into closer contact with one another. The problem was whether a new society should be founded, whether the field should be developed as a section within an existing organization or whether communication should be attempted through other means." In a letter dated May 3, 1953, Alan Merriam suggested to George Herzog that a general inquiry be made regarding interest in a "venture" that would consist of a newsletter presenting publications, monographs, and articles, research in progress, and other pertinent items. Such an inquiry was sent to fifty-eight scholars, many of whom became prominent in the field of ethnomusicology. A general letter, signed by Manfred F. Bukofzer, Frances Densmore, Mieczyslaw Kolinski, David P. McAllester, Alan P. Merriam, Willard Rhodes, Curt Sachs, Charles Seeger, Harold Spivacke, and Richard A. Waterman, was mailed to about seventy persons throughout the world. After an enthusiastic response, the first issue of the *Ethnomusicology Newsletter* was sent to three hundred subscribers in December 1953. As the first issue advised, "The development of a permanent organization with a membership, officers, general meetings and a journal depends upon the active support of those who receive this first communication."[19]

Publication of the first three issues was partly paid out of the treasury of the defunct American Society for Comparative Musicology, with the remainder shared by McAllester, Merriam (secretary pro tem), Rhodes, and Seeger. The second newsletter (August 1954) went to 364 persons and institutions — 227 in the United States and 137 in other countries. Subscribers to the third newsletter (December 1954) had grown to 437 persons and institutions — 286 in the United States and 151 abroad. All three issues offered notes and news about people and institutions in the field, information on courses, bibliographies, and a notice that Merriam served as secretary pro tem pending the development of a permanent organization.

The April 1955 newsletter promised definite news in the fall issue concerning a permanent organization and carried the names and addresses of the 472 individuals and institutions receiving it. Finally, the fifth issue (September 1955) noted that "an organizational meeting for the purpose of forming an ethno-musicological society" would be held at the forthcoming American Anthropological Association (AAA) conference in Boston. The meeting was convened on November 18, following the banquet and the showing of an ethnographic film.

Seeger wrote the constitution for the Society for Ethnomusicology, adopted in 1956, and was elected president in 1960.[20] In 1960 he was surprised by a merger proposal from the American Musicological Society, which had earlier scorned the idea of forming an ethnomusicological branch within its ranks;[21] Seeger speculated that the AMS's motive might be to thwart any possible competition for members. On their side, the ethnomusicologists now resisted the idea of a merger, concerned that they would be engulfed by the larger organization. Only Seeger, among the SEM's founding four, favored amalgamation and tried to push it through — to the displeasure of many. He later reflected that he had ruled the society like a tyrant. This was one of many examples of his growing increasingly at odds with an organization he had helped to create and which he felt had gone awry.

Seeger continued to serve the society and was later the first ethnomusicology delegate to the ACLS in January 1967, but soon found himself sparring with the SEM again. In 1969, President Bruno Nettl established a New Directions Committee that was to function as an "idea" group addressing seven issues: annual meetings, education, membership, representation of minority groups, standards for curricula and teachers, reorganization of the society's administrative processes, and general apathy among the membership. Its report was issued at the 1970 SEM meeting. Seeger dissented with the report on several points and, prompted by the accusation from another member at the meeting (who had also objected to the report) that he and others of like mind did not speak up at the time, wrote a lengthy critique, dated December 31, 1970, which he sent to selected members. I present a considerable portion of this letter—not unlike many others written over the years—because it provides considerable insight into Seeger's ideas on numerous subjects.

Seeger acknowledged that he had been remiss in not speaking up, but he had hoped that discussion on the issue would be tabled. Since it was not, he took the opportunity to dissent. He expressed disapproval in three judgments. In his words:

1. The authors of the Report seem not to understand the nature of the learned society in the humanities;

2. The authors seem unfamiliar with the Constitution of the Society for Ethnomusicology;

3. Submission of the Report to the Membership (a) prejudices the authority of the Council of the Society and (b) exhibits a bias contrary to the letter and the spirit of the Constitution. Submission of the Report to a general session without the consent of the Council was inadvisable; without it, out of order.

Before defending these three judgments I wish to state unequivocally that I am 100 percent in agreement with the motivation and objectives of the Committee. . . . It is the *means by which* this motivation is expressed— action by the Society—that I believe is improper, undesirable and impractical.

1. *The Learned Society in the Humanities*

Of all the institutions created by man—excepting, perhaps, the marriage of man and woman—that of the learned society in the humanities is one of the most fragile. It is by nature a kind of marriage: of a field of study and student of it. Typically, it is very small as organizations go in mass societies.

It is organized and functions so that no person recognized by the highest standards as professionally competent in the field will have any qualms about joining it or, once a member, will feel *his freedom of thought and action in, as well as out of, the organization will be in any way hampered or prejudiced*. Scholars are by the very nature of their calling highly individualistic. In their devotion to their study they are often vehemently partisan and biased with respect not only to the affairs intrinsic to study but also to those extrinsic to it in the world at large. To hold . . . such individuals together all possible impediments and sources of prejudice have become gradually eliminated. There remain just three socially organizable functions for the traditional learned society: (a) to bring about meetings of persons; (b) to facilitate discussion; (c) to publish the results of research and study. . . .

Typically, all the great existing learned societies have been founded by scholars, for scholars. Unlike guilds and unions, amateurs and scholars from other fields are usually welcome as members. But these have gravitated around the nucleus of scholars and usually are aware of the fact that only by leaving this nucleus the freedom of action and thought it sought in founding the society and by submitting gladly to its leadership that they may profit from their membership. For they know — or should know — that if either of these conditions are hampered or prejudiced the scholars would resign and form another organization where their object could be pursued in peace. The bulk of the amateurs and professionals from other fields would then melt away, too.

The exploitation of the learned society for purposes extrinsic to its object or the infiltration of ignorance into its councils is, therefore, traditionally avoided. . . . "To promote" anything, "to recommend" anything or anybody, [and other suggestions to provide financial assistance, to arrange for lectures and exhibits, etc., p. 2 of the mimeographed Report] have no place among the functions of a learned society. In the first place, a large paid staff would be necessary. . . . In the second place, any attempt to do such things would turn the society into a business. . . . In the third place, scholars, like other people, hold varied views. It is utterly visionary and impractical to expect that the leadership of any learned society could agree upon or spare the time to administer such a congeries of education, commercial and political enterprise [as has been suggested].

"Recruitment" (p. 4) is not a proper function of a learned society.

2. *The Society for Ethnomusicology*

The Society for Ethnomusicology was founded by four persons who had long regretted that there were no successors to the Gesellschaft fur

Vergleichende Musikwissenschaft and its affiliate, the American Society for Comparative Musicology, and were deeply concerned that the study of music in the Western World was dominated by a Europocentric viewpoint and a social-classcentric bias. These four persons paid for publication and distribution (gratis) of a mimeographed newsletter for three years, 1953–56. They never sought or expected reimbursement. After surrounding themselves with a few like-minded persons professionally interested in music as a worldwide form of human behavior and communication, they founded the Society for Ethnomusicology. Scholars of many "races, creeds, colors, and national origins" and national citizenship joined. The field of interest of this aggregate had already become one in which well-intentioned amateurs and some out-and-out charlatans had been active. To assure control of the new organization by serious and capable students, they wrote a constitution and served in predetermined succession as the first four presidents. The Constitution was built around a Council composed of "persons who are scholars and have contributed to the object of the Society" (Art. IV.A). The object of the Society was and still is "advancement of research and study in the field of ethnomusicology" (Art. II). Article IV.B. states, "The Council shall determine the general policies of the Society." If this does not mean "directions" new, current, old, what does it mean? . . . In short, *the Council is the seat of power in the Society*. In our Society, as in any other viable learned society, if the nucleus of scholars—about one hundred in our case—ever gives up or adulterates this concentration of power, the Society *as a company of scholars* will cease to function as such. . . . And our Report asks, "Do we need the Council? What specific role does it play in the administration of the Society? Should the membership play a more direct role in administering the Society?" Did it never occur to the authors of the Report that the answers to these questions were already in the Constitution of the Society? . . . Are they not wasting their and their fellow members' time by this putsch, for that is what it seems to be?

3. *The Question of Parliamentary Order*

(a) One hazard in such a putsch lies in the unleashing of divisive factionalism, always latent in all groups, particularly of such individualistic persons as students who not only love study but love what they study, in our case, the beautiful musics of the world. There is already a very delicate balance in our Society between the two principal kinds of scholarly approach to this object as stated in its Constitution: that from outside the universe of music; . . . and that from inside the universe of music. . . . We can be trusted, under the leadership of the best we have in the Society, to keep a fair balance between these two equally important approaches. . . . Instead of saying "the Society should do this, do that," we should do it ourselves.

The Report is unrealistic, whatever one thinks of the worth of its objectives. And it seems that its authors were not aware of the fact that it invades the authority of the Council, which was set up precisely to formulate and keep check upon the directions in which the Society should move or might be moving. On this account, therefore, I find *the Report is out of order*.

(b) The Report is also out of order in that it proposes to inject into the affairs of the Society only the United States national aspects of present world crises of race and color, of poverty and injustice, of minorities and majorities, of youth and age. How many of us realize what the Committee has done? *The Report is starkly nationalcentric*, an attempt to put us back into the 19th century—a strange happenstance for an organization pledged to the opposing of centrism of all kinds! I hate to think of what will be thought of it in other countries. Although to best of present understanding no formal statement of its position with regard to the concepts "national" and "international" have been made by it, the Society is indeed *national in form*. It was founded by citizens of the United States in Philadelphia, Pennsylvania. . . . But it is clearly *international in content*. Its interest is worldwide. Its Constitution does not provide for representation by nationality.

I cannot bring this critique of the Report of the New Directions Committee to a close without endorsing some of its recommendations that are eminently practical and desirable. By all means let us set up an Archive and a post of Archivist. . . . Let us have more papers and panels on ethnomusicology and current events and movements. And let us have more sessions at which papers are distributed well ahead of meetings, with discussions of them *viva voce*. (But none, please more than twenty minutes. Thirty is too long.) And let us memorialize the Council to set up a *Long Term Planning Committee* (a much better name than "New Directions") with special emphasis upon our relations with other learned societies, institutions of learning, libraries and archives throughout the world, and upon *ways and means of preserving our identity and continuity in the face of counterrevolution and repression from outside and above, no less than of putsches from inside and below*. But let us remember: a learned society—and the Society for Ethnomusicology is on the way to being one—is not a completely democratic organization. As a cold matter of fact, it is constituted by a formally non-democratic hierarchy of four classes: scholars of recognized repute; student members who may be candidates for such repute; amateurs and professionals from other fields who are interested but not involved as are these two classes; and subscribers to publications, status seekers and mere "joiners." Within each class there is formal democracy; but between classes, there is not. Informally, that is socially, there is—and should be—complete democracy. Membership is exceptionally cheap: payment of dues and nonobtrusive behavior at meetings. Councillorship is the goal of the serious student member. . . . Such extremism as is evidenced in most of the "new directions" of this Report and in the procedures for following them recommended in it must surely be against the better judgment of the majority of Councillors, so that the only way of implementing them would be by physical force. . . .

I am not sending you this critique of the Report . . . for publication or to promote a counter-putsch, but only to have its content and implications as thoroughly understood as possible—and to friends whose discretion I think I can trust. For not all Members have taken the Report seriously enough to think the thing through so as to be aware of the trouble it may still bring to the Society.

This critique asks neither for answer nor acknowledgment.[22]

In addition to work on the melograph and music technology, Seeger's seven years of research prior to his appointment at UCLA had resulted in papers that thrust in several directions, undertaken without benefit of institutional support or affiliation. Refining earlier ideas, Seeger wrote of the relationship of European and American music, of the dominance of high art over folk art, the responsibility of educators to make America musical, and the importance of folk music in American society.[23] Seeger claimed that vast majorities of the populations of even the most highly industrialized societies are still musically illiterate. "Music can be *made for* these majorities through written techniques. But it still can be *made by* them only through oral techniques. That a majority will long remain content exclusively with music *made for it* is now to be doubted." Seeger laid responsibility for music illiteracy with educators who "joined the forces of destruction and by condemnation and ridicule sought to substitute, throughout the areas it can influence, not only the products but even the process of the written tradition for those of the oral."

In an article extremely important for its awakening of his identity, "Music and Class Structure in the United States,"[24] Seeger attempted to document the start of the integration of musical traditions and idioms in American culture. He focused on "two large historical processes that have taken place throughout the New World since the advent of the Europeans": first, *acculturation*, or "prolonged contact of *masses* of individuals carrying different musics; the "second has accompanied the prolonged contact of these same individuals in new societies thus formed, but in their roles as members of social *classes* carrying different music-social traditions." Seeger argued that American musical life had been neatly polarized along the lines of class structure and that there has been in America, and consequently with its music, a neo-European class structure and a classless, Euro-American egalitarian society. At first, folk art survived "in the colonies upon a broad basis of general social use, both urban and rural. . . . The fine and popular arts, however, could not be given the professional cultivation and patronage, the material plant and equipment that had serviced them in the mother countries." He implied that in tandem with the development of the United States came also the development which would "make the once new American way of musical life become the old," under the auspices of members of the well-to-do classes (or those who aspired to be), the "make-America-musical movement."

[The adherents of the] make-America-musical group, with its fine art, were comparatively few but they became highly organized and very aggressive. The sell-America-music group [music publishers, instrument makers, concert managers, i.e., the music industry] with its popular art, likewise was secure in its profits and urban compactness. The rural population that carried the folk tradition was large. But owing to its seclusion . . . was not . . . extensively subjected either to being converted to "good" music or being sold the "bad."

Seeger noted the changes in these counterprocesses, with the appearance of mechanical and electrical projection of music and the transformation of the two pressure groups:

It seems to me that it was the sell-America-music group, composed of manufacturers, merchants, bankers, and engineers, which by large-scale exploitation of the new means of mass communication served as the catalytic agent in bringing together not only the art and the industry but the three principal music idioms I have distinguished and the classes consuming them and, in musical terms at least, set back the nearly successful drive to create a purely neo-European music class structure in the United States. Big business was—at least until about 1950 (since then it has become more autocratic)—more of a democraticizing than an authoritarian agent in music. . . . One of the largest—perhaps the largest—single market became the public school.

The rapprochement of the urban music idioms and business organizations that exploited them, Seeger observed, had left behind the rural population and its old-time folk songs and dance tunes, and neither of the urban pressure groups "gave back to the rural areas exactly what they had taken from it." He added, "It is risky to compare music with speech fuunctions in any society" and then provided a dense, nearly one-page-long assessment of literacy/illiteracy, passive/active, recreative/creative elements among the various classes. He concluded:

A general rule in the subaccultruation of music idioms seems to be that the receiving (or taking) class must add something of its own to the products of the donor (or taken from) class [which produced it so that] the net result as I see it, might be said to be that the United States is beginning to come of age musically speaking [and that]. . . . From a situation in which music values were imprisoned in mutually exclusive compartments of an increasingly rigid class structure, we seem to be moving into one in which the formation of a unitary music idiom may be taking place.

In tandem with and intertwined with his interest in American studies, theoretical and methodological concerns with folk music comprised a major dimension of Seeger's work during this period. His was the main entry in *Grove's Dictionary* on "Folk Music: USA,"[25] a densely woven essay. He began with the statement that one could not speak of a single American or United States folk music, but that one could speak

(1) about the survival, in oral tradition within the U.S.A., of various European folk musics; (2) about the acculturation of these among themselves and among survivals of *primitive* music idioms within the area; and (3) about their relation to the development in the New World of *popular* and *fine art* music idioms of European provenance.

Peter and Charles, Los Angeles, 1962

Further, he contended that in the United States we can accept the propositions that "(1) dominant folk music traditions are European; (2) secondary traditions of increasing importance are African; (3) while American-Indian traditions are isolated, fragmentary and probably recessive."

The article is packed with information presented elsewhere with different refinements, but here offered as a comprehensive single statement.[26] After a brief chronology of the development of a folk music tradition, Seeger detailed the characteristics of each tradition and how they differed, the rise and development of certain traditions, the best sources available for each, and the prominent scholars and performers of each tradition and category. He concluded,

It may appear that a general integration of an American music — folk, popular and fine art — is eminent; . . . the fact of survival, at all, of some ancient traditions in the U.S.A. has stimulated a movement of revival that cannot but affect the course of that survival. . . . The nature and extent of the revival is strongly affected by the study, both amateur and professional. The relationship between written and oral traditions, not only in music but in speech as well, thus becomes the key problem. Whether these two opposed forms of tradition (that continually borrow from one another) should or must continue to exist side by side has never been thoroughly investigated. [Here he refers readers to his 1950 article, "Oral Tradition."] If, as there is some reason to believe, there are involved not only two techniques but two ranges of content, it can be readily seen that our whole concept of the nature of the art of music and its history must be broadened and more closely integrated with the study of culture as a whole. It is to such studies, therefore, that the question posed in the first paragraph of this section must finally be referred: whether or not the repertory of oral music tradition in the U.S.A., or any part of that tradition, can be termed a true folk music of that politically defined area or whether it merely belongs to the vague class called *populaire* by French scholars—that is to say, "of the people," though not necessarily "ancient," "primitive," or of a centuries-old lowest possible social class.

A decade later, Seeger offered "Folk Music,"[27] which contained the basic elements of his *Grove's* piece, with additional insights from research completed since publication of the earlier article. Part 1 was divided into several telling subsections: "The Origins of Folk Music," with subcategories entitled "The Importance of Oral Transmission" and "Folk-Song Study." He surveyed "The Vitality of the Folk Tradition" and "Factors Making for Change," with subcategories "Verbalization, Industrialization, and Professionalism"; "The Future of Folk Music;" and "Classification." In "European Folk Music" he wrote on eastern Europe, including Russia and the Balkans, south-western Europe, and northwestern Europe. Finally, in "The Diffusion of European Music Traditions" he discussed Latin America, within which he commented on African influences; in "English-Speaking America" he highlighted "Contemporary Developments" and "Other Diffused Music Traditions." This article discussed folk music quite differently from the more scholarly *Grove's* article, demonstrating that Seeger could address a less academic readership.

Seeger expanded on his work in American studies, American music, and folk music instruments and songs. "The Appalachian

Dulcimer"[28] includes historical and technical information on the development of the instrument — its construction, origin, and ancestors, how it was played, and how (judging from field recordings) it might sound. He was enamored of the Appalachian dulcimer as a "pure" folk instrument: it functioned (was constructed and played) "within the currency of an oral tradition of music and no printed directions for its manufacture or notations of its playing have appeared."

In "Singing Style," Seeger emphasized the importance of folk musicians (and others) in America and indicated how they should be studied.[29] Although he acknowledged that most musicians and folklorists would have a rudimentary idea of what is meant by *singing style*, he proposed

a theoretic base comprising four equally important categories of data, any one of which can be approached from either extrinsic or instrinsic viewpoints. . . . These four categories comprise data: 1. of the culture-community in which the tradition of song flourishes; 2. of the singer who carries the tradition; 3. of the repertory; 4. of the singing style.

Anthropology, ethnology, and communications theory may be relied upon to handle the first category; physics, physiology and psychology, the second; linguistics and musicology, jointly and separately, the third and fourth.

In analyzing these data and in reference to category two (the singer), Seeger was already well into his work on phonophotography; he discussed the singer who carries the tradition through noting the electronic aids available to capture the techniques of this process. He explained that in equating and integrating extrinsic and intrinsic viewpoints and data lay the answer to getting the humanities out of the doldrums, and he intended to use singing style as an example. He proposed three sets of hypotheses for treating as a single unit the structural and functional aspects of speech and music in song that appeared to be *identical*, *similar*, and *different*. Commenting on each hypothetical framework, he provided a brief account of the problems encountered in studying singing style. As he summed it up:

I have cited: first, the ease with which a rudimentary notion of it can be formed and refined; second, the four main categories of data whose identification, pertinence, and evaluation must be assessed before this notion can be organized as the kind of concept required by serious study; third, the importance of attaching equal weight to extrinsic and intrinsic viewpoints and methods of study; fourth, the intimate synthesis of speech and music in song; fifth, the problem of isolating the factors of repertory and singing style—what is sung and how it is sung; sixth, I have proposed three sets of working hypotheses for the distinguishing of the roles of speech and music in song as, respectively, identical, similar, and different. . . .

The details of singing style as recognized by the ear of the student and of the singer (especially when anyone transgresses the limitations of the tradition he carries) are on the one hand too fine for verbal expression in terms of existing music theory, which concerns itself very little with the single melody, and on the other, too coarse for the delicate equipment of the psychophysical laboratory. The task here, it seems to me, is to refine the music theory and to coarsen the technological aids until they meet at a point where they both match the auditory sense. . . . In separate papers I have described electronic equipment for the instantaneous graphic representation of the unaccompanied song together with its singing style by a strictly descriptive sound-writing and differentiating between it and our conventional symbolic music notation.

Seeger noted that sophisticated electronic means were being developed that would advance the analysis of singing style. While considerations of repertoire lie above the threshold of consciousness, he observed, those of singing style lie chiefly below it; that is, he saw folk songs functioning on both the conscious and subconscious level.

Seeger's investigations into folk and American musics had a dual focus: on *singing style* and *speech plus song*. Of his articles on these topics, perhaps the two most important were "Versions and Variants of Barbara Allen" (1966) and "The Folkness of the Nonfolk vs. the Nonfolkness of the Folk" (1966). "Barbara Allen" is a "repertory" study, an analysis of speech plus song, not of singing style, and is the most comprehensive examination of a single ballad and its numerous versions.[30] Seeger used seventy-six recordings of the ballad, made on unsophisticated equipment, to notate numerous traditional singing styles. He concluded that considering present knowledge and the state of research techniques, "No such entity as "*the* 'Barbara Allen' tune" can be set up other than for temporary convenience," and that with "a few intermediate steps we can easily change one version into the other." His basic points were that musical folklore should turn to variants; that individual performance is very important; and that performance style is more important than pitches and note durations. He conceived of folk songs as a process, not structure, a creative item, not an artifact.

If "Barbara Allen" was a paean to American music and American studies, "The Folkness of the Nonfolk vs. the Nonfolkness of the Folk" was a more abstract and theoretical expression of Seeger's ideas on folk art as a musical and social phenomenon.[31] One familiar target was the dichotomy in U.S. musical culture between the masses and the elite that has fostered a belief that "one is worth more than the other and the two have nothing in common." Seeger acknowledged differences in attitude toward the study of folk art and high art, but also believed that all scholarly fields have more than their share of folklore.

Following both a structural and a functional approach, Seeger spoke of his "very general realization of the widened and widening gulf between a rapidly changing urban variant of the culture, and a slowly stabilizing rural variant of that culture. For at least a century, individual carriers of each variant had been groping for what they felt they had lost and were losing." The essay, a delightful piece, discusses how the folk appropriate all the nonfolkness they can assimilate, and the nonfolk patronize much of the folk: "Nonfolkness is that which tries not to be folkness"; "folkness is that which knows of no more nonfolkness than it can try to be. . . . Perhaps the two are not mutually exclusive opposites but overlapping complements or, perhaps, two aspects of one unbroken continuum." He ends, "Musically speaking, the people of the United States are divided into two classes: a majority that does not know it is a folk; a minority that thinks it isn't."

Seeger also expressed in print his continuing concern for ownership and legitimate rights in the music sphere.[32] It began with a call to battle: although "only a few feeble voices have spoken up for the integrity of folklore," "Now is a time for all folklorists of good will to step forward and pledge their agreement in substance with Mr. Legman's impassioned attack upon the nefarious practice of 'copyrighting' folk songs." He saw the problem under two different aspects—the legal and the ethical. "They are inextricably intertwined." Because the verbal and melodic texts of conventional popular or fine art songs can be protected by copyright, he wrote, some believe that this applies to folk song as well. "Of course, what we should all look forward to would be a really knotty question of whether the two tunes are the same tune or two different tunes. . . . *What we need is a law penalizing deliberate intent to claim copyright in an item known to be in the public domain.*"

More important for Seeger, however, was that no law "respects the basic rights at issue. Fundamentally, these laws are all exclusively concerned with the rights of individual carriers of a socio-cultural tradition of communication and they pay no attention to the basic equity of that tradition's source. They ignore the continually chang-ing succession of individual, mostly unknown, carriers of a bundle of traditions, millions living at the time of any copyright claimant, millions of others dead or not yet born."

On the printing, performance, and release of pressings of collec-tanea, Seeger took exception to Legman's pathetic portrayal of singers such as Molly Jackson and other "unpaid" informants of the profes-sional and amateur folklorist by asking:

Were they not all themselves collectors? Did they not build their consider-able repertories by a method similar to that of the folklorist collectors? Of course they did. Some gave credit. . . . Some claimed they composed the song themselves. . . . Most singers, however, just appropriated. And many of them picked up money for the retailing of their collectanea. . . . The early singers for the commercial recording companies . . . made what was considered good money in their day. Their disciples still do.

Seeger also referred to people who concerned Legman:

If the Lomaxes, like many others, make money from their books incorporat-ing their own collectanea and from anthologies of the garnerings of other collectors, it can be said, I believe, that they deserve their profits. It takes a lot of work to make a good anthology. But that is where, ethically, the moneymaking should stop.

One surely has a right to claim copyright in a table of contents, an arrangement of titles, one's headnotes, or in editorial and critical comment. But one has no right to try, thereby, to limit the normal currency of a folk song unless one has "arranged and adapted" it beyond all semblance of folk song — in which case it is a fraud to publish it as a folk song. Furthermore, if one places in the headnote or comment "adapted and arranged by . . ." and then prints below it a variant of a song as like two dozen other singings recorded thirty years earlier as peas in a pod, one is just as guilty of fraud as if one placed on sale a "harmless" sleeping pill that in reality was chock full of barbituates.

The *diabolus ex machina* in this miserable business is, I surmise, the publisher, the recording company, the broadcasting office, or the lot.

Seeger then warned that in being agitated by the activities of urban collectors, we should be careful not to impute ownership of folk song to rural collectors. He suggested that the repertory of Anglo-American folk song belonged to all Americans. He agreed with Legman that all serious students have a responsibility on this issue and he concluded with three suggestions:

1. AS A MATTER OF FACT, no one can be enjoined from "doing anything he pleases to or with a folk song" . . . as far as the singing and playing of it is concerned.

2. AS A MATTER OF LAW, copyright should not subsist in the texts of any folk song or in that of any song published as a folk song. In either case, statement of claim of copyright should be penalized as fraudulent.

3. AS A MATTER OF ETHICS, payment should be given at the source when payment is expected to be received, or as it is received, from the profits. . . . In any case, the representation of it in written, printed, or recorded form should be accompanied by due credit line to the source, regardless of any considerations of payment or nonpayment.

N.B. 1. Acoustic dubbing of a particular singing or playing or recording thereof should be licensed under a more general law comprehending a larger aggregate of which folk song is only one item.

N.B. 2. No person can compose a folk song. Consequently, he should not label a composition "a folk song." A composed song may become a folk song, but only by currency among the people, and by a process of aging and adaptation.

Seeger also brought together some ideas on folk, American, and Latin American musics.[33] He pursued his argument about "the hegemony of European culture," noting the trend toward interdependence of Neo-Europeanism and Euro-Americanism into a single, integrated occidental music. He thought that a worldwide vernacular might develop through the influence of mass communications and oral/aural transmission; a methodology was needed to enable scholars to study the acculturation process, not simply in Europe and America, but also in the Americas with African and Amerindian influence. Again displaying his predilection for the vertical, for the north-south axis, he noted two major trends that had affected the acculturation process in the Americas: mass communication and the tendency for ideas to move on an east-west, west-east continuum. His constant questioning of the meaning of music within the American context early on made him the first to define *a distinctly American and modern approach to the study and organization of music*.

Seeger also dealt with hierarchy and social and cultural values in relationship to music, with Latin America as a focus; he shared the notion that collective values, as evinced in folk traditions, should rank more highly than individual values, as reflected in art music. Malena Kuss holds that this 1961 article represented a change in Seeger's thinking about Latin American music since 1946, as well as his belief (to which she took exception) that Latin American art music should be studied ethnomusicogically.[34] Always concerned with acculturative processes, in "Cultivation" Seeger featured transplantation as the context for discussion of Latin American musics, identifying three stages of European music transplantation as traditions, individuals, and reinsemination.

Above all, what emerged in "Cultivation" were two central themes present in all his writings on Latin America. One was a concern to develop an approach to Latin American music that would account for the acculturation of all native American music traditions with the traditions of European art music (a synthesis he suggested would provide an integrated and diverse neo-European tradition of occidental music). The other theme focused on the need to investigate how transplanted European music traditions established their dominance over both native American and imported African traditions in Latin America by assessing the impact of the transplantation on the music composed in Latin America from the time of the Conquest to mid-twentieth century.

Seeger always worked to bridge communications between ethnomusicology and musicology by analyzing precisely what (as he understood it) transpired in the study of music. He presaged his appointment at UCLA's Institute of Ethnomusicology with two major articles: "On the Moods of a Music Logic" and "Semantic, Logical, and Political Considerations Bearing Upon Research in Ethnomusicology."[35]

The first was a proposition for a system of pure "musical logic" based on the function of compositions, a system founded on "analysis as design" (form), and "synthesis as logic" (compositional process), as modes and moods/emotions in music. Seeger set up a series of symbols as guidelines for discussing musical processes and the moods implied by them. He noted that throughout history the Western world has been in "persistent search for a rationale for its music" both in terms of "the inner organization of its compositional process as in the outer organization in the communities that have cultivated it." Speaking of musicology in the West, Seeger said, the inner order, or form, of Western music was most frequently seen as design borrowed from visual art, and less so as logic, a speech factor. The concept of design dealt with structural and spatial aspects of order in music, while the concept of logic considers the functional and temporal aspects of music order. He posited that "a gap exists between any effective analysis as design and any affective synthesis as logic." The two concepts should seem equally valid to the musicologist, since

both require identification of units of form: design, in an order from large to small; logic, from small to large. What the concepts refer to, surely is, in the hands of the competent musician not too dominated by speech-thinking, equally one single collection of maximal units into medial and medial into minimal, and of minimal units combinable into medial and medial into maximal.

Once the maximal unit has been established for design, as for example, a symphony in four movements, or the minimal, for logic, its initial measures or so, a vast number of possibilities of intension and extension present themselves. . . .

With the intension of analysis as design and the extension of synthesis as logic into the body of a product, the degree of uncertainty increases, that is, the uncertainty in the speech report of the progress of the two speech concepts. We cannot assume that the separate functioning of the two concepts in a speech rationale of music is the same as the integration of the two—or whatever must be the music process so referred to—in the actual operation of a music rationale. To the best of present knowledge, no documentation of the music compositional process has been made.

Seeger proposed that the units of music design and music logic can be regarded as identical and can be represented in a speech rationale as a single, partly closed system, made equally of patterns of design and moods of logic.

Ideally, a completely new terminology should be invented for the presentation of such a system. But mindful of the resentment that often greets such innovations, I shall concentrate upon its treatment as a logic, using a minimal vocabulary of terms borrowed from speech logic. This is done for three reasons. First, although the concept of design has beeen conventionally the more exploited with the study of musical form, the general concept of logic has been given in recent years far more comprehensive and precise general theoretical development. And, a logic is prerequisite to an overall rationale. Second, the term *design* has been used more for pedagogical purposes, especially in inexpertly verbalized courses in "music appreciation." Third, the term *logic*, in referring to the compositional processes of both speech and music, implies an approach in the order in which products are actually presented to a receiver and, so, received by him, that is, from a beginning, through a cursus to an end.

A book could be written about this article; this summary merely provides some guideposts by which the reader can acquire a grasp of Seeger's proposition. The article is organized into several sections with titles indicating the categories by which he developed his idea: "The Speech-Concept of a Music-Logic"; "Speech Logics and Music Logic"; "Compositional Functions—Direction and Extent of Variance"; "Compositional Functions in Minimal Extension"; "Compositional Functions in Medial and Maximal Extensions"; "Formation of the Basic (Minimal) Binary and Ternary Moods by Variance of Direction and/or Extent of their Constituent Progressions"; and "Inflection of the Twelve Basic Binary and Ternary Moods by Variance in Direction of Tonal Progression and in Extent in Rhythmic Progression." Seeger also provided six tables and twenty-seven music and graphic examples to highlight his analyses.

He argued that it should be possible to describe in the art of speech a factor in the art of music that serves as a counterpart of the factor in the art of speech known as *logic*—that is, music logic. To him, identities (homologies) are very general; similarities (analogies) somewhat less so; and differences (heterologies) more concrete and of two distinct categories: those that can be clearly distinguished and those that cannot be, but of necessity must be inferred. It might be said that music is, above all, affirmation, truth, and concordance. He found that the moods of a music-logic are best described in terms of a minimal vocabulary about two-thirds drawn from homologues and analogues current in general speech use, and one-third from music—technical terms. Seeger structured his system from the smallest unit of form in music—that initial unit or mood of music-logical form—to the measure, phrase, double-phrase, period, double period, part of a section, section, and finally to the entire piece. His idea was that "at the level of the section, the point had been reached where synthesis seems to be a prescription in speech that is belied by the music process supposed to fill it out." Such prescription in speech required new symbols and terms.

In this analysis, value in the abstract is the equivalent of a fact; that is, it is a concept, in the universe of speed discourse.[36] There are several dispositions:

   a. accept musicians' knowledge of music-discourse universe;

   b. regard units of form of a music-logic as compared to those of speech-logic;

   c. report on those units as facts or data for a *science of music* (or, more precisely, music-communication);

   d. regard combo and transformation of these units of form in any particular music-communicatory product as act of free will by a producer;

   e. report on such production as evidence for a *critique of music*, therefore

   1. music compositional process may be equally music-scientific and music-critical;

   2. unitary music-presentation can be dealt with only successively in speech-presentation, i.e., as either music-fact or music-value, but

3. a music-tradition is what is at any given time and place as a result equally of its having been recognized by past generations of musicians as a fact—a traditional way of doing things—and of its having been used by them for communication of value;

4. the extent that past generations adhered to norms of traditions they contribute to continuity; as they depart, they contribute to variation;

5. both continuation and variation of traditions are a result of music-critical activity;

6. study of music-compositional style equally scientific and critical;

7. critique reaches back to domain of science for definition of possible and available patterns and moods, variants and qualifications;

8. science can reach into critique for probability that one variety will be selected rather than some other in any particular case.

When he first wrote "Moods" (about 1956), Seeger believed that a completely new terminology should be invented for the presentation of such a system, but felt that it would be unacceptable to the music establishment. When he reworked the essay in June 1976, he believed that "comparative (ethno-) musicology has advanced to a point where it would support a proposal that a universal music lexicon could be organized along the lines of such a music logic."

"Semantic, Logical, and Political Considerations Bearing Upon Research in Ethnomusicology" focused on the variety of definitions of ethnomusicology and the problems created by such diversity.[37] He developed three major categories:

1. Semantic. Two meanings of the term "ethnomusicology" are current. One equates the prefix "ethno-" with the adjective "ethnic," meaning "barbarous, non-Christian, exotic"; the other, with the prefix "ethno-" as in ethnology. The former implies that the study now known as "ethnomusicology" is limited to musics *other* than the student's *own*; the latter, that it is limited to the cultural functions of music. Both of these meanings lead to unacceptable situations when applied to a musicological discipline *as a whole*; the first, because, in accord with it, if the study of a student's own music is to be known as musicology, the same music studied by another student who does not carry its tradition, must be known as "ethnomusicology"; the second, because no relatively independent academic discipline can be expected to confine itself to the view of a thing *in a context* to the exclusion of the view of the *thing in itself*.

Seeger recommended that the first meaning of *ethnomusicology* be discouraged and that the second clarified in the strict sense to refer to a *view* and in the broader sense to a *study* or discipline. Ethnomusicology, in these terms, is a study of music in a culture and music in view of itself.

Under "Logical," Seeger noted that we accept the axiom that the view of any area in its contexts and in itself is equally relevant. Further, music must be observed in three general classes of context: as concept, as phenomenon, and as medium of communication. Grappling once again with the speech-music problem, Seeger suggested that "it is not logical, therefore, to attempt to organize music-research in too close association with the universe of speech-discourse and its traditional home, the occidental university. . . . On the other hand, it would not be logical to attempt to organize music-research entirely apart from the universe of discourse and its modern offspring, speech-study of the universe of nature." He recommended that "the optimum relationship between speech- and music-techniques in ethnomusicology would seem to be one of half-independence and half-interdependence, in which the limitations of speech-conceptualism and speech-phenomenalism must be unremittingly subjected to question and non-definition."

Under "Political," Seeger proposed that the study of music throughout the West has been dominated by speech, Eurocentrism, the idiom of the learned or elite art, and the past rather than present practice of that idiom. Because the intersection of conventional (European) historico-musicology and ethnomusicology has been under way since 1950, the time (1961) was ripe for a push to remove the remaining barriers. Seeger noted that "prerequisite to both of these objectives is more general recognition of the fact that continuation of the custom of regarding musicology and ethnomusicology as two separate disciplines, pursued by two distinct types of student with two widely different—even mutually antipathetic—aims is no longer to be tolerated as worthy of Occidental scholarship." His recommendation:

Whether organized independently or within a university, integrated ethnomusicological-musicological research should be continually on guard against the encroachment of the hidden assumption that speech knowledge can comprehend all knowledge and can or should control the use of all knowledge. Organized within a university, it should be afforded an exceptional degree of independence or administrative self-autonomy. In any case, it would be *in fact* musicological in the strict sense of the word, . . . including in its purview all musics in all their idiomatic diversification, their internal relations and external relations, and above all their interrelations in all relevant contexts. But it would probably have to bear, for the present, at least, the designation "ethnomusicological" alone. For if the term "musicological" were used, or even if both terms were used in conjunction (perish the thought!), there would still be a possibility that the "disease of excessive historicism" (as Constantin Brailioiu put it), would take over and invalidize the new departure envisaged here. Eventually, when preoccupation with the musical museum has somewhat abated, as it surely will, and has taken a secondary place in proper perspective to the overall study of music, the prefix "ethno-" could be dropped.

During his years at the institute, Seeger undertook research and wrote on a number of areas of interest to him, bringing to fruition new ideas and refining old ones. His work on the melograph culminated there, with the availability of money, facilities, personnel, and most important the graduate students and their professors whose fieldwork provided the raw material for the melograph laboratory. Hood referred to the core of his twenty-five-year friendship with Seeger as the eleven years at the institute, with Hood, Seeger, and Klaus Wachsmann joined by fellow faculty from various departments at UCLA, as well as visiting colleagues from around the world. As Hood recalled, Wachsmann once referred to those years at UCLA as "the Golden Age of ethnomusicology." Further reflecting on that time, Hood said,

Thanks especially to Seeger's penetrating probing, reasoning and logic the horizons of all participants in the Wednesday seminar kept expanding in all directions. In the field of music he was our unique crystalographer of words, of the very art of speech—in conversation, in eloquent argument, in the written word. The memory of his presence and its catalytic powers on ideas and discussion are still with us.[38]

Although Seeger continued to be active personally and professionally in a range of enterprises, the bulk of his time and energy at the institute was directed toward the philosophical and theoretical considerations of music in general and musicology in particular. Such essays as "Music as a Tradition of Communication, Discipline and Play" (1962), "On the Tasks of Musicology" (1963), "The Music Process as a Function in a Context of Functions" (1966), "Tradition and the (North) American Composer" (1967), "Factorial Analysis of the Song as an Approach to the Formation of a Unitary Field Theory for Musicology" (1968), "On the Formational Apparatus of the Music Compositional Process" (1969), and "Toward a Unitary Field Theory for Musicology" (1970) addressed various components of his overall concern.

In "Music as a Tradition of Communication, Discipline and Play"[39] Seeger's hypothesis was that the three terms in the essay's title—among which there was no accepted hierarchy—should be considered as underlying all others and thus could be "useful to a rational approach to the study of music in any or all of its aspects, from any viewpoint, in any manner, for any purpose. Succinctly stated, it could read: people make music, why? to communicate; what? a discipline; how? by play." As with "Semantic, Logical and Political Considerations," Seeger's essay advanced a series of propositions. The first part again confronted the speech-communication and music-communication dilemma, with a subsection entitled "Concepts and Conceptual Operative Techniques Necessary for the Description of a Tradition of Music as Communication" that included an additional set of propositions. Seeger summarized:

Thus far, in this paper, I have begun formulation of an interdisciplinary vocabulary for an integrated textual-contextual approach to the study of music as a tradition of communication. Part II will continue this formulation and will deal with the concepts of discipline and play together, for distinction between them should not, perhaps cannot, be finely drawn. Eventually, it may be found that in music itself the distinction is often only speech-made, occasional, trivial or non-existent. As a speech-concept, discipline is understood to be a system by which a traditional order is maintained in the activity of the individual man and of the society of which he is a member, toward some significant end; play, the exercise of the capacities for activity, of the society no less than that of the individual member of it, in which that activity is limited only by the nature of the capacities for it, regardless of any end. Contextually to music, both concepts may have well-defined socially organized referents: discipline, as ritual; play, as game. Either, in excess, may serve for dissipation: the one, as regimentation; the other, as entertainment.

"On the Tasks of Musicology"[40] was a brief commentary written in response to "Purposes of Ethnomusicology" by Alan Merriam, the preeminent American anthropologist-ethnomusicologist of his era, whose views and whose followers were frequently at odds with the musicologist-ethnomusicologists represented by Mantle Hood. Merriam was "out to box the compass of ethnomusicological endeavor in this year of 1962," and Seeger responded to the laying down of the gauntlet. He offered four answers to Merriam and two major reasons for studying ethnomusicology. First: music is a human phenomenon deserving to be studied in its own right. Second: music is human behavior and thus deserves to be studied for the physiological aspects of music-making as well as the cultural contexts that shape music-making.

In "The Music Process as a Function in a Context of Functions,"[41] Seeger pursued two increasingly persistent issues in his writing. The major thrust was on the fundamental difficulty of describing music through the distorting medium of speech. But he also demonstrated his interest in the sociocultural matrix of music, which naturally expanded to "the folk," for which he defined his strictures on classifying peoples according to social strata and on the limitations of the expression *national music*. Seeger examined the resources from which music was created—mostly the lower social classes—and tried to note how music works in a way that does not evaluate content by any particular aesthetic system. Thus, music viewed as a quantitative product, not confined to the narrow written tradition of the West, establishes a new value system for music.

But the emphasis in this article is evident. It is one of Seeger's major statements regarding the quandary of music versus speech communication. He intended it to be read in tandem with "On the Moods of a Music Logic."[42] The development of auditory signals, Seeger began, is a basic trait of many species; it is impossible to know when our primate ancestors separated their presumably single sets of auditory signals into the two that we can trace back a few millennia. He noted the "continuing interdependence and complementarity of the two arts. Not the least significant, today, are the novel auditory constructions produced by electronic means which are neither traditional speech nor traditional music, but are planned, often in great detail, (1) in terms of mathematical, logical, or even poetic language under (2) direction of imagination trained or at least accustomed in the composition of traditional music." Seeger then outlined the principal categories commonly found in music-technical and historiographical literature as points that are locatable on the parameter of speech semantic variance defined (or limited) by the terms *structure* and *function*. He presented them in a table:

A. *Extrinsic*	B. *Intrinsic*
1. G eographical Area	1. Own and not-own traditions
2. C ulture area	2. Own and not-own tastes
3. P olitical area	3. Expert and less expert
4. S ocial strata	4. Creative and re-creative
5. S ex, age group, occupation, etc.	5. Written and unwritten
6. S ocial function	6. Self-made and made by others
7. F ocuses of interest	7. Free and priced
	8. Traditional and nontraditional
	9. Music-technical functions

These terms tell us a good deal about the *why* and the *what* of music, Seeger wrote, but not *how* the inward forming is done and how what is formed perform the functions attributed to it. He acknowledged, "The inward function of forming, which is, after all, musicality in concrete manifestation, is a *complex* one" and that the situation required a set of hypotheses, of which he initially offered six. He continued:

The argument will surely be brought forward that an art in which tension, tonicity, and detension constitute virtually the essence of its communicatory content must be not predominantly asymbolic but totally symbolic; for it obviously symbolizes the tensions, tonicities, and detensions of the human beings who practice it and those who receive, hear, or listen to it.

Seeger proposed three additional hypotheses and concluded, "Equal attention [should be paid] to and valuation of both speech and music knowledge and valuation, and extensive and unremitting comparative study of the compositional processes of the two arts." Further,

(1) The extensive structuralization of music throughout the world by the art of speech and (2) the many social uses and functions it is said to serve (3) tend to blind one to the possibility that music functions in a universe of its own as well as an item of attention distinguished as a phenomenon in the physical universe and named as both a concept and as a percept in the universe of speech discourse. In this model of the case, music . . . would mainly paradromize—run parallel to the dynamics (tensions, tonicities, and detension) of what is not music, in the manner peculiar to its signal-message syndrome.

Seeger's preoccupation with music and language was ever present in many of his later writings and frequently linked to the sociocultural matrix. As he said when talking about the musicological juncture,[43]

The situation in which we place ourselves when we talk or write about music must be regarded in barest outline as a sixfold complex that may be referred to as "the musicological juncture": (1) As students, each with our own singular competences and conceptual and perceptual banks of factual and valual behavior, (2) we meet, within certain limited extents of space and time, (3) in a particular biocultural continuum and social context, two of its principal traditions of communication, (4) of a music, (5) of a language, (6) and a subtradition, a musicology, the extents of whose spatial and temporal currencies are, in the constantly renewable collectivity of biocultural continuum, to the best of our knowledge unlimited.

For Seeger, music was more than a worthwhile or well-preserved tradition; it functioned in society at different, interdependent social levels and in different contexts. While he claimed never to have grasped—nor did he work with—musics outside the Western tradition, his acceptance and encouragement of the value of studying them gave his work a broader definition. He set about to define how music operates in society and in the larger world, and he also experimented with techniques for handling music in this larger context. As a result, he understood how judgments about music are conditioned by language, for language is always assessing music, but the reverse is not true. As he interpreted it, "Music is not easy with language to provide exact definitions," so music had been viewed in a subjective light and as a dispensable secondary feature of "culture." Language is a recognitive technique linking symbols into meaning-chains, and thus has tried to portray music in its own image. This has been an important element in the development of the formal Western musical tradition, but it has led to a distorted view of how music works because it has ignored the functional, semiotic, and connective features of music, its essential features. Applying principles of linguistics to music, Seeger at once had a larger canvas on which to work. He also saw that music functions as a connective bridge and can be used to exchange and synthesize cultural values.

Seeger's eclecticism had a point: all musics should be studied. While he never agreed with the separation of music study into two branches, *musicology* (commonly perceived in academic circles as the study of a repertoire of Western art music within limited time frames—medieval to nineteenth century) and *ethnomusicology* (commonly perceived as the study of all other musics), he continued to argue that what ethnomusicologists did and how they did it was what all "-ologists" of music should do, and they should all be called musicologists. But he recognized the resistance to this concept from those who had now become keepers of the Western art music tradition qua musicology, so he appropriated, when necessary, the term *ethnomusicology*.

While Seeger himself emphasized the "ethnomusicological" study of Western music, his overall premise was that the theoretical and methodological constructs of the study of all musics should be, in fact, ethnomusicological. He alluded to these precepts in several articles. For example, in "Tradition and the (North) American Composer,"[44] he wrote, "Ethnomusicology, as I see it, cannot logically or practically be restricted to the music of tribal cultures. . . . It is the ethnomusicology of our own folk, popular, and fine arts music, i.e., the occidental traditions as a whole, that must be our prime consideration." In this article Seeger also directed his theoretical and methodological attention to music as a general whole, drawing indiscriminately on all musics as equally worthy of study because each is valued by its own culture. He spoke of *tradition* as a way of doing something that is inherited, cultivated, and transmitted by human beings living together in a society and carrying a common *culture*, defined as "a bundle of traditions" with geographic coverage and temporal continuity far exceeding that achievable by individuals. But neither is known except when carried by individual members of the society.

Earlier, in "Preface to the Critique of Music,"[45] Seeger had criticized the habit of assessing both art and folk music in value judgments in the absence of an objective descriptive method. He noted that the evaluation of all music in terms of Western art music is a cultural anachronism and emphasized that in much non-Western music the performer, rather than a "composer," is the main creator or re-creator. He spoke of the valuation of music in extrinsic terms, the valuation of music in intrinsic terms, the phenomenology of juncture—music as fact, and the axiology of juncture—music as value. Later, in "Factorial Analysis of the Song as an Approach to the Formation of a Unitary Field Theory,"[46] he maintained that factual analysis takes its departure from a unity—the parameter of physical-musical density while valual analysis begins by recognizing the adversity of criteria. Thus, Seeger set another preface to his magnum opus in this discourse, "Toward a Unitary Field Theory for Musicology."

In the meantime Seeger pursued these themes in other writings. In the foreword to a major text, *Studies in Musicology*, he noted the split between musicologists and educators, concluding with a hope for reconciliation between the fields of musicology and ethnomusicology:

The term "ethnomusicology" [then] will still be valid and useful to designate an *approach* to the study of music in its social-cultural context. But the term 'musicology' should cease to be considered valid to designate only the historical orientation in the study of but one of the multitude of music idioms in the world, even if its adepts would still like to regard it subjectively and ethnocentrically as the best of all possible musics merely because it is their own, or equally subjectively, but egocentrically, as the best merely because they like it.[47]

Implied in this essay was his perceived distinction between musicologists and music historians: he deemed the former the holders of a monographic, monolinear concept of music history, the latter, standard-bearers of the view that synthesis is essential.

Seeger revised "On the Formational Apparatus of the Music Compositional Process"[48] from the spoken version in response to suggestions made at the 1968 SEM meeting for redefinition of the phrase and a linguistic-type transformational grammar for music, with commentary by a linguist. Seeger's paper had "presented a roster of the minimal units that must be dealt with by a formational apparatus for the music compositional process, unitary rather than multipartite, numerate and functional rather than literate and structural." His article declared that this should be seen as "a generative lexicon of successive orders of tonal-rhythmic movement, simple to complex, that can be written in symbols, numbers, or visual signs. Their inflection could serve the music compositional process in a manner analogous to that served by the four-part lexicon-grammar-syntax-rhetoric apparatus of the speech compositional process."

The article discusses "Speech in Terms of Speech"; "Music in Terms of Speech"; and "Esthetics and Semantics." First, he indicated that as long as musicologists know speech they should keep ahead of linguistics, which is several generations in advance of musicological theory. As for the second category, synthesis is additive, analysis divisive. Western music yields most of this, for it is less open-ended. Finally, esthetics has to do with the material form of both compositional processes while semantics has to do with their content. Speech, especially written expression, is a monophonic chain of symbols (structures); music is a polyphonic stream of signs (functions). Speech symbolizes not-speech, music identifies itself with not-music; it does not say so, it does so. Seeger noted, "We pretend to study the whole of music with only part of speech. As a consequence we can propose the two following propositions whose validity is claimed only for the case in hand, namely: (our) speech analyzes its semantics but not its esthetics; (our) music analyzes its esthetics but not its semantics."

He suggested four items in support of the first proposition: "(1) Speech names. . . . Music does not name; (2) Speech relates names; (3) Speech names relationships among distinctions that are named; and (4) Speech relates the relationships among names and the relationships among the named. In support of the second proposition, he suggested four other items: (1) Speech . . . is a monophonic chain of symbols (structures); music is a polyphonic stream of signs (functions); and (2) [while] speech symbolizes not-speech . . . , music identifies itself with not-music; (3) The lexicon of a language is a repertory of esthetic-semantic symbols; the lexicon of a music is a repertory of esthetic-semantic signs; and (8) proposals for both multipartite and unitary formational apparatuses for particular musics and for music as a universal concept should be equally sought. In concluding, he suggested four signposts, two theoretical, two practical: a principle of complementarity, a principle of parity, a principle of indeterminacy, and a principle of compensation."

Seeger posited two types of formational apparatus: literate-structural and numerate-functional, both of which must be expressed in terms of the speech compositional process, the former in the discursive, the latter in the mathematical mode. He asked: how do we best study the intrinsic music text so as to integrate text and context in a comprehensive meaningful report? The answer: transcribe, analyze = or − ; the first two are not enough because it only leaves poorly prepared data.

Seeger explained that in the companion essay, "On the Moods of a Music Logic," he had preferred the term *mood* to *neume* or *motif* for the orders of movement and/or pattern

because it has at once the sanction of long use in the study of speech logic and wide currency in reference to the deeper-seated affective states of man's behavior, changes in which we commonly refer to as 'emotions,' of both of which the visual signs are pictures. The inflection of these moods was considered to be both intensive (by tension, tonicity, and detension of the six necessary functions or resources of the process) and extensive (minimal, medial, and maximal) over the total span of a whole, from the simplest children's song to the hours-long Western oratorio or Indonesian gender ageng.

In an endnote, Seeger noted his tightening of concepts, admitting to a recent view of the roster of moods as a lexicon. Further, in what is a major prelude to "Toward a Unitary Field Theory," Seeger wrote, "Full development of the speech report of such an apparatus must accord with the ultimate goal of musicology. This, as I conceive it, is to adumbrate a unitary field theory for the discipline — one in which the study of music as music knowledge can be carried on upon an equal footing with the study of music as a factor in speech knowledge."

The generative lexicon he had in mind was primarily functional: "Once these functions are presented in symbols and signs, patterns, that is, structures can be discerned," and he provided a synoptic table with several orders to help to explain his ideas. Interestingly, while Seeger saw language as a focus on communication, another great ethnomusicologist, John Blacking, saw music as a "primary modeling system," implying that language focuses on cognition.

Many of Seeger's essays of the previous decade and a half had been aimed at providing a concluding observation about the field of music. The refinement of these concepts appeared in "Toward a Unitary Field Theory for Musicology."[49] He begins in the middle and works outward; the middle in musicology is the musicological juncture. Substitute for the functional term *world view* a structural *universe*, referent to "what is viewed." There are universes of individual thinking and individual feeling. Speech is representational, symbolic, semantic.[50] Value is the relationship so set up — structural, not functional. Our modus vivendi is to live with the linguocentric predicament; to do so, we "(a) develop the dialectic to an extent comparable to that to which he has developed a logic; (b) develop our axiology to be on a par with our phenomenology; (c) impose strict limits on relevance of speech and not-speech; (d) depend more on other means of communication and in so doing free them of some of the bonds we have imposed on them through speech."

The essay is set in an imaginary dialogue between Seeger, Boris Kremenliev, a faculty member at the UCLA Institute of Ethnomusicology, and one of Kremenliev's student's, Jim Yost. The essay is a model of Seeger's use of the dialectic and his penchant for considering the myriad angles abounding in theories. It developed around a discussion of an abstract of the same name in the 1947 *AMS Bulletin*. In the dialogue, Seeger established a design of five basic areas, or universes, that could encompass the entire universe of musicology. As was his wont, Seeger set up symbols to represent his universe of musicology:

(P) physics
(S) speech (I) individuality (M) music (C) culture

Using these symbols of the universe, Seeger defined musicology as

(1) *a speech study*, systematic as well as historical, critical as well as scientific or scientistic; whose field is (2) *the total music* of man, both in itself and in its relationship to what is not itself, whose cultivation is (3) *by individual students* who can view its field as musicians as well as in terms devised by non-musical specialists of whose fields some aspects of music are data; whose aim is to contribute to *the understanding of man*, in terms both (4) of human *culture* and (5) of his relationships with the *physical universe*. A prime methodological postulate would be that there is a limited compatibility between the semiotics of speech communication and of music communication, so that musicological findings, when sought with sufficient rigor, will constitute a comparative study of the communicatory processes of the two arts and a potential factual and valual view of speech, by the musicologist as a carrier of a tradition of music, no less than a factual and valued view of music, by him as a carrier of a tradition of speech.

Each universe is related to each of the others and includes all others. Each exists in a big circle, represented graphically as follows:

(P)	(P)	(P)	(P)	(I)
(I)S(M)	(S)M(I)	(S)I(M)	(S)C(M)	(S)P(M)
(C)	(C)	(C)	(I)	(C)

Inclusion S is representational, symbolic, semantic. Inclusion M is presentational, embodied, semiotic, but not symbolic. Inclusion I is experimental, solipsistic, aesthetic. Inclusion C is axiological, consensual, valual. Inclusion P is phenomenological, existential, factual.

The essay elaborates on these universes and continues the discussion of systems of music study. Seeger then suggested a sixth universe, V, a universe of value made out of four of our original universes, S, M, I, and C, all of which are valuative—that is, value-giving with respect to P, which is neither valuative nor value-giving. We have come to talk about music in terms of fact and value, Seeger wrote, but that is looking at music from the outside; we need to look at music from the inside. "Valuing is the relating, by a living organism, of itself to what is not itself and, equally, of what is not itself to itself, with a view to the continuance of its individuality. Value is the relationship so set up." The basic fact here is that when universe V is substituted for universe P, the theory is changed from fact to value.[51]

Ultimately, said Seeger, the field of musicology is "one of talk rather than of music. But then I remember that the musicologist can say things about music (because he is adept in both the intrinsic and extrinsic views of music) which neither the musician nor the nonmusician can." In diagram, then, he saw the field of musicology as follows:

|||||||||||||| - - - - - - - - - - - -

||||||(S)|||||| - - - - - - -(M)- - - - - - -
||||||||||||||||| - - - - - - - - - - - - - - -

He concluded that the linguocentric predicament is insoluble, but that a MU for individual and collective man, dominated by speech might be to develop the dialectic, develop our axiology to be on a par with phenomenology, to impose strict limits upon the relevance of speech and not-speech, and to depend more on other systems of comunication, freeing us of the bonds of speech.

Mantle Hood encouraged Seeger to produce a book of his ideas and writings. After some thought, Seeger announced a year or so later that he had a title for the book: *Principia Musicologica*—one he had planned to use decades earlier. "With some persuasion" he began putting in order and editing representative writings. In Hood's words:

Principia he envisioned as a major work. After a number of false starts . . . he finally managed an acceptable lead paragraph, the reflective labor of possibly two years. In the third year, he came to me one day and said

"I'm at least fifteen years out of date in the field of philosophy. I must take a year off from *Principia* to read." And he did.

After about five years he announced with surety that he had decided on the format of this budding tome. "First I'll write a book about this thick." He held up thumb and forefinger about a half-inch apart. "Fifty paragraphs. The publication will be sent to certain colleagues in the United States and abroad. After they've had time to read it and think about it, I'll travel from one to another to get their reactions." The Seeger smile was as much in the eyes as in the mouth. "Then I'll come home and write one *this* thick!" He held up forefinger and thumb about three inches apart.[52]

Seeger's work at the Institute of Ethnomusicology and his intense involvement with its students during the 1960s fit hand in glove with the confluence of forces propelling the field of ethnomusicology into prominence worldwide—first by the school of comparative musicology in Europe, then in the development of sophisticated technology for field work, and finally by the increasing realization of the need to study music in its social and cultural context. Seeger noted in 1966 that in the next ten to fifteen years such musical elements as tone and rhythm would have to be redefined. He suggested (characteristically) a conference on a cross-disciplinary and cross-cultural music vocabulary, with participants from each music system—in addition to those in ethnomusicology—who approached their field from either anthropology or music. Participants could include representatives from psychology and physiology and a small nucleus interested in computers and information theory. He further suggested that musicology, or its historiographical branch, was running out of major subjects for research. Professional or fine art music is *made for* the audience, the audience does not, itself, make it. Seeger's slogan was: the crux of historical method is how the present is coming to be what it is going to be.

Coincidentally, Mantle Hood was writing a book that Seeger noted was the first book or article he had ever seen written by someone who knew music as a musician. This seemingly outrageous statement is understood from the perspective of Seeger's interest in the whole spectrum of music as a balance: the view of music seen from the outside as a cultural product, that is, seen from a multidisciplinary

Charles Seeger and Mantle Hood, 1977

stance. He thought that, as of 1967, he and Mantle Hood were the only people in the United States to say in print that musicology is the musicality of humanity, of all music in the world, and that all are related to either. In Seeger's view, the study of music had reached the point where the general type of study was done by one who "looked at music from the outside as a speaker using one art, language, to deal with another, music. Speech is only half the approach to music; the other half is the knowledge of music in its own terms, and the only way you can know music in its own terms is by making it."

At the famed Institute for Ethnomusicology, which graduated so many of the major international figures in the field, the Wednesday Main Seminar was the focal point for such deliberations on music. Seeger's opinion was that the seminar reached its apogee between 1965 and 1968. It was a time for examining major thrusts in ethnomusicology, exploring new ideas, and testing old ones to move the field forward. And it certainly did that for participants in the Main Seminar: participation was required of all graduate students until they successfully completed their oral examinations.

In the seminar, students were privy to magnificent dialogues between Seeger and Klaus Wachsmann, and discussed a plethora of ideas with Hood, Seeger, Wachsmann, and the eclectic collection of linguists, anthropologists, folklorists, historians and others who were perennial participants in the seminar.[53] One wrote,

Hood, Klaus Wachsmann, and Seeger all participated in that seminar, with faculty from other departments [William Bright, linguistics; Leon Knopoff, physics; D. K. Wilgus, English (folklore) and others] coming in on an ad hoc basis. The seminar was a time for thought-provoking discussion among us all, more or less on the topic established by Hood. If Seeger were bored, he turned off his hearing aid and thought his own thoughts though in his 70s–80s, his mind never seemed to be idle). If he were interested, he would join in the discussion at which point we usually encouraged him to talk on and on. He didn't like to talk on and on, however, because his favorite activity was dialectic discussion. His article "Toward a Unitary Field Theory" gives a very clear picture of that style.

In fact, one always had the distinct impression that he was trying to learn from us rather than the other way around. He wanted to know about *our*

Charles Seeger and Klaus Wachsmann, 1971

work. And he wanted us to challenge his thoughts and writing (in fact, he insisted that we do so).

As to whether his "teaching approach" was historical, theoretical, or experimental, I would say that it was all those three, in a kind of integrated flow. And, of course, it depended on the topic at hand. All discussion eventually led to the linguo-centric predicament, however.[54]

The period from 1953 to 1970 was one of diversity and a growing return to respectability for Seeger. Academics with short memories might have forgotten his role in earlier, major academic and professional societies. But he had become the elder statesman in music, particularly in ethnomusicology, with which he had more recently been associated. These were, once again, the "California years." He had survived the blacklisting and the ugly repressive aspects of the

1950s and in the 1960s had been able to fully immerse himself in the scholarly aspects of music. While he was sympathetic to the social and political vision and ideas of the 1960s, he remained at a leveraged distance from such events. He entertained elegantly at his little house near the beach in Venice, and kept careful accounting of the rentals earned by the house he had purchased in the Pacific Palisades section of Los Angeles. His own children had gone on to make their own marks in the music world. Indeed, for Seeger, his new family were the students, ever fascinated by his ideas and energy, reveling in his presence. He had survived numerous storms and fulfilled a deserved role "above the madding crowd."

In a letter to a friend he wrote,

Go to Berkely next week-end to get an honorary at the 100th anniversary of the founding of the university. The best of the year is the ripening friendship with Klaus Wachsmann and his wife. In Mantle Hood's absence, he carries on the main seminar and invites me to participate freely. He is a man after my own heart; a real scholar, whereas I am not, but rather a systematist, who fits what he can pickup into a pattern of belief, a way of living, and can't remember any too well where he got most of it from. We complement each other beautifully. [55]

8

New England Revisited,

1970–1979

◦◦◦

S EEGER'S CAREER and life had many facets and touched many people. By the time he had reached eighty, he had attained a new respectability. Friends and family marked his reaching that milestone with a bouquet of greetings that served to mark his accomplishments to date. As Harold Spivacke wrote,

An enumeration of your accomplishments could never do justice to your real contribution to the musical life of our country. I could write "Happy birthday" to the inventor of the melograph and let it go at that. If I were more articulate I could precede that with pages of specifics, including your presidency of the New York Musicological Society and later the American Musicological Society; your work in the U.S. Government and later in the Pan American Union; your work in music education, to say nothing of your successful teaching career that took place quite a while ago and your work in folklore and ethnomusicology in general.

A list of your accomplishments, offices held, writings completed (including excellent musical compositions which everyone, even yourself, seems to have forgotten) would not give a true picture of your contribution to the development of American musical life. It has been my opinion that your greatest contribution has been the influence you exerted on the very many persons who had the good fortune to work with you, and I feel lucky that I was one of these. Your advice and encouragement have led to a great many important developments. Your own enthusiasm for all types of music served as an inspiration to so many people young and old. All this help you have always given quietly, willingly, with kindness and a friendly smile. I really should not use the past tense because you are still doing it. [1]

Another international colleague wrote:

At any gathering Charles Seeger inevitably assumes a leading role. His wide experience as a musician, a musicologist, an educationist and an administrator gives him an unquestioned authority; but his power to influence his fellow-workers lies even more in his passionate idealism, his far-seeing vision, his selfless integrity and his practical commonsense. 'What would Charles Seeger think of this or that?' is a question which scholars are constantly asking themselves. It is almost as though he wields an invisible yardstick against which we feel constrained to measure our pet theories and projects.

Charlie is about to be eighty, so we are told. But in his case time is an illusion. Judging by his achievements, we should be justified in adding several decades to his present age. But, when we consider the zest with which he continues his own researches and his lively interest in those of his fellow-scholars, we know him to be in the prime of life. When he was seventy, he wrote me of the need to concentrate more intensely on his work since he could hardly reckon on more than another twenty years of active life. Now, on his eightieth birthday, we thank him for all that he has already done, and we wish him at least another twenty years in which to place us still further in his debt. [2]

Son John noted, "All of us, his children, valued his imagination in story and hypothesis. I remember best his age of intense idealism, am convinced my originality in approach and creativity in ideas stems from the fact he delighted in each new point of view we boys came up with—and came up with so many himself! All of us felt he was great fun to be with."

Son Peter said, "Impossible to single out any one phrase or anecdote typifying his contribution to my intellectual life—they have been too varied. I wish I could remember verbatim one of the hundred or more hilarious stories he told me when I was young, but the handful I recall have been too re-told—such as the Foolish Frog, still one of my most requested performance stories."

Daughter Peggy observed, "In my own life I try to reproduce Charlie's extraordinary synthesis of theory and practice, of thought and action. We profited as children from the fact that his childhood was Victorian and regimented, for our childhood was easy, joyful and discipline could be relaxed. He read Boccaccio and the Bible to us on Sundays. We had days off from school when Pete came down and we could clamber over the banjo strings to our heart's content. We were talked *to*, not *at*. Of course, he had to provide a foil to Dio [Ruth] as you would well know—anything he did was a combination of the two temperaments, so a tribute to him would have to be a tribute to Dio as well. I disagree with [Lear's] Cordelia on one point—it is the duty of a child to love a good father: not just the man who lit the spark of life but who tended the fire for years."

Blessed with remarkable good health and energy, he seemed to many indestructible—as if he would go on forever. But Seeger's work at the Institute of Ethnomusicology eventually had to end. It no longer was possible for Hood to obtain administrative approval for the reappointment of a person approaching eighty-five years of age—no matter how exceptional. In 1971 Seeger packed up his belongings and moved back to New England to live with his sister, Elizabeth.

Elizabeth's home in Bridgewater, Connecticut, was the eighteenth-century farmhouse that Grandfather Edwin Seeger had bought a century earlier. Seeger had the upstairs remodeled to suit his living and working situation, while his sister occupied the entire downstairs section. They were to content themselves with this arrangement until Elizabeth died in 1973. The house was a brisk ten-minute walk from the home of Gladys Brooks, widow of Van Wyck Brooks, Seeger's old friend from college days. In neighboring towns lived many other old colleagues, including two musicological giants: Paul Henry Lang, in nearby Washington, and Carlton Sprague Smith, in Ridgefield. He graciously entertained visitors and scholars at his Bridgewater home.

Seeger decided that his major undertaking during this phase of his life would be the book that he had been hoping to publish for many years. He conceived it to be an elaborate tome, in two volumes, that would be the culmination of his life's thinking about music. He also hoped to carry out several other projects, smaller monographs, also dedicated to his thinking. In addition, he kept busy with a variety of other intellectual activities. He wrote numerous papers for collections, encyclopedias, festschrifts, chapters, and public lectures. He taught a variety of guest courses and presented occasional lectures at neighboring institutions such as Yale and Harvard, his alma mater; he offered an annual seminar at Brown University and became an

Charles Seeger, October 1973

"honored presence" in the ethnomusicology graduate program there. He continued to try out new ideas, reading papers at various venues throughout the country, one of the last being a June 11, 1978, lecture at the Library of Congress on "Song and the Compositional Process" in which he sought further to refine his "Principia." Seeger attended local and national meetings of the Society for Ethnomusicology, the American Musicological Society, the American Folklore Society, and other organizations. He often traveled abroad to meetings, frequently moderating or acting as critic at sessions.

On my visits I would accompany him on long daily walks; together we discussed a range of intellectual and personal topics. I can recall plodding along the Connecticut landscape on hot, muggy days, swatting at flies and mosquitoes, stopping at the local playing fields to watch Little League games in progress, or bundling up in the heaviest gear to slog through snow and ice, always fueled by conversation and ideas. One's endurance really was tested as Charlie, walking stick in hand, effortlessly strode the terrain at a rapid lope, all others with him panting to keep pace.

The conversations on foot were continued before the hearth, and some provided the occasion for chuckles and a reminder of his historic timeline. In the autumn of 1975, the late James Koetting, Bonnie Wade, and I traveled to Bridgewater to visit Charlie. A football game of some importance to his three visitors was about to be broadcast on the television. While Charlie hustled providing refreshments, we settled down to watch the game. When Charlie returned to the room, he peered into the set just as a group of players had gone into a huddle. He asked, with great innocence, "What are those men doing, wearing those silly little hats standing around in a circle doing nothing right in the middle of the playing field?" After moments of hilarity we informed him that it was a football game; he replied that it certainly did not resemble the football he had remembered as a young man. It served to remind us that more than a half century had elapsed since Seeger had seen his last football game and the enormous changes that had occurred since then.

During the last few years of his life, one had the sense that, finally, Seeger was admitting to and displaying a broader sense of family affection. He took great pleasure in learning of the adventures of his grandchildren and great-grandchildren and would gleefully recount some "outrageous" Seeger offspring's defiance of social convention. He had often kept his distance from his kin, while being as open as he wished with friends and colleagues. He himself frequently remarked that his role of teacher was always more important to him than his role as father, a fact that did not go unnoticed or uncommented upon by his children. He cited instances, particularly during his marriage to Ruth, when he would have students in to the house regularly to the "neglect" of his own children. He confessed that he often left children and wife — both Constance and Ruth — at home many an evening to indulge in intellectual conversations, sometimes lasting through the night, with students and colleagues. In his nineties he looked back at his behavior with some regret.

Given his genteel nineteenth-century upbringing and prevailing attitudes about the relationship between husband and wife, the proper role of women in the household, and women's primary obligation to their husbands and children, Seeger embodied a very traditional view of marriage. This had caused conflict in his first marriage, and perhaps had emerged even in his union with Ruth. No doubt he was aware of the view that his brilliant student Ruth Crawford could have been a productive twentieth-century composer if she had not chosen to cast her lot with his. Somewhere, deep down, Seeger seemed to feel that this opinion was justified and to wish that things could have been different for her; however, such moments were apparently few and fleeting.

The patrician distance in Seeger's manner was combined with a warmth that was spontaneously given. Almost indiscriminately, he dealt with family and friends in a similar manner. One summer day in 1975 when I was visiting Seeger at a gathering at his home in Bridgewater, a visitor arrived. It was Anthony, child of Seeger's second son, John, whom Seeger had seen only irregularly. Noticing a newcomer on his lawn, he went up to the young man and inquired who he might be. "Mr. Seeger," said Tony, "I'm your grandson, Anthony." Charlie hesitated, peered closely, and said, "Oh, by gosh, so you are."

After his sister Elizabeth's death in 1973, Seeger's home became even more of an open house, and he welcomed young students and old colleagues alike to exchange ideas, share a meal. It was vintage Seeger. It seemed that he had worked out a perfect balance among an assortment of activities: work on his tome; writing various additional essays; preparing lectures; keeping current with his voluminous correspondence; traveling to conferences or to visit family, traveling to Europe, California, and Mexico. He was almost always in astoundingly good health; once when he had to return from a conference early because of feeling unwell, he told me, "Ann, I'm so disgusted with myself. I haven't been sick since nineteen ought eight!"

Holidays were now spent mostly at his son Peter's home, in nearby Beacon, New York. Seeger kept to an almost commuterlike schedule for shorter professional and personal excursions to New York City, Boston, Providence, New Haven, and Middletown. There was, of course, "never enough time," even during the last several years when he hired a typist for his correspondence. On his desk in Bridgewater he kept the ubiquitous manila folder into which went a variety of materials, mostly of a proscrastinative or problematic nature, which he labeled "Suspense."

Through his various endeavors, Seeger was most steadfastly concerned with his ongoing scholarly contributions, his long-awaited book, and new papers that, together with older essays that would not fit into *Studies in Musicology*, would appear in a second volume. Seeger's plan was that *Studies*—reprints of eighteen articles published over forty years—should coincide with the Charles Seeger Celebration to be held in the summer of 1977, during his ninetieth year.

The second and culminating volume, "Principia Musicologica," was planned for 1981–1982. His idea for the volume was that it would serve musicology as Newton's *Principia* had served physics, Russell's for philosophy, and Whitehead's for mathematics. "Principia" was to appear before his ninety-sixth birthday, because Seeger felt sure that he would live to at least that age; any time beyond that, he reckoned, he could devote to beginning new projects. Each statement that appeared in print during this time was a step toward the refinement of *Studies* and "Principia"; for this reason, some of his articles cover the same ground.

With six of seven children, 1977; Peggy, Mike, Peter, son Charles, and Charles Seeger in back row; John and Barbara in foreground

This was Seeger's approach toward publishing, and one should take a similar approach of seeking versions and variants when reading his articles. One of these was "Reflections Upon a Given Topic: Music in Universal Perspective,"[3] developed from a session he had chaired at the 1970 SEM meeting where he had expressed concern that the presenters would presume that the topic, universal perspective, meant nothing more than "worldwide view." He saw his responsibility as chairman of the session to present a context for discussion. As he noted:

I planned to present a brief overview of the range of verbalization available to, even inviting, us in talk about music to consider conceptualization of universals and perceptualization of particulars as equally necessary links in discussion of the topic. Under the circumstances it seemed that this could best be done by projecting upon a screen a chart that would show in relation to music: how, as the universality of concepts increases their particularity decreases; how, as the particularity of percepts increases their universality decreases; and, finally, how the two cases can be shown as a single two-way logical process, *tantôt libre, tantôt recherchée*, charted over a common range, gamut or parameter of speech meaning between its two defining terms, the "pure" concept and the "pure" percept. But in talking over the prospects the day before the session with my two panelists it seemed clear that this might cast a wet blanket of formality over what we had agreed would be a spontaneous and informal exchange of words designed primarily to open an annual meeting by alerting the membership to participation in free discussion. The recording made by a member of the audience with a miniature electronic device did not permit satisfactory transcription. My introduction of the two panelists was not worth printing. I accept the invitation of the editor of *Ethnomusicology*, therefore, to present here an improved version of the original chart together with somewhat more organized comment that I would have made *viva voce*. I must add, however, that I am not entirely happy with the wording of the six boxes under the heading "Judgment" that mark arbitrary stages in the hierarchy of interest from the more particular to the more general experience and from individual to social criteria that might comprehend such worldly values.

Seeger published an elaborate chart entitled "Outline of a Taxonomy-Hierarchy of the Parameter of Speech Semantic Variance Abstract-Universal-Concept/Concrete-Particular-Percept," with several pages explaining the structures of the chart. He noted in the midst of his explanation, "The chart on page 387 pretends to be an outline that can accommodate all possible taxonomies and hierarchies expressed in terms of this parameter [Speech Semantic Variance]." Later, he commented: "The chart presented here is not committed to any philosophy or to the possibility or impossibility of the search for a solution of the impasse. It is designed solely to accommodate as many possibilities as can be foreseen. It is not a philosophical system but a chart of the resources of speech communication viewed by one who is not a philosopher but a musician who has tried to find a way of using the art of speech to deal with the art of music and avoid as many errors of his predecessors as possible."

Further explaining his chart with additional dialogue on the problem of universals and the speech and musicological juncture, he concluded:

In speech, the universals constitute one of the two best devices of language to escape from its own limitations. They function equally well in science, in criticism and in poetry. But they have their limitations. They don't get along any too well with each other. And we . . . are bound in the chains in the orders we put them in. . . . The one escape is to understand how to make them break the very chains we have forged of them. The other escape is the twentieth century knowledge of the percept which has given musicology a point of attack upon the domination of man by his art of speech. Humanity does not have to continue in bondage to this one means of communication and make only minimal use of the others. There are at least five others. Because they are musicians, musicologists know music. And music, though not a universal language, is without question more nearly universal in all senses of the word, including worldwide perspective, than speech.

Of all six, music is in the best position to be the base for a critique of speech. It uses the same medium—sound. Only one of the aims of musicology is more music knowledge of music. Equally important is more speech knowledge about speech. For it is only in terms of speech and of its universals that we can direct the latter in pursuit of the former. There is no escape from the fact that musicology should be—even though it cannot yet be said to be a speech discipline. . . . Everywhere we turn speech and music are ineluctably related. . . . Equal competence in both would seem to be too much to ask for either musician or musicologist. But a sufficient competence in the other can be asked of each. . . . The way out of the double risk would seem to be to balance the quantitative and the qualitative factors in both cases. . . . By the very nature of the act . . . the particulars of one's own music become worldwide universals and, as an almost automatic reflex, those worldwide universals distort one's understanding of one's own music.

A year after the appearance of this complex philosophic-linguistic tract, Seeger was in print with "World Musics in American Schools: A Challenge to be Met."[4] The journal issue in which it appeared provided articles in response to the question:

What, if anything, shall we do in our schools about the impact on our people—especially upon our young people—of musics other than our own, now for the first time in history grown to mass proportions by the low cost of commercially available discs, many of them of excellent quality, and by the frequent well publicized tours of virtuosi from Asia and Africa? From the musician's point of view, I believe there are very good reasons to open the doors as wide as we can, but there are equally good reasons from the non or extra-musical point of view to lock them tight.

On the first issue, the musical point of view, Seeger stated that the prime concern in education should be the acquisition of competence in a child's own music, just as one should learn one's own language first before learning another. On the second point, the non- or extra-musical viewpoint, Seeger observed that whether or not to introduce musics other than our own into schools—and one can learn more about one's own music through learning about other musics—is tangled in questions of ability, competence, and availability of resources. On the politics involved, he noted the controversy over whether traditional musical education has failed and referred to larger issues regarding the control of music, the mass communications business, and the role of statism in music education around the world. Finally, Seeger discussed the historical moment: in the early 1970s the United States was participating in one of the great musical renaissances of history, despite the "reactionary, 'music-is-a-frill' contingent" and the liberal cadres concerned with preserving the Western musical tradition through music appreciation courses. He believed that schools must do the whole job: enactment of the culture is behavior and communication. Seeger's conclusion: "From now on . . . music education in the schools, colleges, and universities must pull every stop in the organ. Its job has become cultural-political on a large scale. Efforts to national-politicize the country in terms of music are harmless and can be made more so by the introduction of non-Western musics. The drive to internationalize the world economically, politically, intellectually—that is, as one cultural whole—is in full swing. Music is an integral factor in the process."

Seeger celebrated his ninetieth birthday in December 1976 in Bridgewater with a party attended by family and friends.[5] He was buoyant. *Studies* was in press, and he was presiding over the meticulous plans for his professional party, the celebration, scheduled for the following year.

Seeger had ambitious plans for the Charles Seeger Conference, over which he presided like a major domo, even overseeing song arrangements for the concert presenting his music. In 1976 he wrote to me about the upcoming event: "What I would like most to do would be to steer the discussions . . . into what is the course of the development of musicology during the coming years—a subject surely in everybody's minds during the joint meeting [1977 IMS-SEM-AMS] but not a topic of any paper."[6]

In March 1977, he reported having changed his mind on the conference format:

I did what I so often have done quite without forethought, turned a somersault and perceived that Ann's original idea was the best: not to invite people to be prepared for *another three days* of scheduled talks when they had already—some of them—gone through eight but to face a familiar kind of situation, a celebration of the 90th year of a colleague. My resistance to the original idea can be laid to (pusillanimous) humility, although at the same time my (sinful) pride, vainglorious in the turn of my vendetta with the music historians to at least a profession of a world-wide scope for musicology, suggested the change of locale and time.

Avaunt (pusillanimous) humility! All hail (sinful) pride! You know as well as I do (and you said so in Berkeley), I do relish the casus, so we may call a spade a spade and make it clear that the additional two or three days is something different from the preceding eight. The plans (we—CS, A, B, and Klaus] worked out would look really tactless to most of the members of the three societies who might give them even passing attention. The implications would clearly be . . . that we planned to hold a separate little meeting to show hoi polloi what they had not been able to excogitate. Of course, this is precisely what we are preparing to do; but there's no use being tactless and saying so. To be shockingly frank, after so many years—the present year included—of being snubbed as a black sheep (which I am) it is sweet to be celebrated and I might as well thank you from the heart (modestly).[7]

In April 1977 he wrote to me, "I am sure that you realize quite as well as I do the low depth to which our musicological colleagues have sunk in techniques of discussion, except of the most informal kind. We are proposing in the sessions a fairly formal kind of discussion. You must sit next to me and kick me when I talk too much—a habit I have gotten into because people are reluctant to ask questions. . . . This, I think, may be the first of its kind in musicology in this country."[8] At the conference he wanted to have copies of his comprehensive graphic outline of the field of musicology, the inverse alignment of conceptualization and perceptualization, and the synoptic table of historical and systematic orientations available for reference.

At the end of April 1977, Seeger elaborated on his ideas about the individual and society which, he believed, needed to be central in the conference discussions:

I am going to go quite thoroughly into this "Individual Versus Society" business and you may be amused with my own strategem. As well as dividing society very sharply from culture and culture from the individual so that they automatically, as it were, set up contradictions between the terms, my procedure, as you know, is to also regard the terms as limit, of parameters over which both extremes range as variable, themselves—when regarded alone—serving as the limits (unreachable) of the parameters, as is, of course, the "50–50" perfectly balanced judgment. The next step is to set up subsidiary parameters within each extreme: proto-, meso-, holo-. The protosocial would be mere collectivity, as are molecules of iron oxide in sufficient profusion in an area making it worthwhile enough for man to mine it, or gold nuggets in a Sacramento Valley riverbed, for man to look for them. (The total parameter, here, I neglected to say, is utter-diffusion-as-is-hydrogen-in-interstellar-space/the-utmost-in-human-individuality that I refer to as singularity par excellence.) Thus we can correlate our three parameters—society/culture, society/individual and culture/individual—with some hope of rationality. Schools of fishes, concentrations of Burmese fireflies in a tree upon which they all flash their signals simultaneously, and other such would be protosocial. But I would say that when the male salmon fights off the female who is trying to eat the eggs she has just laid and he has fertilized, we might have a case of the protosocial in the male but not in the female or, perhaps, even a sign of protoindividuality, in the male. (This is going to be too lengthy to put in a letter, suffice it to say, our three parameters overlap: for example, a mesosociety such as some African termites, with its rigid class system of queen, males (drones?), nurses, workers, soldiers, captured slaves, might be considered protocultural but decidely not protoindividual. An African aggregate of baboons (or is it chimpanzees?) might be considered holosocial, sometimes nearly mesocultural and certainly protoindividual, perhaps even mesoindividual—it would take a biosociologist to tell us just how to name these various points on the three parameters.

As is collectivity to the protosocial, so, I would suggest, is the pecking order to culture and is communication understood as perception of value to the individual. There is an embarrassment, here, in the nature of the English and other IndoEuropean languages: that society and culture are "manies" but the individual a oneness. We, as individuals, are well-known to be about as much manies as onenesses; but the language doesn't let us use the word *individuality* without losing some of the sense of *the* individual. . . . [Speaking about two of his friends, giants in the field] All the dozens of dichotomies impinge upon our Wachsmann/Blacking confrontation, particularly that of the "a priori *Wiedererkennungsurteil*" one/what is not one. Strange, isn't it, that [Klaus], who will see the whole activity of scholarship to be at best guesswork, as he did at the end of his [UCLA] address, cannot see himself as being guessed at—an indecipherable concatenation of a one (or, perhaps, of indeterminate ones) and a many. You know? I wouldn't be surprised if he and [Blacking] wind up close friends after August. [They did. Their difference revolved around Wachsmann's siding with theories of individuality and Blacking with theories of sociality; Seeger agreed with Blacking on this point.]

I must add, however, that I am as aware as you probably are that a good deal of the foregoing is not as unheard of in the ethnology of the preceding decades as much of it will appear to be to many in our audience. The proto-, meso-, holo-, parameter is, to best of my knowledge, new. And, as well, perhaps the concept of culture as a superstructure upon society and that society is primarily a biological concept and culture a nonbiological. Neither is generally accepted but I am certain as I can be certain of anything that both have been already adumbrated and are well on the way to acceptance. I believe we shall profit by accepting them as working propositions if we are going to make any sense out of the discussion that [Klaus] made and would want to raise.[9]

Further anticipating the discussions on the theme of the individual and society, he wrote to Klaus Wachmann:

You would understand more thoroughly than anyone else my adjustment of the dilemmas of my theory of the linguocentric predicament — particularly, the one which might present the issue upon which we feared there might arise too vehemently opposed views, the primacy of individuality *or* sociality. . . . [That matter is] the "problem" of the one and the many, exemplified by the dichotomy individual/society. As I am sure you know, along with every other user of our Western European languages (and, possibly, all others) in what I have called the reasoned mode of usage, has the obligation to regard the terms of dichotomies as contradictory and to deal with them by the rules of formal logic, but at the same time has the obligation to regard them as complementary, as limits defining parameters of semantic variance over which both terms are used in relations that can be, if not measured, at least estimated in terms of other dichotomies and their parameters of semantic variance, in the present case by that of fact/value.

It seems we must admit that societies evolved upon the biological level from the concentration of elements upon the physical level. Both must be assumed to be causally motivated. On the biological level of the evolutionary continuum the individual is completely subordinate to the collective, even in such elaborate societies as those of hiving bees, termites, etc. Communication is strictly doing the job of the social class, for the feeding of him while in the pupa stage fitted him. The only pecking order is the battle of queens and the flight of the successful drone in mating. Both of these are purely superior strength, as far as we know.

The pecking order in a troop of higher apes is much more complex. Sheer physical strength is not always the order. There was an interesting study of this in the October 1976 *Scientific American*, p. 94. "The Social Order of

Japanese Macaques" by G. Gray Eaton in which "Arrowhead" ranked 1 among the males and he was neither the strongest nor the most often chosen as a mate. Was he wise? Holy? Just (he settled disputes)? (Hinduism bases its caste system on such.) Females choose their mates sometimes regardless of strength. Mothers cherish their own offspring—sometimes one above the others. Why?

The rigid determinist will claim all such acts are mechanical—consequents of previous facts. There is no point in arguing with him. We don't know all the preceding facts. But neither does he. He has an imposing method, by now expressed in such elaborate mathematical jargon that we are no match for him unless we can get him to admit that the whole deterministic argument necessarily includes the assumption that it is worthwhile, that it is valuable, in the attempt to express reality in terms of speech. And this is an absolutely unscientific, unreasonable, undemonstrable assumption—a pure value judgment. We can put beside it an opposite value judgment: that because neither he nor we can know all the facts leading to the simplest value judgment, it is equally worthwhile (valuable) to regard values as teleologically motivated. Have we any criterion for the ranking of one of these judgments over against the other? Or against the judgment of the disciplined ecstatic that neither is worthwhile—that both transgress the limits of all parameters of speech semantic variance, that not even all man's other communicatory systems in addition can comprehend the wholeness of things. . . . (You came close to this at the end of your LA lecture.)

We have, however, in this dilemma, recourse to plain common sense. What I have called the "discursive mode of speech usage" and the mode in which the humanities are cast. It is essentially the critical mode. Its criterion is the balanced judgment: between fact and value, the individual and society, and all the rest of the fifty or sixty that we use every day.

Let us take stock of the procedure of our argument. Are we yet ready to undertake the matter of the relation of music to these two parameters of speech semantic variance, fact/value and individual/society? No. We must examine two questions: (1) are there biological values; (2) are wisdom, holiness, justice, most preferred mate, care of particular child biological values or some other kind of value?

(1) from the rigidly determinist viewpoint, there would be values such as the necessaries for survival and procreation: bodily prerequisites (unimpaired strength, food, shelter, protection from enemies, territory, etc.). Granted, these are causally motivated; but not knowing all the causes we fall

back, in use of the discursive mode of speech usage, upon appetite to live, hunger, suffer, fear, have our own way, etc., which we regard as end-motivated, teleological. To the extent this is held valid, there are biological values. And in terms of daily life in the more extended and elaborated industrial societies they are called values.

(2) From this platform and in terms of the discursive mode of speech usage, the emergence of recognition of the *singularity of the individual* in pre-hominid societies could seem to constitute foretokens of what we call *culture*, culture being man's very considerable development of a veritable superstructure upon the infrastructure of his biological being, primarily achieved through his elaboration and extension of the compositional processes of systems of communication as traditions inherited by succeeding genera-tions, cultivated by them and transmitted, sometimes in comparatively stable, sometimes in comparatively rapidly changing forms, but always led by the more and most singular individuals; for singularity is a hierarchy of excellence and these excellencies shape and preserve the highest cultural values conceived, experienced and communicated by man.

A note on the nature of value. Value is always a relationship between an individual, either as a biological organism or carrier of a culture, or both, and what he *must* do to live and what he *wants* to do to enact the culture he has inherited. The continual interplay between the biological infrastructure and cultural superstructure imposes certain restraints and offers oppor-tunities for enhancement of both *musts* and *wants* in the form of *oughts*. In the course of the sociocultural continuum, tradition dominates the activity of the individual; when the stability—either from decay within or challenge from without—unleashes the creative *wants* of the individual in direct proportion to the degree of his singularity; and the *musts* and the *wants* modify old or create new tradition.

The controversy that you wish to avoid between the dominance of one or the other, between individuality/sociality, and the one I wish to avoid, between intellection and affection in music would seem handleable on the basis of these considerations, the only arguable point being the judgment whether the present century is one of stability or change in the sociocultural continuum. And it seems unlikely that anyone would ascribe stability to the known human world in our day. [10]

The entire Charles Seeger Conference, from beginning to end, was an official reentry for Seeger into the ranks of the music establishment. It was a high point for Seeger. Hosted at the University of California, Berkeley, the celebration was planned to follow the 1977 meeting of the International Musicological Society that brought scholars from around the world. Seeger himself drew up the list of participants to be invited to the four-day *festspraache* of his ideas and his works.

Seeger had frequently rued the fact that people did not read his scholarly articles—or, if they did, had no comments or criticisms to make about them. He thought of the conference as a forum for clarifying and expounding on his ideas—giving cohesion to all facets of his life.

The four-day conference opened formally at a party at the home of the chairman of the Music Department, Richard Crocker, at which the president of the American Musicological Society, James Haar, presented formal salutations to Seeger. A prepublication copy of *Studies in Musicology* was given to him at this time. One evening was devoted to performance of Seeger's own compositions—since available on recordings—a musicale held at the home of the eminent musicologist, Professor Joseph Kerman. Another evening was given over to music-making by Seeger's children at a party hosted by Professor Bonnie Wade, an ethnomusicologist at Berkeley.[11]

The celebration was laden with emotion for Seeger. It was held at the university that had first welcomed and then disdained him.[12] It was sponsored by the department he had structured and whose curriculum he had developed. He was officially re-recognized by a society he had co-founded (the AMS) but, because it had moved in directions different from its original intent, did not know quite what to do with him. And he was honored by another society he had helped to found (the SEM). Yet he had sparred with the SEM (he believed it should not be separate from a larger music society) but in his final decades, it gave him an official home and platform from which to speak.

The celebration brought attention to Seegers's ideas and works, both printed and musical, in verbal, visual, technological, oral, and aural forms. It also delineated and repeated themes which, in rondo-like form, had constantly preoccupied him. It has been observed elsewhere that despite the variety of subjects upon which Seeger

Charles Seeger with Gertrude Rivers Robinson, 1977

focused, and the broad range of intellectual interests, much of his writing informally links "an interrelated set of propositions: the hegemony of Old World over New World music, the dominance of high culture over folk culture and the missionary role of educators in 'making America musical.'" Further, Seeger wrote and knew he wrote for different audiences. His dense, complicated epistemological and ethical formulations presumed the academic audience:

To the extent that we can predict futures in scholarship, we can assume that young musicologists, for decades to come, will explore his extraordinary leads and his borrowings across disciplinary barriers. Seeger was well aware of his challenge to musicology, for he employed difficult language in essays and lectures, and fully enjoyed scholarly discourse which flowed from his strategic and semantic choices. [13]

But Seeger also could reach his "other" (nonacademic) audience and championed the folk and popular traditions both nationally and internationally in his choice of venues for publishing his commentaries and proselytizing lectures. Seeger was most concerned with the relationship of man, music, and society and was constantly exploring new ways of conceptualizing and perceptualizing music and discussions about it.

Regardless of whether it was folk, popular, art, or whatever form it took, American music was never far from his attention. As Wiley Hitchcock noted:

The most eloquent spokesman for this new view [Americans newly interested in their own past; partly from the nationalist sentiments evoked by World War II; and finally from a more liberal view of what historical musicology—especially in a fluid, diverse, and democratic society like that of the United States—could or should concern itself with] of the proper approach for American musicologists to take vis-à-vis their own culture's music has been Charles Seeger. . . . Seeger has asserted bluntly that "the majority of musicologists are not primarily interested in music, but in the literature of European fine art music, its grammar and syntax (harmony and counterpoint) ["Oral Tradition in Music"].

Seeger's point of view has been that of a pan-cultural historian. Rejecting the older, exclusive concern with only a cultivated tradition, an educated culture, an elite art—the best that has been thought and said by the few in a civilization, as Matthew Arnold once put it—Seeger has argued for a concern also with the vernacular tradition, popular culture, mass art—"the run of what is thought, felt, and liked by the many," as Max Lerner has put it [in *America as a Civilization*]. Seeger's ideas have opened the way for a new interest in American music by American music historians, for they offer new standards of scholarly value and invite investigation in areas different from those of the traditional European historical musicology—the Adlerian tradition—in which American music historians have been schooled for so long. Essentially, what Seeger has challenged us to do is to write about the history of *music* rather than the history of a music, i.e., the history of musical culture in the large rather than the history of a single musical idiom. [14]

The first of Seeger's two planned major volumes, *Studies in Musicology 1935–1975* (1977), appeared in concert with the celebration and contains eighteen essays published over forty years in various places. Each addresses a particular facet of music that had earned Seeger's attention. The volume is heavy with theoretical discourse and his constant preoccupation with the linguocentric predicament: speech, music, and speech about music. He introduced the book with his synchronic and diachronic orientations in musicology, and the first seven essays, which comprise half the volume, are some of the heavy guns of his musicological work.[15] The other eleven essays which he selected for inclusion target his interest in notation and automatic transcription tools, the relationship between music and society, cultural sources for music in the New World, American music studies, and folk music in general.[16]

Once the celebration was finished and *Studies* had appeared, I believe that Seeger never regained the momentum to finish "Principia Musicologica." Now that he had public recognition and respect, perhaps he felt it was time to rest a bit on his laurels. Shortly after the celebration, in the winter of 1977, Seeger underwent a cataract operation that temporarily prevented him from driving. Because I was expected in December for the traditional birthday visit to celebrate his birthday, he told me that I would find him at the hospital in New Milford. I was to drive him home. Upon my arrival, I learned that he had checked himself out of the hospital. It was a particularly icy December evening. When I reached his home in Bridgewater I found him on the porch, a big white patch over one eye, shoveling snow. He hadn't needed to stay at the hospital any longer, he explained, so he had driven himself home. On that night he refused help in bringing logs in from the porch to supply our usual nighttime fire.

During that visit we talked about his biography and also about what needed to be done to bring "Principia Musicologica" to fruition. But his urgency to published his projected second volume seemed to be gone. "I'll get to it," he said. It was an attitude that lingered throughout 1978. By December he was saying that he might not need to do much more work on it, simply send it off to the press.[17]

The crux of "Principia Musicologica" was to be one of his two last major works, "Tractatus Esthetic-Semioticus: Model of the Systems of

Human Communication."[18] In "Tractatus" Seeger was concerned with semiotics. Semiotics in general is the speech study of communication by members of a society living in that society; in this particular instance, communication is among men as a system. The concern of semiotics — indeed, of all use of languages — is the extent to which linguistic bias must be admitted and ways in which it may be avoided, tempered, or compensated for and/or accepted. Seeger "outlined a general theory in accord with which the communicatory systems — that is, the arts and crafts — of man and their cultivation in their common physical and cultural context may be presented with least distortion by the inescapable bias of the system in which the presentation is made — the art of speech. Both theory and model are speech constructs. But, except for speech, the arts and crafts and their compositional processes are not speech constructs. Their names are; but, except for speech, they do not name themselves. Speech names them; that is, we name them by means of speech."

Again, Seeger resorted to figures to discuss three modes: "The first, general, discoursive, is the mode of 'common sense,' and its more sophisticated versions, sometimes referred to as 'uncommon sense.' The second and third are specialized — one is belletristic, poetic, mystical, and the other, logical, mathematical, scientific. . . . The present undertaking is written in the discoursive mode of speech usage. The core of this mode is the critique. It is the particular job of the critique to try to resolve the contradictions of the two specialized modes, to show their complementarity, and to construct a unitary speech concept of reality that takes into account the realities of the full roster of communicatory systems other than speech.

The essay, he acknowledged, owed considerable inspiration to Wittgenstein. In fact, Seeger even commandeered the title of one of Wittgenstein's major thought pieces. As with Hegel, Kant, and others who influenced his thinking earlier in life, Seeger borrowed liberally from Wittgenstein and reworked extensively to serve his own purposes.

Happily, Seeger noted, "To aid the reader in threading his way from the abstract concept of Title 1 to the concrete percept of Title 33 [a listing of thirty-three key concepts, some with several propositions, all of which he used to demonstrate his points], I append a genealogical tree of the family 'human communication' (fig. 2) and a summary of titles." All of what was promised followed and was the crux of the essay.

In "Sources of Evidence," Seeger focused on the import of judgment qua choice as a factor in the compositional process of all eight or nine principal systems of human communication. He began:

By the word *judgment* I name the act of making distinctions and of choosing between distinctions with a view to further action or inaction. A distinction is a namable or potential namable that is not judged to be another name. A choice is to relate two distinctions to a third as a measuring stick or criterion for action or inaction.

Understood in this dual sense, judgment seems to be a factor in the compositional processes of all eight or nine principal systems of human communication, tactile, visual and auditory. In musicology, a study conducted mainly in terms of the system of speech, the basic distinction is between fact and value. Music is a namable that we can talk about both in terms of fact and in terms of value. Naming is possible in speech alone.

As fact, music is a datum or bundle of data that is existent in the physical universe. . . . As value, music is an element in two universes: the physical and the human cultural built by man on top of or within it. The two make strange bedfellows. . . . In musicology, we must distinguish two special kinds of speech value: general value distinguished in terms of speech referent to music, in itself and in its many contexts . . . and particular values constructed in terms of musicological theory.

Seeger used visual means to present his thoughts as much as the points he was making. In "Sources" he provided several figures (also in his chart for the "Unified Field Theory") as "sources of evidence and criteria for judgment of value in musicology under eight headings." These sources were: individual valuer; arbitrage general; arbitrage musical; historics general; historics musical; systematics general; systematics musical; and law, discussed under the rubric of six figures. After providing an analysis of each of those sources, he then tackled the category of criteria. Noting the ambiguity of the word "criterion," he suggested, "A criterion of any particular judgment would seem to be a generalization of funded experience drawn from more than one or even all eight of the sources shown in figures 2 to 6—a complicated process the nature of whose operation we are for the most part unaware. The more serious the judgment, the more criteria it may involve."

For our edification, Seeger provided figure 7, "Sources of Criteria and Evidence of Musical Value," a synthesis of figures 2 to 6, "enclosed in the embraces of the two specialized criticisms [which] presents a skeletal visual outline of the judgmental act in the compositional process of speech in reference to music in the English language." Figure 8 followed, in the form of a vertical scale. The top line, measuring 10 ———————————— 0, was labeled "Conceptualization in terms of percepts of outer experience"; the bottom line, 0 ———————————— 10, was labeled "Perceptualization in terms of concepts of inner experience." These were followed by figures 9, 10, and 11, circles of medial overlapping among the designates M for Music, S for speech, G for graphics, A for artifacture, D for dance, and C for corporeality. Finally, he offered eight points of summary on the aims of the critique followed by a twelfth and final figure, which indicates the growth of speech and society paripassu.

In both *Studies in Musicology* and the proposed "Principia" the items are heavily weighted to a few extraordinary themes. One is the linguocentric predicament. His introduction of "Studies" with the essay "Speech, Music, and Speech about Music" makes a final statement about the importance he attached to this philosophical assessment regarding music. Another concern was the dichotomy in musicology first between historical musicology (diachronic) and systematic musicology (synchronic), later between musicology and ethnomusicology. Also persistent was the space-time continuum, both music space-time and general space-time. In integrating these ideas, Seeger saw systematic musicology as occurring within music space-time and historical musicology as occurring within general space-time. And, within this structure Seeger further juxtaposed phenomenon and normenon (his own term) suggesting that any musical event that exists in general space-time is a phenomenon and any musical event that exists in music space-time is a normenon.

The most characteristic trait in all Seeger's work was an intellectual inquisitiveness that sought to understand music in its own terms as well as in its cultural context. Striving for a total view of music shaped his professional life; it has been a powerful force in modern music studies. Henry Cowell had said,

Charles Seeger is the greatest musical explorer in intellectual fields which America has produced, the greatest experimental musicologist. Ever fascinated by intricacies, he has solved more problems of modern music theory, and suggested more fruitful pathways for musical composition . . . than any other three men. He has rarely been given public credit for the ideas which he has initiated, since with a perverse humor which is very characteristic of him he always presents his important new ideas in such a way, at such a time, or to such people that they are never accepted at first; later when the ideas have proved to be singularly adaptable, their users often forget the source.

He is personally a bundle of contradictions; but where a majority of people are self-contradictory without suspecting themselves of it, he knows it of himself and is satisfied! All his vagaries are quite self-conscious. He is outstandingly (and to many people obnoxiously) intellectual, but with a leaning toward sentimental outpouring. Here again he sees the tendency in himself plainly, but instead of frowning on it as a thing to be hidden, he takes prankish delight in it. He is rigidly conservative in many ways, never accepting thoroughly anything until it has been entirely proved, believing in precedent, training, even bookishness. Yet no one else has taken as great an interest in the new, the unexplored, the modern. He is aristocrat and radical, but nothing between.

One could go on indefintely and not exhaust the number of subjects in which he has been a pioneer. Probably his most important standpoint, however, is his open advocacy of the intellectual point of view in approaching music. This he started at a time when such a thing was utterly inconceivable—when it was considered that music had value only if it had nothing to do with the intellect, that the most damning thing that could be said against music was that it is intellectual, and that *thinking* about music not only has no value but destroys the musical impulse. Seeger almost proved this old-fashioned notion to be right by allowing over-intellectualism to stultify him. But he has brilliantly recovered, and has renewed activity in a great new outburst of fertility. And, as in the other cases, the public is gradually following him in this, his most important stand.[19]

Seeger's major intellectual concerns focused on the relationship between music and culture; the relationship of language and music; the relationship among the people who are involved in the creating, making, teaching, buying, selling, controlling, and studying of music. Growing up in a Europe-dominated world, Seeger was not naturally inclined to question the preeminence of "the fatherland." However, his desire to be a composer was, I believe, a major force in influencing him not only in the context of his own particular compositional style but also helped him realize the contradiction of being an American composer in an imported music tradition. From that point he was determined to influence the cultural attitudes in the United States and was the first to define a modern and distinctly American approach to the study and organization of music. His friend Klaus Wachsmann wrote:

C. once said: . . . "Music is the tune in my head." As the years went by, he talked more and more about his compositions . . . C. showed me his sonata for violin and piano and various other compositions of his. . . . I did not prompt him to do this—I would not presume that kind of intimacy—but it was all the more overwhelming to be aware of his wish to analyze his own creations.

The interesting question—is whether one really can separate C's concern on the one hand for composition and on the other hand his "unitary field theory of music." But that's the trouble with everything—there are no clearly defined boundaries. [20]

In tandem with promoting the American tradition while not eschewing the European, Seeger pushed beyond those limits. He expanded the notion of what was worthwhile music; he understood that music is more than a well-preserved *written* tradition—it is, after all, sound—but that music had different functions in cultures at different social levels and in different contexts, all interdependent. He came to believe that not only was it important to understand all the music facets of one's tradition, but that to know at least one other music tradition was of special value to understanding one's own.

He saw musicology as

comprehending the study equally of the music of man and of man as a maker of music. Unfortunately, owing to the peculiar development of European academic fashions during the 19th and early 20th centuries, the term became restricted to the study alone of the history of the fine, elite, "high," or professional art of Europe. When, tardily, the study of musics and music idioms other than that began to interest an increasing number of students, they were reluctant to challenge the established discipline of the historicomusicology of Europe and sought first the name "comparative" and then "ethno-"musicology . . . as ethnomusicology gathers within its purview the physics, the biology, the ecology, the anthropology and sociology, the aesthetics and so forth of music, it will produce an ethnomusicology of the fine art of European music which will supersede what is now known as "musicology" and by dropping the prefix "ethno-" itself become the properly named study known as "musicology."[21] . . .

Ethnomusicology is itself an interdisciplinary study. True, in many of its outstanding documents ethnological contexts are not considered. Intrinsically, these are strictly musicological; it is only on account of the peculiar ways of academe that they are currently classed as ethnomusicological. . . . Some of the contributors however, are neither musicians or musicologists. We hope they will not feel at any disadvantage on that account. If the term "interdisciplinary" means anything (of, course, some hold that it does not) it means a two-way relationship in which any field must expect to be looked at in terms of any other and, in turn, may look at any other or the whole collection of fields in its own terms.[22]

It was at this point of realization that Seeger began developing a new descriptive approach to defining how music operates in society and the world at large as well as formulating techniques for handling music within this larger purview. Herein was the crux of his attention to the problem of language and music.

Language and music have an uneven relationship. As a recognitive technique linking symbols into meaning-chains, language, as the most important tool in the Western music tradition because it portrays music in its own image, has led to a distorted view of the way music operates because it tends to ignore the functional, semiotic, and connective features that are the essence of music. Seeger thus sought to raise consciousness by making music an art that is equal and complementary to language. He did this by seeking to show that music functions as a connective bridge among groups of people and that music is strongest precisely when it is used to enhance and synthesize cultural values. As a result, one can try to uncover the way music works in a given context without evaluating its content by any particular esthetic system but, at the same time, it sets up a new value system for appraising the nature of music: by substituting an unbiased criterion—"quantity"—for an unbiased criterion—"quali-ty," that is, accepting music as a product, in and of itself, and trying to discover how it works, without being confined to judgment by a specific value system.

Seeger the organizer, the curious seeker, the missionary, sought to spread these ideas between music and its external spheres, to make more musics and knowledge about those musics available to much larger audiences than would normally be the case, and to foster a universal perspective by encouraging respect for diversity. It was an impetus to his initiating new societies, to linking cultures as well as disciplines, to making government agencies socially useful, to prod-ding educators to take risks with new ideas and approaches, to experimenting with new techniques, to reconciling producers and consumers and middlemen in music. In candid self-assessments he wrote:

Folklore and folk music are only temporary bypaths for me and I sometimes rile up a bit when I am referred to as a student of folk music. . . . I make this sole and last appeal *not* to represent me as a student of folk music except as a neces-sary fulfillment of the ordinary task of the musicologist as I see it, namely the study of *all* the music of a culture, a geographical area, or the whole world. . . . Strictly speaking, I do not regard myself as a scholar, I am a systematist. The two are very different. For one thing, the scholar is primarily interested in knowing everything he can of other peoples' work; the systematist, in appropri-ating everything he can lay his hands on in the continual task of fortifying his World View. The scholar may be a creator; the systematist must be.[23]

Seeger's universal approach to music, his grasping of all the parts and the whole, possibly stems from the dreams of his youth—possibly the agonies of his earaches—when he frequently saw heavenly bodies in collision and saw it as his responsibility to bring order out of such chaos, both in a linear and particle fashion. This was contributed to by his affinity for Aristotelian logic and Hegelian dialectic cum synthe-sis, and later by his cursory fascination with the yin and yang of Eastern philosophies. His thought and writings were infused with the juxtaposition of dichotomy in singularity, structure and function, critical and scientific, esthetic and semiotic, prescriptive and de-scriptive.

Seeger's career, informed by intellectual curiosity of such enormous proportions, touched every aspect of the music world. The underpinning motive was to understand music both in its own terms and in a sociocultural milieu. He did not eschew specialized studies—as one would call ethnographic works in anthropology or bibliographic studies in musicology—indeed, he saw them as necessary building blocks. But his primary bent was to see music studied within the total context. Mantle Hood suggested, "For the new students in music, for the mature colleague, for all in between I make bold to offer advice: *read all Charles Seeger has had to say before claiming to have a new idea.*"[24]

The last months of Seeger's life found his mind still restless with ideas, still appreciative of his longevity, and persistent possessor of a grand wit. He wrote: "I am through the cataract ordeal, having left behind me about six months of my ordinary life. What a gorgeous time in which to simply lie still with my eyes closed and think!!!"[25]

In preparing for what was to be our last visit together, he wrote detailed instructions on what to do followed by a suggested improvisation, as one might expect from him.[26]

This is the time for snow and ice storms. I'll meet you at Kennedy [Airport] weather and traffic permitting. If I am not on hand as you arrive, telephone me at once. If there is no answer, take it for granted that I am on my way. If I don't show up, watch a message center (if there is one) and wait as long as you feel like, but try telephoning once more before you leave New York. Call me up once again before putting up for the night. The last two trains leave Grand Central at 11:15 and 12:30 and I could met you in Brewster. (I enclose time table probably correct, give or take a minute.) If I can't drive, there are taxis. If the unforeseeable happens we'll act unforseeably.

VML [very much love]

He was at Kennedy to meet us.

Two particular images will resonate with all who knew him. Sidney Robertson Cowell recalls:

As to the Seeger influence on musicologists . . . at dinner with Carlton Sprague Smith and Raymond Kendall in Los Angeles about 1950, Seeger was discussed with a respect, even a reverence, that the two men accorded to nobody else. His conspicuous energy and good health came up and I mentioned that Charlie had a regular exercise routine and had once told me that what he considered contributed most to his well-being was the ten to twelve minutes a day that he spent standing an his head.

I then offered to make after-dinner coffee. When I came back with the coffee tray, Carlton and Ray were at opposite ends of the room, quietly engaged in doing headstands. If the ability to stand on one's head is desirable for a musicologist, they wanted to make sure that they qualified. [27]

Mantle Hood writes:

An image that will never die is of Charles seated cross-legged (or sometimes in lotus position) on the floor pursuing an abstract idea with students and colleages . . . : the scarf at his throat, a beautiful beard . . . Bass moccasins on his feet, the posture of an erect young man, the stride of Paul Bunyan, blue, blue eyes that twinkle or snap—depending on the course of discussion—this is the Charles Seeger everybody loves and remembers. [28]

During the early decades of his life, historical events drew Seeger's attention and participation. Once he settled in Washington, however, it seems as if he decided to be a part of history in the making rather than reacting to historical events. His ideological preferences became subsumed under doing; he had a chance to change the historical canvas to suit his vision of the way the world should run.

The last decades of his life were propitious for Seeger. The first half of the 1970s brought to a climax various movements for rights and challenges to government policies by a generation of mostly young Americans who abhorred the moral hypocrisy of their elders. With the protest movements, Seeger was totally in sympathy.

It is fitting that when Seeger died his desk was covered with work to be done. The chronicle of his achievements was noted in the Berkeley Citation, highest honor bestowed at the University of California, Berkeley, which had been presented to Seeger in 1968:

Musician and profound student of . . . the musics of the world, he has inspired whole generations of colleagues and students through the breadth of his humanity and vision, the insight and fertility of his ideas, and the contagious excitement of his personality. Author of numerous articles, a pioneer in the scientific analysis of melody, and lodestone to folk singers and ethnomusicologists everywhere, he is also distinguished in the offices he has held and honors received. The time spanned by his service to the University bridges more than half a century: coming to Berkeley in 1912 as chairman of the Music Department, which he revolutionized, he left in 1919, returning in 1957 to UCLA . . . a vigorous worker and wise counsellor in the Institute of Ethnomusicology. This one is especially dear to the community of musicians.

Peter once related to me a vignette which I think also applies, although Charlie might not entirely agree. Pete remembered that when he was a child, Charlie, in one of the bedtime stories he told to the boys, related a story that ended with a cowboy's epitaph on a gravepost someplace in the far West: "He done his damndest."[29]

Notes
Bibliography
Index

~

Notes

❧

Chapter 1. New England, New York, and Mexico, 1886–1908

1. Richard Hofstadter, *The Age of Reform* (New York: 1955), p. 9.

2. Charles Seeger, dictated to Penny Seeger Cohen, April 22, 1977.

3. Seeger referred to Dr. Karl's wife again as Lucy, not Sally (letter to Charles Evans, 20 February 1976), although later he identified her correctly as Sally. Genealogical information comes from a letter to Seeger from Henry Leland Clarke, February 12, 1976.

4. Letter supporting his son Michael's appeal to be classified 1A on the grounds of conscientious objection to war, Nobember 23, 1952. (The letter includes a reference to Mayflower ancestors, denied elsewhere.)

5. Charles Seeger, dictated to Penny Seeger Cohen, April 22, 1977.

6. Charles Louis Seeger, Jr., was born to Charles and Elsie Seeger on December 14, 1886. His brother Alan was born June 22, 1888, and Elizabeth (also known as Elsie, or Sister) on December 9, 1889). Alan, a volunteer in the French Foreign Legion, was killed in France in 1916, where a monument to his memory was dedicated in 1923. Elizabeth died in Bridgewater, Connecticut, in 1973.

7. Charles Seeger, dictated to Penny Seeger Cohen, April 22, 1977.

8. Mexico, for the first three-quarters of the nineteenth century, had passed through several stages of revolt, independence, foreign rule, loss of lands to several of the United "States," and a quasi-independence under Beníto Juarez and his successor, Lerdo, who ruled until November 21, 1876, when he fled Mexico in the face of an alliance of caudillos with allegiance to Díaz.

9. Charles Seeger, letter to Belden Wigglesworth, who was doing a biography of Alan, April 18, 1953.

10. Elizabeth commented, "I gather that Miss Nourse was a strict teacher and that the school was a good one; but Mother was *not* a good student. I believe that it was she who vastly preferred the novel to the textbook. There is the famous story that when Mother saw Miss Nourse much later, and told her what a good student I was, Miss Nourse said sternly, 'She must take after her father.'"

11. Charles Seeger, "Boyhood on Staten Island."

12. Seeger kept hundreds of pictures for stagings for family performances both in Mexico and New York.

13. Charles Seeger, dictated to Penny Seeger Cohen, April 22, 1977.

14. Letter to Malena Kuss, August 27, 1978.

15. Charles Seeger, dictated to Penny Seeger Cohen, April 22, 1977.

16. The American Foreign Legion Post in Mexico City was named the Alan Seeger Post.

17. Seeger, "Boyhood on Staten Island."

18. Elizabeth Seeger, letter dated January 13, year unspecified.

19. Brooks's widow Gladys lived in Bridgewater in later years, where Charles Seeger spent his last decade. Other friends in the area included the noted musicologist Paul Henry Lang and musicologist-historian Carlton Sprague Smith.

20. Seeger's reminiscences of residence in Apthorp House, letter to the master of Adams House, Reuben A. Brower, July 28, 1959.

21. Charles Seeger, dictated to Penny Seeger Cohen, April 22, 1977.

22. Ibid.

23. Ibid.

24. Ibid.

25. Charles Seeger, in *Records of the Class of 1908* (Harvard University, 1958).

Chapter 2. Europe, Constance, and the University of California, 1908–1918

1. Charles Seeger, dictated to Penny Seeger Cohen, April 22, 1977.

2. Ibid.

3. Roger Shattuck, *The Banquet Years: The Origin of the Avant-Garde in France, 1885 to World War I* (New York, 1961), p. 10.

4. Ibid., p. 115.

5. The following paragraph is based on ibid., pp. 119–31, 161.

6. The following paragraph is based on ibid., pp. 135–42.

7. Ibid., p. 329–32.

8. The following paragraph is based on ibid., pp. 332, 349.

9. H. Stuart Hughes, *Consciousness and Society: The Revolution of European Social Thought, 1890–1930* (New York, 1958), p. 13.

10. Ibid., pp. 13–14.

11. Ibid., p. 15.

12. Ibid., p. 4.

13. Ibid., pp. 64–65.

14. Ibid., pp. 191.

15. Charles Seeger, dictated to Penny Seeger Cohen, April 22, 1977.

16. Seeger related to me details about Constance's family in an interview.

17. Walter Damrosch became conductor of the New York Symphony, and Frank Damrosch director of the prestigious Institute of Musical Art, where Constance studied and where both Charlie and Constance were employed.

18. Charles Seeger, dictated to Penny Seeger Cohen, April 22, 1977.

19. Charles Seeger, "Toward an Establishment of the Study of Musicology in America," manuscript, [1913], Seeger Collection, Library of Congress, pp. 1–2, later revised.

20. Ibid., pp. 2–3.

21. Glen Haydon, *Introduction to Musicology* (New York, 1941), p. viii.

22. Charles Seeger, dictated to Penny Seeger Cohen, April 22, 1977.

23. Vincent Duckles, preface to UCB Music Library Catalogue for the 1977 meeting of the International Musicological Society.

24. Frederick J. Teggart, "The Circumstance or the Substance of History," 1910; See also Teggart's *The Idea of Progress—A Collection of Readings Selected by Frederick J. Teggart.*

25. H. M. Stephens and H. H. Bolton, eds., *Prolegomena to History—the Relation of History to Literature, Philosophy, and Science* (Berkeley: University of California Publications no. 4, 1916–17); *Processes of History*, 1918.

26. Commonwealth Club of California, *The Population of California* (San Francisco, 1946), p. 21.

27. See Frank L. Beach, "The Transformation of California," Ph.D. diss., University of California, 1963, esp. for the period 1900–1920; and James Gregory, *American Exodus: The Dust Bowl Migration and Okie Culture in California* (Oxford, 1989).

28. Walter J. Stein, *California and the Dust Bowl Migration* (Westport, Conn., 1973), p. 34.

29. See Carlton Parker, *The Casual Laborer* (New York, 1920), a classic study of U.S. migratory farm labor. See also Fuller's study on agricultural labor and the evaluation of California agriculture (1940); the *San Francisco News* for this period; and A. L. Kroeber, *Configuration of Culture Growth* (Berkeley and Los Angeles, 1944).

30. Richard Hofstadter, *The Age of Reform* (New York, 1955), p. 5.

31. Richard Reuss, "American Folklore and Left-wing Politics, 1927–57," Ph.D. diss., Indiana University, 1971, pp. 224–25.

32. Ibid., p. 225; the quotation may be a paraphrase.

33. For a concise summary of Cowell's life and achievement, see *The New Grove Dictionary of American Music* (New York: Macmillan, 1986).

34. Henry Cowell's comments were described in Sidney Robertson Cowell, letter to Charles Seeger, 1960, about Cowell's interview with Hugo Weisgall in the *Music Quarterly*, October 1959.

35. Seeger, letter to a Dr. Godwin, who was doing a study of Cowell, December 13, 1974.

36. Sidney Robertson Cowell, "Recall," letters to Charles Seeger's biographer in 1965–1966. Cowell left Berkeley in early 1918 to enlist in the army.

37. Ibid.

38. Henry Cowell, "Charles Seeger," in *American Composers on American Music—A Symposium* (New York, 1962), p. 121.

39. Charles Seeger, letter to Dr. Godwin, December 13, 1974.

40. See Sidney Robertson Cowell, "Charles Seeger 1886–1979," *Musical Quarterly* 65 (April 1979), 305.

41. Ibid., pp. 305–06.

42. H. Cowell, interview with Hugo Weisgall, 1959 (see S. R. Cowell, letter to Charles Seeger, 1960).

43. Charles Seeger, "Henry Cowell," *Magazine of Art* 33 (May 1940): 288.

44. Robert Stevenson, professor of music at UCLA, writes, "While head of the UC Music Department [Charles Seeger] also performed. In the San José newspapers he was listed for a performance of the Brahms F minor Sonata" (letter to Bonnie Wade, 9 September 1976, in author's possession).

45. The Parthenia were also said to have been given in the Greek Theater as public productions. See H. Cowell, "Charles Seeger," pp. 120–21.

46. Author's notes.

47. Ronald Erickson, *Music of Charles Seeger, 1886–1979*, Arch Records, no. 1750, Berkeley, Calif., c. 1984.

48. H. Cowell, "Charles Seeger," pp. 120–21.

49. Ibid., pp. 121–24.

50. Charles Seeger, dictated to Penny Seeger Cohen, April 22, 1977. These cylinders have only recently been copied, with the aid of a National Endowment for the Humanities grant.

51. The first lecture was titled "Introduction to Musicology: Scientific Methodology"; the other "Introduction to Musicology: Critical Methodology."

52. Reuss, "American Folklore and Left-wing Politics," p. 226.

53. Charles Seeger, in *Records of the Class of 1908* (Harvard University, 1933), pp. 628–29.

54. Charles Seeger, in *Records of the Class of 1908* (1938), p. 121.

55. Charles Seeger, in *Records of the Class of 1908* (1958).

Chapter 3. A Decade of Reckoning, 1918–1930

1. Henry Cowell, "Charles Seeger," in *American Composers on American Music — A Symposium* (New York: Ungar, 1952), pp. 122–23.

2. Charles Seeger, dictated to Penny Seeger Cohen, April 22, 1977.

3. H. Cowell, "Charles Seeger," pp. 119, 122–23.

4. Charles Seeger, dictated to Penny Seeger Cohen, April 22, 1977.

5. Richard Reuss, "Folk Music and Social Conscience: The Musical Odyssey of Charles Seeger," *Western Folklore* 38 (October 1979): 221–38.

6. Charles Seeger, "Henry Cowell," *Magazine of Art* 33 (May 1940), 288–89.

7. Charles Seeger, letter to Richard Reuss, June 18, 1977.

8. Much of the material in this chapter is based on personal interviews with Charles Seeger.

9. Charles Seeger, dictated to Penny Seeger Cohen, April 22, 1977.

10. Ibid.

11. In 1923, all of Seeger's stored music and important papers were destroyed, along with the family's belongings, in the disastrous Berkeley fire.

12. Charles Seeger, dictated to Penny Seeger Cohen, April 22, 1977.

13. H. Cowell, "Charles Seeger," p. 121.

14. Ibid.

15. Charles Seeger, in *Records of the Class of 1908* (Harvard University, 1958).

16. "Music in the American University," *Educational Review* 66 (September 1923), 95–99.

17. ""On Style and Manner in Modern Composition," *Musical Quarterly* 9 (July 1923), 423–31.

18. Ibid., p. 423.

19. Ibid.

20. ""On the Principles of Musicology," *Musical Quarterly* 10 (April 1924), 244–50.

21. Ibid., p. 250.

22. Charles Seeger, "Reviewing a Review," *Eolian Review* 3 (1923), 16–23.

23. Charles Seeger, "Prolegomena to Musicology: The Problem of the Musical Point of View and the Bias of Linguistic Presentation," *Eolus* 4 (May 1925), 12–24.

24. Charles Seeger, "A Fragment of Greek Music," *The Baton* 8 (May 1929), 5–6.

25. Charles Seeger, "Dissonance and the Devil: An Interesting Passage in a Bach Cantata," *The Baton* (May 1930), 7–8.

26. Charles Seeger, "On Dissonant Counterpoint," *Modern Music* 7 (June–July 1930), 25–31.

27. Charles Seeger, "Lines on the Grace Note," *The Baton* 10 (February 1931), 6–7.

28. Seeger, "On Dissonant Counterpoint," p. 26.

29. Ibid., pp. 26–29.

30. Ibid., p. 31.

31. In 1926 the Julliard School was founded with a bequest from the estate of a wealthy silk merchant and patron of the arts named Augustus D. Juilliard. In the early 1930s it took over the IMA.

32. Charles Seeger, in *Records of the Class of 1908* (Harvard University, 1933).

Chapter 4. *Ruth and the New York Scene, 1930–1935*

1. The information contained herein, unless otherwise cited, is culled from materials in the Seeger Archive collection in the Library of Congress, which I had earlier reviewed with Seeger before his death; conversational and written information by Seeger himself on facets of Ruth's life and work; correspondence and conversations with Michael Seeger; other restricted access items of Ruth Crawford and Charles Seeger, including their love letters; and personal and family correspondence between Charlie and Ruth, first when all of these were with Seeger, himself, and later, in the possession of Michael, the executor of Charlie's estate. I have referred also to Matilda Gaume, *Ruth Crawford Seeger: Memoirs, Memories, Music* (Metuchen, N.J.): Scarecrow Press, 1986). See also "Ruth Crawford Seeger," *The New Grove Dictionary of Music*, ed. Wiley Hitchcock and Stanley Sadie (New York: Macmillan, 1986); and Herbert Mitgang, ed., *The Letters of Carl Sandburg* (New York, 1968), for comments on Ruth.

2. Ruth suspected that the bequest was the gift of a cousin, Nellie Hastings, who later supported her during her Guggenheim Fellowship year in Europe.

3. In June 1933 Ruth's *Three Songs* were chosen to represent the United States at the International Society of Contemporary Music Festival in Amsterdam.

4. Ruth Crawford, letter to "Alice," January 24, 1930.

5. Charles Seeger, "Ruth Crawford," in *American Composers on Music: A Symposium*, ed. Henry Cowell (New York: Frederick Ungar, 1962), p. 118.

6. Ibid., p. 116.

7. Ruth Crawford [Seeger], "New York Jottings," February 22, 1930.

8. Seeger's treatise on composition went through several revisions. There are four versions, two in the Music Library at the University of California, Berkeley, and two in the Library of Congress. The few composers who have examined it think it is a work of genius. It will be published by the University of California Press.

9. Ruth Crawford [Seeger], letter to Henry Allen Moe, January 22, 1931.

10. At this time, in 1932, Constance had a studio on West Sixty-fifth Street and she and Charlie lived at East Eighty-ninth Street.

11. Serge R. Denisoff, *Great Day Coming: Folk Music and the American Left* (Urbana: University of Illinois Press, 1971), p. 42.

12. Archie Green, "Charles Louis Seeger," *Journal of American Folklore* 90 (1979), 393.

13. Ibid., p. 363.

14. Unless otherwise cited, information on the Composers' Collective is derived from many conversations and notes made from conversations with Seeger as well as interviews with the late Norman Cazden (June 1976, Berkeley, California). It should be noted that Seeger gave many interviews and much the same information — some verbatim — to other people doing research on the subject, or on members of the family, usually of a similar nature. See also "Composers' Collective," *The New Grove Dictionary of Music*.

15. Siegmeister, Copland, Clarke, and Seeger wrote for the Collective under assumed names for professional or political reasons. Also involved in the Collective was Charlie's and Ruth's Latin American friend, Lan Adomian. With a group of radical musicians, Lan had formed another organization that also had begun composing songs for strikers, unemployed picketers, and other workers.

16. Richard Reuss, "American Folklore and Left-wing Politics, 1927–1957," Ph.D. diss., Indiana University, 1971, p. 266.

17. David K. Dunaway, "Charles Seeger and Carl Sands: The Composers' Collective Years," *Ethnomusicology* 24 (May 1980), 164.

18. "Hanns Eisler," *The New Grove Dictionary of Music*; see also "Composers' Collective," ibid.

19. "Hanns Eisler," *The New Grove Dictionary of Music*.

20. Ibid. See also "Composers' Collective," ibid.

21. They were performed in Philadelphia on March 27, 1933, by the Society for Contemporary Music, to poor reviews and unfavorable audience reaction.

22. *The Red Song Book*, published by the Workers Library Publishers of New York in 1932.

23. *The New Workers' Song Book*, compiled by Seeger and Lan Adomian and issued in 1934; see Denisoff, *Great Day Coming*, p. 45.

24. *Songs of the People*, 1935.

25. Charles Seeger, letter to Richard Reuss, June 18, 1971. See Reuss, "American Folklore and Left-wing Politics."

26. Henry Leland Clarke, response to Steven E. Gilbert, "'In Seventy-Six the Sky Was Red': A Profile of Earl Robinson," presented to the annual meeting of the American Musicological Society, November 7, 1976. In "Composers' Collective," *The New Grove Dictionary of Music*, Clarke lists Schaefer as a member.

27. Charles Seeger, "On Proletarian Music," *Modern Music* 11 (March 1934): 121–27, was an outgrowth of an invited lecture Seeger had delivered at a union meeting on the dictatorship of language. All quotations in this paragraph are from this article.

28. Joseph Yasser, *A Theory of Evolving Tonality* (New York, 1932).

29. *New York Musicological Society Bulletin* 1 (November 1931).

30. Charles Seeger, letter to a Dr. Godwin, December 13, 1974.

31. American Musicological Society, 1934. On December 1 a constitution and by-laws were drawn up and officers elected for 1935–1937: Kinkeldey, president; Seeger, senior vice-president; Oliver Strunk, vice-president.

32. Charles Seeger, letter to the author, April 12, 1976.

33. The dubbing that George List and Moses Asch made in their famous edition were mainly from Cowell's two sets.

34. Helen Roberts, with a Carnegie Endowment grant, had designed electronic equipment for comparative musicology at her laboratory in Yale's Institute of Human Relations. When she and George Herzog were dismissed, Herzog took his collection, part of which had been left to him by von Hornbostel, to Columbia.

35. Seeger served simultaneously as president of the ACSM (1935) and vice-chair of the Gesellschaft für Vergleichende Musikwissenschaft from 1934 through 1936, when it ceased functioning. Lachmann departed for Palestine, where he offered to start up a new journal but stipulated, "We are not going to compare anything." No more comparative musicology! Two-thirds of the dues of the nearly 150 members had been sent to Berlin to keep the *Zeitschrift* going. Also, the ASCM gave $100 toward the new journal, and Spivacke and the ACLS provided $100 for the fourth issue of the journal. But when Lachmann died, Chancellor Magnes of Hebrew University instead used the money to publish Lachmann's work on the Djerba. (All ACSM records are now housed at Wesleyan University.)

36. Charles Seeger, Helen Roberts, and Henry Cowell, "Music and Musicology" and "Music Occidental," *Encyclopedia of the Social Sciences* (New York, 1933), 11:143–50.

37. Charles Seeger, "Preface to All Linguistic Treatment of Music," *Music Vanquard* 1 (March–April 1935), 17–31. The following quotations all come from this source.

38. Charles Seeger, in *Records of the Class of 1908* (Harvard University, 1933).

39. Charles Seeger, in *Records of the Class of 1908* (1938).

40. Irving Howe and Lewis Coser, *The American Communist Party: A Critical History* (New York, 1962), p. 217.

41. See Reuss, "American Folklore and Left-wing Politics," p. 229.

42. Green, "Charles Louis Seeger," pp 393–95.

43. Charles Seeger, letter to Sidney Robertson [Cowell], in S. R. Cowell, "Charles Seeger (1886–1979)," *Musical Quarterly* 65 (April 1979), 305–06.

44. Benton's mural was dedicated jointly with José Clemente Orozco's frescoes, January 19, 1931. See Green, "Charles Louis Seeger," pp. 393–94; also Charles Seeger, dictated to Penny Seeger Cohen, April 22, 1977.

45. Charles Seeger, dictated to Penny Seeger Cohen, April 22, 1977.

Chapter 5. The New Deal and Music, 1935–1941

1. Executive Order 7072, April 30, 1935.

2. Charles Seeger, dictated to Penny Seeger Cohen, April 22, 1977.

3. Charles Seeger, letter to to Archie Green, June 24, 1975.

4. Charles Seeger, dictated to Penny Seeger Cohen, April 22, 1977.

5. Archie Green, "A Resettlement Administration Song Sheet," *JEMF Quarterly* 2 (1979), 393.

6. Charles Seeger, letter to Richard Reuss, June 18, 1971.

7. Adrian Dornbush, *First Annual Report of the Resettlement Administration* (Washington, D.C.: 1936), pp. 88–91.

8. Charles Seeger, *General Considerations for Music Directors in Leading Community Programs*, rev. and exp. as *Musical Manual, 1937*, unpublished.

9. Richard Reuss, "Folk Music and Social Conscience: The Musical Odyssey of Charles Seeger," *Western Folklore* 38 (October 1979), 233.

10. Possibly Great Lakes Lumberjack, Peter suspects. (Interview.)

11. Sidney Robertson Cowell, "Recall," letters to Charles Seeger's biographer in 1965–1966.

12. Green, "A Resettlement Administration Song Sheet."

13. Dornbush, letter to Inglis, November 23, 1936.

14. Charles Seeger, *Music Manual*, pp. 27–28.

15. Charles Seeger and Margaret Valiant, "Journal of a Field Representative," *Ethnomusicology* 24 (May 1980), 169–210.

16. A major result of this work was a recording expedition in the Southeast, carried out by Herbert Haufrecht, that yielded more than 300 discs (deposited in the Archive of American Folk Song.)

17. Charles Seeger, dictated to Penny Seeger Cohen, April 22, 1977.

18. Ibid.

19. Margaret Valiant, *Journal of a Field Representative*, with foreword by Seeger (Washington, D.C.: Resettlement Administration, 1937).

20. Seeger and Valiant, "Journal of a Field Representative."

21. Ibid.

22. S. R. Cowell, "Recall."

23. Sidney Robertson Cowell, "Charles Seeger 1886–1979," *Musical Quarterly* 65 (April 1979), 306. A full set of field disc recordings made by Sidney Robertson and

supplemented by Seeger and Valiant, now deposited in the Library of Congress Archive of Folk Song, is the major body of work surviving from this period. These discs, recorded between June 1936 and September 1937, are accompanied by field notes; Seeger himself supervised the checklist of nearly 160 discs and three volumes.

24. Catalogued as AFS 3155 to 3313, June 1936 to September 1937, accompanied by Resettlement Administration field notes.

25. S. R. Cowell, "Recall."

26. These were $6^1/_4 \times 8^1/_4$ inches in size.

27. Charles Seeger, report to Adrian Dornbush, December 10, 1935.

28. Seeking financial support, Dornbush asked Seeger to send a set of the pamphlets to the Carnegie Foundation, for by January 4, 1937, he was told that there was no more agency money for song sheets. Seeger had sought aid from the Civilian Conservation Corps (CCC) and the Works Progress Administration (WPA). After applying to the Department of Agriculture, Dornbush attempted unsuccessfully to have the WPA's Federal Theater Project issue the remaining song sheets.

29. Charles Seeger, letter to Archie Green, June 24, 1975.

30. S. R. Cowell, "Recall."

31. Seeger and Valiant, "Journal of a Field Representative," p. 178.

32. S. R. Cowell, "Recall."

33. Seeger's twenty-two months with the RA is documented in a file of 500 pages of memoranda and reports, mostly by Seeger to Dornbush, bound as "Records, Music Unit" under "U.S. Farm Security Administration, Special Skills Division, Music Unit, Miscellaneous," in addition to the discs, documentation, and song sheets noted above.

34. Seeger's contacts with the WPA when seeking support for the RA song sheets project probably helped to secure him a post with the agency when the RA folded. Among its programs were the Federal Theater Project (FTP), the Writers' Project (FWP), and the Arts Projects, which included the Folksong and Folklore Department, directed by Herbert Halpert (of the FTP); the Folklore Studies Project, under Ben A. Botkin (of the FWP); the leisure-time program of the Recreation Division under Nicholas Ray; the Historical Records Survey, and the Federal Music Project.

35. "Composers' Forum-Laboratory," *The New Grove Dictionary of Music*, ed. Wiley Hitchcock and Stanley Sadie (New York: Macmillan, 1986). The first concert, given on October 30, 1935, included works by Aaron Copland, Edgard Varèse, George Antheil, and Roy Harris.

36. More contemporary evidence of this problem is the recent (1989, 1990) controversy over the funding of art and taste in art, with the National Endowment for the Arts being held hostage for reauthorization and funding through an act of censorship by reactionary politicians.

37. Seeger's guidelines were as follows:

1. recreation always was more concerned with the effect of work or play on the individual or community;
2. there should be leisure time pursuits;
3. musicians do *not* agree on the relationship of recreation and music;

4. we need to know all music resources and needs in a community;

5. the main job of a recreation leader is to get music out of people;

6. we should see what people like by what they *do* more than what they *say;*

7. recreation leaders should continue all going activities, aid the weak ones, and start new ones;

8. we need to recognize that two traditions are at play, oral and written, and each have different values;

9. in such recreational settings, emphasis should be on folk and popular material;

10. there is a legitimate musical activity for every social, education, economic, and age level, i.e., there are several "musics," therefore music need not be a highly specialized activity.

Charles Seeger *Music as Recreation* (Washington, D.C.: Works Project Administration, Technical Series, Community Service Circular no. 1, 1940).

38. The California WPA materials are in the Music Library, University of California, Berkeley.

39. Charles Seeger, ed., *Check-list of Recorded Music in the English Language in the Archive of American Folk Song to July, 1940,* 3 vols. (Washington, D.C.: Library of Congress, 1942).

40. Charles Seeger, address to teachers of District 1, Florida Music Project, Jacksonville, 21 March 1939. Quotations in the following paragraphs are all from this source, which was sent to the author by Joseph Hickerson at the Library of Congress.

41. Michael Seeger, letter to the author, June 28, 1985.

42. Ibid.

43. Charles Seeger, "Music in America," *Magazine of Art* 31 (July 1938), 411–13, 435–36. Three excellent photographs accompanying the article confirm Seeger's eclecticism. One shows Josef Hofman at the piano with the caption, "Academic music is typified by the austere expertness of virtuoso pianist Josef Hofman. . . . The American audience for "good" music is small but constantly increasing." Benny Goodman's swing band is accompanied by the caption, "Popular music today usually is swing. . . . Much of swing's vitality and lasting power are derived from the content it takes from folk music and from the technical inventiveness and skill taken from the academies." And Ben Shahn's photograph of square dancers and guitarists at the Skyline Farms, Alabama, claims, "The music of the masses is still going strong in America, losing, as it goes, many old songs but healthily adding many new."

Later Seeger noted the need to understand the technical and cultural functions of the various musical idioms in the United States. He wished to see a unified American tradition from whence all these idioms arose and reiterated that only with such a comprehensive understanding could American music be perceived as a unified tradition, but it would not be easy, since each one of the idioms is like a language that must be learned in order to understand and determine its value (Frank L. Harrison, Mantle Hood, and Claude V. Palisca, *Musicology* [Englewood Cliffs, N.J.: Prentice-Hall, 1963], p. 281).

44. Charles Seeger, "Grass Roots for American Music," *Modern Music* 16 (March–April 1939), 143–49.

45. Charles Seeger, "The Importance to Cultural Understanding of Folk and Popular Music," in *Digest of Proceedings*, Conference on Inter-American Relations in the Field of Music (Washington, D.C., 1940), pp. 1–10. All quotations are from this source.

46. Charles Seeger, "Contrapuntal Style in the Three-Voice Shape-Note Hymns," *Musical Quarterly* 26 (4 October 1940), 483–93.

47. "Folk Music as a Source of Social History," in *The Cultural Approach to History*, ed. Caroline Ware (New York: 1940), pp. 316–23.

48. Charles Seeger, "Music and Culture," in the *Proceedings of the Music Teachers National Association*, 35th ser. (1940), 112–22.

49. Charles Seeger, "Systematic and Historical Orientations in Musicology," *Acta Musicologica* 11 (1939), 121–28.

50. Charles Seeger, "Music and Government: Field for an Applied Musicology." In *Papers Read at the International Congress of Musicology Held at New York, September 11–18, 1939*, 12–20. New York: Music Educators National Conference for the American Musicological Society, 1940. (The AMS co-hosted with the MENC the First International Congress of Musicology, where Seeger made the lead-off address.)

51. Charles Seeger, Records of the Class, statement for his 1938 Harvard reunion.

52. Charles Seeger, letter to parents, December 20, 1939.

Chapter 6. The Pan American Years, 1941–1953

1. During its first year, the Committee on Inter-American Relations was under the auspices of Nelson Rockefeller's Office of Inter-American Affairs and, for the next two years, functioned through the Pan American Union. During this period the Carnegie Corporation provided $15,000 in funding.

2. The organizing committee for music also included William Berrien; Evan Clark (who had the largest collection of Latin American records at the time); Eric Clarke; N. Colier; Howard Hanson of the Eastman School of Music); a Mrs. James, chief of the PAU Intellectual Cooperation Division; Eric Moore of the Federal Music Project; Carlton Sprague Smith of the New York Public Library Music Division; Harold Spivacke, head of the Library of Congress Music Division; Davidson Taylor of CBS; a representative from NBC's international division; and another from the ACE movie projection service. Charles Seeger, "The Importance to Cultural Understanding of Folk and Popular Music." In *Digest of Proceedings*, Conference on Inter-American Relations in the Field of Music, 1–10. Washington D.C.: U.S. Department of State, 1940.

3. Charles Seeger, dictated to Penny Seeger Cohen, April 22, 1977.

4. Charles Seeger, "Inter-American Relations in the Field of Music: Some Basic Considerations." *Proceedings of the Music Teachers National Association*, 36th ser. (1942), 41–44. The quotations that follow are taken from this article, in which Seeger gave details of the funding of the PAU as an example of new international music organizations.

5. Seeger credited Lawlor's success in part to her "staying in the background," reflecting his old-fashioned skepticism about women in positions of power and influence.

Her stint was intitially to be six weeks, then six months, finally six years; half of her salary was paid by the PAU and half by MENC.

6. Seeger hired Cowell for about a year and had him work out of New York. Charles Seeger, letter to the previously mentioned Dr. Godwin, December 13, 1974.

7. Charles Seeger, dictated to Penny Seeger Cohen, April 22, 1977.

8. Ibid.

9. See Vanett Lawlor, *Educación musical en 14 repúblicas americanas* (Washington, D.C.: Pan American Union, 1945), which summarizes all these efforts.

10. *Music in Latin America*, PAU Club and Study Series 3 (Washington, D.C.: Pan American Union, 1942).

11. See A. T. Luper, *The Music of Argentina*, PAU Music Series 5 (Washington, D.C.: Pan American Union, 1942); and *The Music of Brazil*, PAU Music Series 9 (Washington, D.C.: Pan American Union, 1943).

12. See Gilbert Chase, *Partial List of Latin American Music Obtainable in the United States with a Supplementary List of Books and a Selective List of Phonograph Records* (1941); 2d ed., 1942; and Leila Fern Thompson, *Selected References in English on Latin American Music*, PAU Music Series 13 (Washington, D.C.: Pan American Union, 1944).

13. Gustavo Duran, *Recordings of Latin American Songs and Dances*, PAU Music Series 3 (Washington, D.C.: Pan American Union, 1942).

14. See Charles Seeger, "Notes on Music in the Americas. Property Rights in Musical Works," *Bulletin of the Pan American Union* 79 (1945), 3.

15. Charles Seeger, "UNESCO, February 1948," *Music Library Association Notes*, 2d ser., 5 (March), 165–68. The following quotations are from this article. UNESCO was formalized in London, November 16, 1945. Seeger lauded its magnificent preamble and organs and its intent to secure mass participation from each nation's citizens. U.S. music was represented by Howard Hanson, then president of the National Music Council, while Waldo Leland of the ACLS (American Council of Learned Societies) he judged a friend of musicology.

16. The latter also had a project under way to prepare a catalog of world music, listing music already available in recorded form and music which should be recorded to supplement existing materials; $8,000 had been budgeted for that).

17. Charles Seeger, dictated to Penny Seeger Cohen, April 22, 1977.

18. Charles Seeger, "The Musician: Man Serves Art. The Educator: Art Serves Man," *UNESCO Courier* 6 (1953), 15–16. The following quotations are from this source.

19. Charles Seeger, "A Proposal to Found an International Society for Music Education," *Music in Education* (Paris: UNESCO, 1955), 325–31, outlined the project to develop an agency to act as an international interest group for music educators.

20. One was a project that interested Seeger greatly—a proposed encyclopedia of music to replace the *Grove Dictionary of Music and Musicians*, to be published by Macmillan at a cost of over a million dollars. This was an opportune time, Seeger believed, for American scholars to demonstrate their worth, particularly on cultural and idiomatic areas of music other than Western art music.

21. In "Music and Musicology," *Encyclopedia of the Social Sciences* (New York, 1933), 11:143–50, and later in revised editions.

22. This was published as "Systematic Musicology: Viewpoints, Orientations, and Methods," *JAMS* 4 (Fall 1951), 240–48.

23. In an earlier talk at the AMS (1935), Seeger had chided musicologists for segmenting and categorizing to excess and explained the (to him) abhorrent division of music study as "a symptom of an attachment to a linguistic convention that separated fixed categories" (Frank L. Harrison, Mantle Hood, and Claude V. Palisca, *Musicology* [Englewood Cliffs, N.J.: Prentice-Hall, 1963], p. 108). He returned to this theme time and again, and developed it into a more sophisticated theory.

24. Charles Seeger, "Preface to the Description of a Music," *Kongressbericht*, International Gesellschaft für Musikwissenschaft (Amsterdam, 1953), pp. 360–70.

25. Between 1940 and 1953, Seeger's bibliography lists twenty-three publications; he wrote extensively for U.S. and Latin American journals, many focusing on education. In fact, all but one of his writings on education appeared during this time, published in journals such as the *Music Educators' Journal, Proceedings of the Music Teachers National Education Association*, the *Music Education Source Book,* and UNESCO publications.

26. "Wartime and Peacetime Programs in Music Education," read at the Sixth General Session of the Conference of the National Institute on Music Education in Wartime (Chicago, 1942), published in *Music Educators' Journal* 29 (January 1943), 12–13.

27. "Music Education and Musicology," *MENC Journal*, May–June 1945, included an addendum, "The Music Historian," by Curt Sachs (pp. 78–79). (See note 29.)

28. Seeger pointed to the MENC's recognition of the need to work more closely with musicologists by establishing, at the 1944 St. Louis conference, a Committee on Music Education and Musicology, of which Seeger was named chair. At the December 1944 AMS meeting, a similar Committee on Musicology and Music Education was authorized, with Arnold Small as chair; the Music Teachers' National Association also had a committee on Musicology and Education, with Glen Haydon as chair. Regional MENC committee meetings were planned for the spring of 1945, but never convened because the Office of Defense Transportation prohibited conventions due to the war effort.

29. Curt Sachs's points followed his general view that the MENC expected more, and less, of the AMS. He disclaimed the title *musicologist*. "Any girl that manufactures a newspaper article by transcribing Grove's Dictionary without too many misspellings presents herself as a musicologist. . . . The essential point is that we music historians in graduate schools have just been placed, with some friendly irony, at the top of the hierarchy of music education. This implies honors and duties that we cannot accept." He said that musicologists are not only trained in the disciplines but must also be musicians, seeing the contribution of "musicologists" as twofold: vocational and humanistic. In the former realm they can add to the knowledge of music educators in width and depth. In the latter role, "A teacher might never be given the oppportunity to "use" what he once learned in graduate school about oriental or medieval music, about old instruments or aesthetics. But he will acquire that surplus of knowledge and insight which is the privilege of all higher education; . . . Here we meet. And we would be rightfully

presented with one of the numerous ivory towers which lately have been on sale, did we not gladly take into serious consideration all the suggestions that music educators care to make" (Sachs, "The Music Historian," p. 79).

30. "Inter-American Relations in the Field of Music"; "Wartime and Peacetime Programs in Music Education"; "Musicology and the Music Industry"; "The Arts in International Relations"; "Music and Government: Field for an Applied Musicology" (1944); "Music in the Americas: Oral and Written Traditions in the Americas" (1945); and "Folk Music in the Schools of a Highly Industrialized Society" (1953).

31. Charles Seeger, "Folk Music in the Schools of a Highly Industrialized Society," *Journal of the International Folk Music Council* 5 (1953), 40–44.

32. Charles Seeger, "Music and Class Structure in the United States," *American Quarterly* 9 (Fall 1957), 281–94. It was presented several years earlier.

33. Charles Seeger, "Inter-American Relations in the Field of Music: Some Basic Considerations" (March–April 1941), 17–18, 64–65.

34. Charles Seeger, "American Music for American Children," *Music Educators Journal* 29 (November–December 1942), 11–12, presented at the biennial MENC conference in Milwaukee in the spring of 1942 as "American Songs for American Children."

35. Charles Seeger, "The Arts in International Relations," *Journal of the American Musicological Society* 2 (Spring 1949), 36–43, first read at the 1947 AMS meeting. The following quotations are from this source.

36. "Musicology and the Music Industry." *Bulletin of the National Music Council* 5 (May 1945), 8–10.

37. Charles Seeger, "Professionalism and Amateurism in the Study of Folk Music," *Journal of American Folklore* 62 (April–June 1949), 107–13; Charles Seeger, "Oral Tradition in Music," *Standard Dictionary of Folklore, Mythology and Legend* (New York: Funk and Wagnalls, 1949), pp. 825–29; Charles Seeger, "Music in the Americas: Oral and Written Traditions in the Americas," *Bulletin of the Pan American Union* 79 (May), 190–93; ibid. (June), 341–44.

38. Seeger provided a chart of the Dynamics of Music Tradition, with categories of the field, the operations, and the environment. Within the field, briefly, these are (a) *Families of tradition* (in which he included cultural and geographic areas) and (b) Traditional *Idioms* (defined by social stratum (types of music); within the operations, they are (c) Traditions of music *Technique* and (d) Traditions of *Control* (intrinsic); and within the environment, (e) Traditions of *Control* (extrinsic), and (f) Total physical *Environment* of a total culture ("Oral Tradition in Music," p. 827).

39. Seeger's concern for notation at this time, companion to his interests in technological resources and technical development in music, was presaged by "An Instantaneous Music Notator," *Journal of the International Folk Music Council* 3 (1951), 103–06.

40. Seeger viewed the sound recording as the solution to this problem, as a primary objective datum for study particularly when it was accompanied by a film ("Oral Tradition in Music," p. 829).

41. In fact, his first article in the *Journal of American Folklore* (*JAF*, April 1948) was an untitled review of four 78 rpm ten-inch record albums: *Listen to Our Story* and *Mountain Frolic*, which were ballads and hoedowns originally released in the 1920s and 1930s, and *Sod Buster Ballads* and *Deep Sea Chanteys*, which were works by revival singers then based in Manhattan. The review, a model of clarity and complementary to his essays on folk music, became a standardbearer for academic assessment of commercial sound recordings, particularly with the shift in the recording industry to LPs and tape.

42. See Charles Seeger, "Music and Society: Some New-World Evidence of Their Relationship," *Proceedings of the Conference on Latin-American Fine Arts*, June 14–17, 1951, pp. 84–97.

43. The definition adopted in 1935 by the Social Science Research Council (SSRC) confirmed acculturation as comprehending "those phenomena which result when groups of individuals having different cultures come into continuous first-hand contact, with subsequent changes in the original cultural patterns of either or both groups" (Robert Redfield, Ralph Linton, and Melville J. Herskovits, "Memorandum on the Study of Acculturation," *American Anthropologist* 38 [1935], 149). Seeger included "any oral traditions that form a culture, including those of social organizations," and as operational "not only in contacts between more or less distinct culture groups but also between more or less distinct social strata within each group, that is, not only in social extent but in social depth as well, and of course, over considerable duration of time" ("Music and Society: Some New-World Evidence of Their Relationship," p. 184).

44. "Music and Musicology in the New World." *Proceedings of the Music Teachers National Association*, 40th ser. (1946), 35–47. Exp. and rpt. in *Hinrichsen's Musical Yearbook* 6 (1949–50), 36–56. London: Hinrichsen, 1949.

45. An early project was *19 American Folk Tunes* (1936–38), arranged for piano and for use in elementary schools. Ruth compiled and edited *American Folk Songs for Children* (1948), *Animal Folk Songs for Children,* (1950), and *American Folk Songs for Christmas* (1953).

46. Two were posthumously published. *Let's Build a Railroad* (1954) and *Folklore Infantil de Santo Domingo*, ed. Edna Garrido de Boggs (Madrid, 1955), for which Ruth transcribed the songs.

47. Apparently, Ruth and Alan Lomax disagreed seriously about the proprietorship of songs and their transcriptions and publication, as well as others' appropriating Charles's ideas. (Restricted materials, Seeger Collection, Library of Congress).

48. A work that was never completed was entitled *1001 Songs*—approximately half of which Ruth and Charles transcribed from field recordings—a project in which they collaborated with Duncan Emrich of the Archive of American Folklore at the Library of Congress.

49. Michael Seeger, letter to the author, June 28, 1985.

50. Ruth Seeger, letter to Edgard Varèse, May 22, 1948, Seeger Collection, Library of Congress.

51. Ruth Seeger, letter to a Mr. Ussachevsky, June 17, 1952, Seeger Collection, Library of Congress.

52. *Suite for Wind Quintet* won first prize in a competition sponsored by the D.C. chapter of the National Association of American Composers and Conductors and was premiered on December 2, 1952.

53. Charles Seeger, letter to the headmaster of Hackley School, a Mr. Newell, May 26, 1953, Seeger Collection, Library of Congress.

54. Charles Seeger, in *Records of the Class of 1908* (Harvard University, 1953).

55. Michael Seeger, letter to the author, June 28, 1985.

Chapter 7. California Dreaming, 1953–1970

1. David K. Dunaway, in *How Can I Keep From Singing: Pete Seeger* (New York, 1981) discusses the HUAC and red-baiting tactics used against Pete and others.

2. Charles and Ruth decided that they could live comfortably on her income from teaching, his small pension from the Pan American Union, limited social security, and other income from royalties and investments.

3. It was a bitter irony that the FBI agents appeared at the Seeger home to question him on the very day that Ruth's incurable cancer had been discovered. As Seeger recalled, the agents "grilled" him and, in his emotional state, he "confessed" to membership in the Composer's Collective and to activities that by the 1950s had taken on sinister overtones far distant from the idealistic spirit of the thirties. However, he would give the FBI the names of no other Collective members. He told the FBI, "I'm willing to undress, figuratively speaking, myself, but I will not tell you anything about anyone else."

4. Charles Seeger, in *Records of the Class of 1908* (Harvard University, 1958).

5. The study had been designed, as part of the renovation of the house, by the architect of the Hackley School in Tarrytown.

6. Charles Seeger, "An Instantaneous Music Notator," *Journal of the International Folk Music Council* 3 (1951), 103–06.

7. The melograph and other technological apparati useful to the study and explication of music were of considerable fascination to him. See his own oral history, dictated in 1971. "An American Musicologist," pp. 427–39, for information on the melograph (copy in author's possession).

8. See Milton Metfessel, *Phonophotography in Folk Music* (Chapel Hill, N.C., 1928).

9. See Olav Gurvin, "Photography as an Aid in Folk Music Research," *Norveg* 3 (1953), 181–96.

10. Alan P. Merriam and Barbara W. Merriam, *Voice of the Congo*, Riverside World Music Series: Riverside Records RLP 4002 (1951–52).

11. The model A, using a pen of an oscillograph moving at 120 cycles per second, was operated on a Bush Development Corporation Double Channel Magnetic Oscillograph, BL 202. But it reproduced only whistling sounds.

12. Charles Seeger, "Toward a Universal Music Sound-Writing for Musicology," *Journal of the International Folk Music Council* 9 (1957), 63. See also "Prescriptive and Descriptive Music Writing," *Musical Quarterly* 44 (April 1958), 184–95.

13. Charles Seeger, letter to George Herzog, 29 January 1961.

14. Charles Seeger, letter to Rose Brandel, 9 November 1969.

15. Its major limitation is that it records only one melodic line at a time. Another criticism of the melograph is that it presents both significant and insignificant musical features indiscriminately. For example, electronic notations are perfectly legitimate with music traditions we know, but are not nearly so successful with music traditions with which we have little familiarity. Also, as a student of ethnomusicology noted, Seeger had a mystical view of what he called music knowledge; one either has it or not. Perhaps because he possessed a monolithic conception of music knowledge he could devise a device to try to represent music objectively, as more "unitary than multitary."

16. Charles Seeger, "Prescriptive and Descriptive Music Writing," *Musical Quarterly* 44 (April 1958), 184–95. Seeger did little more on cantrometrics, leaving development of its theory and practice to Alan Lomax, in whose hands it became a different and controversial system.

17. Mantle Hood, "Reminiscent of Charles Seeger," *Yearbook of the International Folk Music Council* 11 (1979), 77.

18. Materials on the development of the Society for Ethnomusicology are found in the Archives of Traditional Music at Indiana University.

19. *Ethnomusicology Newsletter* 1 (December 1953), 1.

20. The early years of the Society for Ethnomusicology (SEM) very much reflected, as Seeger observed, "the American anthropological style of administration, as opposed to the European-oriented musicological style. The SEM was run in a very democratic fashion and with much cooperation. Merriam put the heaviest work into the society and also edited the newsletter." Despite a preponderance of anthopologists, Seeger was assigned to write the SEM's constitution, adopted in Philadelphia, November 5, 1956, patterning it after that of the AMS so that, as he thought, when the inevitable amalgamation came, it would be easy to incorporate the two societies.

21. In 1954 Seeger suggested to the AMS the formation of a society for ethnomusicology; the AMS said one should be formed, but outside the confines of the AMS.

22. Copy in author's possession.

23. Charles Seeger, "Folk Music in the Schools of a Highly Industrialized Society," *Journal of the International Folk Music Council* 5 (1953), 40–44.

24. Charles Seeger, "Music and Class Structure in the United States," *American Quarterly* 9 (Fall 1957), 281–94.

25. Charles Seeger, "Folk Music: USA," *Grove's Dictionary V* (1955), 3:387–98.

26. Sections were titled: The Euro-American Music Community; The Afro-American Music Community; Field Collection of Folk Music; The British Element in British-American Folk Music; The American Element in British-American Folk Music; Stylistic Idiosyncrasies of American Folk Music; Folk Music of Foreign-Language Minorities; Hispanic-American Folk Music; French-American Folk Music; Folk Music of Other Minorities; and Folk Music in Composition.

27. Charles Seeger, "Folk Music," *Collier's Encyclopedia* (1965), 10:132–40.

28. Charles Seeger, "The Appalachian Dulcimer," *Journal of American Folklore* 71 (1958), 40–51.

29. Charles Seeger, "Singing Style," *Western Folklore* 17 (January 1958), 1, 3–11, based on a paper read at the American Folklore Society in 1956.

30. Charles Seeger, "Versions and Variants of 'Barbara Allen' in the Archive of American Folk Song in the Library of Congress," *Selected Reports* no. 1 (Los Angeles: Institute of Ethnomusicology, UCLA, 1966), pp. 120–67. Rpt. with phono disk album L54 (Washington, D.C.: Library of Congress, 1966).

31. Charles Seeger, "The Folkness of the Non-Folk vs. the Non-Folkness of the Folk," in *Folklore and Society*, ed. Bruce Jackson (Hatboro, Pa.: Folklore Associates, 1966), pp. 1–9.

32. Charles Seeger, "Who Owns Folklore?—A Rejoinder." *Western Folklore* 21 (April), 93–101.

33. Charles Seeger, "The Cultivation of Various European Traditions in the Americas," *Report of the Eighth Congress of the International Musicological Society, New York, 1961* (New York: IMS, 1961), 364–75.

34. Malena Kuss, "Charles Seeger's Leitmotifs on Latin America," *Journal of the International Folk Music Council* 31 (1979), 83–99. Through new evidence or reinterpretation, Kuss basically refutes Seeger's theories. I stress this complementary discussion of Seeger's essay and its analysis by a devoted friend of his because Kuss, an Argentinian, writes from the viewpoint of a trained historico-musicologist who believes that her discipline is as valid an approach to the study of Latin American musics as ethnomusicology—or, as she puts it, the difference between the qualitative and quantitative approaches, respectively.

35. Charles Seeger, "On the Moods of a Music Logic," *Journal of the Amerian Musicological Society* 13 (1960), 224–61; and "Semantic, Logical, and Political Considerations Bearing Upon Research in Ethnomusicology," *Ethnomusicology* 5 (May), 77–80.

36. A good example is Ralph Barton Perry, *A General Theory of Value*.

37. Charles Seeger, "Semantic, Logical, and Political Considerations Bearing Upon Research in Ethnomusicology," *Ethnomusicology* 5 (May), 77–80.

38. Hood, "Reminiscent of Charles Seeger," pp. 78–79.

39. Charles Seeger, "Music as a Tradition of Communication, Discipline and Play," *Ethnomusicology* 6 (September 1962), 146–63, originally read as "Music as a Tradition of Communication" at the 1961 SEM meeting.

40. Charles Seeger, "On the Tasks of Musicology," *Ethnomusicology* 7 (September 1963), 214–15.

41. Charles Seeger, "The Music Process as a Function in a Context of Functions," *Yearbook: Inter-American Institute for Musical Research* 2:1–36. New Orleans, La.: Tulane University, 1966, revised and published as "The Music Compositional Process as a Function in a Nest of Functions and in Itself a Nest of Functions" in *Studies in Musicology, 1935–75* (Berkeley and Los Angeles: University of California Press, 1977), pp. 139–67.

42. "On the Moods of a Music Logic" certainly stands by itself as a tour de force of hypotheses and analyses on the music and language problem. Gilbert Chase referred to the article as "extraordinarily far-reaching and deeply probing" (Chase, "An Exagmina-

tion Round His Factification for Incamination of Work in Progress," *Yearbook of the International Folk Music Council* 11 [1979], p. 143.)

43. The musicological juncture refers to a chart that was a conspectus of "On the Formational Apparatus," "Systematic Musicology," "Factorial Analysis," "Preface to the Critique of Music," and "The Music Process as a Function in a Nest of Functions. . . ." The following quotation is taken from an appended typed analysis to his chart "Conspectus of the Resources of the Musicological Process" (1975).

44. Charles Seeger, "Tradition and the (North) American Composer," in *Music in the Americas*, Inter-American Music Monograph Series no. 1 (Bloomington: Research Center in Anthropology, Folklore, and Linguistics, Indiana University, 1967), pp. 195–212.

45. Charles Seeger, "Preface to the Critique of Music," *Interamerican Music Bulletin* 49 (September 1965), 2–24.

46. Charles Seeger, "Factorial Analysis of the Song as an Approach to the Formation of a Unitary Field Theory," *Journal of the International Folk Music Council* 20 (1968), 272–77.

47. Charles Seeger, foreword to *Studies in Musicology, Essays in the History, Style and Bibliography of Music in Memory of Glen Haydon*, ed. James W. Pruett (Chapel Hill: University of North Carolina Press, 1969), pp. vi–iii. In a short paean to Haydon, Seeger provided a brief chronology of the "coming of age" of musicology in the United States, noting the passage from the early days of music study to the creation of the first chair in musicology, created for Otto Kinkeldey at Cornell in 1930. At that time, a national society had not yet been formed, but from the mid-1930s on, under the impetus of war refugees, the field moved forward. Haydon was a compelling force behind that movement and in other activities that brought the study of music out of the narrow confines of academic departments.

48. Charles Seeger, "On the Formational Apparatus of the Music Compositional Process," *Ethnomusicology* 12 (September 1969), 230–47, first drafted as a sequel to "On the Moods of a Music Logic."

49. Charles Seeger, "Toward a Unitary Field Theory for Musicology," *Selected Reports* (Los Angeles: Institute of Ethnomusicology, UCLA, 1970), 1:171–210.

50. See ibid., p. 180, for definition of figures 1 and 2.

51. I have been told by members of that famous Wednesday afternoon seminar at the Institute of Ethnomusicology, that Seeger asked them if anyone could find the "joke" in the pattern he produced. The first to do so, I am told, was either Jim Koetting or Ron Wolcott. The "joke" was that the pattern spelled MUSIC!

52. Hood, "Reminiscent of Charles Seeger," p. 78. Seeger frequently received complaints about his writing style, which most people found difficult to penetrate. It reminded me of a story he told me that when his daughter-in-law Toshi (Peter's wife) complained to him about his writings — in this particular situation referring to "Folk Music in the Schools of a Highly Industrialized Society" — "Charlie, I needed a dictionary to read your paper!" He responded, "But Toshi, I wrote that for the masses!"

53. Seminar participants included Lois Anderson, Robert Garfias, William Malm, Robert Brown, Akin Euba, Bonnie Wade, Roderic Knight, James Koetting, Jose

Maceda, Willem Adriaanz, Frederic Lieberman, Ric Trimillos, Reis Flora, Cynthia Tse Kimberlin, Josef Pacholczek, Sara Stalder, and many other notable first- and second-generation leaders in the field of ethnomusicology.

54. Bonnie Wade, letter to Lucia Core, 18 March 1982, in author's possession.

55. Charles Seeger, letter to Denise Venturi, 16 March 1968.

Chapter 8. New England Revisited, 1970–1979

1. Harold Spivacke, letter to Charles Seeger, November 29, 1966, in author's possession.

2. Maud Karpeles, letter to Charles Seeger on the occasion of his eightieth birthday. Following quotations are taken from letters written by sons John and Peter and daughter Peggy to Sidney Robertson Cowell.

3. Charles Seeger, "Reflections Upon a Given Topic: Music in Universal Perspective," *Ethnomusicology* 13 (September 1971), 385–98.

4. Charles Seeger, "World Musics in American Schools: A Challenge to be Met," *Music Educators Journal*, October 1972, pp. 107–11, also titled "Ethnomusicological Materials in Music Education in the United States."

5. Seeger's year-long ninetieth birthday celebration began with his delivery in Philadelphia (in November 1976) of the Society for Ethnomusicology's first Distinguished Lecture at a joint SEM-AFS (American Folklore Society) conference. This lecture, now called the Seeger Lecture, is an annual event in the Society for Ethnomusicology meetings.

6. Charles Seeger, letter to author, 20 September 1976. In an earlier letter (6 February 1976), he suggested the following topics:

(1) The Linguocentric Predicament and the Musicological Juncture

(2) The Three Modes of Speech Usage

(3) Fact and Value, Science and Criticism in Musicology

(4) Historical and Systematic Orientations in Musicology

(5) The Music View of Speech and the Place in it of the Other 8 or 9 Systems of Human Communication

(6) The Unitary Field Theory and the Unified Theory of Operations

(7) The Classical Speech Logic and the Proposal to Outline More Concisely a Dialectic of Value

Later he hoped the conference would undertake "a comparison of music as one of the humanities, one of the sciences and one of the most mystical undertakings that man can get involved with. . . . What I would especially enjoy would be a confrontation of the two viewpoints that the times make the man and the man makes the times and that society has more to do with the making of music than individuals" (letter to author, 13 October 1976).

7. Charles Seeger, letter to author, 25 March 1977.

8. Charles Seeger, letter to author, 1 April 1977.

9. Charles Seeger, letter to author, 29 April 1977.

10. Charles Seeger, letter to Klaus Wachsmann, 5 June 1977.

11. When the announcements of and invitations to the conference were sent out, there was an immediate outpouring of response from many people from many decades in Charlie's life. Examples follow.

From Bertrand Bronson (4 October 1975): "I have great admiration for Charles, and would delight at any time to do him honor. . . . Charles is absolutely unique, and well deserves all the honor we can pay him."

From Gilbert Chase (6 October 1975): "I've known Charlie since 1938 and was associated with him particularly in his inter-American activities. Nevertheless, I believe my best contribution would be to discuss his influence on me as a historian of American music."

Alan Lomax wrote (13 October 1975):

Of course I am delighted that my dear friend and admired mentor, Charles Seeger, is going to have the kind of celebration he wants; . . . he and I worked together on the collection of protests and became fast friends in relation to our shared views in relation to political and social matters. I was present very much and close to him during the Washington period and shared his struggles and achievements there. I had the great pleasure, of course, of teaching him and his family many of the songs that they came to love.

Malena Kuss (14 October 1975) noted Charles's contribution to the field of Latin American music: "He practically created the Music Division of the Pan American Union with Vanett Lawler, a wonderful woman who died a few years ago. He established strong connections with some countries, among them Chile."

Barbara Krader observed (21 October 1975), "What a stimulating *focus* his life and work make!"

From Frank Callaway (23 October 1975):

It was Charles Seeger who drafted the original constitution of ISME [International Society for Music Education] which he presented to the UNESCO Conference on The Role and Place of Music in Education of Youth and Adults held in Brussels in 1953.

I have a special reason to be interested in [his] initiative at that time, for early in 1949 (my diary tells me it was March 7th) when I was a guest in the U.S.A. as the holder of a Carnegie Travel Grant a dinner was held at the Lord Baltimore Hotel in Baltimore during an MENC Regional Conference. This dinner was for foreign guests and was attended by UNESCO Fellows from Norway and Holland, two visitors from Uruguay and myself—then a young teacher from New Zealand. Also present were the late Clifford Buttelman and the late Vanett Lawler (MENC Executive Secretary and Assistant Executive Secretary respectively), Henry Cowell and Charles Seeger. The chief topic of conversation was the idea of establishing an international organization for music education. A week later I met with Charles Seeger over lunch in Washington (he was then Chief, the Division of Music and Visual Arts of the Pan American Union) and we talked further on those ideas.

For supporting evidence of [his] significant part in the launching of ISME, I refer you to the Report in the Brussels Conference which was published in 1954 by UNESCO, Paris.

From Juan A. Orrego-Salas (28 October 1975):

Nothing could be more rewarding than to contribute to such an occasion and express my feelings towards a person that I have for many years so deeply admired as a human being, as a musician and as a promoter of freedom and social justice.

As a composer I would like to participate in a dialog with him on . . . the creation of music and training of the composer. As a person involved in the field of Latin American music would certainly like to participate in sections of the program dealing with Seeger's work in strengthening the links with the Latin American nations. And as a simple human being I am most deeply interested in Seeger the man, the sociologist, the organizer, the social protester and the political radical.

From Domingo Santa Cruz (28 October 1975):

[Charles Seeger is] not only my best and more admired friend there, but a man for whom I have the highest respect. . . . My personal acquaintance with Charles took place in 1941 when he was still in the WPA work. From this day we became real intimate friends. I remember many wonderful hours with him, a little later, at the PAU and also with the Seeger family at Chevy Chase where I knew well Ruth and the growing little tribe. Charles understood better than anyone else our music life and needs, and helped us so generously that he received an honorary degree from our University of Chile, and a decoration from Chilean government. Our correspondence has never stopped during 34 years.

Mercedes Reis Pequeno wrote (24 November 1975): "I consider it a privilege to have had the opportunity to work with Charlie for two years (1947/49) at the Music Div. of the Pan American Union—a unique experience at the beginning of my working career, and from which I keep the most interesting and unforgettable recollections."

From Juana de Laban (4 Deceember 1975): "Charles Seeger is a most unique human being."

From Edward N. Waters (14 January 1976): "I know of no person more deserving of such treatment than the subject proposed [the CSC]. I have long been one of Mr. Seeger's most ardent admirers. His genial spirit, his boldness of thought, his sheer musicality, his humor, his vivacity, his innate kindness—all of these qualities combine in him to form a truly unique personality."

From William Lichtenwanger (22 January 1976):

I first met Charlie when he befriended me, as a friend and student of his nominal boss of the year, Earl V. Moore, Director and later Dean of the University of Michigan School of Music, in connection with the New York IMS meeting of that damnable month. I came to work in the Library of Congress just a year later, but the Army soon snatched me and I don't remember much about Charlie until the winter of 1945–46, when I was back in Washington though still in uniform, and Charlie and Ruth gave a pair of very abstruse papers to the local AMS chapter. I came back to the Music Division in December 1945, and from then on as a reference librarian and especially as associate editor of *Notes* from 1946 to 1964 I saw a fair amount of Charlie and was proud to have him as a contributor in *Notes* from time to time. I especially remember him in the sad months after Ruth's death in November 1953; at the AMS meeting at Chapel Hill in December he was not his usual sassy self, but in characteristic fashion he threw off his depression before much time had passed. . . . Charlie's qualities and influences as a writer about music are to me much more important than his teaching or social consciousness or his work as a composer. I am perfectly sure—well, as sure as one has a right to be about anything in the distant future—that 50 years from now Charlie will be known for some of these writings when the other aspects have—not disappeared, no, but become indirect in the milieu of that time.

From Ruth Katz (February 22, 1976): "My colleague, Dalia Cohen, and I well remember his visit to Jerusalem in the mid-60s when he 'hopped over' from London to see for himself the working of the Jerusalem Melograph. That a man of his age and stature should take such a detour to visit two beginners was a source of lasting encouragement to us. It reflects his well-known dedication to the essence of things and not to meaningless glamor and showy paraphernalia."

From Charles Haywood (14 September 1976): "I first met him—it may seem incredible—in 1928; and my life assumed a new meaning and direction ever since those early days. And I have much to tell! . . . Charles Seeger is a very warm, sensitive, *social human being,* endowed among other gifts with a subtle and delightful sense of humor, whose life was not totally spent in secluded corners of libraries; who lived fully and richly."

From Isabel Pope Conant (2 April 1977): "A dear friend and a great man; . . . my best wishes for a joyous time of celebration and success of the sessions worthy of the distinguished musician they honor."

From Krister Malm (27 June 1977): "Charles Seeger is one of the persons in ethnomusicology who have influenced me most. I first met him personally in 1962 and have since now and then communicated with him, mostly on melograph matters."

Carlton Sprague Smith, one of the first respondents to queries about the Charles Seeger Conference, provided a statement that serves to frame the atmosphere of the proceedings (25 August 1977):

Charlie is a very old and dear friend. . . . Few men have contributed more to the analysis of musical research along with its goals and possibilities than Charles Seeger. . . . The emphasis of the seminars is on Seeger the theorist and philospher of music and that is an important aspect of his life. However, since it seems to me important that those present recognize the all-around man—I include A SALUTE which, if there is an appropriate moment, might be read.

Regretting my absence

A SALUTE TO CHARLES SEEGER

• Mexican-born Yankee interested in people and ideas—the Harvard graduate who learned about European music in Cambridge, Massachusetts—the lanky young man who in 1912 came to the West Coast and Berkeley where his horizon broadened. Harmonic Structure and musical invention were searchingly analyzed and songs and instrumental music composed. Here Henry Cowell was one of his students and folk music took on new importance.

• The musician who, following World War I, taught for a decade at the Institute of Musical Art and lectured at the New School for Social Research and was a founder of the American Musicological Society.

• But let not historical and ethno- musicologists forget that besides being a philosopher and theorist in their fields, he has been a man of action and for several decades was Chief of the Music and Visual Arts programs of the Pan American Union. There he showed remarkable skill as a diplomat and his experience and judgment were also of great value to UNESCO.

• Again let us particularly remember the father of gifted children who have made significant contributions in the field of folk music—and the husband and teacher of Ruth Crawford Seeger, one of this country's most talented composers in the 1930s and 1940s.

In short, for these and other reasons and above all — for his friendship, tact and absolute integrity — let us cherish, applaud and salute him with a hemispheric *abrazo* in this his 90th year.

12. The sessions were held at the Alumni House, in a paneled room that opened out to a large, comfortable seating area accommodating a few hundred people, but was a cozy environment. Seeger sat at the seminar table and participants moved from audience to table, depending on the topic discussed. Sessions were videotaped, with microphones distributed unobtrusively about the room. Chalkboards were available for the charts and other visuals Seeger delighted in. He set the topic for each morning and afternoon session, dividing them into large categories. Written questions from the floor stimulated more discussion. Later he said he was distressed to realize that he had done most of the talking.

13. Archie Green, "Charles Louis Seeger." *Journal of American Folklore* 90 (1979), 397.

14. Wiley Hitchcock, "Americans on American Music." *College Music Symposium* 8 (1968), 138–39.

15. These include "Speech, Music, and Speech about Music;" "Music as Concept and Percept;" "The Musicological Juncture: Music as Fact;" "The Musicological Juncture: Music as Value;" "On the Moods of a Music Logic;" "Toward a Unitary Field Theory for Musicology;" and "The Music Compositional Process as a Function in a Nest of Functions and in Itself a Nest of Functions."

16. These are "Prescriptive and Descriptive Music Writing;" "Music and Society: Some New-World Evidence of Their Relationship;" "The Cultivation of Various European Traditions of Music in the New World;" "Music and Musicology in the New World;" "Music and Class Structure in the United States;" "Contrapuntal Style in the Three-voice Shape-note Hymns of the United States;" "The Appalachian Dulcimer;" "Versions and Variants of "Barbara Allen" in the Archive of American Song to 1940;" "Professionalism and Amateurism in the Study of Folk Music;" "Folk Music in the Schools of a Highly Industrialized Society;" and the lovely short tongue-in-cheek analysis "The Folkness of the Nonfolk and the Nonfolkness of the Folk," with which he ended the volume.

17. "Principia" will be published as *Studies in Musicology II* by the University of California Press, overseen by the author.

18. "Tractatus Esthetico-Semioticus: Model of the Systems of Human Communication," orig. publ. in *Current Thought in Musicology*, ed. John Grubbs (Austin: University of Texas Press, 1976), pp. 1–39. In a letter to me of February 23, 1976, he advised that the first three chapters of the "Principia" should be: "Tractatus," "Sources of Evidence and Criteria for Judgment in the Critique of Music," *Essays for a Humanist* (New York, 1977), pp. 261–76, and the paper he read in Mexico, which was to be published, and the occasional papers should include the following earlier articles: "Preface to All Linguistic Treatment of Music" (1935); "Music and Government: Field of Applied Musicology" (1944); "The Arts (Music) in International Relations" (1949); "Systematic Musicology: Viewpoints, Orientations and Methods" (1951); "Preface to a Critique of Music" (1965);

"Tradition and the (North) American Composer" (1967, the title of which he proposed to change to "Nationalism, Traditionalism, and the American Composer"); "Factorial Analysis of the Song (Musical Event)" (1968) "On the Formational Apparatus of the Music Compositional Process" (1969) qua "Preface to the Compositional Process of Music;" and "World Musics in American Schools," to be changed to "Ethnomusicological Materials in Music Education in the United States" (1972).

19. Henry Cowell, "Charles Seeger," in *American Composers on American Music: A Symposium* (New York: Frederick Ungar, 1962), pp. 119–24.

20. Klaus Wachsmann, letter to author, 15 October, 1974.

21. Charles Seeger, letter to Ralph Rinzler, 5 October 1969.

22. Charles Seeger, Memorandum to Wachsmann Festscrift contributors.

23. Charles Seeger, letters to Richard Reuss, 20 May and 18 June 1971.

24. Mantle Hood, "Reminiscent of Charles Seeger," *Yearbook of the International Folk Music Council* 11 (1979), 79.

25. Charles Seeger, letter to author, 22 May 1978.

26. Charles Seeger, letter to author, 8 December 1978.

27. Sidney Robertson Cowell, "Charles Seeger (1886–1979)," *Musical Quarterly* 65 (April 1979), 307.

28. Mantle Hood, "Reminiscent of Charles Seeger." *Yearbook of the International Folk Music Council* 11 (1979), 79.

29. Peter Seeger, interview with the author.

Bibliography

∽

Primary Works

Published Papers by Charles Seeger

1913   *Outline of a course in Harmonic Structure and Musical Invention as Elementary Composition.* With Edward G. Stricklen. Berkeley, Calif.: Privately printed.

1916   *Outline of a course in Chromatic Harmony and Intermediate Types of Musical Invention.* With E. G. Stricklen. Berkeley, Calif.: Privately printed.

1923   "On Style and Manner in Modern Composition." *Musical Quarterly* 9 (July) 423–31.

1923   "Music in the American University." *Educational Review* 66 (September), 95–99.

1924   "On the Principles of Musicology." *Musical Quarterly* 10 (April), 244–50.

1925   "Prolegomena to Musicology: The Problem of the Musical Point of View and the Bias of Linguistic Presentation." *Eolus* 4 (May), 12–24.

1929   "A Fragment of Greek Music." *The Baton* (Institute of Musical Art, New York) 8 (May), 5–6.

1930   "Dissonance and the Devil: An Interesting Passage in a Bach Cantata." *The Baton* 9 (May), 7–8.

1930   "On Dissonant Counterpoint." *Modern Music* 7 (June–July), 25–31.

1931   "Lines on the Grace Note." *The Baton* 10 (February), 6–7.

1932   "Carl Ruggles." *Musical Quarterly* 18 (October), 578–92. Rpt. in *American Composers in American Music,* ed. Henry Cowell, 14–35. Stanford, Calif.: Stanford University Press, 1933.

1933   "Music and Musicology" and "Music Occidental." In *Encyclopedia of the Social Sciences* 11:143–50, 155–64. New York: Macmillan.

1933   "Ruth Crawford." In *American Composers on American Music,* ed. Henry Cowell, 110–18. Stanford, Calif.: Stanford University Press.

1934   "On Proletarian Music." *Modern Music* 11 (March), 121–27.

1935   "Preface to All Linguistic Treatment of Music." *Music Vanguard* 1 (March–April), 17–31.

1938   "Music in America." *Magazine of Art* 31 (July), 411–13, 435–36.

1939   "Charles Ives and Carl Ruggles." *Magazine of Art* 32 (July) 396–99, 435–37.

1939   "Grass Roots for American Music." *Modern Music* 16 (March–April), 143–49.

1939   Program notes for GPO White House concert in honor of the king and queen of England.

1939   "Systematic and Historical Orientations in Musicology." *Acta Musicologica* 11, 121–28.

1940   "Contrapuntal Style in the Three-Voice Shape-Note Hymns." *Musical Quarterly* 26 (October), 483–93.

1940   "Folk Music as a Source of Social History." In *The Cultural Approach to History*, ed. Carolyn F. Ware, 316–23. New York: Columbia University Press.

1940   "Henry Cowell." *Magazine of Art* 33 (May), 288–89, 322–25, 327.

1940   "The Importance to Cultural Understanding of Folk and Popular Music." In *Digest of Proceedings*, Conference on Inter-American Relations in the Field of Music, 1–10. Washington D.C.: U.S. Department of State.

1940   *Music as Recreation*. Works Project Administration, Technical Series, Community Service Circular no. 1, Washington, D.C., May 20.

1941   "Inter-American relations in the field of Music: Some Basic Considerations." *Music Educators Journal* 27 (March–April), 17–18, 64–65.

1941   "Music and Culture." *Proceedings of the Music Teachers National Association*, 35th ser., 112–22.

1942   "American Music for American Children." *Music Educators Journal* 28 (November–December), 11–12.

1942   "Inter-American Relations in the Field of Music." *Proceedings of the Music Teachers National Association*, 36th ser., 41–44.

1943   "Wartime and Peacetime Programs in Music Education." *Music Educators Journal* 29 (January), 12–14.

1944   "Music and Government: Field for Applied Musicology." In *Papers Read at the International Congress of Musicology Held at New York, September 11–18, 1939*, 12–20. New York: Music Educators National Conference for the American Musicological Society.

1945   (With Curt Sachs) "Music Education and Musicology." *Music Educators Journal* 31 (May–June), 78–79.

1945   "Music in the Americas: Oral and Written Traditions in the Americas." *Bulletin of the Pan American Union* 79 (May), 290–93; (June), 341–44.

1945   "Musicology and the Music Industry." *National Music Council Bulletin* 5 (May), 8–10.

1945   "Notes on Music in the Americas. Property Rights in Musical Works," *Bulletin of the Pan American Union* 79 (March).

1946   "Music and Musicology in the New World." *Proceedings of the Music Teachers National Association*, 40th ser., 35–47. Rpt. as "Musica y musicología en el Nuevo Mundo," *Revista Musical Chilena* 22 (September 1946), 7–18. Rev. and rpt. in *Hinrichsen's Musical Yearbook* 6 (1949–50), 36–56. London: Hinrichsen, 1949.

1947   "Music Education and Musicology." In *Music Education Source Book*, ed. H. N. Morgan, 195–98. Chicago: Music Educators National Conference.

1947   "Toward a Unitary Field Theory for Musicology" (abstract). *Bulletin of the American Musicological Society* 9–10 (June), 16.

1948   "UNESCO, February 1948." *Music Library Association Notes*, 2d ser., 5 (March), 165–68.

1949   "The Arts in International Relations." *Journal of the American Musicological Society* 2 (Spring), 36–43.

1949   "Oral Tradition in Music." in *Standard Dictionary of Folklore, Mythology and Legend*, 825–29. New York: Funk and Wagnalls.

1949   "Professionalism and Amateurism in the Study of Folk Music." *Journal of American Folklore* 62 (April–June), 107–13. Rpt. as "El profesional y el aficionado en el estudio de la musica folklorica," *Revista Musical Chilena* 13 (November–December 1959), 70–79. Rpt. in *The Critics and the Ballad*, ed. McEdward Leach and T. P. Coffin, 151–60. Carbondale, Ill.: 1961.

1951   "An Instantaneous Music Notator." *Journal of the International Folk Music Council* 3, 103–06.

1951   "Music and Society: Some New World Evidence of Their Relationship," *Proceedings of the Conference on Latin-American Fine Art, June 14–17*, 84–97. Austin: University of Texas Press. Rev. and rpt. by the Pan American Union, Washington, D.C., 1953.

1951   "Systematic Musicology: Viewpoints, Orientations and Methods." *Journal of the American Musicological Society* 4 (Fall), 240–48.

1952   Foreword to George Pullen Jackson, *Another Sheaf of White Spirituals*. Gainesville: University of Florida Press.

1953   "Folk Music in the Schools of a Highly Industrialized Society." *Journal of the International Folk Music Council* 5, 40–44. Rpt. in *The American Folk Scene*, ed. David A. De Turk and A. Poulin, Jr., 88–94. New York: Dell, 1967.

1953   "The Musician: Man Serves Art. The Educator: Art Serves Man." *UNESCO Courier* 6 (February).

1953   "Preface to the Description of a Music." In *Kongressbericht, Internationale Gesellschaft für Musikwissenschaft, Utrecht 1952*, 360–70. Amsterdam: Vereneging voor Nederlandse Muzikgeschiedenis.

1955   "Folk Music: USA." In *Grove's Dictionary of Music and Musicians*, 5th ed., 3:387–98. New York: St. Martin's.

1955   "A Proposal to Found an International Society for Music Education." In *Music in Education*, 325–31. Paris: UNESCO.

1957   "Music and Class Structure in the United States." *American Quarterly* 9 (Fall), 281–94.

1957   "Toward a Universal Music Sound-Writing for Musicology." *Journal of the International Folk Music Council* 9, 63–66.

1958   "The Appalachian Dulcimer." *Journal of American Folklore* 71 (January–March), 40–51.

1958   "Musicology." Representing the American Musicological Society. No. 23 in the broadcast series *The World of the Mind*, American Council of Learned Societies and the American Association for the Advancement of Science. New York: Broadcast Music, Inc.

1958   "Prescriptive and Descriptive Music Writing." *Musical Quarterly* 44 (April), 184–95.

1958   "Singing Style." *Western Folklore* 17 (January), 3–11

1959   "Otto Kinkeldey." *Acta Musicologica* 31:7–8.

1960   "On the Moods of a Music Logic." *Journal of the American Musicological Society* 13, 224–61.

1961   "The Cultivation of Various European Traditions in the Americas." *Report of the Eighth Congress of the International Musicological Society, New York, 1961*, 364–75. New York: IMS, 1961.

1961   "Semantic, Logical and Political Considerations Bearing Upon Research in Ethnomusicology." *Ethnomusicology* 5 (May), 77–80.

1962   "Music as a Tradition of Communication, Discipline and Play." *Ethnomusicology* 6 (September), 156–63.

1962   "Who Owns Folklore?—A Rejoinder." *Western Folklore* 21 (April), 93–101.

1963   "On the Tasks of Musicology." *Ethnomusicology* 7 (September), 214–15.

1963   "Preface to the Critique of Music. In *Primera conferencia interamericana de etnomusicologia: Trabajos presentados* Cartagena de Indias, Colombia, 24–28 February 1963. Rpt. in *Boletín Interamericana de Música* 49 (September 1965), 2–24.

1964   "La Realdad sobre la Educación Musical y el Profesorado de la Música Culta." *Revista Musical Chilena* 18 (January–June), 14–19.

1964   "Symposium on Transcription and Analysis: A Hukwe Song with Musical Bow . . . Report of the Chairman-Moderator." *Ethnomusicology* 8 (September), 272–77.

1965   "Folk Music." *Collier's Encyclopedia* 10:132–40.

1965   Introduction to *Primera conferencia interamericana de etnomusicología, Trabajos presentados*. Cartagena de Indias, Colombia, 24–28 February 1963. Washington, D.C.: Pan American Union.

1966   "The Folkness of the Non-Folk vs. the Non-Folkness of the Folk." In *Folklore and Society*, ed. Bruce Jackson, 1–9. Hatboro, Pa.: Folklore Associates.

1966   "The Music Process as a Function in a Context of Functions." *Yearbook: Inter-American Institute for Musical Research* 2:1–36. New Orleans, La.: Tulane University.

1966   "Versions and Variants of 'Barbara Allen' in the Archive of American Folk Song in the Library of Congress." *Selected Reports* 1:120–67. Los Angeles: Institute of Ethnomusicology, UCLA. Rpt. with phono disk album L54. Washington, D.C.: Library of Congress, 1966.

1967   "Tradition and the (North) American Composer." In *Music in the Americas*, 195–212. Inter-American Music Monograph Series no. 1. Bloomington: Research Center in Anthropology, Folklore, and Linguistics, Indiana University.

1968   "Factorial Analysis of the Song as an Approach to the Formation of a Unitary Field Theory." *Journal of the International Folk Music Council* 20:272–77.

1969   Foreword to *Studies in Musicology: Essays in the History, Style, and Bibliography of Music in Memory of Glen Haydon*, ed. James W. Pruett. Chapel Hill: University of North Carolina Press.

1969   "On the Formational Apparatus of the Music Compositional Process." *Ethnomusicology* 13 (September), 230–47.

1970   "Toward a Unitary Field Theory for Musicology." *Selected Reports* 1:171–210. Los Angeles: Institute of Ethnomusicology, UCLA.

1971   Foreword to Mantle Hood, *The Ethnomusicologist*. New York: McGraw-Hill.

1971   "Reflections Upon a Given Topic: Music in the Universal Perspective." *Ethnomusicology* 13 (September), 385-98.

1972   "In Memoriam: Carl Ruggles." *Perspectives of New Music* 10:171–74.

1972   "World Musics in American Schools: A Challenge to be Met." *Music Educators Journal* 58 (October), 107–11.

1976   "Tractatus Esthetico-Semioticus." In *Current Thought in Musicology*, ed. John Grubbs. Austin: University of Texas Press.

1977   "The Musicological Juncture: 1976." *Ethnomusicology* 21 (May), 179–88.

1977   "Sources of Evidence and Criteria for Judgment in the Critique of Music." In *Essays for a Humanist*, ed. Seeger, 261–76. New York.

1977   *Studies in Musicology, 1935–75*. Berkeley: University of California Press. (Includes complete bibliography of Seeger's writings and 18 essays.)

1980   "Folk Music USA." *Grove's Dictionary of Music and Musicians*, 6th ed. London.

1980   (With Margaret Valiant.) "Journal of a Field Representative." *Ethnomusicology* 24 (May), 169–210.

Works Edited by Charles Seeger

1930–1934   *Bulletin of the New York Musicological Society*, nos. 1–3.

1933–1936   *American Library of Musicology: Joseph Yasser, a Theory of Evolving Tonality*. New York, 1932.
                 Helen H. Roberts: Form in Primitive Music. New York, 1933.

1936–1937   *A Series of American Folk Songs Rarely Found in Popular Collections*, nos. 1–8, 10. Washington, D.C.: Resettlement Administration: Special Skills Division.

1941   *Army Song Book*. Washington, D.C.: Adjutant General's Office, in col-
            laboration with the Library of Congress.

1941   *Boletin latinoamericano de musica*. Vol. 5, pt. 1: *Estudios estado unidenses*,
            25–434; *Suplemento musical* 12–161. Montevideo: Instituto inter-
            americano de musicología.

1942   *Check-list of Recorded Music in the English Language in the Archive of Ameri-
            can Folk Song to July, 1940*. 3 vols. Washington, D.C.: Library of Con-
            gress.

1942–1952   *Music Series, Pan American Union*, nos. 1–16.

1949   *National Anthems of the American Republics*. Facsimile edition. Official
            versions. Washington, D.C.: Pan American Union.

1943–1953   *Handbook of Latin American Studies, Music Section*.

1947   *Folk Song, U.S.A.* By John A. Lomax and Alan Lomax. Music editors,
            Charles Seeger and Ruth Crawford Seeger. New York: Duell, Sloan, and
            Pearce. Rpt. as *Best Loved American Folk Songs*. New York: Grosset and
            Dunlap, n.d.

1945   "Four Christmas Songs," *Bulletin of the Pan American Union* 79:700–03;
            ibid., 81 (1947): 691–94.

c. 1948   *Folk Music of the Americas*. Album 15: *Venezuelan Folk Music*. Ed. with
            Juan Liscano. Washington, D.C.: Library of Congress.

1950   *Cancionero popular americano: 75 canciones de las repúblicas americanas*.
            Washington, D.C.: Pan American Union.

1957   *American Folk Songs for Christmas*. Ed. with Peggy Seeger. New York:
            Folkways Records and Service Corp. Phonodisc no. FC 7053.

1957   *American Folk Songs: Sung by the Seegers*. Ed. with Peggy Seeger. New
            York: Folkways Records and Service Corp. Phonodisc no. FA 2005.

1960   *Journal of the American Musicological Society* 13.

Reviews by Charles Seeger

1923   "Reviewing a Review," pt. 2 of "The Revolt of the Angels." *Eolian Re-
            view* 3:16–23.

1940   "New York at the Coolidge Festival." *Modern Music* 17 (May–June),
            250–54.

1942   *Bosquejo del proceso de la musica en el Peru* by Abraham Vizcarra Rozas
            (Cuzco: Universidad Naiconal del Cuzco, 1940); *Los origenes del arte mu-
            sical en Chile*, by Eugenio Pereira Salas (Santiago: Imprenta Universita-
            ria, 1941); *Panorama de la musica mexicana desde la independencia hasta la
            actualidad*. In *Hispanic American Historical Reivew* 22 (February), 171–73.

1942   *Mission Music of California* by Owen Francis da Silva (Los Angeles: War-
            ren F. Lewis, 1941. In *Hispanic American Historical Review*.

1944   "Latin American Music." In *The American Annual*, 393–94. New York:
            Americana Corporation; ibid., 1945; 1946, 423–24; 1947; 1948, 375–
            76; 1949, 378–79.

1944   *Papers Read at the International Congress of Musicology Held at New York, September 11–18, 1939.* New York: Music Educators National Conference for the American Musicological Society, 1944. In Music Library Association *Notes*, 2d ser., 2 (December), 62–66.

1945   *A Guide to Latin American Music* by Gilbert Chase (Washington, D.C.: GPO, 1945). In Music Library Association *Notes*, 2d ser., 2 (June), 170–71.

1945   *Harvard Dictionary of Music* by Willi Apel (Cambridge, Mass.: Harvard University Press, 1944). In *Music Educators Journal* 31 (April), 38.

1945   *Music of Latin America* by Nicholas Slonimsky (New York: Thomas Y. Crowell).

1945   *The Schillinger System of Music Composition* by Joseph Schillinger, ed. Arnold Shaw (New York: Carl Fischer, 1945). In Music Library Association *Notes*, 2d ser., 2 (September), 299; ibid., 4 (March 1947), 183–84.

1945   "Sonata da Chiesa" by Virgil Thomson, *New Music* 18 (October), 1944. In Music Library Association *Notes*, 2d ser., 2 (June), 180–81.

1946   *Twelve American Preludes for Piano* by Alberto Ginastera (New York: Carl Fischer). In Music Library Association *Notes*, 2d ser., 4 (December), 102–03.

1947   *Ozark Folksongs*, collected and ed. by Vance Randolph (Columbia: State Society of Missouri, 1946–50. 4 vols. In Music Library Association *Notes*, 2d ser., 4 (June), 330–32; ibid., 5 (September 1948), 576; ibid., 6 (June 1949), 469; ibid., 7 (June 1950), 469–70.

1948   *A Dictionary of Musical Themes*, comp. by Harold Barlow and Sam Morgenstern and intro. by John Erskine (New York: Crown Publishers, 1948). In Music Library Association *Notes*, 2d ser., 5 (June), 375–76, with Richard S. Hill.

1949   *A Collection of Ballads and Folk Songs* by Burl Ives (New York: Decca Records, 1945; Personality Series album no. A-407; *Ballads and Folk Songs* vol. 2 by Burl Ives (New York: Decca Records 1947; Personality Series album no. A-481; *Ballads and Blues* by Josh White (New York: Decca Records, 1946, Personality Series album no. A-447; *American Folk Music Series* by Richard Dyer Bennett (New York: Decca Records 1947; Personality Series album no. A-573. In *Journal of the American Folklore Society* 62 (January–March), 60–70.

1949   *Living Music of the Americas* by Lazare Saminsky (New York: Howell, Soskin and Crow, 1949). In Music Library Association *Notes*, 2d ser., 7 (December), 110–11.

1949   *Music and Society: England and the European Tradition* by Wilfred Mellers (London: Denis Dobson, 1946). In *Journal of the American Musicological Society* 2 (Spring), 56–58.

1950   *Joseph Schillinger* by Frances Schillinger (New York: Greenberg). In Music Library Association *Notes*, 2d ser., 7 (June), 476.

1950   *Sinfonia India* by Carlos Chavez (New York: Schirmer, 1950). In Music
        Library Association *Notes*, 2d ser., 7 (September), 627–28.

1950   *Tone Roads No. 1 for Chamber Orchestra* by Charles I. Ives (New York:
        Peer International Corp., 1949). In Music Library Association *Notes*, 2d
        ser., 7 (June), 432–33.

1951   *Folksongs of Florida*, collected and ed. by Alton C. Morris (Gaines-
        ville: University of Florida Press, 1950); *Texas Folksongs* by William
        Owens (Austin: Texas Folklore Society, 1950); *Folksongs of Alabama*,
        collected by Byron Arnold (University of Alabama Press, 1950). In
        Music Library Association *Notes*, 2d ser., 8 (June),
        523–25.

1951   *Journal of the International Folk Music Council*, 5 vols., ed. Maud Karpeles
        (Cambridge: W. Heffer, 1949–53.. In Music Library Association *Notes*,
        2d ser., 8 (June), 525–26; ibid., 9 (December 1951), 129; ibid., 10
        (March 1953), 282–83; ibid., 10 (September 1953), 642–43.

1951   *Terzetto for Two Violins and Viola* by Richard Donovan (South Hadley and
        Northampton, Mass.: Valley Music Press, 1950). In Music Library As-
        sociation *Notes*, 2d ser., 8 (June), 568.

1952   *Manual for Folk Music Collectors* by Maud Karpeles and Arnold Bake
        (London: International Folk Music Council, 1951). In Music Library
        Association *Notes*, 2d ser., 9 (March), 294.

1952   *Serbo-Croatian Folk Songs* by Bela Bartok and Albert Lord. Columbia
        University Studies in Musicology no. 7 (New York: Columbia Univer-
        sity Press, 1951). In *Journal of the American Musicological Society* 5 (Sum-
        mer) 132–35.

1953   *Cancionero Popular del Provincia de Madrid*, collected by Manuel García
        Matos (Barcelona and Madrid, 1951). In *Musical Quarterly* 39 (April),
        289–93.

1953   *Collection Musée de l'Homme. Catalogue etabli par . . . C.I.A.P.* Archives
        de la musique enregistrée, ser. c: Musique ethnographique et folklor-
        ique no. 2 (Paris: UNESCO, 1952). In Music Library Association *Notes*,
        2d ser., 10 (March), 283–84.

1953   *Harmony* by Heinrich Schenker (Chicago: University of Chicago Press,
        1954). In Music Library Association *Notes*, 2d ser., 11 (December), 53–
        55.

1953   *Music in Mexico: A Historical Survey* by Robert Stevenson (New York:
        Thomas Y. Crowell, 1952). In Music Library Association *Notes*, 2d ser.,
        10 (March), 269–70.

1953   *Rhythm and Tempo: A Study in Music History* by Curt Sachs (New York:
        Norton, 1953). In Music Library Association *Notes*, 2d ser., 10 (March),
        435–38.

1954   *Bibliografia musical brasileira (1820–1950)* by Luis Heitor Correia de
        Azevedo, Cleofe Person de Matos, and Mercedes de Moura Reis (Rio de

Janeiro, 1952). In Music Library Association *Notes*, 2d ser., 11 (September), 551–52.

1954   *Die Schwedische Hummel: eine instrumentkunliche Untersuchung* by Stig Walin (Stockholm: Nordiska Museet, 1952). In Music Library Association *Notes*, 2d ser., 11 (September), 567–68.

1955   *America's Music: From the Pilgrims to the Present* by Gilbert Chase (New York: McGraw Hill, 1955). In Music Library Association *Notes*, 2d ser., 12 (June), 431–34.

1956   Columbia World Library of Folk and Primitive Music, ed. Alan Lomax. Columbia Records SL-204-SL-217 (New York: 1955). In *Journal of the International Folk Music Council* 8:113–13.

1958   *Les Colloques de Wegimont: Cercle Internationale d'Etudes Ethno-Musicologiques*, ed. Paul Collaer (Brussels: Elsevier, 1956). In *Ethnomusicology* 2:38–41.

1958   *Music in Primitive Cultures* by Bruno Nettl (Cambridge, Mass.: Harvard University Press, 1956). In *Journal of American Folklore* 71 (January–March), 90–91.

1958   *The Music of the Ballads*, ed. Jan Philip Schinhan (Durham, N.C.: Duke University Press, 1957). In Music Library Association *Notes*, 2d ser., 15 (June), 399–401.

1959   *An Introduction to Research in Music* by Allen M. Garrett (Washington, D.C.: Catholic University, 1958). In *Journal of Research in Music Education* 7 (Fall), 221–22.

1959   *The New Oxford History of Music*. Vol. 1: *Ancient and Oriental Music* by Egon Wellesz (London: Oxford University Press, 1957). In *Ethnomusicology* 3 (May), 96–97.

1959   *The Traditional Tunes of the Child Ballads*, vol. 1, by Bertrand Harris Bronson (Princeton, N.J.: Princeton University Press, 1959). In Music Library Association *Notes*, 2d ser., 16 (June), 384–85.

1960   *New Methods in Vocal Folk Music Research* by Karl Dahlback (Oslo: Oslo University Press, 1958). In *Ethnomusicology* 4:96–97.

1960   *Norwegian Folk Music*. Ser. 1: *WSlattar for Hardin Fiddle*, ed. Olav Gurvin (Oslo: Oslo University Press, 1958). In *Journal of the American Folklore Society* 73 (January–March), 73–74.

Writings under a Pseudonym

Unless otherwise indicated, the following reviews were published in the New York Daily Worker *in 1934–1935, often under the heading "In the World of Music."*

1934   "The Concert of the Pierre Degeyter Club Orchestra." 2 January, p. 5.
        "A Program for Proletarian Composers." 16 January, p. 5.
        "The International Collection of Revolutionary Songs," 31 January, p. 7.
        "Stirring Songs of Struggle in International Collection." 1 February.

"For Revolutionary Music Criticism in our Own Press." 5 March, p. 7.

"Proletarian Music Is a Historic Necessity." 6 March, p. 5.

"The Broad Scope of Revolutionary Music Criticism." 7 March, p. 5.

"The Function of the Revolutionary Music Critic." 8 March, p. 7.

"Copeland's [*sic*] Music Recital at Pierre Degeyter Club." 22 March, p. 5.

"Workers Audience Applauds Gold's Poem Set to Music." 26 June, p. 5.

"The Internationale." 31 October, p. 5.

"In the World of Music: Business, Business, Business." 8 November, p. 5.

"Zimbalist Concert to Aid Anti-Nazi Fighting Fund." c. 14 November, p. 5.

"On Opera." 15 November, p. 5.

"Philadelphia Orchestra Plays Dawson's Negro Folk Symphony." 23 November, p. 5.

"Shostakovitch's Opera Receives Ovation." 28 November, p. 5.

"Westminster Chorus Sings Roy Harris Composition." 6 December, p. 5.

"More About Roy Harris." 20 December, p. 5.

"Music Division in the Workers' School." 31 December, p. 5.

1935   "Stokowski and His Trustees." 9 January, p. 5.

"Songs by Auvilles Mark Step Ahead in Workers' Music." 15 January, p. 5.

"DeGeyter Club of Philadelphia Forging Ahead." 7 February, p. 5.

"Shostakovitch's Brilliant Opera and the New York Music Critics." 19 February, p. 5. [On *Lady MacBeth of Mensk (sic)*]

"Shostakovitch and the Critics." 20 February, p. 5.

"World of Music." 23 February, p. 5. [On the Workers' Music School concert]

"Concert and Reception for Hanns Eisler." 6 March, p. 5.

"The Freiheit Gesang Ferein." 22 March, p. 5.

"A Week of Music." 22 April, p. 5.

"Hanns Eisler." Letter to the editor, *The New Masses*, 23 April, p. 21.

"Eisler Farewell Concert Highly Successful Event." 23 April, p. 5.

"Freiheit Mandolin Orchestra." 3 May, p. 5.

"Concert Arranged to Build Workers' Orchestra in N.Y." 8 May, p. 7.

"Pierre Degeyter Concert and Ball." 16 May, p. 5.

"All-Copland Concert." 16 October, p. 5.

"Schonberg's Latest Composition," 23 October, p. 5.

"All-Harris Concert." 31 October, p. 5.

"Organizing Workers' Bands." 7 November, p. 5.

"Music League Plans New Book of Songs." 18 November, p. 5.

"All-Thomson Program." 20 November, p. 5.

Other Works by Charles Seeger

1971   *An American Musicologist.* Oral History Office, University of California, Los Angeles. Typescript.

1977   "Charles Seeger speaking from Bridgewater, Conn., with Penny Cohen recording." Short memoir, 1886–1930s, April 22, 1977.

n.d.   "Boyhood On Staten Island." Library of Congress. Typescript and manuscript.

n.d.   "Toward the Establishment of a Study of Musicology." Library of Congress. Typescript. (Also noted as "Toward an Establishment of the Study of Musicology in America.")

Musical Compositions by Charles Seeger (Library of Congress)

Note: The scores and parts of two masques, a string quartet (1910), and other compositions were burned in the Berkeley fire of 1923.

1908   Overture to an unfinished opera, "The Shadowy Waters." Text by William B. Yeats. For orchestra, 51 pages. Seeger's honors composition, "Graduation Overture." Performed at a Boston Symphony Orchestra Pops concert, June 1908; Munich, 1908; Bohemian Grove, Sonoma County, California, 1912.

1908   "Sonata for Violin and Pianoforte." Revised in 1915. 1. Moderato con moto. 2. Dialogue—Grave. 3. Academic Rondo—Allegro. 37 pages.

1911   *Seven Songs for High Voice and Pianoforte.* New York: G. Schirmer. "Asleep," Keats; "Endymion," Wilde; "The Price of Youth," Scott; "Till I Wake," Hope; "Song to—," Wheelock; "When Soft Winds and Sunny Skies," Shelley.

1907–1912   "Twelve Songs for High Voice and Pianoforte." "On a Faded Violet," Shelley; "Sampan Song," Hope; "To Helen," Poe; "The Lady of the South," Shelley; "From the Arabic," Shelley; "Song," Hartley Coleridge; "Ach, die Qualen," Adam Mieckiewicz; "Wie ein Schiff," Anon.; "Think not of it," Keats; "When as in Silks my Julia goes," and "My Love in her attire doth shew her wit," Herrick; "Alguna vez," de Castillejo; "Encouragement to lover," Suckling.

1914–1915   "Two Parthenias." With Ruth Cornell Cook. Pageants presented by the women students of the University of California, Berkeley. 1. "Derdra," orchestral score, 180 pages. 2. "The Queen's Masque," for orchestra, harpsichord, and voices, 164 pages.

1933–1935   "A Baker's Dozen Rounds on the Undepressed."

1936   "The Middleman," Nicholas Ray. Three recitatives and three arias, for one or four voices and guitar.

1937   "Three songs for Mezzo-Soprano, Microphone and Orchestra." "John Riley," "Wayfaring Stranger," and John Henry." Composed for the 75th anniversary of the founding of the U.S. Department of Agriculture. Performed at the Department of Agriculture. 47 pages.

1940   "John Hardy." Variation for a small orchestra. Commissioned by the Columbia School of the Air (CBS).

1941   "Danza Lenta." For violin. In *Boletín Latinamericano de música*, suplemento musical, 5:89. Instituto interamericano de musicología. Montevideo.

1953   "Two Songs." "The Letter," John Hall Wheelock, for solo voice; "Psalm 137," for solo voice. In *New Music* 26 (April), 10–15.

1953   *100 Arrangements of American Folk Songs for Pianoforte and Voice.*

Other Compositions by Charles Seeger

1906   "Valgovind's Boat Song." For voice. 2 manuscripts, 3 pages each.
1907   "Chanson de Bohème." For voice. 2 pages.
n.d.   "Encouragements in Love." For voice. 2 pages.
1909   "Song: She is not fair to Outward View." For voice. 2 pages.
n.d.   "Song to——." For voice. 2 manuscripts, 2 pages each.
1911   "Encouragements to a Lover." For voice. 2 pages.
1912   "Think not of it." 2 manuscripts, 4 pages, 5 pages, 1 page.
n.d.   "Slow Dance." For violin and piano. 2 pages.
n.d.   "Sonata." For unaccompanied clarinet. 1-page fragment.
1913   "Le Roy d'Yvetot" and "The Men of Gotham." For chorus and piano. 3 pages.
1931   "Two Complaints and a Grumble." 3 pages.
1934   "Lenin, Who's that guy?" For voice and piano. Published under the pseudonym "Carl Sands" by Workers' Music League.
n.d.   "By the Rivers of Babylon." For unaccompanied voice.
c. 1930   "Gloria tibi Vanderbilt." 3 stanzas. Stanzas 4–9 and accompaniment written in 1977.

Other Materials Consulted

Restricted

Letters and personal correspondence between Charles and Ruth Seeger, in Michael Seeger's possession.

Photographs of the Seeger family, in Michael Seeger's and the author's possession.

Nonrestricted

SEEGER COLLECTION, LIBRARY OF CONGRESS

Music by Charles Seeger; music by Ruth Crawford Seeger; music by other composers; book manuscripts; letters; programs; clippings; financial records; medical records; melographs; transcriptions; drafts of papers; photographs; music journals; scholarly works by others.

SEEGER COLLECTION, UNIVERSITY OF CALIFORNIA, BERKELEY

Syllabus for course in musicology (1916). "Tradition and Experiment: Occidental Fine Art of Music, Part I: Critique and Technique of an Experimental Method in Musical Composition; Part II: Manual of Dissonant Counterpoint." (Also referred to as "Tradition and Invention in Musical Composition" or "Treatise on Musical Composition and Manual of Dissonant Counterpoint" (1930).

"Tradition and Experiment in the New Music," coauthored with Ruth Crawford Seeger [1931?].

"Tradition and Experiment in Musical Idiom, Part I: Critique and Technique of Experimental Method in Musical Composition; Part II: Manual of Dissonant Counterpoint," typescript [ca. 1931].

"Tradition and Experiment in the New Music," typescript [ca. 1931].

Short "oral history" of Charles Seeger.

Miscellaneous materials.

WPA MATERIALS

American orchestral works recommended by WPA music project conductors, 1941. Library of Congress.

Check List of California songs under WPA auspices. Sidney H. Robertson, supervisor, 1940. Archive of California Folk Music, University of California, Berkeley, Department of Music.

Federal Music Project Reports. Library of Congress and University of California, Berkeley.

WPA Music Program catalogue of 230 master electrical transcriptions produced by the WPA and broadcast coast to coast from April 1930 up to and including the release of November 6, 1939. Recorded by RCA. Library of Congress. Typescript.

WPA Music Project, various states. University of California, Berkeley.

WPA National Advisory Committee digest of meetings. University of California, Berkeley.

WPA Writers Program, California. Anthology of Music Criticism. University of California, Berkeley.

MISCELLANEOUS MATERIALS

Address by Charles Seeger to teachers of District 1, WPA Florida Music Project, Jacksonville, March 21, 1939. In author's possession.

Charles Seeger's parents' memoirs. In Peter Seeger's possession.

Karl Ludwig Seeger's (Charles Seeger's great-grandfather) antifederalist oration. In Peter Seeger's possession.

Secondary Sources

Aaron, David. *Writers on the Left*. New York; Harcourt, Brace, 1961.

Achter, Barbara Z. "Americanism and American Art Music, 1929–45." Ph.D. diss., University of Michgan, 1978.

Adler, Guido. *Methode der Musikgeschichte*. Leipzig, 1919.

––––––. "Umfange, Methode und Ziel der Musikwissenschaft," *Vierteljahrschrift fur Musikwissenschaft* 1 (1885).

Allen, Barbara, and Lynwood Montell. *From Memory to History: Using Oral Sources in Local Historical Research*. Nashville, Tenn.: American Association for State and Local History.

Allen, Frederick Lewis. *Only Yesterday*. New York, 1964.

––––––. *Since Yesterday*. New York, 1939.

Bachelder, Marilyn Meyer. "Women in Music Composition." M.A. thesis, Eastern Michigan University, 1973.

Baldwin, Sidney. *Poverty and Politics: The Rise and Decline of the Farm Security Administration*. Chapel Hill: University of North Carolina Press, 1968.

Banfield, Edward. *Government Project*. Glencoe, Ill., 1951.

Bauer, Marion. *Twentieth Century Music*. New York, 1933.

Beach, Frank L. "The Transformation of California." Ph.D. diss., University of California, Berkeley, 1963.

Bentley, Eric, and Earl Robinson, eds. *The Brecht-Eisler Song Book*. New York, 1967.

Billington, Ray. "Government and Art: WPA Experience." *American Quarterly*, Winter 1961, pp. 466–79.

Blake, David. "Hanns Eisler." *The New Grove Dictionary of Music*, ed. Wiley Hitchcock and Stanley Sadie. New York: Macmillan, 1980.

Blum, S. "Toward a Social History of Musicological Technique." *Ethnomusicology* 19 (1975), 208–24.

Bohle, Bruce. "Charles Seeger." *The International Cyclopedia of Music and Musicians*, 10th ed. New York: Dodd, Mead, 1975.

Botkin, B. A. *A Treasury of Western Folklore*. New York, 1951. With 32 transcriptions with suggested chord letters for possible accompaniment by Ruth Crawford Seeger.

––––––. "WPA and Folklore Research: Bread and Song." *Southern Folklore Quarterly* 3 (1934), 7–14.

Bukofzer, Manfred. *The Plan of Musicology in American Institutions of Higher Learning*. New York, 1957.

Canon, Cornelius Baird. "The Federal Music Project of the Works Progress Administration: Music in a Democracy." Ph.D. diss., University of Minnesota, 1963.

Cassirer, Ernst. *Language and Myth*. New York, 1946.

Chase, Gilbert. *The American Composer Speaks*. Baton Rouge, La., 1966.

––––––. "American Music and Musicology." *Journal of Musicology* 1 (1982), 59–62.

————. *America's Music*. New York, 1955.

————. "Charles Seeger and Latin America: A Personal Memoir." *Latin American Music Review* 1 (1980), 3–5.

————. "An Exagmination Round His Factification for Incamination of Work in Progress (Review Essay and Reminiscence)." *Yearbook of the International Folk Music Council* 11 (1979), 138–44.

————. *Partial List of Latin American Music Obtainable in the United States with a Supplement List of Books and a Selective List of Phonograph Records*. Washington, D.C.: Pan American Union, 1941.

Chennevière, Rudhyar D. [Dane Rudhyar]. "The Rise of the Musical Proletariat." *Musical Quarterly* 6 (1920), 500–09.

Chomsky, Noam. *Reflections on Language*. New York, 1976.

Clarke, Henry Leland. "Composers' Collective," *The New Grove Dictionary of Music*, ed. Wiley Hitchcock and Stanley Sadie. New York: Macmillan, 1986.

Cole, Rossetter G. "Adolf Weidig." *Dictionary of American Biography*, ed. Dumas Malone. New York, 1936.

Commonwealth Club of California. *The Population of California*. San Francisco, 1946.

Conkin, Paul. *Tomorrow a New World: The New Deal Community Program*. Ithaca, N.Y., 1959.

Cord, Nicholas John. "Music in Social Settlement and Community Music Schools," Ph.D. diss., University of Minnesota, 1970.

Cowell, Henry. *American Composers on American Music: A Symposium*. Palo Alto, Calif.: Stanford University Press, 1933.

————. "Charles Louis Seeger, Jr." *The Fortnightly* 1 (January 15, 1932), 5–7.

————. "Charles Seeger." In *American Composers on American Music: A Symposium*, 119–24. New York: Frederick Ungar, 1962.

————. *New Musical Resources*. New York, 1930.

Cowell, Sidney Robertson. "Charles Seeger (1886–1979)." *Musical Quarterly* 65 (April 1979), 305–07.

————. "Recall." A collection of letters to Charles Seeger, 1965–1966. In author's possession.

————. "Ruth Crawford Seeger, 1901–1953." *International Folk Music Journal* 7 (1955), 55–56.

Daniels, Robert V., ed. *Documentary History of Communism*. New York: Random House, 1960.

Deitz, Robert. "Marc Blitzstein and the 'Agit-Prop' Theatre of the 1930s," *Yearbook for Inter-American Musical Research* 6 (1970).

Denisoff, R. Serge. "Christianity, Communism, or Commercialism: The Song of Persuasion Revisited." In *Sing a Song of Social Significance*, 19–37. Bowling Green, Ohio, 1972.

————. *Great Day Coming: Folk Music and the American Left*. Urbana, Ill., 1971.

————. "The Proletarian Renascence: The Folkness of the Ideological Folk." *Journal of American Folklore* 82 (1969), 51–65.

Dornbush, Adrian. *First Annual Report of the Resettlement Administration*. Washington, D.C.: 1936.

————. "Records of the Farmers Home Administration, Resettlement Division, General Correspondence, 1936–1942." Special Skills (Music), entry 948–07. Washington, D.C.: National Archives and Records Services, Record Group 96.

Drinker, Sophie. *Music and Women*. New York, 1948.

Dunaway, David K. "Charles Seeger and Carl Sands: The Composers' Collective Years." *Ethnomusicology* 24 (May 1980), 159–68.

————. *How Can I Keep from Singing: Pete Seeger*. New York, 1981.

————. "Protest and Political Song in the United States: A Selected Bibliography." *Folklore Forum* 10 (April 1978).

————. "Unsung Songs of Protest: The Composers' Collective of New York." *New York Folklore* 5 (Summer 1979), 1–19.

Duran, Gustavo. *Recordings of Latin American Songs and Dance*. Washington, D.C.: Pan American Union, 1942.

Eisler, Hanns. "History of the German Workers' Music Movement from 1848." *Music Vanguard*, 1935, pp. 33–48.

————. *Musik und Politik: Schriften 1924–48*. Leipzig, 1974.

Ekirch, A. A., Jr. *Ideologies and Utopias: The Impact of the New Deal in American Thought*. Chicago, 1969.

Erickson, Ron, et al. *The Music of Charles Seeger, 1886–1979*. Arch Records no. 1750. Berkeley, Calif., 1984.

Ferris, William R., Jr. "Folk Song and Culture: Charles Seeger and Alan Lomax." *New York Folklore Quarterly* 29 (1973), 206–18.

Fuller, Levi Varden. "The Supply of Agricultural Labor as a Factor in the Evolution of Farm Organization in California." Ph.D. diss., University of California, Berkeley, 1940.

Gaume, Matilda. *Ruth Crawford Seeger: Memoirs, Memories, Music*. Metuchen, N.J.: Scarecrow Press, 1986.

Goldston, Robert. *The Great Depression: The United States in the Thirties*. Greenwich, Conn., 1968.

Gornick, Vivian. *The Romance of American Communism*. New York, 1977.

Grabs, Manfred, ed. *A Rebel in Music*. New York, 1978.

Greater New York American Musicological Society. *1935–1965 Retrospective*.

Green, Archie. "Charles Louis Seeger." *Journal of American Folklore* 90 (1979), 392–99.

————. "John Neuhaus: Wobbly Folklorist." *Journal of American Folklore* 71 (1960).

————. *Only a Miner*. Chicago: University of Illinois Press, 1972.

————. "A Resettlement Administration Song Sheet." *JEMF Quarterly* 2 (Summer 1975).

————. "Thomas Hart Benton's Folk Musicians." *John Edwards Memorial Foundation Quarterly* 12 (1976), 74–90.

Gregory, James. *American Exodus: The Dust Bowl Migration and Okie Culture in California*. Oxford: Oxford University Press, 1989.

Gurvin, Olav. "Photography as an Aid in Folk Music Research." *Norveg* 3 (1953), 181–96.

Harrison, Frank L., Mantle Hood, and Claude V. Palisca. *Musicology*. Englewood Cliffs, N.J.: Prentice-Hall, 1963.

Harvard University Alumni Office. *Records of the Class of 1908*. Reunion statements for 1933, 1938, 1948, 1953, 1958. Cambridge, Mass.: Harvard University.

Haydon, Glen. *Introduction to Musicology*. New York: Prentice-Hall, 1941.

Herzog, George. "Song: Folk Song and the Music of Folk Song." *Standard Dictionary of Folklore* 2:1032–50. New York, 1950.

Hitchcock, Wiley. "Americans on American Music." *College Music Symposium* 8 (1968), 138–42.

———. *Music in the United States: An Introduction*. Englewood Cliffs, N.J.: Prentice-Hall, 1969.

Hofstadter, Richard. *The Age of Reform*. New York, 1955.

Hood, Mantle. *The Ethnomusicologist*. Los Angeles: McGraw-Hill, 1971.

———. "Reminiscent of Charles Seeger." *Yearbook of the International Folk Music Council* 11 (1979), 76–82.

Howard, John Tasker. *Our American Music*. New York, 1929.

———. *Our Contemporary Composers*. New York, 1941.

Howe, Irving, and Lewis Coser. *The American Communist Party: A Critical History*. New York, 1962.

Hughes, H. Stuart. *Consciousness and Society: The Revolution of European Social Thought, 1890–1930*. New York, 1958.

Jackson, George Pullen. *White Spirituals in the Southern Uplands*. Chapel Hill: University of North Carolina Press, 1933.

Jepson, Barbara. "Ruth Crawford Seeger: A Study in Mixed Accents." *Feminist Art Journal*, Spring 1977, pp. 13–16.

Kerman, Joseph. *Contemplating Music: Challenges to Musicology*. Cambridge, 1985.

Kingman, Daniel. *American Music: A Panorama*. New York, 1979.

Kirkendall, Richard. *Social Scientists and Farm Politics in the Age of Roosevelt*. Columbia, Mo., 1966.

Koch, Raymond, and Charlotte Koch. *Educational Commune: The Story of Commonwealth College*. New York, 1972.

Kodish, Deborah. *Good Friends and Bad Enemies: Robert Winslow Gordon and the Study of American Folksong*. Urbana: University of Illinois Press, 1986.

Korson, George, with Ruth Crawford Seeger, music editor. *Anthology of Pennsylvania Folklore*. Philadelphia, 1949.

———. *Coal Dust on the Fiddle*. Philadelphia, 1943.

Kowenhoven, John. *The Arts in Modern American Civilization*. New York, 1967.

Kroeber, A. L. *Configuration of Culture Growth*. Berkeley and Los Angeles, 1944.

Krummel, D. W., Jean Geil, Doris J. Dyen, and Deane L. Root, eds. *Resources of American Music History*. Urbana, Ill., 1981.

Kuss, Malena. "Charles Seeger's Leitmotifs on Latin America." *Yearbook of the Interna-*

tional Folk Music Council 11 (1979), 83–99.

Lange, F. C. "Charles Seeger and Americanismo Musical." *Inter-American Music Review* 1 (1972), 245–51.

Larson, Gary O. *The Reluctant Patron. The United States Government and the Arts, 1943–65*. Philadelphia: University of Pennsylvania Press, 1983.

Lawlor, Vanett. *Educación musical en 14 repúblicas americanas*. Pan American Union Music Series no. 12. Washington, D.C.: Pan American Union, 1945.

Lévi-Strauss, Claude. *The Raw and the Cooked*. New York, 1969.

List, George, and Juan Orrego-Salas. *Music in the Americas*. Bloomington: Indiana University Press, 1967.

Lomax. Alan. *The Folk Songs of North America*. New York, 1960.

———. *Folk Song Style and Culture*. Washington, D.C., 1968.

———. "Historical Origins of the Revival." *New York Folklore Quarterly* 19 (1963).

———. *The Penguin Book of American Folk Song*. London, 1964.

Lomax, John. *Adventures of a Ballad Hunter*. New York, 1947.

Lomax, John A., and Alan Lomax. *Our Singing Country*. New York: Macmillan, 1941. With 205 transcriptions by Charles Seeger and Ruth Crawford Seeger, music editors.

Lomax, John A., Alan Lomax, and Ruth Crawford Seeger. *Folk Song, U.S.A.* New York, 1947. With 111 songs, piano arrangements by Charles Seeger and Ruth Crawford Seeger.

Luper, A. T. *The Music of Argentina*. Pan American Union Music Series no. 5. Washington, D.C.: PAU, 1943.

———. *The Music of Brazil*. Pan American Union Music Series no. 9. Washington, D.C.: PAU, 1943.

McDonald, William F. *Federal Relief Administration and the Arts*. Columbus: Ohio State University Press, 1969.

Malone, Bill C. *Country Music, U.S.A.: A Fifty-Year History*. Austin, Texas: American Folklore Society, 1968.

Mandel, Alan, and Nancy Mandel. "Composers to Re-emphasize." *Clavier* 14 (1975), 14–17.

Mangione, Jerry. *The Dream and the Deal: The Federal Writers' Project, 1935–1943*. New York, 1972.

Mason, Daniel Gregory. *The Dilemma of American Music and Other Essays*. New York, 1928.

McKinzie, Richard D. *The New Deal for Artists*. Princeton, N.J.: Princeton University Press, 1973.

Mead, Rita. *Henry Cowell's New Music 1925–1935*. Ann Arbor: University of Michigan Press, 1981.

———. "Henry Cowell's New Music Society." *Journal of Musicology* 1 (1982), 449.

Merriam, Alan P. *The Anthropology of Music*. Chicago: 1964.

Merriam, Alan P., and Barbara W. Merriam. *Voice of the Congo*. Riverside World Folk Music Series, Riverside Records RLP 4002, 1951–52.

Merton, Robert. *Social Theory and Social Structure*. New York, 1968.

Meyer, Leonard. *Music, the Arts and Ideas: Patterns and Predictions in Twentieth-Century Culture*. Chicago, 1967.

Metfessel, Milton. *Phonophotography in Folk Music*. Chapel Hill: University of North Carolina Press, 1968.

Mitgang, Herbert, ed. *The Letters of Carl Sandburg*. New York, 1968.

Moore, Michael. "The Seeger Melograph Model." *UCLA Institute of Ethnomusicology Selected Reports* 2 (1974), 2–13.

Morgan, Hazel. *Music in American Eduation*. Chicago, 1955.

Mueller, John. *The American Symphony Orchestra: A Social History of Musical Taste*. Bloomington: Indiana University Press, 1951.

Musselman, Joseph. *Music in the Cultured Generation: A Social History of Music in America, 1870–1900*. Evanston, Ill.: 1971.

Netzer, Dick. *The Subsidized Muse: Public Support for the Arts in the United States*. New York, 1978.

Neuls-Bates, C., and A. F. Block, comps. and eds. *Women in American Music: A Bibliography of Music and Literature*. Westport, Conn., 1979.

New York Musicological Society. *Bulletins* 1, 2.

Oinas, Felix J., ed. *Folklore, Nationalism, and Politics*. Columbus, Ohio: Slavica, 1978.

Osgood, Charles E., and Thomas A. Sebeok. *Psycholinguistics*. Bloomington: Indiana University Press, 1969.

Overmyer, Grace. *Government and the Arts*. New York, 1939.

Pan American Union. *Music in Latin America*. Club and Study Series no. 3. Washington, D.C.: PAU, 1942.

Parker, Carlton. *The Casual Laborer*. New York, 1920.

Penkower, Monty N. *The Federal Writers' Project: A Study in Government Patronage of the Arts*. Urbana: University of Illinois Press, 1977.

Pettis, Ashley. "The WPA and the American Composer." *Musical Quarterly* 26 (1940), 101–12.

Pfaff, Timothy. "The Measure of a Man: Charles Seeger Across the Centuries." *California Monthly* 88 (1978).

Pool, Jeannie. "American Women Composers." *Music Educators Journal* 65 (1979), 28–41.

Purcell, Ralph. *Government and Art: A Study of the American Experience* Washington, D.C., 1956.

Redfield, Robert, Ralph Linton, and Melville Herskovits. "Memorandum on the Study of Acculturation." *American Anthropologist* 38 (1935), 149–52.

Reed, Oliver, and Walter Welch. *From Tin Foil to Stereo*. New York, 1959.

Reis, Claire. *Composers, Conductors, and Critics*. New York, 1955.

———. *Composers in America*. New York, 1938.

Reuss, Richard. "American Folklore and Left-Wing Politics." Ph.D. diss., Indiana University, 1971.

———. "Folk Music and Social Conscience: The Musical Odyssey of Charles Seeger." *Western Folklore* 38 (1979), 221–38.

————. "The Roots of American Left-wing Interest in Folksong." *Labor History* 12 (1971), 259–79.

Ringer, Alexander. "Guidelines for the Doctor of Philosophy Degree in Musicology." American Musicological Society, 1969.

Rosen, J., and G. Rubin-Rabson. "Why Haven't Women Become Great Composers?" *High Fidelity/Musical America*, February 1973, pp. 47–50.

Rosenfeld, Paul. *An Hour with American Music*. Philadelphia, 1929.

————. *Musical Portraits*. Freeport, N.Y., 1968.

Salzman, Eric. *Twentieth-Century Music: An Introduction*. 2d ed. Englewood Cliffs, N.J.: Prentice-Hall, 1974.

Saminsky, Lazare. *Living Music of the Americas*. New York, 1949.

Sandburg, Carl. *An American Songbag*. New York, 1927.

Sapir, Edward. *Language*. New York, 1921.

Saussure, F. de. *Cours de linguistique générale*. Paris, 1972.

Schmid, Will. "Reflections on the Folk Music: An Interview with Pete Seeger." *Music Educators Journal* 66 (1980), 42–46, 78–81.

Seashore, Carl. "Why No Great Women Composers?" *Music Educators Journal* 65 (1979), 42–44.

Seeger, Peter. "Charles Seeger: A Man of Music." *Sing Out* 27 (1979), 18–25.

Seeger, Ruth Crawford. *American Folk Songs for Children*. New York, 1948. Rpt. 1980.

————. *American Folk Songs for Christmas*. New York, 1953.

————. *Animal Folk Songs for Children*. New York, 1950.

————. *Folklore Infantil do Santo Domingo*. Madrid, 1955.

————. "Keep the Song Going!" *NEA Journal*, February 1951, pp. 93–95.

————. *Let's Build a Railroad*. New York, 1954.

————. "Making Folklore Available." In *Four Symposia on Folklore*, ed. Stith Thompson, 191–94. Bloomington: Indiana University Folklore Series no. 8, 1953.

————. "New York Jottings." 22 February 1930. In Seeger Collection, Library of Congress.

————. Review of John N. Work, *American Negro Songs for Mixed Voices*. Music Library Association *Notes*, December 1948, pp. 172–73.

Shattuck, Roger. *The Banquet Years: The Origin of the Avant-Garde in France, 1885 to World War I*. New York, 1961.

Siegmeister, Elie. *Music and Society*. New York, 1938.

Slonimsky, Nicholas. *Music Since 1900*. 4th ed. New York, 1971.

Society for Ethnomusicology. *Newsletter*, 1–5.

Stein, Walter J. *California and the Dust Bowl Migration*. Westport, Conn., 1973.

Steinberg, Stephen. *The Ethnic Myth: Race, Ethnicity, and Class in America*. Boston: Beacon Press, 1989.

Stephens, H. M., and H. H. Bolton, eds. *Prolegomena to History — The Relation of History to Literature, Philosophy, and Science*. Berkeley: University of California Publications no. 4, 1916–17.

Sternsher, Bernard. *Rexford Tugwell and the New Deal*. New Brunswick, N.J.: Rutgers

University Press, 1964.

Stryker, Roy, and Nancy Wood. *In This Proud Land: America 1935–43 as Seen in the FSA Photographs*. Greenwich, Conn., 1973.

Teggart, Frederick J. *The Theory of History as Progress*. Berkeley: University of California Press, 1925.

Teggart, Frederick J., ed. *The Idea of Progress — A Collection of Readings Selected by Frederick J. Teggart*. Berkeley: University of California Press, 1949.

Terkel, Studs. *Hard Times: An Oral History of the Great Depression*. New York, 1978.

Thomson, Virgil. *American Music Since 1910*. New York, 1971.

Thompson, Leila Fern. *Selected References in English on Latin American Music*. Pan American Union Music Series no. 13. Washington, D.C.: PAU, 1944.

Thompson, Stith. *Four Symposia on Folklore*. Bloomington: Indiana University Folklore Series no. 8, 1953.

Toffler, Alvin. *The Culture Consumers: Art and Affluence in America*. Baltimore, 1965.

Valiant, Margaret. *Journal of a Field Representative*. Foreword by Charles Seeger. Washington, D.C.: Resettlement Administration, 1937.

Valiant, Margaret, and Charles Seeger. "Journal of a Field Representative." *Ethnomusicology* 24 (May 1980), 169–210.

Warren-Findley, Janelle Jedd. "Of Tears and Need: The Federal Music Project, 1935–1943." Ph.D. diss., George Washington University, 1973.

————. "Musicians and Mountaineers: The Resettlement Administration's Music Program in Appalachia, 1935–1937." *Appalachian Journal* 7 (1979).

Weidig, Adolf. *Harmonic Material and Its Uses: A Treatise for Teachers, Students and Music Lovers*. Chicago, 1924.

Weisgall, Hugo. "Interview with Henry Cowell." *Music Quarterly*, October 1959.

Wilgus, D. K. *Anglo-American Folk Song Scholarship Since 1898*. New Brunswick, N.J.: Rutgers University Press, 1959.

Williams, J. A. "Radicalism and Professionalism in Folklore Studies: A Comparative Perspective." *Journal of the Folklore Institute* 12 (1975).

Woodworth, William Harry. "The Federal Music Project and the WPA in New Jersey." Ed.D. diss., University of Michigan, 1970.

Workers Songbooks I (Red Song Book). New York: Workers Library Publishers, 1934.

Workers Songbooks II (New Workers Song Book). New York: Workers Library Publishers, 1935.

Yasser, Joseph. *A Theory of Evolving Tonality*. New York, 1932.

Zuck, Barbara. *A History of Musical Americanism*. Ann Arbor: University of Michigan Press, 1980.

Index